"Amid so much empty rhetoric and shallow theory about capitalism, pro and contra, Delanty and Harris have provided us with a book that is as lucid as it is incisive. Understanding capitalism as an intrinsically historical phenomenon, they trace its development as a concrete historical formation but also explore the evolutions in theory that have sought to understand it. This is a book that should be read widely especially by those today who would seek to create a politics to confront the destructive effects of capital.".

Michael J. Thompson, *Professor of Political Theory, William Paterson University, USA*

"This outstanding book is a comprehensive guide to theories and critiques of capitalism, by two leading critical theorists."

William Outhwaite, *Emeritus Professor of Sociology, University of Newcastle, UK*

"In concise and clear prose, Delanty and Harris line up all the great authors of the past to understand the past, present and future of capitalism. This is the book you need if you want to anticipate the coming crash!"

Frederic Vandenberghe, *Professor of Sociology, Federal University of Rio de Janeiro, Brazil*

Capitalism and its Critics

Capitalism and its Critics offers an accessible account of major theories of capitalism from the industrial revolution to the present day. The book provides a comprehensive account of the economic and social thought of key theorists from Adam Smith and Karl Marx to David Harvey and Thomas Piketty.

Capitalism has long been the subject of passionate debate, and today such contestations are perhaps more timely than ever. For its advocates, capitalism brings democracy and freedom and is the cornerstone of modernity and of progress. For its critics, capitalism is based on the exploitation of labour and is responsible for the destruction of the environment as well as colonialism. Whether capitalism survives the century, or whether an alternative social system emerges, may very well determine the fate of humanity. *Capitalism and its Critics* gives a comprehensive critical analysis of the most important theorists of capitalism, including Adam Smith, Karl Marx, Max Weber, Joseph Schumpeter, Karl Polanyi, F.A. Hayek, J.M. Keynes, David Harvey and Thomas Piketty. The book discusses some of the main debates about capitalism and considers alternatives in the twenty-first century. The 12 chapters are loosely chronologically organized around the main approaches and historical phases in the history of capitalism. Central themes of the book are the ideas of capitalist crisis and of tensions between democracy and capitalism in the making of modernity.

A highly readable, informative and engaging text, *Capitalism and its Critics*, is essential reading for anyone interested in understanding capitalism and its alternatives.

Gerard Delanty is Emeritus Professor of Sociology at the University of Sussex, UK. His research explores social theory and the cultural and historical analysis of social and political questions, particularly the comparative analysis of modernity in global perspective and in social change in Europe. He is the author of *The Cosmopolitan Imagination* (Cambridge University Press, 2009), *The European Heritage: A Critical Re-Interpretation* (Routledge, 2017) and *Critical Theory and Social Transformation* (Routledge, 2020). He is also co-editor of the *Routledge International Handbook of Contemporary Social and Political Theory* (Second Edition, 2021).

Neal Harris is Senior Lecturer in Sociology at Oxford Brookes University, UK. His research explores the relationship between critical social theory (particularly the Frankfurt School) and a range of social problems, including global warming, capitalism, nationalism, patriarchy and digital totalitarianism. He is the author of *Critical Theory and Social Pathology: The Frankfurt School beyond Recognition* (Manchester University Press, 2022). He is also the editor of *Pathology Diagnosis and Social Research: New Applications and Explorations* (Palgrave Macmillan, 2021) and co-editor of *Thinking beyond Neoliberalism* (Palgrave Macmillan, 2022).

Capitalism and its Critics

Capitalism in Social and Political Theory

Gerard Delanty and Neal Harris

Routledge
Taylor & Francis Group
LONDON AND NEW YORK

Cover image: © Getty Images

First published 2023
by Routledge
4 Park Square, Milton Park, Abingdon, Oxon OX14 4RN

and by Routledge
605 Third Avenue, New York, NY 10158

Routledge is an imprint of the Taylor & Francis Group, an informa business

British Library Cataloguing-in-Publication Data
A catalogue record for this book is available from the British Library

Library of Congress Cataloging-in-Publication Data
Names: Delanty, Gerard, author. | Harris, Neal, author.
Title: Capitalism and its critics : capitalism in social and political theory /
Gerard Delanty and Neal Harris.
Description: Milton Park, Abingdon, Oxon ; New York, NY : Routledge, 2023. |
Includes bibliographical references and index.
Identifiers: LCCN 2022026541 (print) | LCCN 2022026542 (ebook) |
ISBN 9781138497863 (hardback) | ISBN 9781138497870 (paperback) |
ISBN 9781351017671 (ebook)
Subjects: LCSH: Capitalism. | Economics | Political science.
Classification: LCC HB501 .D417 2023 (print) |
LCC HB501 (ebook) | DDC 330.12/2–dc23/eng/20220624
LC record available at https://lccn.loc.gov/2022026541
LC ebook record available at https://lccn.loc.gov/2022026542

ISBN: 978-1-138-49786-3 (hbk)
ISBN: 978-1-138-49787-0 (pbk)
ISBN: 978-1-351-01767-1 (ebk)

DOI: 10.4324/9781351017671

Typeset in Bembo
by Newgen Publishing UK

Contents

Preface

This book had its origin in a postgraduate course, 'Capitalism and Its Critics', that Gerard Delanty taught for ten years at the University of Sussex, from 2010 to 2020, as part of the MA in Social and Political Thought. The course as well as the present book was a response to the new interest in capitalism that followed in the wake of the financial crisis of 2008–10. While there are now many books on capitalism, there is little by way of a comprehensive survey and appraisal of major theories of capitalism. Our book aims to bring together approaches to capitalism in social and political theory, extending back to the classical political economy theories of Karl Marx and Adam Smith. The book is therefore organized around major theorists of capitalism.

The introduction and first six chapters were written by Gerard Delanty and the latter six by Neal Harris.

We are grateful to the following for reading and commenting on the final draft: Michael J. Thompson, William Outhwaite and Frederic Vandenberghe.

Neal would like to thank Maïa Pal, James Stockman, Angus Reoch, Robin Jervis, Andy Kilmister, Chris Hesketh, Miriyam Aouragh and Denis C. Bosseau for their helpful comments and suggestions.

Gerard would also like to thank Johann Arnason, Charles Masquelier and Sam Sadian, for reading parts of the manuscript and making helpful comments.

Preface

Introduction

Capitalism, Crisis and Critique

It is almost impossible to separate the notion of capitalism from its many theories. There is no acceptable definition of capitalism, a term which is widely used but without any clear meaning. It invariably tends to be used more by its critics and therefore suggests a critical attitude. Yet, the term is not entirely lacking in specificity, even if there is little consensus on the political questions that capitalism raises. It was a key concept in classical sociology (Giddens 1973). In mainstream economics and modernization theories since 1945, the preference was for 'the economy' or 'development' and as a result capitalism waned as a term. Interest in capitalism has returned in recent years in the social sciences as well as in history. Kershaw (2020) notes the emergence of a 'new history of capitalism' as a subfield in history especially in the USA, despite no substantial engagement with the concept. Since the financial crisis of 2008–10, interest in capitalism has returned after a long interval. Its revival has led to a re-examination of theories of capitalism and the return of political economy to the forefront of social and political theory.

As with many concepts in social science, capitalism is a contested concept. But it is nonetheless a concept and as such is not self-defining. Almost any definition of capitalism invokes a theory that has furnished the elements of its definition. As a concept, it is therefore best approached from the perspective of a theory. In this book, we look at capitalism through the lens of the most important theories of capitalism. Our focus is on critical theories of capitalism, but we also consider its advocates, such as the enigmatic Joseph Schumpeter and, its staunch defender, F.A. Hayek, a critic of capitalism's critics. The book offers a reconstruction of the theory of capitalism from Adam Smith and Karl Marx to the main theories of the present. Although we attempt to be reasonably comprehensive, we do not offer a systematic history. As with any narrative, there is some selection.

The term capitalism itself presents a problem to begin with. It was not used in the English language until the mid-1850s but was hardly used at all until the end of the nineteenth century.[1] So, a question is whether we are talking about the modern economy or something more specific, or perhaps a more general phenomenon. Is capitalism the name for the modern economy as a whole or a specific kind of economy or even a specific kind of society? Since today, capitalism is more or less universal and seemingly here to stay, it may be argued there is little point in using the term (Wark 2019). We do not agree with this view. The rationale for the continued use of the term capitalism is that it is a concept of critique: it is less a descriptive term than a critical one. It entails analysis, interpretation and critique. This does not necessarily mean a negative attitude. Milton Friedman used the term capitalism in a positive sense, as did Schumpeter. In the 1990s, it was popular term amongst the nascent new right in central and eastern Europe, as in the book, *Building Capitalism*, by the Czech proponent of privatization, Tomáš Ježek (2002).

DOI: 10.4324/9781351017671-1

Thrift (2005) has argued that capitalism now produces theories about itself, which can also be critical. Branko Milanović (2019) more recently says capitalism has triumphed simply because it has worked. In a similar vein, Iversen and Soskice (2019) argue that the 'advanced capitalist democracies' are resilient and anchored in the modern knowledge society because they have secured prosperity, at least for the educated workforce. Campbell and Hall (2021) see the success of capitalism residing in social cohesion, which when undermined through, for example, increased levels of social inequality, leads to economic instability. However, it is difficult to avoid a sense of a critical edge to the use of the term capitalism. Donald Sassoon has made the interesting observation that before the First World War, capitalism, in spite of its success, was in fact quite unpopular in culture, and still remains so. Many writers who were not favourable to socialism despised capitalists and financiers and regarded competitive capitalism as irrational or inhuman or vulgar (Sassoon 2019: 511). This is reflected in much of the literature of the pre-1918 period. Perhaps, as capitalism became tempered by democracy and the welfare state, elite cultural disdain for competitive capitalism decreased. The allure of wealth prevailed and it became a key part of the American Dream since the 1920s.

In almost every account of capitalism, there is a general recognition of the interconnected nature of the economy to society as a whole. Capitalism does not reside in a specific area of society such as the economy. It has a wider political and cultural significance in that it is interconnected with other spheres of life. Thus, in the Marxist tradition, it is generally seen as a political economy encompassing a system of social relations; in the work of Max Weber, it is part of the wider context of rationalization; and for others, ranging from Schumpeter to the Frankfurt School to Baudrillard and Jameson, it has a cultural logic that brings it out of the economic domain into the wider cultural fabric of society. Weber also stressed that capitalism as an economic activity is embedded in a 'spirit' that gives it a moral legitimation. Schumpeter, following Weber, argued it had a civilizational dimension.

One of the reasons why it is so hard to pin capitalism down is that it is a term that also captures 'the non-contractual in the contract'. It not only concerns economic activity but also goes beyond the strictly contractual. This idea was reflected in Marx's theory of commodity fetishism and the wage labour contract. It was also accepted by Talcott Parsons, who effectively created the discipline of sociology out of what economics could not explain, though he did not use in any significant sense the term capitalism.[2] In modern sociology, especially since Durkheim and Mauss, the non-contractual was captured by the theory of social representations and the symbolic nature of all social activity. Mauss, who was a socialist,[3] drew attention to the centrality of the gift in social relationships in his seminal essay in 1925, 'The Gift' (Mauss 1990). Although he never developed a theory of capitalism, he showed how the symbolic form of the gift – which requires, giving, receiving and reciprocating – is implicit in all social relationships. The gift and the commodity, while being different, are often intersecting, and many gifts are themselves also commodities.[4] But neither are reducible to the other. The gift is also a reminder of the danger of seeing capitalism lurking everywhere.

Recent accounts of capitalism often emphasize its variable nature. There is no one single type of capitalism but a multiplicity of forms. As Thrift (2005) has also argued, capitalism is not a total system but is more akin to a project that is continuously under construction. All the classical accounts noted the historical evolution of capitalism, from mercantilism to entrepreneurial or liberal capitalism to various kinds of protective or state capitalism to monopoly capitalism to late capitalism.[5] Capitalism emerged in a long historical process that goes back to the twelfth century when some features of capitalism were present in the northern Italian city states. Capitalistic activity can be found as far back as in antiquity. Early capitalism emerged from commerce and trade and the rise of finance, which made possible a web of relationships defined by debt and credit (Graeber 2011). However, the existence of capitalist activities prior to the modern period does not necessarily mean that capitalism as such existed, since such enterprises were fairly marginal to the pre-modern economy as a whole. As the dominant and comprehensive form of economic organization, it is a modern phenomenon. The consolidation of capitalism as such occurred in the early modern period under mercantilism, so-called political capitalism, under the control of the absolute state (mercantilism of course also persisted, as did the *ancien regime*).

In this period, the rise of capitalism in Europe can be seen as part of a more general advancement of commercial activity world-wide (Goody 2004). The 'Great Divergence', to use Pomeranz's term, when Europe overtook the rest of the world did not occur until much later, arguably as late as the nineteenth century (Pomeranz 2000). In the western context, we cannot speak of a transition to capitalism until at least the late sixteenth century. Marxist historians have emphasized the importance of agrarian capitalism that came with the commercialization of farming in late Tudor England as a key step in the emergence of capitalism, along with war as a mechanism for the opening up of markets, which are potentially global.[6] Wallerstein drew attention to capitalism as a world system. He argued that capitalism is not just an economic system as such, but a world system and embraces many other dimensions of the social world beyond the economic (Wallerstein 1974). But the high age of modern capitalism was in the nineteenth century with the rise of the free market and industrialization. The twentieth century began with the growth of monopoly capitalism and the giant corporation, above all in the USA.

The historical development of capitalism did not proceed in one direction. The older approaches, going back to Smith and Marx, tended to see the rise of the modern economy in terms of stages. We are more sceptical of this view, which persisted well into the middle of the twentieth century. There is no one trajectory and capitalism today exists in a variety of cultural and political forms. Barrington Moore in a classic work, *Social Origins of Dictatorship and Democracy*, drew attention to the various combinations of capitalism, democracy and dictatorship (Moore 1996). Recent scholarship has stressed global varieties of capitalism, with the Asian varieties perhaps the most significant (Hamilton and Shin 2015; Coates 2005; Amable 2004). In a narrower sense, capitalism is also mediated by its relation to the state (Hall and Soskice 2001). This pluralization of types of capitalism does not mean that it does not have a defining core. It would not make any logical sense to say something exists only in a plurality of forms without any common characteristics. In the terms of the French Regulation School, following Michel Aglietta (1979), a possible solution to this problem is to see the varieties in terms of different modes of regulation interacting with different regimes of accumulation. Whatever the solution, the problem of diversity underlies the need for conceptual clarity on what capitalism as a term means.

It is hopefully not too contentious to suggest, at least for the heuristic purpose of a working definition, that capitalism is an economic system based on (1) free enterprise and the competitive market; (2) the pursuit of profit and its private appropriation; (3) wage labour and the production of commodities; (4) property rights; (5) the financial infrastructure of money and investment that makes possible credit and debt; (6) a highly variable degree of state regulation; and (7) a propensity for growth as the productive reinvestment of profit. To refer to an economic activity as capitalist is to say that it is driven by the pursuit of profit as opposed to other ends, for example charity. Capitalism entails a system of production of commodities, which are produced by wage labour and distributed through markets for mostly private consumption (but not neglecting public uses). It is underpinned by the legal institution of private property, in the sense of the private ownership of, what Marx referred to, as the means of production. In historical perspective, it was based on formally free labour as opposed to other kinds of labour, such as slavery or serfdom. For a long period, trans-Atlantic slavery was an essential component of modern capitalism. It may be the case that in the future wage labour will be less important as a result of technological advancement. It is a gigantic global system in terms of the organization of production, markets for tangible and non-tangible commodities, consumption. The opening sentence of *Capital* vol. 1 captures this emphasis on the commodity: 'The wealth of societies in which the capitalist mode of production appears, presents itself as an "immense collection of commodities"'. But the commodity is not just an economic phenomenon. As with money, as Georg Simmel in *The Philosophy of Money* [1900] showed, the commodity has a symbolic form, which brings it into the sphere of culture and social relations. Theorists such as Arnason, drawing on Castoriadis have stressed the presence of imaginary significations in the make-up of capitalism and which ramify across the social world. In this vein, Deutschmann (2001b) has drawn attention to 'the promise of absolute wealth' that capitalism presents.

Defining the economic dimension of capitalism opens up the wider context of capitalism. Once consumption is brought into the picture, the economic unavoidably encroaches on the social world, for capitalism is ultimately anchored in something other than the system of production. Commodities need to be desired and bought and the people who buy them need to be in a position to do so. The acquisitive spirit as much as the system of production drives capitalism. This brings capitalism into the domain of wealth creation and prosperity, which in turns provides democracy with a basis since it makes possible stability without which democracy fares badly. But, capitalism, turbo-driven by growth, does not always achieve stability. The reality is often turmoil and upheaval.

To invoke the notion of capitalism is at the same time to refer to problems. This is because capitalism, in reaching into other areas of society necessarily causes problems, such as poverty, exploitation, inequality, greed, and environmental destruction. As a system of production, it necessarily depends on access to vast supplies of energy, which today as oil and gas slowly gives way to lithium and other minerals, are perhaps the greatest challenges of all. Also, the new sources of energy bring with them new kinds of power (Mitchell 2011). Depending on where one stands politically, these problems may be seen as integral to capitalism or regarded as by-products that can be ameliorated. But that is exactly the issue. It is not possible to separate the economic from the political: the problems that capitalism produces are not just problems of organization or management; they are political ones and are not therefore easily remedied by non-political means. This means that capitalism is unavoidably embroiled in social struggles and political contestation (Delanty 2020).

Not only is capitalism inextricably connected to other aspects of society, for example the state, but also it became entangled in democracy. More or less every theory of capitalism includes a theory of the relation of the economy to the state. It is impossible to conceive of capitalism without an account of the state, which creates the legal framework that makes possible market transactions. Markets preceded capitalism but capitalism relies more on markets than any economic system ever did. Markets are in effect sustained by states. Even Marx did not question the basic rationality of the state and the neoliberal attack on the state also did not in reality reject the state as such which was critical to the delivery of neoliberal goals. It was Weber, along with Sombart, who most clearly showed how the emergence of capitalism was facilitated by the 'legal rational' state, which provided it with the necessary instruments, including banking systems, the regulation of finance, legal guarantees for contracts etc. Imperialism was also a major feature of earlier capitalist development and entailed a close link between the state and capitalist firms. With the rise of the 'tax state', the state came to depend on capitalism to provide it with its principal source of revenue (Cardoso and Laitin 2013). Inescapably, much of the rest of society came to depend on capitalism, since the tax state sustained public provision of key institutions such as the modern welfare state.

Capitalism increasingly became entwined in democracy, which was linked to the rise of taxation and helped to stabilize capitalism. As the labour force increased in size, it also acquired more power and intensified democratization. This was also related to the increased importance of the skilled working class, which had invested in education and citizenship. As the work force became more educated and as capitalism became more and more entrenched in technology with the so-called knowledge society, not only a symbiotic but also a fraught relationship emerged between capitalism and democracy. But this tendency was not specific to the skilled working class, as Mitchell (2011) has argued, for the old coal-based capitalism led to 'carbon democracy' as a result of the power of the coal workers and other industrial workers. The era of industrial capitalism was based on a fairly homogenous working class – the coal and steel workers at its core – while today the new sources of energy and production have led in part to a more heterogeneous system of wage labour in which the 'precariat' is more central. Service workers in the gig economy are as likely to be migrants and female, in contrast with the demographic typifying the proletariat in industrial capitalism.

While the philosophical idea of democracy preceded capitalism, the later took precedence in terms of the organization of society. So when democracy emerged as a political system, it did so in the context of societies that were largely capitalist. There was henceforth a certain co-development of democracy and capitalism, though with considerable variation. So far, every democracy has been capitalist. Both capitalism and democracy were underpinned by the idea of freedom, at least in the western world. But it was a relation of tension, if not of contradiction, since capitalism has a natural tendency to lead to inequality, while democracy – which is in part legitimated by a normative idea – is based not just on freedom but also equality. Liberty and equality are not always compatible. Consequentially, two rival political philosophies emerged, liberalism and socialism. Many of the major theories of capitalism in the twentieth century were framed by these philosophies. While rival systems, coherent positions did emerge that combined elements of both, as in the case of social liberalism of which Durkheim was a representative. In practice, modern democracies when they finally consolidated attempted to fuse different normative projects. Today, a major question is whether capitalism and democracy can co-exist or whether there is a fundamental incompatibility (Bowles and Gintis 1986). It is widely believed that the era of harmony – suggested by the idea of democratic capitalism – is in crisis since the turmoil produced by neoliberalism and financial capitalism in 2008–2010, as well as increased levels of inequality (Streeck 2014). Capitalism may no longer be producing the conditions favourable to democracy – equality, cohesion, social progress. But it is also not self-evident that there is a general and irreversible slide towards neo-liberalization, as theorists such as Streeck believe is the case (Thelen 2014, Sadian 2022). It also remains to be seen if the Chinese path to modernity, capitalism counter-balanced by the Leninist state, will survive the world-wide push for democracy.

According to Branko Milanović, there are now two types of capitalism competing with each other, liberal meritocratic capitalism and political capitalism (Milanović 2019). The latter is amply represented by different varieties of authoritarianism, as for example in Russia and China. There is no natural tendency for capitalism to lead towards democracy. For much of the history of capitalism, democracy was suppressed. Yet, it is also incontrovertible, as Schumpeter recognized, that capitalism produced the conditions favourable to democracy, as in the example mentioned of the creation of a knowledge-based working class, whose interests and motivation cultivated an inclusive and democratic idea of society. The result was tendencies that resisted capitalism while at the same time facilitating its reproduction. Schumpeter was of course mistaken in thinking that the emergence of democratic currents would be detrimental to capitalism.

There are other powerful forces at work, especially the ecological and the implications of datafication. The classical theories of capitalism, in fact more or less every theory of capitalism until very recently, did not see the relation with the natural world as a relevant consideration. The exploitation of the worker, not the exploitation of nature, was considered to be the main problem of capitalism. It is true that Marx recognized the violent nature of capitalism in appropriating the natural environment in its relentless search for raw materials, but this remained a background consideration. Today, one of the most important critiques of capitalism questions growth, which was the very condition of the possibility of capitalism, namely continued growth based on carbon energy. Until now, this was taken for granted since it acquired its legitimacy from its capacity for improving individual living conditions and social progress (Borowy and Schmelzer 2017). Today the engine of growth, which was based on carbon capitalism as well as, what Mitchell (2011) has termed, 'carbon democracy' is breaking down in low growth economies at a time when the ecological challenge has changed the political landscape in far-reaching ways (see also Di Muzio and Ovadia 2016).

In this book, we have placed at the centre of the narrative the pivotal role of crisis in capitalism. The major historical moments of crisis defined the trajectory of capitalism. In terms of economic crises – that is crises that developed primarily from the economic rationality of capitalism – there were three major ones: first, the Wall Street Crash of 1929 and the subsequent Great Depression of the 1930s; second, the fiscal crisis in the early 1970s and third, the financial crash of 2008–10.[7] Each of these led to major changes in the organization of capitalism. The first led to the end of what Karl Polanyi called the 'Great Transformation' in which nineteenth-century liberal capitalism came to an end in a new era of protectionism and various forms of state capitalism along with the rise of monopoly capitalism (Polanyi 2001 [1944]). This set the stage for new theories of capitalism, since the economic and the political were entangled in each other. Along with Polanyi's classic work of 1944, *The Great Transformation*, F. A. Hayek produced a new conception of capitalism that was to become the bedrock of neoliberalism in later decades. The period saw the emergence of J. M. Keynes' proposals for the organization of capitalism by a more benevolent state. The onset of the crisis of the 1970s saw the rise of new Marxist theories of late capitalism[8] – Habermas, Mandel, Jameson – and the beginnings of new critical theories, such as those associated with French post-structuralism and the cultural left, including feminism. The period witnessed the emergence of neoliberalism, whose triumph in part solved some of the systemic problems of capitalism and global finance capitalism. But the resolution of the problems was simply postponed, as Wolfgang

Streeck has shown (Streeck 2014). The early promises of globalization faded and by 2007 a new crisis emerged in the finance sector and rapidly pervaded the wider social and political spectrum culminating in a new era of austerity and precarity (Azmanova 2020). The crisis was mostly averted by c. 2010 but it has opened up new critiques of capitalism and the prospects of post-capitalism have once again been posed. While the economic crisis as such ended, the political crisis continued since the economic question became inextricably entwined in the ecological question, which had gained a new momentum. The Covid-19 pandemic introduced an additional layer of complexity and crisis since lockdowns were also shutdowns (Delanty 2021). In the wake of the Russian invasion of Ukraine in February 2022, an energy crisis, followed by food crisis, suddenly emerged as the western world woke up to the dire implications of dependency on Russian gas.

This entwinement of the economic and the political has been central to the dynamics of capitalism. Going back to Marx, as outlined in Chapter 1, the economic analysis of capitalism was part of an account of political modernity that began in the spring of 1848 when 'Bourgeois revolution' swept across Europe. For Marx, this prepared the way for 'Proletarian revolution', which would be hastened by the systemic crises of capitalism. Polanyi, who we discuss in detail in Chapter 4, argued that the 'great transformation' brought about by the rise of the market and its dominance over society, led to a political counter-movement to re-embed the economy in protective social institutions. To make a general claim, the economy is always necessarily political and embedded in society. This has been persuasively argued by many authors, such as Fraser and Jaeggi (2005) and Joerges et al. (2005), who have taken up the Polanyian argument, shorn of some of its more problematical aspects. The French Regulation School offered a far-reaching theory and analysis of how capitalism overcomes its inherent tendency towards crisis by creating modes of regulation that enable it to stabilize over time, until new crises emerge leading to a new mode of accumulation. One of the major examples, as in the classic study by Michel Aglietta, is the way Fordism became embedded in the Keynesian state, which provided it with a model of regulation (Aglietta 1979). This approach within institutional economics and international political economy – pioneered by Aglietta along with Robert Boyer and Alain Lipietz – sees capitalism as an economic system unable to stabilize itself without a mode of regulation, which organizes or normalizes capitalism without ever reaching a perfect equilibrium. Markets are embedded in Non-markets social relations as well as civil society. As the French theorists and others such as Bob Jessop demonstrated, capitalism is an instituted order that also draws on pre-capitalist logics. It requires not just co-ordination, but also regulation to manage its contradictions.[9] However, the tensions remain, within what the regulation school refer to as the mode of development, and eventually lead to crises and breakdowns.

Drawing on the philosophy of Cornelius Castoriadis, Johann Arnason has shown in a similar vein that modernity more generally should be theorized as a field of tensions arising from a central conflict, which can be characterized in terms of an economic and political conflict between capitalism and the political striving for autonomy (Arnason 2001, 2015). The latter can be related to processes of democratization. Modernity should not be conflated with capitalism, as is a tendency more broadly, but specifically within Marxist inspired literature. Braudel in his major survey of the sources of capitalism tended to see western civilization in terms of the rise of capitalism (Braudel 1978). This is also the case with Wallerstein for whom capitalism and modern civilization are more or less synonymous (Wallerstein 1983). Inspired by Castoriadis's idea of capitalism as an expression of unlimited rational mastery, power and rationality, Arnason sees capitalism as having an inbuilt dynamism that allows it to undergo continuous transformation. But it is also characterized by contradictions within its bureaucratizing drive and which are not fully explained by the Marxist theory of class conflict, nor by Weber's theory of rationalization. Capitalism runs up against counter-movements that seek to affirm human autonomy, as for example democracy, and it cannot entirely domesticate, what Castoriadis called, the 'radical imaginary', which all societies have, namely the projection of a positive vision of their future which serves to orient them (Castoriadis 1987 [1975]). This topic of the imaginary that runs through and empowers capitalism is closely related to the question of the place and significance of culture in the development of capitalism. Since Weber, capitalism has been seen as linked to religion, even in part as an expression of religion (see Deutschmann 2001a, 2001b, 2015). In recent times since the post-modern critique of capitalism, but going back to the Frankfurt School's critique of capitalism, the cultural dimension of capitalism has been given much emphasis. In a major work, Boltanski and Chiapello (2006) showed that capitalism has acquired new spirits, which bring the struggle for autonomy into the heart of capitalism, giving it a new justification. Beckert (2016) has demonstrated how the realm of the imagination is central to the operative functions of capitalism especially today with the complex and crisis prone nature of finance capitalism. Fictional expectations are often what drives capitalism, which is far from being entirely rational.

The relative neglect of the economy has been an unfortunate development in contemporary social theory and in particular in critical theory. This is in contrast to the classical tradition both in sociological theory and in the older critical theory of the Frankfurt School, which was very much concerned with the critique of capitalism, at least until the mid-1940s when the *Dialectic of Enlightenment* and later Adorno's *Minima Moralia* brought about a change of direction towards cultural critique. The separation of the economy from the social and the political domain has been in part an outcome of disciplinary specialization. However, this does not quite explain the neglect of the economy in social theory, since contemporary social theory is itself very much the result of inter-disciplinarity. It would appear to be case that inter-disciplinarity in the culturally oriented social sciences has not always included economic theory. In this book, we have attempted to bring economics into the broad field of social and political theory. Capitalism cannot be understood only in terms of cultural phenomena or political struggles without engagement with political economy.

A key question that the very notion of capitalism raises is its possible end (Wallerstein et al. 2013). Since Marx, the notion of capitalism has generally been seen as an economic system or form of society that will one day come to an end. The chapters in the book engage with the various positions on this question. One thing is clear. Today it is no longer possible to envisage the end of capitalism in the way that it was in the nineteenth century. When Marx predicted the end of capitalism in the middle of the nineteenth century, it was at this time possible to image an alternative to capitalism, which had not yet become global. Large parts of the world were still pre-capitalist and pre-capitalist modes of production persisted alongside capitalism in the western world.[10] Perhaps more significantly, Marx was writing in the age of revolution when it was possible to imagine an existing political order swept away by direct mass political action. Four conditions had to be fulfilled for transition to a socialist order for Marx: there had to be a certain development of democratization (initially achieved by bourgeois revolution); an advanced economic development of capitalism (leading to ever more systemic crises) and the struggle between labour and capital had to be advanced with labour highly organized; additionally, socialist political organization had to be available to provide leadership. By the end of the nineteenth century, and even before Marx's death in 1883, it was already difficult for these conditions to be met. The failure of Marx's four conditions to materialize led to the search for substitutes. The one that prevailed was the Leninist idea of revolutionaries taking power to do what was not going to happen as a result of class conflict. For the non-Leninist left for whom there had to be continuity with the democratic project, the result was that the revolutionary moment was perpetually postponed, while the memory of its pursuit remained engraved in the political imagination of the left. According to Traverso (2016), this led to a culture of left-wing melancholy arising from a sense of a loss and is expressed in mourning and resignation; yet, for much of the twentieth century it was possible to imagine an alternative to capitalism, simply by virtue of the existence of a rival economic and political system to western capitalism.

Today it is rather more difficult to image a revolutionary event in the same way (Wallerstein et al. 2013). Societal complexity, the vastly more expansive nature of the deep state and the pervasiveness of capitalism make it unlikely that there will be a revolutionary transition to a post-capitalist order. The major experiment in history with an alternative to capitalism failed with the collapse of the USSR in 1991. The end of the Soviet experiment is also a reminder than an alternative order is not necessarily better. The demise of Soviet communism and state socialism in central and eastern europe should not be mistaken for the end of ideology or some such notion of the 'end of history'. Many new ideological conflicts followed, but these were less organized on economic issues and class struggle than on cultural ones concerning identity (see Castells 1997, 1998). It is also clear that capitalism has a greater capacity to absorb opposition than was believed for much of the twentieth century. In the final chapter of this book, some visions of post-capitalism are discussed.

It is arguably the case that today there is more questioning of capitalism than ever before. Nineteenth-century socialism was not primarily or exclusively anti-capitalist. Much of it was driven by anti-industrialization and rooted in the customs and institutions of a vanishing world. Marxism and revolutionary socialism represented the most important challenge to capitalism. But where it triumphed after 1917, it was in a largely pre-capitalist part of the world. With the institutionalization of the left in the post-1945 period, capitalism anchored itself in modern society. In western societies in the decades following the end of the war, there was a general acceptance of capitalism so long as it served social interests. In this period, there was not considerable questioning of social and political order in the western world, where a pact had been made with capitalism, which had managed to sustain its growth trajectory. Patriarchy and religion ensured relative political domestication. By the 1970s that had changed: late capitalism was less functional, continued economic growth could no longer be assumed and new cultural developments led to widespread questioning of authority, including those sources of authority that capitalism indirectly depended on. Yet, despite the rise of the New Left and new critiques of capitalism, capitalism endured. This is perhaps because in the latter three decades of the twentieth century other political currents were more significant than anti-capitalism, for example the various rights movements, the anti-nuclear movement, feminism and environmentalism. Marxism also moved away from a concern with the political economy of capitalism to engage with wider social struggles. It is possible that today there is a new interest in questioning capitalism. There is also the spectre that capitalism may have abolished itself in all but name, as suggested by recent accounts of digital capitalism, surveillance capitalism and cognitive capitalism. In these accounts of the digital economy, a 're-feudalization' has taken place whereby capitalism has been replaced by the techno-feudalism. In this new order there are not workers as such, as everyone works for a rentier minority who control the intellectual property rights of the digital economy.[11] But one must not lose sight of the fact that capitalism also endured for due to its intrinsic strength and adaptability, including its ability to 'buy time', as argued by Wolfgang Streeck (2014).

In this light, for this book the notions of crisis and critique are closely linked. We have identified four major critiques of capitalism in the classical literature unto the 1970s. To begin, Marx's conception of capitalism was articulated as a critique of political economy. This was continued by many of the major Marxist theorists of the first half of the twentieth century, such as Georg Lukács, Rosa Luxemburg, the British Marxists, such as Maurice Dobbs, and the Austro-Marxists, such as Karl Renner and Rudolf Hilferding. It was taken up by later Marxists, including Paul Sweezy and Harry Braverman. Second, Max Weber's theory of capitalism can be characterized as a conservative cultural critique of capitalism, even if it does not capture all his writings on the subject, which were a mix of defence and critique. Conservative cultural critique was also reflected in Joseph Schumpeter's theory of capitalism, which was also cast in the terms of a conservative cultural critique of the new era of monopoly capitalism and the decline of the creative spirit that was supposedly the basis of liberal capitalism. The third critique of capitalism is essentially a moral critique. This is based on the idea of what E. P. Thompson termed the moral economy and best exemplified by Karl Polanyi's *The Great Transformation*. The moral critique of capitalism, while compatible with Marxism, captures the spirit of democratic socialism (Rogan 2017). It may also be compatible with a more socially responsible kind of capitalism, as in Tony Judt's vision in *Ill Fares the Land* (Judt 2010). The fourth critique is a weaker one that is essentially a plea for a more benevolent kind of capitalism. This vision of capitalism was nurtured by was nurtured by John Maynard Keynes, whose work was also tinged by a civilizational critique of capitalism (see Mann 2019). In his work, discussed in Chapter 6, a rationale was established for a more controlled capitalism regulated by experts. For this reason, due to the strong emphasis on fiscal policy, what emerged was a technocratic critique of capitalism that was opposed to unregulated markets.

As mentioned at the beginning of the Introduction, this book offers a reconstruction of major writings on capitalism. This aim is not for its own sake, but to provide a basis for understanding the nature of capitalism in the times in which we live. We endeavour to show the limits as well as the relevance of the classical and more recent theories of capitalism for the present day. We show in later chapters the relevance of other perspectives, such as critiques of capitalism emanating from the Black radical tradition – Cedric Robinson for example – as well decolonial/postcolonial and feminist critiques.

The world in which many of these writings were produced has vanished and we need to be especially mindful of the limits of the older theories. Capitalism in the times of Adam Smith, Karl Marx and Max Weber was very different from today. We live in vastly different times. The world's population is now approaching 8 billion and is much more mobile and interconnected than ever before. The wealth that capitalism has produced remains desirable, while its negative consequences are not easily overcome. The non-western world is no longer marginal and there is now the challenge of climate change compelling the need for a post-carbon future, either for capitalism, or for an alternative. Yet, for all their limits, the authors we look at in this book provided illuminating works that shaped how we think about capitalism.

Notes

1 See for a general survey, Hartwell and Engerman (2003) and Ingham (2008/2011). Also Williams (1976).
2 His main substantive discussion of capitalism as such was in 1929 in a discussion of Weber and Sombart. Interestingly, the term 'capitalism' appears in the title in quotation marks (Parsons 1929).
3 Durkheim was politically a social liberal.
4 See Carter and Benson (2008) and Gregory (1982). The work of David Graeber is also relevant to this question. See Graeber (2011).
5 On the historical emergence of capitalism, some useful accounts can be found in Arrighi (1994), Baechler (1976), Baechler et al. (1988), Fulcher (2004), Kocka (2016) and Wallerstein (1983).
6 This is the so-called Brenner thesis (see Aston and Philpin 1985). See also Hilton (1978) and Wood (2002).
7 See Aliber and Kindleberger for a discussion of other crises, which they refer to as 'panics' (Aliber and Kindleberger 2015. Originally Kindleberger 1978).
8 The term is of an older vintage, going back to Sombart, but was revived in the 1970s by Marxist theorists, especially Ernst Mandel (see Chapter 8).
9 On the regulation school, see also Aglietta (1998), Boyer (1990), Boyer and Sailand (2002) [1975]), Jessop (1997, 2001), Jessop and Sum (2006) and Neilson (2012).
10 This is still the case today: over half the land in the UK is still a result of feudal ownership, especially in Scotland.
11 For a discussion, see Morozov (2022).

References

Aglietta, M. 1979. *A Theory of Capitalist Regulation: The US Experience*. London: New Left Books.

Aglietta, M. 1998. 'Towards a New Regime of Growth'. *New Left Review*, 232. Nov/Dec.: 41–90.

Aliber, R. and Kindleberger, C. 2015 [1978]. *Manias, Panics and Crashes: A History of Financial Crashes*, 7th edition. London: Palgrave.

Amable, B. 2004. *The Diversity of Modern Capitalism*. Oxford: Oxford University Press.

Arnason, J. 2001. 'Capitalism in Context: Sources, Trajectories and Alternatives.' *Thesis Eleven*, 66: 99–125.

Arnason, J. 2015. 'Theorizing Capitalism: Classical Foundations and Contemporary Foundations'. *European Journal of Social Theory*, 18 (4): 351–67.

Arrighi. G. 1994. *The Long Twentieth Century: Money, Power and the Origins of Our Time*. London: Verso.

Aston, T. H. and Philpin, C. H. E. (eds.) 1985. *The Brenner Debate: Agrarian Class Structure and Economic Development in PreIndustrial Europe*. Cambridge: Cambridge University Press.

Azmanova, A. 2020. *Capitalism on Edge: How Fighting Precarity Can Achieve Radical Change Without Crisis or Utopia*. New York: Columbia University Press.

Baechler, J. 1976 [1971]. *The Origins of Capitalism*. Oxford: Blackwell.

Baechler, J., Hall, J. and Mann, M. (eds) 1988. *Europe and the Rise of Capitalism*. Oxford: Blackwell.

Beckert, J. 2016. *Imagined Futures: Fictional Expectations and Capitalist Dynamics*. Cambridge: Harvard University Press.

Benson, M. and Carter, D. 2008. 'Introduction: Nothing in Return: Distinctions between the Gifts and Commodities in Contemporary Societies'. *Anthropology in Action*, 15 (3): 1–7.

Boltanski, L. Chiapello, E. 2006 [1999]. *The New Spirit of Capitalism*. London: Verso.

Borowy, I. and Schmelzer, M. (eds.) 2017. *History of the Future of Economic Growth: Historical Roots of Current Debates on Sustainable DeGrowth*. London: Routledge.

Bowles, S. and Gintis, H. 1986. *Democracy and Capitalism: Property, Community, and the Contradictions of Modern Social Thought*. London: Routledge & Kegan Paul.
Boyer, R. 1990. *The Regulation School: A Critical Introduction*. New York: Columbia University Press.
Boyer, R. and Sailard, Y. (eds.) 2002. *Regulation Theory: The State of the Art*. London: Routledge.
Braudel, F. 1978 [1967–1973]. *Civilization and Capitalism, 15th-18th Century*. Vol. 3. London: Fontana.
Campbell, J. and Hall, J. A. 2021. *What Capitalism Needs: Forgotten Lessons of Great Economists*. Cambridge: Cambridge University Press.
Cardosa, J. and Lains, P. 2013. *Paying for the Liberal State: The Rise of Public Finance in Nineteenth-Century Europe*. Cambridge: Cambridge University Press.
Castells, M. 1997. *The Information Age: Vol. 2 The Power of Identity*. Oxford: Blackwell.
Castells, M. 1998. *The Information Age: Vol 3. The End of the Millennium*. Oxford: Blackwell.
Castoriadis, C. 1987 [1975]. *The Imaginary Institution of Society*. Oxford: Blackwell.
Coates, D. (ed.) 2005. *Varieties of Capitalism, Varieties of Approaches*. London: Palgrave.
Delanty, G. 2020. *Critical Theory and Social Transformation: Crises of the Present and the Future Possibilities*. London: Routledge.
Delanty, G. (ed.) 2021. *Pandemics, Society and Politics: Critical Reflections on the Pandemic*. Berlin: De Gruyter.
Deutschmann, C. 2001a 'The Promise of Absolute Wealth: Capitalism as a Religion?' *Thesis Eleven*, 66 (1): 32–56.
Deutschmann, C. 2001b. 'Capitalism as Religion? An Unorthodox Analysis of Entrepreneurship'. *European Journal of Social Theory*, 4 (4): 387–403.
Deutschmann, C. 2015. 'Disembedded Markets as a Mirror of Society'. *European Journal of Social Theory*, 18 (4): 368–81.
Di Muzio, T. and Ovadia, J. S. (eds.) 2016. *Energy, Capitalism and World Order*. London: Palgave.
Fraser, N. and Jaeggi, R. 2005. *Capitalism: A Conversation in Critical Theory*. Cambridge: Polity.
Fulcher, J. 2004. *Capitalism: A Very Short Introduction*. Oxford: Oxford University Press.
Giddens, A. 1973. *Capitalism and Modern Social Theory*. Cambridge: Cambridge University Press.
Goody, J. 2004. *Capitalism and Modernity: The Great Debate*. Cambridge: Polity Press.
Graeber, D. 2011. *Debt: The First 5,000 Years*. London: Melville House.
Gregory, C. 1982. *Gifts and Commodities*. Chicago: University of Chicago Press.
Hall, P. and Soskice, D. 2001. *Varieties of Capitalism: The Institutional Foundations of Comparative Advantage*. Oxford: Oxford University Press.
Hamilton, G. and Shin, S. 2015. 'Demand-Response Industrialization in East Asia: A New Critique of Political Economy.' *European Journal of Social Theory*, 18 (4): 390–412.
Hartwell, R. and Engerman, S. 2003. 'Capitalism'. In: *The Oxford Encyclopaedia of Economic History*. Vol. 1. Edited by J. Mokyr. Oxford: Oxford University Press.
Hilton, R. 1978. *The Transition from Feudalism to Capitalism*. London: Verso.
Ingham, G. 2008 [2011 new edition]. *Capitalism*. Cambridge: Polity Press.
Iversen, T. and Soskice, D. 2019. *Democracy and Prosperity: Reinventing Capitalism through a Turbulent Century*. Princeton: Princeton University Press.
Jessop, B. 1997. 'Survey Article: The Regulation Approach'. *Journal of Political Philosophy*, 5 (3): 287–326.
Jessop, B. (ed.). 2001. *Regulation Theory and the Crises of Capitalism*. Vol. 5. Cheltenham: Edgar.
Jessop, B. and Sum, N.L. (eds.). 2006. *Beyond the Regulation Approach: Putting Capitalist Economies in their Place*. Cheltenham: Edgar.
Ježek, T. 2002. *Building Capitalism: The Transformation of the Former Soviet Bloc*. Cambridge: Cambridge University Press.
Joerges, C., Strath, B., and Wagner, P. (eds). 2005. *The Economy as a Polity: The Political Constitution of Contemporary Capitalism*. London: UCL Press.
Judt, T. 2010. *Ill Fares the Land*. London: Penguin.

Kershaw, P.V. 2020. 'Hamlet without the Prince of Denmark: Bringing Capitalism Back into the "New" History of Capitalism'. *Journal of Historical Sociology*, 33: 61–73. https://doi.org/10.1111/johs.12263
Kocka, J. 2016. *Capitalism: A Short History*. Princeton: Princeton University Press.
Mann, G. 2019. *In the Long Run We are All Dead: Keynesianism, Political Economy and Revolution*. London: Verso.
Mauss, M. 1990 [1925]. *The Gift*. London: Routledge.
Milanovic, B. 2019. *Capitalism Alone: The Future of the System that Rules the World*. Cambridge: Harvard University Press.
Mitchell, T. 2011. *Carbon Democracy: Political Power in the Age of Oil*. London: Verso.
Moore, B. 1996. *Social Origins of Dictatorship and Democracy: Lord and Peasant in the Making of the Modern World*. New York: Bacon Press.
Morozov, E. 2022. 'Critique of Techno-Feudalism'. *New Left Review*, 133–4 (Jan–April): 89–120.
Neilson, D. 2012. 'Remaking the Connections: Marxism and the French Regulation School.' *Review of Radical Political Economy*, 44 (2): 160–77.
Parsons, T. 1929 '"Capitalism" in Recent German Literature: Sombart and Weber'. *Journal of Political Economy*, 37 (1): 31–5.
Polanyi, K. 2001 [1944]. *The Great Transformation*. Boston: Beacon Press.
Pomeranz, K. 2000. *The Great Divergence: China, Europe and the Making of the Modern World Economy*. Princeton: Princeton University Press.
Rogan, T. 2017. *The Moral Economists: R. H. Tawney, Karl Polanyi, E. P. Thompson, and the Critique of Capitalism*. Princeton: Princeton University Press.
Sadian, S. 2022. 'Wolfgang Streeck on Consumption, Depoliticisation and Neoliberal Capitalism'. *European Journal of Social Theory*. https://doi.org/10.1177/13684310221097016
Sassoon, D. 2019. *The Anxious Triumph: A Global History of Capitalism, 1860–1914*. London: Penguin.
Streeck, W. 2014. *Buying Time: The Delayed Crisis of Democratic Capitalism*. London: Verso.
Thelen, K. 2014. *Varieties of Liberalization and the New Politics of Social Solidarity*. Cambridge: Cambridge University Press.
Thrift, N. 2005. *Knowing Capitalism*. London: Sage.
Traverso, E. 2016. *Left-Wing Melancholia: Marxism, History, and Memory*. New York: Columbia University Press.
Wallerstein, I. 1974. *The Modern World System: Agriculture and the Origins of the European World Economy in the Sixteenth Century*. New York: Academic Press.
Wallerstein, I. 1983. *Historical Capitalism*. London: Verso.
Wallerstein, I., Collins, R., Mann, M., Derluguian, and Calhoun, C. 2013. *Does Capitalism Have a Future?* Oxford: Oxford University Press.
Wark, M. 2019. *Capital Is Dead: Is This Something Worse?* London: Verso.
Williams, R. 1976. 'Capitalism'. In: *Keywords*. London: Croom Helm.
Wood, E. M. 2002 [1999]. *The Origins of Capitalism: A Longer View*. London: Verso.

1 From Smith to Marx

Marx's Critique of Capitalism

The very notion of capitalism is difficult to disentangle from the seminal ideas of Adam Smith and Karl Marx. Yet, neither used the term capitalism as such but gave to its analysis some of the most enduring theories about economy and society. Their theories are not just conceptual models; they are also normative critiques in that they sought to evaluate the economic forces shaping the modern world. Their legacies have shaped two very different traditions of thought and political practice. One the architect of modern liberalism and the other the founder of revolutionary socialism are classic figures whose writings have been too quickly reduced to political manifestos and have often been much misunderstood. Perhaps one such misunderstanding is the view that they represent rival systems of thought. Marx was deeply indebted to Smith whose ideas he advanced and he shared much of Smith's Enlightenment humanism. The two thinkers have also suffered the fate of division into early and late phases, with the early works dismissed or deemed incompatible with the later and more important ones (see Avineri 1968).[1]

This chapter will attempt to show that Smith and Marx are more compatible than is often thought. Their ideas need to be disengaged from the political philosophies that claimed their legacy. Many of the differences in their approaches to capitalism can be seen as a result of the very different times and contexts in which they wrote. Smith wrote in what was largely a mercantilist economy making the transition to pre-industrial capitalism and Marx in a more developed but a still limited era of industrial capitalism. The account offered here emphasizes how Marx built upon Smith's analysis rather than providing an incompatible theory. He did so in far-reaching ways. *Capital* [1867] is without parallel the most important analysis of the capitalist system, but would not have been possible without *The Wealth of Nations* [1796]. While historical figures, whose ideas were products of their age, Marx and Smith have a continued relevance for the present due in no small part to the fact that their ideas – or rather interpretations of their ideas – shaped the modern world long after their era had passed.

In this chapter, we see both figures as critics of capitalism, rather than one the apologist and the other the apostle of an alternative order. Both saw the modern economy as endangering social progress and human advancement that were the great promises of modernity. In the final section of this chapter, we reflect on the limits of Marx's critique of capitalism.

The Ambivalent Legacy of Adam Smith

The received view of Adam Smith requires the divorce of the author of *The Wealth of Nations* [1776] from the earlier *The Theory of Moral Sentiments* [1759]. Interpretations of

DOI: 10.4324/9781351017671-2

Adam Smith tend to be divided on whether the perspectives of both works can be reconciled or not. The mainstream view is that Smith discarded his earlier ideas for the more advanced position set forth in *The Wealth of Nations,* which supposedly contains the core principles of neoclassical economics. But this turns out to be a particular and highly selective interpretation of his legacy and of his *magnum opus*. While there can be no doubt that he was the father of modern economics, which hardly existed before him, like many Enlightenment thinkers he did not operate in just one domain. In fact, he held to a very sociological idea of the economy and of society. His contribution to modern economic thought must be placed alongside his social and political theory and his moral philosophy.

Did Adam Smith provide the basic justification for capitalism or not? It is certainly the case that his ideas have helped to define capitalism and in doing so gave to it a certain rationale. The core concepts of neoclassical economics concerning the principles of exchange, equilibrium in the pricing system, supply and demand and the workings of the market economy are certainly to be found in *The Wealth of Nations*, but so are many other ideas. Smith's defence of free trade must be understood in the context of the eighteenth century when crude mercantilist ideas where still influential and which he sought to refute. Letting aside the difficulty that the term capitalism[2] did not exist in his time, not least due to the fact that capitalism as such was in its infancy, it is equally plausible to say that Smith was offering a vision of how the modern capitalist economy could be organized in accordance with desirable principles about how society should be organized.

Smith viewed the economy, which he called 'commercial society', through the lens of moral philosophy. He was first and foremost a moral philosopher concerned with human nature and the problem of how the individual could live in harmony with society. His central concern was the question of how the free actions of the individual could be made to serve the collective interests of society. While he can be rightfully claimed to be the first modern economist, his Scottish Enlightenment heritage shaped his view of the economy as part of society. This idea rested on a basic conception of the social nature of human beings, a position he shared with the other major Scottish thinkers of the era, such as Adam Ferguson and John Millar, all of whom contributed to the emergence of sociology. Society is not an atomized set of individuals but interdependent. It was this insight that also guided his theory of the modern economy and the pursuit of prosperity and liberty. In fact, it is a view contrary to the basic axiom of faith of neoliberalism that the isolated individual pursuing their self-interest creates collective wealth. For Smith, capitalism must be able to create the collective good of all.

Smith saw the emerging commercial society of his time as based on the centrality of exchange and money. Now, exchange is basic to almost every form of economic organization. But, the rise of dynamic markets and with it the money, economy becomes one of the defining features of modernity and makes possible growth and thus wealth. It was reflected in the division of labour, which made possible a more efficient form of exchange, as in the famous example of the pin-maker discussed in the opening pages of *The Wealth of Nations* to illustrate the division of labour: no one person can efficiently make a pin, which requires the input of several workers each performing specialized tasks. So, market efficiency comes with capitalism and leads to wealth creation. Capitalism, he recognized, was leading to a new kind of society organized into three classes: the capitalist, the workers and the landowners, a structure which corresponds to the main dimensions of modern society: capital, labour and land. One major feature of this new order was the emergence of wage labour and with it new kinds of inequalities.

Much of the controversy about how we should evaluate Smith comes down to the question of the alleged primacy of self-interest over the common good. Smith famously asserted the central role of self-interest in modern society. But this is a notoriously elusive concept encompassing instrumental gain, the actions of individuals, liberty as opposed to constraint, the specialization of social functions, efficiency. Perhaps the most famous statement in *The Wealth of Nations* (in Book 1, Chapter 2) captures some of the complexity of the notion of self-interest:

> It is not from the benevolence of the butcher, the brewer, or the baker, that we expect our dinner, but from their regard to their own interest. We address ourselves, not to their humanity but to their self–love, and never talk to them of our own but of their advantages.
>
> (Smith 1976 [1776, 1789])

No other phrase in modern social and political theory has given rise to so much controversy and interpretation. What Smith meant, what he might have meant and what he said is open to interpretation. What we think these sentences mean is this: individuals who occupy different social positions pursue their different interests and in so doing collective advantages result. But this presupposes an order in which self-interest will result in advantages both for the individual seeking to further their interests and society as a whole. Smith took this for granted. The reason is clear. He had in mind a utopia. He was not describing the society in which he lived. The result was a bizarre paradox, as David Graeber pointed out: for at the time Smith was writing most English shopkeepers were relying on credit, which meant that their customers were relying on their benevolence (Graeber 2011: 335). Smith thought an optional model for society was one in which cash was used. To follow Graeber's argument:

> This allowed him to ignore the role of both benevolence *and* malevolence in economic affairs, both the ethos of mutual aid that forms the necessary foundation of anything that would look like a free market...*and* the violence and sheer vindictiveness that had actually gone into creating the competitive, self-interested markets that he was using as his model.
>
> (p. 336)

The received view would see order, even a perfect order, arising from the pursuit of self-interest alone, while another view – which was probably closer to his position – would see the need to create such an order to enable the pursuit of self-interest to generate collective advantages. In other words, self-interest cannot have the primacy that is often attributed to it. It requires for its working a social order in which other values exist. But this was a utopian model, as Graeber has commented, 'an imaginary world almost entirely free of debit and credit' (Graeber 2011: 353). This is both a serious limitation of Adam Smith's thinking and also its advantage – perhaps its only one in that he was not describing capitalism as it existed but as it should exist. Only a very selective reading of Smith – and the implausible separation of his mature work from the earlier *The Theory of Moral Sentiments* – would postulate the primacy of self-interest over other human attributes. In any case, self-interest, as in the above quote, is not reducible to instrumental gain, let alone greed, but is a product of the simple fact of societal specialization that comes with the division of labour. The butcher, the baker and the brewer are different professions and as such they operate according to their own dictates, not greed. As he put it elsewhere, the tailor does not make his own shoes but buys them from the shoemaker. So, what may appear to be logically primary is in fact connected to a greater societal order. The pursuit of self-interest is possible anyway only within a legal order and a value system that respects the public culture. The emerging commercial society is thus not only an instrumentalized economic system but also one embedded in social institutions, which are as much responsible for the collective good as the pursuit of individual gain. Smith also, contrary to the neoliberal doctrine, recognized the necessity for the state to regulate the economy, as in taxation and a banking system. Benevolence doesn't figure in this order, but trust does. Benevolence does not entirely vanish either, as with the modern welfare state a form of benevolence becomes central to the function of the state.

Smith in *The Theory of Moral Sentiments* emphasized the social dimension, the 'moral sentiments' underpinning modern commercial society (Smith 2009 [1759]). He wrote about, for instance, sympathy, prudence, generosity, justice and the public spirit. To characterize moral sentiments as opposed to self-interest would be a simplification of his thought. But they are not just related; they require each other. Self-interest as egoism, which roughly characterized the neoliberal interpretation, would be self-destructive if it were not embedded in social institutions and a moral conception of society. No system of exchange, even one based on egotism, can succeed if it is not based on trust and underlying moral principles. It is absolutely clear that Smith saw moral sentiments such as prudence and sympathy as necessary to correct greed. In that sense, Smith offered a moral critique of a certain kind of capitalism based on greed. It is difficult to characterize this vision of society as the victory of *homo economicus*.

According to Amartya Sen, Smith never abandoned the framework he developed in *The Theory of Moral Sentiments* (Sen 2009; see also 2010). In fact, he produced the sixth edition of that work shortly before his death. This underlies the need to place the later *Wealth of Nations* within the broader philosophical context developed in the earlier work. It implies a theory of economic life grounded in moral philosophy. It is remarkable how neoliberal theory has severed this link, so central to the thought of Adam Smith. Tim Rogan, in a similar vein, argues that Smith saw the science of economics within a moral framework. It was only after him, with Thomas Malthus and David Ricardo in the early 1800s, that the idea of the moral economy became marginalized after which a lapse into naturalism occurred (Rogan 2017: 88). In fact, as Emily Eriksen has shown, the major shift in economic thought that led to the first coherent defences of free trade occurred in England a century before *The Wealth of Nations* (Eriksen 2021). The kind of state regulation he was opposed to was one that benefited the rich.

Smith was a liberal, not a revolutionary socialist. He stood in the tradition of British liberalism, from Hobbes and Locke to Bentham and Mill. His contribution was to bring liberalism in the direction of economics, but for that he has been claimed as the false prophet of neoliberalism. He is in fact better seen as a social liberal who was concerned about social inequality and poverty. As he wrote in *The Wealth of Nations*: 'No society can surely be flourishing and happy, of which the far greater part of the members are poor and miserable' (Book 1 Chapter 8).

He was also opposed to the accumulation of wealth in the hands of the few, though he did believe that society overall benefits if some are rich. Since Milton Friedman's attempt to link the notion of the 'invisible hand' with the price system, Smith's work has been distorted as the champion of *laissez-faire* capitalism. But as often noted, the notion of the 'invisible hand' is mentioned only once in the c. 950 pages of *The Wealth of Nations* and in a discussion of how the pursuit of self-interest leads indirectly to an end that was no one's intention (Book 4 Chapter 11). Merchants, he notes, do not trade for the common good, but for their gain and in doing so, the common good is promoted from the resulting wealth they produce. His argument is thus that the market creates wealth and in doing so establishes the conditions for the common good, which paradoxically requires self-interest. But this works only if the organization of economic life is underpinned by the appropriate morals that check the prevalence of greed and other forces that would endanger the common interest.

The 'hidden hand' can mean several things. It has often been interpreted to be simply the cumulative effects of the market, even the notion of 'trickle-down' economics, but it is also an epistemological concept to refer to the deeper structures of society that in effect amount to social reality, since society is not simply the net sum of the actions of isolated individuals. Nor is it a structure created and orchestrated by the state. The hidden-hand also encompasses the social fact of societal interdependence, which he illustrated with the famous example of the woollen coat:

> The woollen-coat... is the produce of the joint labour of a great multitude of workmen. The shepherd, the sorter of the wool, the wool-comber or carder, the dyer, the scribbler, the spinner, the weaver, the fuller, the dresser, with many others, must all join their different arts in order to complete even this homely production.
>
> (Book 1 Chapter 1)

In the passage, he extends this analogy to encompass global trade. Much has been made of this concept, but it has been stretched beyond what it can reasonably cover.

Adam Smith's legacy in economic thought and in social and political theory has been considerable. In many ways, it is an ambivalent legacy in that his *magnum opus* has been generally interpreted in a limited way that neglected his moral philosophy. He was far from the prophet of market fundamentalism. He shaped not only nineteenth-century liberalism, but political economy and inspired Marx who brought his analysis of political economy to a new and more scientific level.

From Smith to Marx

One of Adam Smith's original insights, which influenced Marx, was that the basis of wealth is ultimately labour. Once the division of labour has taken place, as he argues in a key section of *The Wealth of Nations* (Book 1 Chapter 6), value can be acquired not only in a limited way from one's own labour but also from the labour of others: 'Labour, therefore, is the real measure of the exchangeable value of all commodities'. For Marx, this was an important insight but it did not go far enough: it was the buying and selling of labour for wages that gave to capitalism its key dynamic. Smith tended to see the economy as operating largely harmoniously. In his analysis, the various components interact without major tensions, let alone conflict. This perhaps reflected his benign view of the world and of human nature. He was of course writing at a time when capitalism was not very advanced and when the industrial proletariat had not yet emerged as a significant force in the world. His preoccupation was mostly with trade and with private entrepreneurialism in a society and economy that was still predominantly agrarian. World population was under 900 million during his lifetime. The urban world of industrial capitalism and with it massive population explosion had yet to emerge. While he recognized the tremendous transformation of the world brought about by the market and the fundamental fact of exchange as a key mechanism in modern society, he did not recognize the contradictions and violence in capitalism. By 1700, at least in Britain, agrarian capitalism and mercantilism was already firmly in place. The victory of exchange did not lead to the common good, but to the good of the few.

Anticipating Marx's distinction between use values and exchange values, Smith wrote in *The Wealth of Nations*:

> The word value, it is to be observed, has two different meanings ... The one may be called 'value in use'; the other, 'value in exchange.' The things which have the greatest value in use have frequently little or no value in exchange; and, on the contrary, those which have the greatest value in exchange have frequently little or no value in use. Nothing is more useful than water: but it will purchase scarce anything; scarce anything can be had in exchange for it. A diamond, on the contrary, has scarce any value in use; but a very great quantity of other goods may frequently be had in exchange for it.
>
> (Book 1, Chapter 4)

With capitalism, use values decline and are replaced by exchange values. Marx's innovation was to see that capitalism was bringing about commodification, which is what exchange values generate. The exchange economy was based on the production of commodities, not simply the generation of wealth. As a result, the relationship between individual choice and collective gain is more complicated. Smith recognized, contrary to the received view, that markets are mediated in social institutions, but he did not see that they are also embedded in relations of production and in exploitation. His analysis rested on a separation of production from the market.

For Marx, the major limitation of Smith's analysis of political economy was his failure to explain what he regarded as the defining feature of capitalism, namely profit. The mechanisms of supply and demand do not account for profit. Smith in focussing too much on the level of the market consequently did not see that in the system of production the basic mechanisms of capitalism are established. These mechanisms are not simply technical operations of the market, such as the laws of supply and demand. Moreover, contrary to Smith, the fundamental rationale of capitalism is not to make money, which in itself is useless, but to make profit. The unrelenting pursuit of profit is the motor of capitalism.

There is no 'hidden hand' leading to general prosperity. In whatever way Smith's argument should be understood, Marx's critique of political economy demonstrated that class relations are the real source of power in modern society. Smith tended to see capitalism as superior to mercantilism and the harbinger of a better world. His moral philosophy and his views about the relationship between individual rationality and collective interests were far too harmonious, if not docile. Marx gave much greater attention to conflict and to contradictions in economic analysis. In his approach, there is no harmonious integration of land, capital and labour. Consequently, the market cannot be harmonious.

In terms of the politics of liberalism, Marx accepted the basic principles of liberal thought but was disenchanted with liberalism in its failure to address the root causes of inequality but also its failure to deliver genuine freedom in the sense of the free development of human abilities and potential. Social justice did not greatly figure in the thought of Adam Smith, who believed capitalism was not the root cause of inequality and that social reform would be sufficient to ameliorate social suffering, poverty and inequality. Since the failure of the 1848 revolutions, which led to restorations and only minor concessions for constitutional government, it was clear that the promises of liberalism could ultimately not be delivered by liberalism, which had at most prepared the ground. As a revolutionary socialist, Marx saw capitalism as not the end stage of history, but just one stage. Smith, who characterized human history into the four stages of hunters, shepherds, agriculture and commerce, saw the current stage as the final one. Marx's theory of modes of production postulated a more dynamic movement in which the capitalist stage would destroy itself. In this respect, Marx drew on French utopian philosophy, including 'socialism', which according to Kolakowski (1978: 183) was first used as a term in 1832 by a follower of Saint-Simon. Marx also drew on Hegel's dialectical conception of history to develop a more transformative conception of modernity in which social struggles are pivotal.

Marx's Critique of Political Economy

Marx titled his major work *Capital: A Critique of Political Economy* [1867], not capitalism, for a good reason. He sought to understand the nature of capital. As mentioned earlier, the term capitalism was not in common usage until the end of the nineteenth century. The *Communist Manifesto* [1848] used the term the 'bourgeois mode of production' and 'modern bourgeois society', not capitalism. Marx wrote of the 'capitalist era', 'capitalists' and the capitalist 'mode of production'. The later *Critique of the Gotha Programme* [1875] says '"Present-day society" is capitalist society'. However, by the early twentieth century, especially in German and in English, it was possible to speak of capitalism, to refer to the capitalist mode of production.

But what is capital? It is normally taken to be the assets of society, but for Marx it is the use of money; but it is not just only money, it is the use of money to produce commodities to make more money, generally summed up in Marxist economics as M-C-M. As stated in Part 2, Chapter 4 of *Capital*, M-C-M is the 'general formula for capital'. It is the 'transformation of money into commodities, and the re-conversion of commodities into money: buying in order to sell' (Marx [1867] 1976: 248). Capital seeks to create and expand 'valorization', the creation of new values. Valorization is not just about creating exchange values or a commercial transaction such as the buying of labour; it is about creating additional value. Capitalism as such refers to a form of social and economic organization in which all assets as well as the profit that is realized in the M-C-M process are privately owned. So, capital ultimately resides in the accumulation of profit and the instruments needed to achieve it. In this sense, then, capitalism sucks up everything in its path to transform all content into capital.

Marx also distinguished between constant capital (in essence, raw materials but also machinery) and variable capital (which is basically labour). He held that it was the latter that was the source of profit. Variable capital is variable because of the costs of wages. Capital develops from the accumulation of profit. A feature of the capitalist era is the generation of ever greater profit and thus the growth in capital to a point that capital becomes the dominant feature of the economy. Thus, we can speak of the capitalist era, or capitalism. Contrary to Adam Smith, profit does not lead to collective goods, since it is privately appropriated. Workers are rewarded for their labour by wages; the capitalist class appropriate profit. The resulting inequality is a structural feature of capitalism and cannot be alleviated since it is endemic.

The core of Marx's theory of capitalism has generally been regarded as residing in the labour theory of value which holds that abstract labour produces value. This theory claims that the potential for production is greater than what the worker gets as a wage and as a consequence profit is created. The more specific theory of surplus value, which Marx developed from the work of the British economist David Ricardo and outlined in the early part of *Capital* vol. 1, claims that exchange under the conditions of capitalism involves the chimera of a fair exchange of labour for wages, but what is really exchanged is labour time. It is this exchange, the time the worker spends at producing a commodity that makes possible surplus value and thus profit. Surplus value becomes profit when it is privately appropriated by the capitalist. It is sometimes said that this theory is the defining core of Marx's theory of capitalism, but it is contested and often claimed not central to Marx. It certainly forms the basis of his theory that exploitation is endemic to capitalism in that in so far as the worker is paid for the time producing commodities that earn more value than what the worker is paid. The resulting surplus value is then privately appropriated. Thus, exploitation is necessarily built into the structure of capitalism. It followed from this structural claim that capitalism also requires exploitation in seeking to extract ever more surplus value by forcing down the cost of wages and an increase in the working day. This leads to the so-called immiseration (or pauperization) of the workers, a controversial thesis too, which Marx himself qualified as not an inexorable feature of capitalism, since wages historically have risen as much as they have fallen. However, on the whole, he tended towards the view that while not necessarily an unstoppable downward movement leading to absolute misery, capitalism certainly entailed relative misery for the workers. A modified version of the thesis is that wage-labour is alienated labour, which is not necessarily the same as pauperization. The thesis in whatever way it is understood is a weak spot in Marx's writings for it assumes that the longer the worker works the more surplus wealth is produced. A more favourable reading of Marx is that his theory of capitalism see as the essential fact about capitalism not its exploitation of the worker but the private appropriation of profit. But, Marx's theory of capitalism does reply on the centrality of wage-labour however understood.

Another key feature of capitalism is its 'abstract' character. Both capital and labour have an abstract character in that they are extracted i.e. abstracted from particular contexts and converted into other forms. Thus, abstract labour is greater than 'particular' labour: surplus value is extracted from particular labour making it abstract. This distinction, where particular is somehow more natural, corresponds to the distinction between use values and exchanges values. Work in non-capitalist conditions is particular but under capitalism it is transformed i.e. abstracted into something else, namely a function in the accumulation of capitalism. The growth of abstract labour is achieved through what Marx called 'subsumption' whereby work or particular labour is incorporated into capitalism and is then further transformed to meet the requirements of capitalism. Subsumption describes the process by which Capital becomes the dominant force in society, a process of absorption and transformation.

With this elaborate theory advanced in his later work, especially volume one of *Capital* and the earlier unpublished in his lifetime but often considered to be his greatest work, *Grundrisse* [1857–8], Marx was able to revise his earlier theory of alienation and the ideas in his first work, *The Economic and Philosophical Manuscripts* [1844). The concept of alienation remained an important concept in his work, as did the notion of 'objectification' (*Vergegenständlichung*). The latter was in his view universal and can be found in all kinds of social arrangements, while alienation is something that is more specific to capitalism – it is not clear if it can exist in non-capitalist societies. It is clear however that capitalism exacerbates alienation and extends it to reach into all spheres of life. It follows the logic of capitalism in being a consequence of abstract labour, work that is done to serve the requirements of capital rather than human requirements. It takes its most pronounced form in the way in which the workers become alienated from the objects produced by their labour, which have lost their 'use value'. The worker sees only the wage as the product of work. Instead, everything assumes the form of the commodity. As outlined in what is perhaps the most famous part of *Capital*, in the final section of the first chapter, 'The Fetishism of the Commodity and its Secret', it is the very form of the commodity that conceals the social relations of labour such that workers only see relations between objects.

This process of abstraction through subsumption produces commodification. Capitalism is not just about the production of commodities as goods to be sold on the market to make profit, but it entails the conversion into the form of the commodity, including the workers themselves. Commodification is thus a form of distortion. This is also why capitalism is a mode of production that cannot be understood simply as an economic system; it reaches beyond the economic system itself to shape the wider framework of society and defines the relation between economy and the state. In this relationship, the locus of power is no longer in the traditional site of sovereignty, the state. Unlike in feudalism and in the era of absolutism and the mercantilist state, the centre of power does not reside in the figure of the ruler, the monarch, parliament or in the state more generally. In capitalism, the state serves the needs of capitalism, where the true source of domination rests. But, it is an indirect mode of domination in that it is largely invisible, shielded by the veil of ideology and the form of the commodity. The aim of Marx's critique of political economy is to go behind this veil and the 'super-structure' to reveal the structures of power that are built into the workings of capitalism.

So, for Marx capitalism refers to more than the economy but to a kind of society, a social formation or a societal system. His notion of a mode of production also tries to capture this sense of capitalism as society, viewed as a totality, as is also reflected in the notion of 'bourgeois society'. Now, to say that capitalism is modern society, or modern capitalist society, is not to say that capitalism has achieved the total transformation of all aspects of society into functions of capitalism. It certainly resides in the logic of capitalism to do just that, but it does not succeed in eradicating opposition, since it generates conflict through its contradictions. Capitalism, on the one side, seeks the abolition of 'all that is holy and profane', as in the famous words of *The Communist Manifesto*, such as pre-capitalist traditions (the family, patriarchy, religion, traditional cultural values etc.) but at the time it is requires the support of those traditions, while at the same time giving them new functions, as in the notion of religion as the opium of the people. In a similar way, there is the persistence of what he called 'primitive accumulation', the incorporation into capitalism of pre-capitalist modes of production. Capitalism cannot overcome these tensions and other ones, such as those that might be associated with the legitimating norms of liberalism, democracy and constitutionalism. Once these have been co-opted by capitalism as its ideologies, they continue to stand in a relation of contradiction opening up the political field to contestation and the critique of ideology. There is also the contradiction that lies at the heart of the commodity between use values and exchange values, for the former can never be entirely eradicated. Capitalism thus requires an authenticity that its products lack because they are produced by alienated labour.

Marx's account of capitalism is far from the benign and harmonious world of Adam Smith. It is not only an economic system that rests on irreconcilable contradictions and class conflict, but it also extends its grip over the entire world through violence. This is reflected in the relationship with nature[3]. Capitalism entails the violent extraction of raw materials from the earth for energy and materials for the production of commodities. This in turn requires the extension of capitalism beyond its home in the West to the rest of the world, a thesis developed by Rosa Luxemburg in *The Accumulation of Capital* [1913] as well as by Lenin, in *Imperialism, the Highest Stage of Capitalism* [1917]. Imperialism, which preceded capitalism, now becomes essential to capitalism in its search for both raw materials and new markets, since the home markets are not sufficient to satisfy the productive power of capitalism. As is attested by the violent history of labour relations in its formative period, capitalism also exerts violence in its endeavour to maximize the productivity of labour through the process of subsumption.

We can now offer a general definition of capitalism. It is in the first instance a system that is primarily characterized by the relentless pursuit of profit. Its logic and rationale is the maximization of profit, which is realized through the conversion of everything into capital. Its principal sources derive from surplus value abstracted from labour, but it is not confined to wage labour. The logic of capitalism goes beyond the confines of the economy as such to encompass the social and political domain. As capitalism consolidates, it creates ever worsening crises, sowing the seeds of its own destruction in combination with political agitation.

The End of Capitalism: The Logic of Revolution and Its Economic Preconditions

Since the financial crisis in 2008–10 there has been a revival of interest in Marx's theory of capitalism, especially *Capital*. However, those in search of an alternative economic model to capitalism will be disappointed, since what we find in this work is a detailed analytical account of the functioning of capitalism. As much noted, Marx offered little by way of an alternative since his youthful and more utopian thinking, as in *The Communist Manifesto*, written with Friedrich Engels in the revolutionary fervour of February 1848. In this work, the idea of bourgeois revolution prepared the ground for proletarian revolution, which was also to be world revolution. His mature and more scientific work of the late 1850s and 1860s gave few clues as to what would come after capitalism. The *Critique of the Gotha Programme* [1875] is an exception in that it gives a brief sketch of his mature thought and on issues where he differed from the emerging social democratic movement in Germany[4]. But we do not find a developed theory of revolution. As Perry Anderson wrote in an influential work, *Considerations of Western Marxism*, Marx left behind a well-developed economic theory of the capitalist mode of production, but no comparable political theory, neither of the state nor of strategies and tactics for revolutionary social struggles (Anderson 1974: 4). Why is this? Part of the answer is that Marx was opposed to political designs for the future stemming from intellectuals. This after all was one of his objections against utopian socialism. Change had to come from within social reality, not from the domain of ideas.

Political practice was inscribed in the critique of political economy, linking theory and practice. Nevertheless, Marx had his own practical politics. He was opposed the anarchists of the day, such as Mikhail Bakunin, his main rival in the First International, in his strong conviction that revolutionary change needs political parties to lead the working class.

He accepted the basic rationality of the state. The abolition of the market, as argued by the French socialist, Pierre-Joseph Proudhon, was also inadequate. Marx stood for revolutionary socialism as opposed to the position favoured by one of the key leaders of the German SPD, Eduard Bernstein, of peaceful and gradual transition. Marx's position was closer to that of another key figure in the SPD, Karl Kautsky, who defended the idea of revolution. Yet, while communism beckoned, it was a long way into the future, a utopian aspiration that was also a practical possibility. Marx also disdained purely philosophical analysis, famously proclaiming against the left-wing Hegelians the overcoming of philosophy. The transition to a socialist society could not be accomplished by mere thought alone.

One of Marx's main contributions to radical politics was his analysis of how the capitalist system worked rather than spelling out how an alternative might be created. To abolish capitalism and to create an alternative order, it is necessary to understand the system to be overcome. The alternative may be worse, as is perhaps what happened in the USSR where an ostensible workers' republic was founded but led to a totalitarian form of domination. In the view of the theorists of the Frankfurt School, Marcuse, Adorno and Horkheimer, the version of socialism established in Russia merely took over the worse aspects of industrial capitalism in terms of technical and instrumental rationality but without any project of emancipation. Marx provided the first detailed study of capitalism going far beyond the earlier work of Adam Smith and the major political economists of the day, the so-called Classical Economists, such as David Ricardo. His account of modern society differed profoundly and decisively from the rival theories of modernity such as August Comte's positivistic social science and the emerging functionalist sociology which regarded modern society as primarily characterized by industrialism. Marx persuasively shows that the core features of modern society are those of capitalism. Industrialism developed within the structures of capitalism, which preceded it. Capitalism began earlier, as Max Weber also showed in the context of the rise of rationalization, and for Marx in the commercialization of agriculture. Industrialism, bolstered by imperialism, allowed capitalism to develop on a massive scale since it made it possible to realize what capitalism is essentially all about, namely the production of commodities on a vast scale leading to the accumulation of capital.

So, capitalism is not then just the name for the modern economy or to be reduced to industrialism, which the USSR made the basis of its path to modernity; nor is it to be reduced to the market, as was the tendency in Smith and much of later mainstream Weberian sociology. Capitalism encompasses economy and society; for Marx it is a political economy characterized by the social relations of production. It can also be said in this context that the emerging orthodoxy in the new science of sociology, as reflected in the work of Herbert Spencer, was that modern society is to be understood according to the analogy of the body, with a perfect balance between the differentiation of functions and overall integration. Marx's analysis offered an entirely different account of modernity than this harmonious view of the relation between economy and society. His approach also required the rejection of the Comtean vision of an emerging scientific civilization in which the emerging technical and scientific elites would be the new leaders.

Now, for Marx a feature of modern industrial capitalism as a societal system that extends across the social and political domains is that it is prone to crises, which create spaces for political action. There are several reasons for this. First, in holistic terms as capitalism becomes more and more advanced, it leads to ever greater strain on society, leading to dysfunctional outcomes in the conversion of everything in its path into the service of

Capital. Thus, for instance, Capital cannot secure social reproduction, which depends on other social institutions, which are undermined by capitalism (see Bhattacharya 2007). Economic production cannot achieve social production. Second, political opposition is increased since it cannot be entirely domesticated, as in the tension between democracy and capitalism, the rise in class consciousness, which cannot be entirely controlled, conflicts between capital and labour. Third, specifically economic crises increase due to the systemic nature of capitalist contradiction. Marx believed that capitalism had an inbuilt tendency towards a fall in the rate of profit (not necessarily in profit, but in the rate of profit) leading to a long-term structural decline. This results when constant capital, essentially technology, is substituted for variable capital (i.e. labour). The theory of the fall in the rate of profit – developed in the 1850s and expanded in the posthumously published *Capital* vol 3 [1894] – was related to the tendency for capitalism to over-produce while at the same time pushing wages down. The result is under-consumption, recession and stagnation. Marx also believed that capitalism will one day reach its limits in access to raw materials. In sum, Marx's economic analysis of capitalism points in the direction of the accumulation of crises leading to its final demise. Capitalism in constantly revolutionizing the means of production is sowing the seeds of its destruction out of which grow alternative political forces. Unlike some of the later orthodox Marxists, this logic did not entail an economistic interpretation of social transformation, since dialectics was inscribed in the make-up of the capitalist mode of production.

Capitalism is not a static system; it is a constantly expanding, unstable and turbulent one. Crises are not just periodic problems that can be successfully crisis managed, but a systemic feature of capitalism. On a very abstract level, Marx held that the most fundamental contradiction was that of the relations of production and forces of production, whereby the forces of production refer to technology, natural resources – generally the productive potential deriving from the material base of production including human labour – while the social relations of production are based on ownership and control. In this view, famously put forward in the *Preface to the Critique of Political Economy* [1859], the productive potential is constrained by the existing outmoded relations of production. The result of this contradiction would require the destruction of the existing mode of production:

> At a certain stage of development, the material productive forces of society come into conflict with the existing relations of production or – this merely expresses the same thing in legal terms – with the property relations within the framework of which they have operated hitherto. From forms of development of the productive forces these relations turn into their fetters. Then begins an era of social revolution. The changes in the economic foundation lead sooner or later to the transformation of the whole immense superstructure.

The enduring attraction of Marx is to a large degree that he provided a robust theory of capitalism that contained the key to its destruction (see Boldizzoni 2020). This at least is how he has been taken up by the tradition that he inspired. The end of capitalism does not come entirely from the attraction of a rival system, whether socialism or communism, but from itself. Socialism alone, unless it is connected to the dynamics and politics produced by capitalism, is destined to be unpolitical romanticism. The main obstacle to capitalism is Capital, as Marx observed. For capitalism to grow, it has to increase its labour supply and thus inescapably increases the power of the workers. Perhaps for this reason, he did not need to provide an exclusively normative critique of capitalism. His critique of political economy was a form of immanent critique, whereby the forces of change emanate from the internal workings of the system in conjunction with the political forces produced and released by capitalism. Each crisis portends the end of capitalism, which will finally arrive as a result of the systemic or structural crises within the economic system colliding with political forces responding to the rise of class consciousness. According to Stedman Jones, Marx did not see the transition to socialism as an apocalyptical event; his assumption was that the transition to socialism had already occurred, in a manner analogous to the transition from feudalism to capitalism (Stedman Jones 2016: 510–11).

This vision of the end of capitalism is a good demonstration of Marx's Hegelian inspired method of dialectics. Following Hegel's lead, the dialectical conception of history postulates the self-transformative nature of reality. Reality is not fixed, immutable, unchanging, but rather change is built into the very conception of reality. Human beings are always able to transcend their situation. The experience of alienation gives rise to the capacity to transcend it. In contrast to other accounts, for example utopianism, change is not seen to be entirely transcendent, it does not come from outside society by force of an ideal, but is embryonic in social reality. Marx believed that class conflict, itself the product of the social contradictions of capitalism, would engender the demise of capitalism with a new order emerging from its ruins. Marx departed from Hegel in his endeavour to see dialectics at work in the present and not as a speculative matter that occurs in pure thought, as would appear to be Hegel's position as a philosopher in the idealist tradition. Thus, Marx's call for the overcoming of philosophy was intended to bring idealist philosophy down to earth in the analysis of the real world of social struggles. The critique of political economy sought to identify the emancipatory potentials within the present.

Marx's lack of clarity on the mechanisms that would lead to the end of capitalism is perhaps explained by his belief that socialism, in the sense of the political organization of the working classes of the world, the 'dictatorship of the proletariat', would lead the way out of the morass of problems created by capitalism. The systemic problems of capitalism, as in the theory of the tendency of the rate of profit to fall, are in themselves not sufficient to bring about the demise of capitalism unless there is also the stirring of political agency. Socialism had to have a basis in the dialectical conception of social struggles. But there is no doubt that there is a certain divergence in Marx's thought between the economic analysis of capitalism and its political transformation. The grandiose theory of history in terms of the succession of modes of production is vague on details and timescales. The stalling of the radical socialist movement even in Marx's life-time, especially in France, casts some doubt on the imminent end of capitalism. This is perhaps why Marx thought the trigger might in fact come from outside the capitalist system, though it is difficult to say exactly what lies outside the capitalist system. Yet this notion might explain his belief that the rise of nationalism in Ireland might hasten the decline of capitalism by a major strike against the imperial centre. However, this was at least a hope that had little foundation in historical reality. The dominant nationalist movement in Ireland at the end of the nineteenth century was the home rule movement under the leadership of the Irish Parliamentary Party, which sought home rule within the Union and within the empire, which it supported. When independence finally occurred after 1922, capitalism was struck a near fatal blow only in the early Irish Free State, not in Britain. India was a more plausible possibility where nationalist liberation might be decisive, but this also proved to be a false hope even if it created a basis for Indian Marxism. Marx has been criticized for reducing Indian emancipation from imperialism too much to the interests of western radical socialism, which was his primary interest. It is also clear that he had no developed theory of imperialism.

In 1871, there was a brief moment in Paris when socialism appeared to be on the horizon. The Paris Commune of 1871, which followed in the aftermath of the Prussian victory over France in the short Franco-Prussian war, presented a vision of a possible alternative order, as Marx observed in *The Civil War in France* [1871], written as the revolt happened. The Paris Commune was 'to serve as a model to all the industrial centres of France'. But the two month commune was not the beacon of communism that it had seemed and was defeated by the army of the French republic. While it was an example of the rebellion of the workers, it could not be explained by crisis tendencies in capitalism, and many political actors in addition to socialists were involved in the insurrection. The chaos created by the war was the background, not capitalism. Marx recognized after 1871 that the Paris Commune lacked a political strategy to bring about socialist revolution, which required control over the state. Its ideas were perhaps socialist but it was also an example of an unsuccessful revolt. For Marx, socialism in any case was not possible on a national scale, even if it had to begin on a national basis; it had to be international.

The inescapable conclusion in reading Marx's vast work is that while capitalism is crisis-prone, its systemic problems alone will not bring about the end of capitalism, which can come about only through social struggles along with socialist leadership. Without socialist leadership, it remained a forlorn hope that capitalism would somehow destroy itself. While many Marxists continued to analyse the workings of the capitalist system in the hope of finding signs of its internal crumbling, the main preoccupation of Marxism after Marx was in advancing revolutionary socialism. It is remarkable how much of the later Marxist tradition abandoned the economic analysis of capitalism in favour of a political philosophy of Marxism. The economic theory and the theory of revolution were never satisfactorily linked, at least in a way that preserved the logic of dialectics.

The problem of the lack of congruence between Marx's economic analysis of capitalism, which sets out the historical conditions necessary for socialist transition, and his relatively undeveloped political theory of an alternative can be partly accounted for by the fact that in his life-time the industrial proletariat was only emerging. The revolutionary period since 1789 was almost entirely agrarian or artisanal, including the Paris Commune. The plethora of socialist movements along with the major socialist philosophies – Charles Fourier, Henri Saint-Simon, Robert Owen – of the nineteenth century were operating in largely pre-capitalist social conditions and not all were revolutionary, especially those in England and France (Claeyss 2011). Socialism prior to Marxism was essentially collectivism and often based on localism; it was not, as Marx required for radical political transformation, a quest to attain state power. Some socialists, such as Owen, were reacting to industrialization rather than to capitalism. Their pre-dialectical model was the past not the future. Marx and Engels were scornful of many of these thinkers who did not present a real challenge to capitalism. A more plausible interpretation of Marx's politics is that he saw the need for the political maturation of the working class whose development was part of the development of capitalism. Without such maturation, socialism would be prone to authoritarianism by a self-appointed elite (or it would be docile romanticism). By the time of his death in 1883, only the German working class under the leadership of the German Social Democratic Party, the SPD, founded in 1875, showed any real promise of delivering an alternative. The SPD was inspired by Marxist ideas until it abandoned revolutionary socialism in favour of gradualism. Yet, this was a relatively small industrial working class. In Britain, the economic conditions were more strongly present as regards the size of the industrial working class, but it did not have the same level of political leadership.

The conclusion that both Marx and Engels appeared to draw was while that the optimal conditions were not present for proletarian revolution – in terms of the size of the industrial proletariat and the systemic crises of capitalism – it could still be politically possible if social struggles took place and with the right kind of socialist leadership. The political logic of revolution, since bourgeois revolution began, had a tendency to ameliorate revolt that then takes on a momentum of its own. The shifting positions of Marx and Engels, according to Michael Löwy, must be situated in the context of their view of the incapacity of the bourgeoisie for revolution and the immaturity of the proletariat (Löwy 1981: 28). Marx and orthodox Marxists later wavered between faith in the political momentum providing the necessary spur and the desire to wait for the advancement of capitalism to provide the trigger. This hesitation in coming down fully on the side of political momentum was the main dividing line later between the orthodox Marxists and Lenin. The latter, and generally the position of the Russian Bolshevist Marxists as opposed to the western Marxists, was that proletarian revolution did not have to wait for bourgeois revolution nor for a high degree of industrial advancement. Strategy over-rode preconditions. The path to revolution is not in clear-cut stages but is multi-linear. Lenin held that capitalism was most vulnerable to collapse at its weakest point, not as Marx held, where it was most advanced. His strategy accordingly was to defeat capitalism where it was most vulnerable and wherever that might be (Lane 2020). This problem of the timing, the relation of bourgeois and proletarian revolution and the location of revolution had also to be linked to the question of the relation between peasants and the industrial workers. In a world in which the majority of workers were not industrial proletarians but peasants or various kinds of artisans, the industrial proletariat could not on its own achieve revolution leading to socialist transition but could be a spring-board for revolution into which the peasants could be drawn. This prospect was inextricably tied up with the international scope of socialist revolution, since the working classes in other countries would need to respond to the call. So long as socialist revolution was confined to just one country, the prospects for socialist transition were remote. For Marx, genuine socialism had to be international and not confined to the advanced industrial economies, even if it had to begin in those countries. But could this be possible in the absence of its conditions? For Lenin world revolution could be indefinitely postponed, as a strategic necessity at least for Russia, until the revolutionary vanguard sized power. While the October Revolution was carried out in the name of imminent world revolution, its failure to realize the aim led inevitably to Stalin's principle of 'socialism in one country'.

Marx opened up an avenue of thought and political practice that was central to later Marxism, but did not have a full basis in his own thought. It is best exemplified by Leon Trotsky's quest for permanent revolution in his book, *Permanent Revolution* [1930].[5] The term derived from Marx, who used it in various writings, such as in 'On the Jewish Question' in 1844, with Engels, in *The Holy Family* in 1845 and in various speeches c. 1850, as well as in *The Class Struggle in France, 1848–1850.* In the latter text, in 1850, he wrote revolutionary socialism 'is the declaration of the permanence of the revolution'. For Trotsky, writing almost five decades later, revolution did not have to come from the conditions of capitalism alone, but he recognized the western proletariat was key to world revolution. This more political interpretation as opposed to the economic legacy of Marx's work was arguably more influential for radical politics, since it did not require a theory of the capitalist mode of production breaking down as a result of its systemic contradictions. Perhaps this explains Marx's comment that he was not a Marxist – both Marx and Engels preferred to wait and were sceptical of doctrinaire Marxists. Both Lenin and Trotsky, despite their differences, agreed that revolution could occur in a relatively weak link in the international system, since all countries were one way or the other connected with the dominance of capitalism. This included Russia, even if its industrial capitalist basis was relatively small. Since the peasants were not capable of revolutionary agency, it fell on the industrial workers to take the lead. The peasants had a common interest with the industrial proletariat but only the latter were capable of political agency and would, at the right moment, strike common cause with the peasants, who were a potentially enormous subversive force. Trotsky held that the peasants in fact had 'an exceptional place in democratic revolution' especially in countries with belated capitalist development (Trotsky [1930] 276).

Lenin, in his first major theoretical work, *The Development of Capitalism in Russia* [1899], claimed that capitalism had already gained considerable ground in Russia where it was almost entirely a product of investment by western countries and thus a weak spot in international capitalism. On this question of where the revolutionary impulse comes from, which is not easily separated from doctrinal considerations in Marxist scholarship, Marx himself was ambivalent, since he held to the view that bourgeois revolution creates the impetus for proletarian revolution, which then gains its own momentum as a result of the crisis prone nature of capitalism.[6] This position was deeply ingrained in the political imagination of the Russian Marxists, indeed of all orthodox Marxists, to the extent that the revolution of 1905 was seen as a bourgeois revolution that prepared the path to proletarian revolution in 1917. Trotsky, in 1906 after the revolution of the previous year, was the first to question this misreading of Russia's historical path to socialism.[7]

Michael Löwy, a Marxist theorist in the Trotskyist tradition, in a seminal book on the idea of permanent revolution, *The Politics of Combined and Uneven Development* [1981], has questioned the traditional interpretation of Marx's theory of a two stage movement of revolution, whereby first bourgeois revolution established the conditions for proletarian revolution, which in turn is based on industrialization establishing the required conditions. Following Trotsky's possibly heretical break from the idea that proletarian revolution is an outcome and not the reverse, as was the case in Russia, and in many parts of the non-western world, he suggests that Marx's account of socialist transition in fact was not quite so mechanical and need to be rethought in order to avoid the danger of an overly economistic interpretation of capitalism. The two-stage theory of revolution was ever only stated in *The Communist Manifesto* in 1848 and henceforth took on the status of an article of Marxian faith and its adherence was a disaster for progressive socialism. Marx's famous claim in *The Preface to the Critique of Political Economy* [1859] that 'no social order perishes before all the productive forces for which there is room in it have been developed' sets the bar impossibly high for proletarian revolution anywhere. Moreover, Bourgeois revolution was never a historical necessity for the rise of capitalism, if a broader perspective is taken. Such a perspective would have to give more consideration to the 'uneven development' thesis of capitalism, which the Russian Marxists strongly emphasized. Löwy's argument that permanent revolution is based on uneven and combined development is persuasive and, if correct, it solves the problem of Marx's silence about how revolutionary socialism might be possible as world revolution given the limited size of the world industrial proletariat. Revolution can be triggered by different strategies in different places and sustained through internationalization. After all, the French Revolution opened the gates to revolution, even if it was largely bourgeois. The revolutionary drive goes back at least to the peasant revolts of the sixteenth century (Ree 2013). The French Revolution was not itself unconnected from earlier social struggles and revolutions elsewhere in the world, as the case of the earlier American Revolution shows. The example of the Haitian Revolution, 1791–1804, is another example, though one of a more radical interpretation of 1789, and which had strong reverberations in France where it led to a new turn in radical politics that was not entirely appropriated by bourgeois revolution. A similar dynamic took place in Spain when radicalized republican ideas re-entered Spain from its former dominions in Latin America. In any case, the Russian Marxist perspective required a firm belief in the viability of international links in socialist struggles and that capitalism, uneven in its development, was vulnerable in the pre-capitalist peripheries. Trotsky explicitly eliminated the distinction between 'mature' and 'immature' countries for socialism: 'Insofar as capitalism has created a world market, a world division of labour and world productive forces, it has also prepared world economy as a whole for socialist transformation' (Trotsky [1930] 1969).

Nonetheless, despite the fact that there is no unilinear logic to the revolutionary sequence of events, for Marx, socialism had to be post-capitalist and democratic. There is some indication that Marx later questioned his earlier insistence on stages, as in his correspondence with Vera Zasulich in 1881 on the prospects of socialist revolution in Russia (see Eaton 1980; Shanin 2018). Marx's political legacy, although inconclusive as regards the question of where and when socialist transition occurs, had the great strength in establishing a dialectical conception of social struggles and the permanence of revolution. This could not be easily translated into direct political activism without the temptations of authoritarianism.

Marx and Capitalism Today

Marx's legacy has been huge. No other thinker has exerted as much influence on modern thought. His political legacy has been claimed by Marxism-Leninism and by the western social democratic movement. Within the intellectual tradition often referred to as western Marxism or humanist Marxism, to distinguish Marxism from Soviet Marxism, several rival schools of thought developed Marx's theories. Some of the most influential of these combined Marx's work with Weber's, as in Georg Lukács' *History and Class Consciousness* [1923] with its central concept of reification, which gave a new and lasting significance to the notion of commodification and alienated labour. The synthesis of Marx and Freud, first forged by the critical theorists of the Frankfurt School, especially Herbert Marcuse, was one of the most revolutionary intellectual developments of the twentieth century and which also opened up the path to feminist theory and post-modern theory. Antonio Gramsci represented another important strand in Marxism with his notion of cultural hegemony. Leon Trotsky, as discussed, took up Marx's notion of 'permanent revolution' and made it the basis for new internationalism. This concept provided to be remarkably prescient. Revolutions are all interlinked, once started the revolutionary impetus becomes permanent. Trotsky developed a key insight of Marx that democratic revolution develops into socialist revolution. As he wrote, 'revolutions have a logic of their own' (cited in Löwy 1981: 98).

All these schools of Marxism played a major role in shaping the left and critical thought in the twentieth century and paved the way for later appropriations by feminism and post-colonial liberation movements. Other thinkers in the Marxist tradition – Ernst

Bloch, Herbert Marcuse, Jürgen Habermas, Axel Honneth for example – sought to recover Marx's Hegelianism in an endeavour to develop a more philosophical approach to capitalism that avoided a direct political appeal to the working class as the revolutionary subject. It is not our aim here to assess the cauldron of political and economic upheaval that followed the collapse of the central European powers in the aftermath of the First World War and the October Revolution. The fact that it was the Russian working class along with the stirrings of peasant revolution, not the German working class who championed communism in a country that had barely experienced capitalism remains one of the astonishing occurrences of political modernity. It can be explained only by the success of Lenin's implementation of strong socialist leadership and the effective silencing of alternatives. In the end, socialist revolution was possible in Russia but not in Britain, France or Germany. But the cost was the loss of the democratic spirit. This fact in part confirms Marx's reticence in announcing the transition to socialism, since it had also to be a transition to democracy, which is what the expression 'the dictatorship of the proletariat' was supposed to mean. The subsequent history of the Bolshevik socialism since Stalin confirmed Marx's lingering scepticism, which he shared with Engels, of top down revolutionary transition.

Our concern in this chapter is to access his theory of capitalism rather than the numerous later interpretations of his work. There is in any case a vast scholarship on Marx and Marxism. While much of later Marxism and the critical theory tradition were preoccupied by the disappearance of the revolutionary subject, the problem of capitalism remained. Later chapters in this book will address how Marxists interpreted capitalism after Marx. In these debates, a key question is how much of Marx's analysis of the dynamics of capitalism remains relevant. Many of the axioms of his economic theory have become articles of faith for Marxist theorists and, taken away from the body of thought that constitutes Marxist scholarship, often difficult to translate into other theoretical idioms. But the strength of his analysis of capitalism ultimately resides in the usefulness for scholars not working specifically in the Marxist tradition. An adequate account of capitalism needs to engage with Marx's theory of capitalism since it was this theory that furnished so much of the debate about capitalism. We conclude this chapter with a few remarks on some of the main problems within Marx's analysis of capitalism.

As already indicated, one problem is the notion of the immiseration of the proletariat. It is not at all evident that capitalism necessarily requires the impoverishment of the proletariat. Capitalism in the western world since 1945 witnessed an increase in living standards and in real wages (see Chapter 6). In Marx's terms, exploitation remains on a more general level in so far as capitalism necessarily entails a capitalist class that lives off the appropriation of surplus value. Capitalism since the beginning of the twentieth century also became more reliant on the working class not only as producers, but as consumers. Higher wages thus translated into more consumption fuelling economic growth. Henry Ford was the first to exploit mass consumption with the transformation of the motor car from a luxury item to an affordable purchase for the middle class with the entry of Model T in 1908.

Marx, in correcting the major weakness of Adam Smith in severing the market from production, tended to neglect the pivotal role of consumption in capitalism[8]. This problem is very much related to the question of the middle class, which hardly figured in Marx's theory of capitalism, which pitted Labour versus Capital as the main driver of social change. It is certainly the case, taking a global view of capitalism as a world system that the immiseration thesis is not entirely irrelevant. Poverty and exploitation in many parts of the world that provides cheap labour for the manufacture of commodities for global markets is the reality of capitalism today.

One of the major developments in capitalism in the twentieth century is the enormous expansion in scientific research and technological innovation. Beginning with the post-industrialization and culminating in the electronic revolution in recent decades, the notion of constant capital is hardly adequate to grasp the massive transformation of capitalism, even to the point that much of valorization does not directly depend of the existence of an industrial proletariat.

David Harvey has drawn attention to the centrality of crisis to capitalism. Drawing on but also going beyond Marx's theory of capitalist crisis, he has shown how capitalism not only produces ongoing crises, but crises are as necessary to the functioning of capitalism as money, labour power and capital itself (Harvey 2010: 117). Marx's own account of crisis did not go far enough and was probably too much tied up with the idea that capitalist crisis portends the demise of capitalism. Another view, not necessary contrary to Marx but requiring a corrective, is that it is through crises that capitalism revolves its contradictions. So, for example, 'financial crises serve to rationalize the irrationalities of capitalism. They typically lead to new reconfigurations, new models of development, new spheres of investment and new forms of class power' (Harvey 2010: 11). This does not mean it will resolve its contradictions for perpetuity or postpone indefinitely a terminal crisis; it does suggest that capitalism has more escape routes than in Marx's account, which tended to emphasize the internal crises emanating from largely economic dynamics, such as the falling rate of profit.

One of Marx's most important ideas still remains pertinent: future possibilities are dialectically immanent in the contradictions and conflicts in society. Social struggles are not by-products or marginal but are ingrained in the nature of society. The way in which Marx analysed this was too much bound up with the notion of the relations of production and the forces of production, but it remains a key insight for the understanding of capitalism today. It foregrounds the centrality of social transformation. Marx brought together the analysis of the capitalist economy with the political. Despite the inconclusive and undeveloped nature of his analysis, he showed how democracy could emerge from the capitalist development. His work was the first step in the complicated relation of capitalism and democracy (see Rueschemeyer et al. 1992).

Finally, we assert the compelling definition of capitalism that Marx provided. Capitalism is based on the accumulation of profit. The logic of capitalism is the relentless pursuit of profit through commodification. But the notion of capitalism is not just a concept that needs to be defined for the purpose of analysis; it is also an interpretative and critical concept, in short it is a concept that implies critique. It is perhaps for this reason that the notion of capitalism has been mostly used by its critics rather than by its defenders.

Notes

1 Althusser more than anyone was responsible for the notion of 'an epistemological break' in Marx's late work, with *Capital* representing a break from the earlier humanist work.

2 See Kocka (2016) and Hartwell and Engerman (2003). Marx used the term capitalist relations of production, which effectively amounts to the term capitalism.

3 On the question of Marx and nature, see Bellamy Foster (2000) and Burkett (1999).

4 This was Marx's critical response to the proposals of the German social democrats, Karl Liebknecht, a follower of Marx, and those of Ferdinand Lassalle for socialist transition.
5 Originally written in 1906 as *Results and Prospects*, it was re-published in a revised form in 1930 in Russian in 1931 and in English as *Permanent Revolution* along with the original text (Trotsky 1969).
6 See Ree (2013) for a comprehensive review and discussion of the problem of the sources of revolution in Marx.
7 On Marx and Russian Marxism, see Shanin (1984).
8 *Capital,* Vol. 2 was in part a step in this direction, but remained incomplete in Marx's life. It was published in 1885 by Engels who edited Marx's notes on the market and the circulation of capital. It should be noted that the three volumes of Capital were incomplete by the time of Marx's death.

References

Anderson, P. 1974. *Considerations on Western Marxism*. London: New Left Books.

Avineri, S. 1968. *The Social and Political Thought of Karl Marx*. Cambridge: Cambridge University.

Bellamy Foster, J. 2000. *Marx's Ecology: Materialism and Nature*. New York: Monthly Press.

Bhattacharya, T. (ed.) 2007. *Social Reproduction Theory*. London: Pluto.

Boldizzoni, F. 2020. *Foretelling the End of Capitalism: Intellectual Misadventures since Karl Marx*. Cambridge: Harvard University Press.

Burkett, P. 1999. *Marx and Nature: A Red and Green Perspective*. London: Palgrave.

Claeyss, G. 2011. 'Non-Marxian Socialism, 1815–1914'. In: *The Cambridge History of Nineteenth-Century Political Thought*. Edited by G. Steadman Jones and G. Claeyss. Cambridge: Cambridge University Press.

Eaton, H. 1980. 'Marx and the Russians'. *Journal of the History of Ideas*. 41 (1): 89–112.

Eriksen, E. 2021. *Trade and Nation: How Companies and Politics Reshaped Economic Thought*. New York: Columbia University Press.

Graeber, D. 2011. *Debt: The First 5,000 Years*. London: Melville House.

Hartwell, R. and Engerman, S. 2003. 'Capitalism'. In: *The Oxford Encyclopaedia of Economic History*. Vol. 1. Edited by J. Mokyr. Oxford: Oxford University Press.

Harvey, D. 2010. *The Enigma of Capital: And the Crises of Capitalism*. London: Verso.

Kocka, J. 2016. *Capitalism*. Princeton: Princeton University Press.

Kolakowski, L. 1978. *Main Currents of Marxism – The Founders*. Vol. 1. Oxford: Oxford University Press.

Lane, D. 2020. 'V. I. Lenin's Theory of Socialist Revolution', *Critical Sociology*. 47 (3): 455–73. https://doi.org/10.1177/0896920520958451

Löwy, M. 1981. *The Politics of Combined and Uneven Development: The Theory of Permanent Revolution*. London: Verso and NLB.

Marx, K. 1996 [1976]. *Capital: A Critique of Political Economy*. London: Penguin.

Ree van, E. 2013. 'Marxism as Permanent Revolution'. *History of Political Ideas*. 34 (3): 541–63.

Rogan, T. 2017. *The Moral Economists: R. H. Tawney, Karl Polanyi, E. P. Thompson, and the Critique of Capitalism*. Princeton: Princeton University Press.

Rueschemeyer, D., Huber Stephens, E. and Stephens, J. 1992. *Capitalist Development and Democracy*. Chicago: University of Chicago Press.

Sen, A. 2009. 'Introduction'. In: *The Theory of Moral Sentiments*. Edited by A. Smith. London: Penguin.

Sen, A. 2010. 'Adam Smith and the Contemporary World'. *Erasmus Journal of Philosophy and Economics*. 3 (1): 50–67. https://ejpe.org/journal/article/view/39/36

Shanin, T. 1984. *Late Marx and the Russian Road*. London: Routledge.

Shanin, T. 2018. '1981 Letters of Vera Zasulich and Karl Marx'. *Journal of Peasant Studies*. 45 (7): 1183–1202.

Smith, A. 1976 [1776, 1789]. *An Inquiry into the Nature and Causes of the Wealth of Nations*. Edited by R. H. Campbell, A. S. Skinner and W. B. Todd. Oxford: Clarendon Press.
Smith, A. 2009 [1759]. *The Theory of Moral Sentiments*. London: Penguin.
Stedman Jones, G. 2016. *Karl Marx: Greatness and Illusion*. London: Penguin.
Trotsky, L. 1969 [1930]. *Permanent Revolution and Results and Prospects*. New York: Pathfinder Books.

2 Weber and the Iron Cage of Modern Capitalism

There was a new interest in capitalism after Marx within social science and in economics. It came with the increased use of the term capitalism. The Norwegian-American Thorstein Veblen is one such example of a theorist outside the Marxist tradition who developed a theory of capitalism. The author of the influential *Theory of the Leisure Class* [1899] Veblen advanced the notion of conspicuous consumption as a feature of capitalism. In Germany, Werner Sombart, one of the most important figures, wrote the three-volume *Modern Capitalism* [1902, 1916, 1927] and already after the end of the First World War coined the terms, 'late-capitalism', which became a standard term in Marxist theory in the 1970s, as well as the notion of 'creative destruction', made famous later by Joseph Schumpeter, who borrowed the term from Sombart. His many other works included *The Quintessence of Capitalism* [1913] in which he looked at the psychological and cultural make-up of the modern capitalist (the German title was *Der Bourgeois*) and *Why is there no Socialism in United States* [1906]. His 1930 article on capitalism offers one of the most concise definitions of the term capitalism before its widespread use (Sombart 1930).

While both Sombart and Veblen are considered to be important figures in the sociology of modern capitalism, Max Weber clearly stands out as a monumental figure. His work is essential for an understanding of capitalism, not least due to his huge influence especially in Germany and the USA. *The Protestant Ethic and the Spirit of Capitalism* [*PESC*] [1904–5] is without doubt his most famous contribution, but an exclusive focus on this classic work would obscure some of his other writings on capitalism. Much of his wider work on capitalism is not as accessible as *PESC* as it is spread across his vast corpus of writings, such as the posthumous *Economy and Society* and the *General Economic History* [1923], which was based on his last lectures in 1919–20.

Weber, like Georg Simmel who influenced his work, represents the first comprehensive sociological theory of capitalism, which he called in the Introduction to the *Protestant Ethic and the Spirit of Capitalism* the 'the most fateful force in our modern life' (p. 17). He went beyond Simmel's emphasis on the symbolic nature of money in *The Philosophy of Money* [1900] with a wider conception of capitalism as civilizational. Like Simmel, Weber was concerned with the cultural foundations of capitalism. In this respect, he was different from Marx, whose interest in this aspect of capitalism was marginal. However, it would be a mistake to see Weber only as a cultural sociologist in contrast to the political economy approach of Marx. He also had profound insights into the material foundations of capitalism and the relationship between capitalism and bureaucracy. We will consider the Marx versus Weber debate in the first section of this chapter.

Much has been written on the question of the thematic unity of Weber's writings, which covered many areas ranging from economic history, law, organizations, religion,

DOI: 10.4324/9781351017671-3

music and the methodology of the social sciences. Overall, we concur with the general view that the master concept in his work is the process of rationalization (see Schlucter 1985; Tenbruck 1980). Weber's writings on capitalism, unlike Marx's, were not specifically about capitalism. He was interested in capitalism as an aspect of rationalization and as a particular civilizational feature of the West. This is really the key to an understanding of Weber's work in general and specifically his writings on capitalism. It also provides a clue to his critique of modern capitalism. He was not of course in any sense a radical critic of capitalism in the way Marx was, but he was a critic of modern society that had made a god out of money. In that sense, his sociology was an expression of late nineteenth-century German pessimism with modernity which brought about a loss in freedom. However, it must be noted that his primary objection was not capitalism as such but the blind pursuit of wealth and bureaucratic organization. In this chapter, we locate his theory of capitalism in the context of his wider theory of rationalization as culminating in the famous motif of the 'iron-cage'.

Marx after Weber: Weberian Marxism

Weber has been traditionally seen as a critic of Marx and consequently offering a very different theory of capitalism. There can be no doubt that Weber's politics was different. He was a self-declared 'member of the bourgeoisie'[1] and was famously opposed to linking theory and practice, standing instead for a so-called value-free social science in which science should not become embroiled in the major issues of the day other than advising on practical matters in the domain of social and public policy. Yet he was not quite a mandarin of the established order as he was a strong critic of Wilhelmine order. The focus of his work was also different, concerned as he was with understanding the cultural significance of social phenomena, especially in terms of their 'world historical' significance. One of the abiding themes in his work was the religious underpinnings of economic activity and why it was in the West capitalism that took on the importance that it did. Perhaps, the most important difference was his opposition to the idea associated with Marx that economic forces determine the overall shape of society. The aspects of capitalism that he drew attention to were also very different from Marx's analysis. In general, he offered a more pluralist view of class, power and politics in modern society. There are also of course major methodological differences in that Weber stood in the neo-Kantian tradition rather than the left-Hegelian one and he saw his approach to sociological inquiry to be largely interpretive.

Now, we do not wish to revisit the well-known conflict of the two sociologies in all its dimensions. The account offered here stresses Weber as building rather than departing from Marx. The differences, which are undeniably considerable, can be seen more productively as a broadening of the scope of Marx's theory of capitalism to encompass a more sociological theory of modern society. We can reject as irrelevant the old argument of the idealist Weber versus the materialist Marx, as these are caricatures. The dominant reception of Weber in modern sociology has been strongly influenced by Talcott Parsons, who sought to reconstruct and develop a version of Weber that had severed any possible connection with Marx. Weber himself did not discuss Marx at great length. The *PESC* contains more or less no discussion of Marx, other than critical remarks, mostly indirect, against later appropriations of Marx, the so-called theorists of the superstructure. In view of this and a very different politics, it was not difficult for Parsons – who had the advantage of translating the *PESC* into English in 1930 – to resurrect an image of Weber that reflected his own purposes in shaping sociological theory. In any case, it came about that the legacies of Weber and Marx were claimed by different traditions in the course of the twentieth century. It can also be noted that the major theorists of the Frankfurt School, Adorno and Horkheimer, were influenced by Weber but did not explicitly acknowledge this.

As we have seen in the previous chapter, the theory of capitalism in Marx was centrally about commodification and the accumulation of profit. Now, while Weber largely accepted the centrality of profit to capitalism, he developed a theory of capitalism that was very consistent with Marx's account of commodification. This at least was how György Lukács saw it. It was Lukács who established the most important synthesis of Weber and Marx. The theory of reification developed in *History and Class Consciousness* [1923], while an explicitly Marxist work, drew heavily on Weber's theory of rationalization. The resulting consolidation of Marx and Weber was transmitted via Lukács to the Frankfurt School tradition and was a key idea in the *Dialectic of Enlightenment* whose themes were very much the Weberian one of the disenchantment of the West, modernity as a loss of freedom and an oppressive rationalization and bureaucratization. For Weber too, the worst aspect of modernity was bureaucratization, not capitalism as such. However, the development of capitalism as reflected in the big corporation facilitated the expansion of bureaucracy. While the Frankfurt School are more generally known for their synthesis of Marx and Freud, their reinterpretation of Weber is also important in what has been referred to as 'Weberian Marxism'.

Michael Löwy (1996) has shown that it was Merleau-Ponty in *Adventures of the Dialectic* [1955] who first used the term Weberian Marxism. It is a reminder of the deep influence that Marx had on Weber, an influence which, notwithstanding the differences in their political positions, had a lasting impact on later thinkers in the Marxist tradition. This legacy is important also in that it shows a different reading of Weber in seeking to understand the relationship between capitalism and modernity more generally, especially in its cultural configurations (see also Feenberg 1981; Sayer, 1991). Karl Löwith (1993 [1960]), an influential figure in German social thought, claimed there was a convergence in the work of Marx and Weber (see also Sayer 1991). It is evident, for instance, that Weber saw the relationship between modernity and capitalism as one of interdependence and not an account that sought to offer a cultural alternative. This becomes all the more clear when *PESC* is read alongside his more systematic sociological works, such as *Economy and Society*. As Löwy acknowledges, Weberian Marxism is a heterogeneous field, since few if any later Marxist theorists saw themselves as Weberian even when they drew on his work. They were more likely to claim the Freudian heritage. Habermas's vol. 1 of *Theory of Communicative Action* [1981] changed that neglect in giving Weber a key role in the reconstruction of historical materialism.

It is not the aim here to rehabilitate Weberian Marxism, but to assert a closer relationship between Weber and Marx than in mainstream Anglo-American Weberian sociology, which had expurgated Marx from Weber and exaggerated Weber's departure from Marx. Weber built upon Marx's work and in so doing developed his own distinctive sociology of modern capitalism. His approach is in part a corrective of Marx rather than an outright rejection. His pithy definition of capitalism in the *General Economic History* is close to Marx: Capitalism is the provision of human needs by the method of enterprise' (1961: 207). He also accepted the centrality of wage labour to capitalism and he tended to see the socialist workers movement, as opposed to socialism more generally, as a counterforce to capitalist rationalization It is clear though that his project was a different one, methodologically and theoretically.

Before discussing his key concepts and arguments concerning capitalism, his methodological approach can be briefly clarified, as outlined in the influential 1904 essay, '"Objectivity" in Social Science and Social Policy' and in other writings on the methodology of the social sciences.[2] Absolutely basic to Weber and the neo-Kantian tradition in which he stood and which shaped the philosophy of the social sciences in far-reaching ways, was a strong opposition to empiricism in the sense that empirical knowledge is theoretically based rather than being self-evident or reliant on observation. The facts do not speak for themselves. Capitalism, like all empirical social phenomena, is known to social science as a concept; it is not a reality in itself. Scientific knowledge is conceptually laden and it is through concepts that reality, as he put it, becomes intelligible. While social science is 'an empirical science of concrete reality', it proceeds by means of concepts, in particular 'ideal types', which enable the construction of social reality, rather than, as in the positivist approach to science, by recourse to analytical laws. In line with the Kantian sources of this tradition of social science, social reality cannot be known in itself as an objective reality. It must be conceptually reconstructed. For this reason, Weber argued for an interpretive social science. Such a conception of social science is able to offer explanations, but not explanation that is reduced to primary causes. While there is much controversy on the relation of explanation and understanding in Weber, one key point is incontrovertible, namely that the kind of interpretative explanation he developed sought to demonstrate the relationship between different realms of social life. Thus, in demonstrating the link between Protestantism and capitalism, Weber was postulating what he called 'an elective affinity'. Moreover, his approach did both through the construction of ideal types, the purpose of which was more akin to a heuristic guide to empirical reality than a descriptive account. Thus, capitalism is an analytical concept based on ideal types. We return to this below. It can be mentioned in the present context that Weber's analytical approach was always to establish a pattern of relationships among diverse elements in order to explain the formation and shape of a given social phenomenon. This is the quintessence of the sociological method, the demonstration of what elements need to be present and connect with each other for a specific pattern to develop. Weber went further in developing a probabilistic kind of explanation, that is a reasoning that tries to say, given certain conditions and factors, what a likely outcome will be of a particular action or event.

Rationalization and Capitalism

A basic axiom of Weber's approach to social inquiry is a view that the unit of social reality is social action. Social science seeks to understand why people do what they do. Action is not just behaviour; it is imbued with meaning since people act in accordance with their beliefs and their interests. As such, action requires an interpretive approach. It cannot be simply explained by recourse to laws. Moreover, action is embedded in historical contexts and as such it is historically variable.

This notion of action as meaningful was the central theoretical idea underpinning Weber's work and laid the basis of what was to become action theory in modern sociological theory. Weber's particular approach, in line with his ideal types, was to define social action into four types: traditional action, affectual action, value rational and purposive rational. The first is action guided by tradition, the second is action that is essentially emotionally driven, the third is action that is guided by a belief in certain values and the fourth is the action that is instrumental or purposive. While he defined these in terms of ideal types, he saw them as universal features of human beings and not as historically specific, even if they are historically conditioned. Weber held that the latter two were becoming more dominant in modernity, which entails the declining significance of tradition and emotion in the organization of societies. The latter does not vanish but retreats to the inner world of the individual.

The latter two notions of action brought the theory of social action into the much-confused realm of rationality (see Brubaker 1984; Kalberg 1980; Schluchter 1985). In contrast to later rational choice theory, Weber operated with different notions of rationality and not always consistently. To follow Stephen Kalberg's reconstruction, there is practical rationality, as embodied in everyday life as a pragmatic way of dealing with practical problems; theoretical rationality as reflected in science and intellectual mastery; substantive rationality as embodied largely in values and beliefs; and formal rationality as reflected in procedural and means-ends approaches (Kalberg 1980). Modernity entails the conflict between these forms of rationality and especially between two broad categories of rationality, substantive or value rationality and formal purposive rationality. Much of his work was an attempt to examine the relationship between these two kinds of rationality, which sometimes are reflected in the conflict between interests and values. This was not without some confusion, since the broad definition of rationality that he operated was an expression of the dominance of the latter kind. So rationality is characterized by the application of rules: it is procedural rather than substantive, it is abstract and impersonal. Yet, at the same time, Weber held that action guided by beliefs is also rational in more substantive terms. The apparent contradiction in this can be reconciled by seeing action guided by values in terms of a means-end relationship in that the end, which is a higher value and not in itself rational, requires the application of practical or instrumental means to its attainment. In that sense, then, value rationality may take precedence over instrumental rationality, which in itself is not guided by a value but can be made to serve values. In this way, religious beliefs can be rational, as can the pursuit of money.

Weber's complicated theory of rationality is essential for an understanding of capitalism, since he held that capitalism alone did not create its conditions of existence. Moreover, capitalism did not create the 'economic ethic'. The 'spirit of capitalism' emerged not just from capitalism, but from processes of rationalization in other spheres of life. Thus, for Weber, capitalism evolved to become not just an economic system or, as in Marx, a political economy, but a civilization. Its success, at least in the West, was that it embodied a cultural form that was also present in other spheres of life. Capitalism embodied formal rationality in terms of purposive instrumental rationality but it was also conducive to other forms of rationality, as in theoretical and substantive rationality. Capitalism coincided with the rise of modern science and the kind of intellectual mastery that it fostered and it also coincided with the Protestant Reformation, which similarly exhibited a strong theoretical rationality. But while 'the development of the spirit of capitalism is best understood as part of the development of rationalism as a whole', the situation is more complicated in that 'the history of rationalism shows a development which by no means follows parallel lines in the various departments of life (1978: 76–7).

Before discussing the argument of the *PESC* in the next section, we can now discuss the more general features of capitalism in terms of his broader theory of rationality and processes of rationalization. This discussion will seek to correct the misinterpretation that Weber held to an exclusively cultural conception of capitalism. As Randall Collins has argued, *General Economic History* was his last word on capitalism, which he analysed with very little reference to religious factors and the general argument of *PESC*, which he considers only at the end of the work (Collins 1980). In this, his mature work, he is also considerably closer to Marx's analysis of capitalism. This may have been his 'last word', but Weber never systematized his vast corpus, so it is not possible to say exactly what was his definitive view on many of the topics on which he wrote.

As an economic system, capitalism for Weber is a highly rationalized economic system based on the rational weighing of utilities and costs. As capitalism becomes a more complex system, it comes to depend increasingly on a capacity for calculation. Weber shares with Marx the basic idea that capitalism is an economic system based on private businesses seeking to make profit. But it is more than this. Rational calculation is the driving force of capitalism, not the pursuit of profit alone. The latter may be the rational end and the former the means to that end, but the means dominates. As he wrote in *Economy and Society*:

> It is only in the modern Western World that capitalistic enterprises with fixed capital, free labour, the rational specialization and combination of functions, and the allocation of productive functions on the basis of capitalistic enterprises, bound together in a free market economy, are to be found.
>
> (Weber 1947: 279)

Capitalism becomes closely tied up with the general movement towards bureaucratic organization. Weber recognized the historical transformation of capitalism from what he called political capitalism – essentially premodern and early modern capitalism such as mercantilism which was dominated by the unreformed state and agrarian capitalism – to traditional capitalism towards rational capitalism. Political capitalism was also strongly present in classical antiquity and in premodern times. Traditional capitalism is capitalism proper, the era of entrepreneurial capitalism that was the background to Marx and characterized by the figure of the bourgeois and the family enterprise. This era of entrepreneurial capitalism, as Weber saw it, is being replaced by the new age of rational capitalism and reflected in the big corporation and the separation of owners from managers in the organization of the large-scale capitalist enterprise.

The twentieth century sees the arrival of the large corporation and with it a culture of the rational calculation of profit by accounting. Weber greatly emphasizes the 'formal rationality' of accounting in the evolution of capitalism. From a Marxist perspective, it is perhaps the case that he downplays the pursuit of profit. But this is because he thinks the means to profit-making often dominates, as in, to take a more contemporary example, the way in which neoliberal management techniques have penetrated to the non-profit domain. As he said in the Introduction to *PESC*, 'the impulse to acquisition, pursuit of gain, of money, of the greatest possible amount of money, has in itself nothing to with capitalism'. This impulse, he argues, has long existed before capitalism. Moreover, he notes capitalism may even be identical with restraint from such impulses. The key point is that 'capitalism is identical with the pursuit of profit, and forever renewed profit, by means of the continuous, rational, capitalistic enterprise' (Weber 1978: 17). This could have been written by Marx.

Weber was the first to give serious attention to accounting as critical to the development of capitalism. He emphasized budgetary management through, for example, double-entry book-keeping, as essential for the rational calculation of profit. Increased prediction in production through technological means is another such aspect of rational calculation. Such practices come with the rise of the modern professions, the institutionalization of theoretical rationality and the legal-rational state.

The historical perspective developed by Weber gave a more central role to the state than Marx did. It was more than the 'night watchman' and played an important role in the removal of obstacles in the path of capitalism. This was not necessarily due to complicity with capitalism but it was an outcome of rationalization processes that led to the triumph of the dominant forms of rationality, such as formal and theoretical rationality. This argument was also put forward in a different key, but fully compatible with Weber's, by Albert O. Hirschman in a classic text in 1977, *The Passions and the Interests*. The rise of modern capitalism was greatly aided by developments that resided in the non-economic spheres of life. Hirschman (2013) argued that the removal of cultural-religious barriers to capitalism, such as the prohibition in medieval Christianity on usury, the disdain for luxury and a view of gain as a destructive passion, were critical in facilitating the dominance of new values that brought economic interests closer to a value and to a point at which they became a passion. This also occurred in science with the Protestant Reformation. In contrast to the Catholic Church's opposition to science, the Protestant Reformers embraced scientific explanation as compatible with the search to explain god's plan. Weber also held that a fundamental feature of the civilizations of the world was the desire to explain suffering, which according to Tenbruck was the key to his *opus* (Tenbruck 1980). Science in part helped in this quest, as did more than any other religion, Protestantism, since it encouraged the believer to deal with the material world and to master it.

It was not only the removal of obstacles, such as those associated with Medieval Catholicism and the abolition of slavery and its replacement by formally free labour, that was significant, but also the creation of new values, as in Protestantism, and the extension of practical and formal rationality. In addition to the rise of accounting, of great significance was formal law. Weber also recognizes the importance of banking systems which make possible credit without which buyers have limited capacity to buy. Money itself is a form of credit. The point of money is not to store it but to create more through investments, which require loans. Money links producers and consumers and thus makes possible the extension of exchange. The development of complex monetary systems, different forms of finance, the gold standard, etc. extend the range of capitalism, which is no longer simply about the production of commodities, as in Marx. Weber instead stressed less commodity production and commodification than rationalization as a feature of modernity. His concern ultimately was less alienation than the loss of freedom brought about by excessive rationalization. While associated with capitalism, rationalization did not derive from capitalism but it was capitalism that allowed it to become the dominant force in the modern world.

Finally, capitalism, as Marx also recognized, requires access to markets, which become central to modernity. The acquisitive spirit is nourished by the market and the allure of money. Weber is very close to Marx in his view of the distinctive feature of modern capitalism, as opposed to earlier forms, as the arrival of 'the rational capitalistic organization of (formally) free labour' (1978: 21). But his emphasis was on the market as a power structure. The competitive market provides optimal conditions for calculability. Furthermore, he tended to see capitalism as contained within the nation-state, which even in his time was hardly justified (Stinchcombe 2003).

Why Did This all Happen? The Protestant Ethic and the Spirit of Capitalism

We now turn to the *Protestant Ethic and the Spirit of Capitalism*, which helps to understand how it came about that capitalism came to have taken on the significance that it acquired by the twentieth century. How did it come about that people made capitalism their god? Weber provided an explanation in *PESC* which was both a cultural critique and an explanation. This was to a large degree a historical account of the rise of capitalism and part of his more general comparative historical sociology of the civilizations of the world. Weber's quest was to understand the unique trajectory of the West where certain characteristics of human beings became more dominant than elsewhere. The process of rationalization was not specific to the West: capitalism, he noted, existed in a simple form in ancient China, India, Egypt and in the ancient world in Europe, but it did not develop into anything like the advanced form that emerged in western Europe since the eighteenth century (see also Collins 1997).

The central argument of *PESC* was not a causal explanation as such. Modern capitalism was the product of many forces, but fateful was the 'elective affinity' between Protestantism, especially in its Calvinistic form, and capitalism. Weber may have exaggerated the relationship, but it should be noted contrary to much misunderstanding that he was not claiming that Protestantism caused the rise of capitalism. This would not have made any sense since capitalism as a form of economic organization preceded Protestantism and was relatively advanced in the predominantly Catholic areas. His argument was rather more one of establishing the cultural conditions for capitalism and especially to see how religious factors played a role in shaping the spirit of capitalism. In the stronger version of his thesis, he was establishing a relationship between a cultural ethos and an economic ethic, with the former largely emanating from Protestantism. In the weaker version of the argument, he is demonstrating that capitalism requires a mentality that imbues it with a spirit. In these terms, some of the features of the 'Protestant ethic' come to pervade capitalism as 'influences' that provide 'directions'. Capitalism would have existed without Protestantism, though probably in a less rationalized form. However, Weber does not rule out the possibility of there being causal relationships between religious beliefs and patterns of behaviour and capitalism. Weber was far too careful methodologically to attribute causes when the relationship may be only one of influence or one of cultural selectivity or adaptability. The opening of Chapter 1 of *PESC* notes that in some cases the relationship may be the reverse, with religious affiliation the result and not the cause of economic conditions. The final page of *PESC* also acknowledges that Protestantism was itself influenced in its development by capitalism.

There are good grounds to see Weber's argument as one of cultural adaptation. As he wrote in *PESC*, 'it is worthwhile to ask how this connection of adaptability to capitalism with religious factors may have come about in the days of the early development of capitalism (p. 62). Later in *PESC*, he refutes the strong causal argument and qualifies his position to be that 'we only wish to ascertain whether and to what extent religious forces have taken part in the qualitative formation and the quantitative expansion of that spirit over the world' (p. 91). It is clear that by the end of Part 1 of *PESC*, he sees a causal argument possible only if modern culture can be attributed to religious movements and not just simply that they influenced the development of material culture. Here it should be noted that Weber was also interested in the influence of Protestant ideas not just on capitalism, but on the culture of modernity more generally. He found 'the roots of that disillusioned and pessimistically inclined individualism' (p. 109) were a feature of modernity in Puritanism. It is clear that ultimately his approach was interpretative rather than causal.

The features of Protestantism that Weber found conducive to capitalism included the work ethic, world asceticism, the Protestant idea of a 'calling', the 'methodic manner of life' and rational calculability. Underlying these characteristics was a tendency towards the 'systematic rational ordering of the moral life as a whole' (p. 126). Salvation was brought down from an other-worldly concern to the everyday routines of life in a 'world calling'. Some of the extreme cults, Pietism and Calvinism, penetrated into Protestantism more generally. It was his argument that these orientations then entered the wider culture. Although Weber did not pursue it, the point has been noted by others that modern Catholicism was itself influenced by aspects of Protestantism. The inner asceticism of Protestantism released tremendous energy for private acquisition. Weber notes how wasting time through idleness or excessive sleeping was one of the deadliest of sins for Calvinistic Protestantism. These cultural orientations led to a strong emphasis on work, as in the Puritan dictum, 'Work Hard in your calling'. Capitalism benefited from this religious command that work is a duty. Related to this was the strong compulsion to save money, which made possible the productive investment of capital. One of the most intriguing connections between Protestantism and capitalism was the Calvinistic belief in the Elect. Since the Elect were predestined, nothing could be done about it other than to discover signs that one might be among the predestined. Thus, the believers acted as if they were the Elect, whose piety entailed hard work and frugality.

Weber's argument, which had a somewhat provisional character, can be summed up as this: the work ethic, to take the main relevant aspect of Protestantism, was given a religious significance by Protestantism, which did not itself create the work ethic but gave it a new significance. Capitalism benefited from this cultivation of values that provided capitalism with a moral basis. This was at first a religious condition but soon became a wider cultural orientation in modernity. 'What the religious epoch of the seventeenth century bequeathed to its utilitarian successor was … a good conscience in the acquisition in the making of money'. Thus, the modern bourgeois could follow his pecuniary interests as if he was fulfilling a religious duty (pp. 176–7).

So, Weber postulated a theory of a historical take-off in which cultural rationalization in the sphere of religion translated into economic rationalization. Once this occurred, in the seventeenth and eighteenth centuries, modern capitalism on the basis of this moral and religious uplift could develop without any further need for religious justification. In abandoning the monastery, Christian asceticism with Protestantism 'strode into the market-place of life, slammed the door of the monastery behind it, and undertook to penetrate just that daily routine of life with its methodicalness, to fashion it into a life in the world, but neither of nor for this world' (p. 154). The result was a paradox: capitalist modernity owed its success to religious asceticism but lost any semblance of religion once it became its own master. This paradox has been explained as the transference of cultural rationalization into a self-perpetuating societal rationalization.

It should be noted that Weber was not simply trying to explain the rise of modern capitalism as such, but its 'spirit'. Capitalism needs a certain kind of devotion to the making of money and an ethos that cultivates a rationalistic attitude. It cannot entirely create this on its own, as is evidenced by many earlier instances of capitalism in pre-modern Europe and in other parts of the world. The uniqueness of the West in the end resides in the prevalence of deep and pervasive processes of cultural rationalization that furnished capitalism with what was initially a strong religious motivation but which came with time to be a more general substantive rationality that no longer required a religious foundation. The final pages of *PESC* make the somewhat stronger claim that the spirit of Christian asceticism gave birth to the spirit of modern capitalism and all of modern culture. Whether Weber was right or not, he nonetheless raises the question from where did modern capitalism get the cultural ethos that gave it such a firm foundation in human societies, first in the West and later in the rest of the world. The standard Marxist argument that capitalism anchored itself in society through ideological manipulation is not enough.

Weber's explanation for the rise of modern capitalism as entangled in processes of cultural rationalization does not in the final analysis offer much of a guidance since his conclusion was that capitalism no longer requires a substantive rationality. It would appear that once unleashed in the modern world, capitalism and the 'tremendous cosmos of the modern economic order' became an 'iron cage' into which we are trapped.

Trapped in the Iron Cage?

The famous final three pages of *PESC* convey Weber's cultural pessimism, which is much a conservative critique of modernity as it is of capitalism. The famous sentence that 'fate decreed that the cloak should become an iron cage' expressed the view that societal rationalization had transformed the Protestant concern with material goods and work from a 'cloak' that can be easily discarded into a cage 'stripped of its religious and ethical meaning'. It was never predetermined that the outcome would be a totally instrumentalized world that had severed its connection with spiritual values. Ironically, religious asceticism escaped from the cage but lingers on in the modern world only as a private morality, no longer commanding societal significance.

> Victorious capitalism, since it rests on mechanical foundations, needs its support no longer. The rosy blush of its laughing heir, the Enlightenment, seems also to be irretrievably fading, and the idea of duty in one's calling prowls about in our lives like the ghost of dead religious beliefs.
>
> (pp. 181–2)

The final reflections of Weber – where on his own admission he strayed into the domain of value judgements, contrary to his view of scientific value neutrality – painted a picture of modern society as trapped and with little scope for individual or collective transformation. As in a much-cited passage, he left this prospect open but without any sense of any alternative other than the pursuit of wealth and mundane passions:

> No one knows who will live in this cage in the future, or whether at the end of tremendous development entirely new prophets will arise, or there will be a great re-birth of old ideas and ideals, or, if neither, a mechanized petrification, embellished with a sort of convulsive self-importance.
>
> (p. 182)

This was written before 1918 when capitalism was in fact challenged on many fronts. In Russia after the October Revolution in 1917, an alternative modernity arose and Germany itself descended into chaos in 1918 after the collapse of the *Deutsche Reich*. Weber's attitude was one of resignation to capitalism, which was an inevitable outcome of the disenchantment of the West. After 1918, Weber, who prematurely died in 1920, was more aware of the prospect of an alternative model of modernity to capitalism. However, there are only some glimpses of this in his final writings and the dominant tendency in his work is to see capitalism as here to stay. Yet, he was intrigued that Russia might be an exception to western rationalism and where a new civilization might emerge. Following the Revolution of 1905, he published that year two essays on Russia – he had acquired a reading knowledge of Russian – exploring this prospect, which he moved away from in later years (Pipes 1955). It is clear that he did not share Oswald Spengler's notion of the possible emergence of different kind of civilization in Russia. The historical significance of Bolshevism was not clear to him by the time of his death in 1920, though arguably it did lead to a new civilizational order but not what Weber envisaged as an alternative to rationalization.

Since capitalism is subordinated to the process of rationalization, it is the latter that ultimately determines the shape of modern society. Perhaps it was a reflection of his political conservatism that he did not see capitalism as posing a problem to its survival. He certainly recognised that economic problems are endemic to capitalism, for example over-speculation and over-production, but he did not think these problems were the result of a fundamental contradiction in the nature of capitalism, as Marx believed. The problems of capitalism can in essence be resolved by capitalism since they are largely problems of rationality and technology and it is the nature or rationality that it can steer itself in the right direction. Weber clearly had too much faith in market competitiveness along with technical rationality to steer capitalism.

Today in the age of climate change, it is difficult not to be struck by a sentence at the end of *PESC* that capitalism will continue to determine our lives 'until the last ton of fossilized coal is burnt' (p. 181). The prescience of this sentence of course was lost to Weber, for whom it meant that capitalism would endure. However, he did accept that a political challenge could emerge, as in the rising tide of socialism, but this would not derive from capitalism itself. In this respect, he was in part correct, since both China and Russia embarked on a non-capitalist path without having had much historical experience of capitalism.

Weber's critique of capitalism, as argued, was a conservative cultural critique that did not question the rationality of capitalism. There is little if any sense of social struggles having any significance, other than possibly the potential to rein in capitalist development. While profoundly tuned to problems of meaning and value, he had little sense of justice as a driving force in human affairs. While Weber made the problem of suffering central to his sociology of religion, it is remarkable that he did not extend it to social and economic conditions. Suffering only needs to be explained. He found that Christianity offered one of the most fateful responses to the problem of suffering in that it led to a strong impulse to master the profane world. But this was a theodicy and could only make suffering bearable. Political responses were not systematically considered. Democracy was reduced to a mechanism for the selection of elites who lead the masses. Imperialism hardly impinges on Weber's historical sociology, despite writing at the high tide of worldwide colonialism which Germany also participated in (politically he praised European colonialism in Africa). The result is that capitalism is portrayed as a decidedly passive and almost silent process when the historical reality was one of considerable resistance, violence and upheaval. The 1918 flu – which claimed Weber himself in 1920 along with more than 50 million people worldwide – is one such example of one of the great historical moments of rupture and transformation. It does not fit into a conception of modernity that emphasizes rationalization and business as usual. However, some qualification is in order. Weber's political conservatism was not a coherent political position and changed throughout his relatively short life. In his later years it is clear that he moved towards a position more favourable to the left and strongly embraced democracy. In the context of his time, he was closer to a liberal and was opposed to reactionary conservatism.[3]

Weber's theory of rationalization while on the one side placed a very strong emphasis on the market and bureaucratic organization and, on the other side, placed too much emphasis on religion as supplying modern capitalism with its moral and cultural legitimation. His critique of capitalism was in the end a critique of modernity as entailing disenchantment. This idea of loss was rooted in religious rationalization. As he said in his 1918 lecture 'Science as a Vocation': 'Our age is characterized by rationalization and intellectualization, and above all, by the disenchantment of the world'. Disenchantment, strictly speaking and literally in German, refers to 'de-magnification', that is the progressive loss of magic that first came with the rise of formal religion. Weber sees de-magnification, and not despair with which it is easily associated, carried forwards into modernity by the Protestant Ethic and by processes of rationalization in other spheres of life, ranging from the economy to the state, law and bureaucracy. As Habermas has most persuasively shown, Weber failed to develop a conception of modern culture that could accommodate other expressions of rationality, including everything that could be summed under the category of what Habermas called 'communicative rationality' (Habermas 1984 [1981]). Weber, influenced in no small part by Nietzsche, remained trapped within the limits of late nineteenth-century German cultural criticism that ultimately saw only a personal ethics resisting the Iron Cage. Karl Jaspers regarded him as an existentialist. But he was also a political pragmatist and, as argued, believed in a somewhat constrained form of Anglo-American liberal democracy.

What became of the capitalist spirit? This is unclear. The argument of *PESC* suggests that it had run its course, having furnished capitalism in the seventeenth century with a powerful moral and religious foundation and it lost its rationale by the twentieth century when capitalism no longer required such a spirit. Yet, some of its elements remained, for example the work ethic in an un-ascetic form. Weber's argument here lacks development. If capitalism needed a spirit to sustain it for three centuries, is it really plausible that it can simply discard it? As we will see in Chapter 10, the notion of a 'spirit of capitalism' has remained a pertinent issue, as in, for example, Boltanski and Chiapello's *The New Spirit of Capitalism* (2006). There is also the important and influential argument given by Colin Campbell in *The Romantic Ethic and the Spirit of Capitalism* that capitalism nurtured from early on a spirit of consumerism, which he associates with the Romantic current, which cultivated a certain hedonism that was conducive to modern consumerism (Campbell 1987). The Romantic ethic did not sit comfortably with Weber's ascetic Protestantism and its work ethic.

A longer perspective on capitalism would question the assumption of an iron cage. Modernity is irreducible to economic and bureaucratic rationalization. The many facets of political modernity do not fit easily into Weber's model of rationalization as a unilinear and homogenizing process. It is also difficult to avoid confronting capitalist crisis. By the end of the 1920s, capitalism underwent its first major crisis that emanated directly from its internal workings, which were not smoothly averted by technocratic measures. Weber's work does not provide us with an adequate means to understand the nature of capitalist crisis.

The 'iron cage' has also been questioned as an incorrect translation of the term Weber used, 'stahlhartes Gehäuse'. It is in fact Parsons's term in the 1930 translation and which has become a taken-for-granted rendition of what Weber had written. According to Peter Bahr, the German term should be translated as 'shell as hard as steel'. He also notes that steel is a human-made artefact, suggesting that the shell may not be quite so hard after all and 'steel' has a different connotation to 'cage'. The term 'iron cage' was preferred by Parsons due to its religious connotation; it was first used in John Bunyan's *The Pilgrims Progress* [1678] where it suggests a condition of despair at humanity's turning away from god (Bahr 2001). Whatever the correct translation is, it is evident that Weber saw modernity encased in a steel-like structure. Liberal democracy and personal redemption are all that can be hoped for in the modern world since the triumph of capitalism. The view of capitalism as a hard structure, however defined, and it matters little whether it is steel or iron, fails to see that it takes a wide variety of forms and much of its success resides in its malleability and plasticity. Digital capitalism today cannot be easily seen in terms of hardness. Market efficiency and rationalization is only part of the story of the rise of modern capitalism. But it is undeniably an important part, as is suggested by George Ritzer's *The McDonaldization of Society*. Ritzer (1993) follows Weber in his analysis of the fast-food industry as based on four dimensions of rationalization: efficiency, calculability, prediction and control. This work shows the undoubted relevance of Weber's theory of capitalism and rationalization for the present day. However, this Weberian model with its emphasis on standardization does not give sufficient attention to counter-trends and alternative movements. Nor does it offer a perspective on health risk associated with diet.

DiMaggio and Powell (1983), in a much-cited article, question the assumptions about the iron cage of capitalist rationalization. They argue that the causes of bureaucratization and rationalization have changed. They claim structural change is less driven by market competition or by the need for efficiency, as Weber thought. Instead, the state and professions become the main vehicles of rationalization. Organizations become more and more similar in the way they operate as a result of rationalization, but not necessarily more efficient.

Weber's sociology assumed that the *laissez-faire* market economy was still intact. By the time of his final writings on capitalism, there was in fact very little of the nineteenth-century free market. The era of protectionism had arrived and with it the movement towards the interventionist state. This movement saved capitalism from a terminal crisis, but only to produce further problems. This brings us to the topic of the next chapter, Joseph Schumpeter's theory of capitalism, which we see also as a conservative critique of capitalism but one more attuned to the systemic problems of capitalism.

Notes

1 It should be noted that Weber probably meant here a member of the *Bürgertum*, not the bourgeoise as such, a distinction that is not so clear in English.
2 Most notably the essays written between 1903 and 1917 (Weber 2011).
3 See Weber (1994), in particular the essay written in 1917 'Parliament and Government in Germany under a New Political Order'.

References

Bahr, P. 2001. 'The "Iron Cage" and the "Shell as Hard as Steel" in Parsons, Weber, and the Stahlhartes Gehause Metaphor in *The Protestant Ethic and the Spirit of Capitalism*'. *History and Theory*, 40: 153–69.

Boltanski, L. and Chiapello, E. 2006 [1999]. *The New Spirit of Capitalism*. London: Verso.

Brubaker, R. 1984. *The Limits of Rationality: An Essay on the Social and Moral Thought of Max Weber*. London: Allen & Unwin.

Campbell, C. 1987. *The Romantic Ethic and the Spirit of Capitalism*. Oxford: Blackwell.

Collins, R. 1980. 'Weber's Last Theory of Capitalism: A Systematization. *American Sociological Review*, 80: 925–42.

Collins, R. 1997. 'An Asian Route to Capitalism: Religious Economy and the Origin of Self-Transformation'. *American Sociological Review*, 62 (6): 843–65.

DiMaggio, P. and Powell, W. 1983. 'The Iron Cage Revisited: Institutional Isomorphism and Collective Rationality in Organizational Fields'. *American Sociological Review,* 48: 147–60.

Feenberg, A. 181. *Lukács, Marx and the Sources of Critical Theory*. Totowa: Roman & Littlefield.

Habermas, J. 1984. 1981. *Theory of Communicative Action*. Vol. 1. Cambridge: Polity Press.

Hirschman, A. 2013 [1977]. *The Passions and the Interests: Political Arguments for Capitalism Before its Triumph*. Princeton: Princeton University Press.

Kalberg, S. 1980. 'Max Weber's Types of Rationality: Cornerstones of the Analyses of Rationalization Processes in History.' *American Journal of Sociology*, 85 (5): 1145–79.

Löwith, K. 1993 [1960]. *Max Weber and Karl Marx*. London: Routledge.

Löwy, M. 1996. 'Figures of Weberian Marxism.' *Theory and Society*, 25: 431–66.

Pipes, R. 1955. 'Max Weber and Russia'. *World Politics*, 7 (3): 371–401.

Ritzer, G. 1993. *The MacDonaldization of Society*. London: Sage.

Sayer, D. 1991. *Capitalism and Modernity: An Excursus on Marx and Weber*. London: Routledge.

Schluchter, W. 1985. *The Rise of Western Rationalism: Max Weber's Developmental History*. Berkeley: University of California Press.

Sombart, W. 1930. 'Capitalism'. In: *Encyclopaedia of the Social Sciences*. Vol. 3. New York: Macmillan.

Stinchcombe, A. 2003. 'The Preconditions of World Capitalism: Weber Updated'. *The Journal of Political Philosophy*. 11: 411–36.

Tenbruck, F. 1980. 'The Problem of Thematic Unity in the Works of Max Weber'. *British Journal of Sociology*, 31 (3): 316–51.

Weber, M. 1947. *The Theory of Social and Economic Organization*. Edited with an Introduction by T. Parson. New York: The Free Press.

Weber, M. 1961 [1923]. *General Economic History*. New York: Collier Books.

Weber, M. 1978 [1930, 1904–5]. *The Protestant Ethic and the Spirit of Capitalism*. London: Allen & Unwin.

Weber, M. 1994. *Weber: Political Writings*. Edited by P. Lassing. Cambridge: Cambridge University Press.

Weber, M. 2011 [1903–1917]. *Methodology of the Social Sciences*. Edited by E. Shils and H. Finch. London: Routledge.

3 Schumpeter and Capitalist Crisis

In this chapter, we deal with the first major consideration of capitalist crisis in the twentieth century. Joseph Schumpeter's *Capitalism, Socialism and Democracy* [1942] is one of the twentieth century's seminal texts on capitalism and offers profound insights into the nature of capitalist crisis. Although written in the mid-twentieth century amidst perhaps the greatest crisis of that century when much of the world was falling under the sway of a non-capitalist power and the capitalist liberal democracies were threatened by fascism, many of the insights in this book are of relevance to the current situation as capitalism undergoes another transformation.

Schumpeter was primarily an economist but his economic theory, at least as developed in *Capitalism, Socialism and Democracy* [*CSD*], incorporated a consideration of social processes making it of major relevance to social theory. He saw economics as an integrated social science incorporating sociology and economic history (Shionoya 1997). His work has often been seen as falling within the limits of social theory (Bottomore 1985, Collins 1986, Dahms 1995, 2011). Like Marx and Weber, he argued that the economy is not a separate sphere but is part of society and must be understood in terms of historical processes. This insight, that capitalism is an inter-related system, is less evident in his major works, from the early *Theory of Economic Development* [1911] and the later *Business Cycles* [1939], but it is central to *CSD*, which we concentrate on in this chapter. In this work, which encompasses economics, economic history, sociology, social and political theory, Schumpeter went beyond economics as such to address the wider questions that his economic theory posed but did not answer.

Schumpeter was influenced by Marx's analysis of capitalism. His work shaped the debate on capitalism in far-reaching ways, even if many of his arguments turned out to be wrong. Schumpeter was convinced Marx was mostly right in his prediction of the end of capitalism and the triumph of socialism. He was wrong about the end of capitalism but right about the brief triumph of a particular version of socialism adopted in the USSR but wrong on the reasons for its triumph. In the end, capitalism, since the fall of the USSR and its adoption by the Communist Party of the PRC, eliminated its alternatives.

He was also influenced by Weber, with whom he had worked and who was politically closer to him than to Marx. It should be noted though that Weber did not share Schumpeter's cynicism and ambivalence. While he of course drew on many other traditions of thought, especially the Austrian economic tradition and, with Weber, the German Historical School, his work was in a way a combination of Marx and Weber from the perspective of the political right in a way that Lukács was a combination of Marx and Weber from the left. In that sense, he was not as such a critic of capitalism and claimed to stand for a value-free science. However, he was not politically neutral and we see him like

DOI: 10.4324/9781351017671-4

Weber as a conservative cultural critic of capitalism. For Schumpeter, it was the cultural consequences of capitalism that were detrimental to its survival: the giant corporation brings about cultural changes that silently usher in socialism without a need for revolution. It was a theory about the end of capitalism without a revolution, since capitalism itself furnished the necessary measures for its demise.

Schumpeter: Between Weber and Marx

Weber's work was deeply influenced by the historical context of late nineteenth-century Germany. The context in which Schumpeter, who was of German and Czech background, wrote was initially not Berlin but Vienna and the late Austrian-Hungarian Empire. While he became a US citizen and was a professor of economics at Columbia and later Harvard – *CSD* was written in English[1] – he was one of the great intellectuals of central Europe. His work and idiosyncratic career in many ways reflects the history of that world from the promising 1880s to the disaster of the post-1918 period. In 1919, he was briefly the Finance Minister of the post-war Austrian republic; he was a president of a failed Austrian bank; he was later investigated for pro-Nazi sympathies, which he almost certainly did not have; he was politically of the right, yet the government in which he served in 1919 was led by the Austrian socialists under Karl Renner and he had served on a commission set up to socialize the Austrian coal industry. He admired Marx's economic theory of capitalism without accepting the political consequences while at the same time believing that capitalism would give way to socialism. It is not quite clear if that was what he believed or whether it was intended as a wake-up call for the political right. It is therefore not surprising that he was regarded as politically ambivalent by both the right and the left.

Schumpeter, who was born in 1883, ironically the year of Marx's death, was indebted to Marx's analysis of capitalism. There are striking similarities between his notion of creative destruction, to be discussed below, and Marx's theory of the revolutionary nature of capitalism sweeping away all previous modes of production (see Elliot 1980). However, Schumpeter discussed in much more detail the process by which capitalism would come to an end. He shared Marx's view of capitalism as dynamic and as a revolutionary economic system that sows the seeds of its own destruction. He did not embrace Marx's dialectical view of history but his theory of historical development comes close to it. Schumpeter theorized economies in terms of static and dynamic analysis. His interest in the latter departs from Marx's similar approach in that he regarded the normal condition of economies to include both stagnation and transformation. However, the dynamic core of capitalism resides in its creative capacities, not in the class struggle. He opposed accounts of capitalism, for instance, the work of J. M. Keynes, which seemed to him to advocate a static concept of capitalism.

One of his most important ideas was that capitalism was evolutionary, a position too held by Marx and was possibly derived from his theory of history as a succession of modes of production. Both Schumpeter and Marx, unlike Weber, emphasized the centrality of the system of production over markets and consumption as the source of the dynamism of capitalism. But it was not based on exploitation as such; the central dynamic was innovation in production. He was also critical of what he took to be tendencies towards tautology in Marx whereby every instance of something supporting the interests of capitalism means that capitalism benefits (p. 47).

Like Marx, Schumpeter was intrigued that capitalism would come to an end one day. It is possibly the case that he saw this end coming sooner than what Marx thought, but it was not imminent. However, he did think that capitalism would break down under the weight of its own contradictions and in doing so release alternative cultural forces that could not be contained within the existing framework. But not all crises are anti-systemic. In fact, he sees many crises as normal. Capitalist dysfunctionalities are to be seen as fluctuations and can also serve the evolutionary function of eliminating weak firms. One of his most famous ideas, which defined his legacy for future neo-Schumpeterian, was that innovation was the key to economic development. This can easily be overinterpreted to be a revolutionary force akin to Marx's theory of revolution. Elliot (1980: 64) suggests it is more like a process of transformation. If innovation is normal, it can hardly be revolutionary.

Part 1 of *CSD* is devoted to Marx, who he clearly admires. He refers to his work as a product of the 'bourgeois mind' and superior to that of later socialists. He appears to be praising his sociological analysis over Weber's when he writes: 'The whole of Weber's facts and arguments fits perfectly into Marx's system' (p. 10). Drawing on Marx's economic theory, he argues the

> Capitalist economy is not and cannot be stationary. Nor is it merely expanding in a steady manner. It is incessantly being revolutionized from *within* by new enterprise, i.e. by the intrusion of new commodities or new methods of production or commercial opportunities into the industrial structure as it exists at any moment.
>
> (p. 27)

This is a key insight. Where he sharply disagreed with Marx is that in his view Marx failed to distinguish between the entrepreneur and the capitalist. Schumpeter admired the heroic figure of the entrepreneur over the capitalist. It was as if he saw the ideal model of capitalism to be an economic system run by an entrepreneur imbued with creative energy and dedication. The entrepreneur effectively replaced Marx's capitalist class.

Schumpeter had an important insight into the nature of crisis when he comments that Marx had two notions of crisis.

> In most cases Marx used the term crisis in the ordinary sense, speaking of the crisis of 1825 or 1847 ... but he also used it in a different sense. Believing that capitalist evolution would some day disrupt the institutional framework of capitalist society, he thought that before the actual breakdown occurred, capitalism would begin to work with increasing friction and display the systems of a fatal illness.
>
> (p. 35)

Following Marx, he says that the factors responsible for the ultimate crisis of capitalism cannot be made responsible for every crisis. So, crisis is normal to capitalism, but the final crisis of capitalism will come about due to forces endemic to capitalism. Schumpeter differed from Marx in his view about those forces. In general, as is clear from the end of Part 1 of *CSD*, he tended towards a view of revolution as a process of evolution. His sympathetic but critical reading of Marx was intended to provide a basis for his theory of capitalism as a good system destined to fail for evolutionary reasons.

Schumpeter was in agreement with Marx's analysis of capitalism but rejected his politics. Schumpeter's political philosophy was closer to Weber's view of liberal democracy and the separation of elites and masses. The latter are governed by elites and lack an active role in the political life of democracy. He tended to see capitalism as Weber did as a civilization. He was heavily influenced by Weber and the German Historical School (Love 2017; Swedberg 2002). He can be seen, as mentioned, as a Weberian Marxist of the right.

Weber's theory of rationalization – through calculability, bureaucratization, routinization etc. – is present in Schumpeter in terms of processes of continuity and stability, though Weber emphasized much more stability. Schumpeter has been seen as a key figure in Weberian sociology (see Collins 1986). While Weber acknowledged the creative aspects of capitalism, he did not do so to the same extent as Schumpeter with his notion of creative destruction and accordingly failed to appreciate trends towards instability. However, not every instance of instability is an indication of a catastrophic crisis. It can simply be the elimination of uncompetitive businesses.

Marx, Weber and Schumpeter were theorists of major historical transformations. They differed in their view of how societies undergo transformation. On this question, Schumpeter stood somewhere between Marx and Weber. He shared Marx's emphasis on major transformation as an evolutionary process. He disagreed with Weber's tendency to place historical rupture in the past, with the transition to capitalism in Europe in the seventeenth century as the apotheosis of historical transformation. Schumpeter saw capitalism as a gradual process of development, at least until its maturation when it will come to an end through its 'decomposition'. Weber, on the whole, was convinced that the process of rationalization, embedded in modern capitalism, was irreversible. Although he entertained the prospect of a socialist overcoming of capitalism, this would only be due to its political attraction. It was not an evolutionary necessity. The USSR, to the extent it can be referred to as socialist, it was fighting for its very existence and it was by no means clear that in 1942, when he published CSD, that its future was guaranteed. In any case Schumpeter saw socialism as a development of capitalism than from a rival political system. Weber's thesis of total rationalization is present in Schumpeter's account of the tragic loss of creativity in the large corporation where creativity vanishes with the rise of the bureaucratic manager and too by the decadent rentier. In the tension between rational action versus creative action, it is the latter that will eventually win the battle. Interestingly, Weber did not have a theory of creativity as a form of action, though arguably his notion of the role of charisma in political life incorporates creativity. However, capitalism itself in his analysis did not require creativity.

Schumpeter developed Weber's account of capitalist rationalization through credit creation. Ingham (2003) stresses that Schumpeter followed Weber but developed his argument, seeing credit-money as an essential dynamic force in capitalism. Money is created by banks making possible transferrable debt without which capitalism cannot operate. In *Business Cycles* [1939], he gave a definition of capitalism that reflected the significance of finance: 'Capitalism is that form of private property economy in which innovations are carried out by private means of borrowed money, which in general, though not by logical necessity, implies credit creation' (cited in Bottomore 1985: 36).

One final point can be mentioned on the influence of Weber on Schumpeter: the spirit of capitalism in Schumpeter's account is carried not by ascetic Protestantism but by the creativity of the entrepreneur, who progressively succumbs to the disenchantment of modernity.

Creative Destruction and Capitalist Crisis

'Can capitalism survive? No, I do not think it can'. On the basis of this self-declared opinion with which the Prologue to Part 11 of *Capitalism, Socialism and Democracy* (hereafter *CSD*) opens, Schumpeter provides an analysis of the demise of capitalism that does not rest on notions of inevitability or necessity, but on tendencies present that point to an observable pattern whereby the success of capitalism generates the seeds of its destruction.

His argument is boldly stated:

> The thesis I shall endeavour to establish is that the actual and prospective performance of the capitalist system is such as to negate the idea of its breaking down under the weight of economic failure, but that its very success undermines the social institutions which protect and "inevitably" creates conditions in which it will not be able to live and strongly point to socialism as the heir apparent.
>
> (Schumpeter 2010: 53–4)

So, his argument is not one based on economic failure, as in Marx, but essentially it is a sociological argument about the cultural consequences of capitalism.

Schumpeter admits that his argument does not differ much from that of Marxists, but to accept it, one does not have to be a socialist, since prognosis does not say anything about the desirability of the course of events. Paradoxically, his argument is directed as much to those fatalistic socialists who think that capitalism does not harbour any tendency towards destruction having become entrenched. He was also a critic of neoclassical economics with the argument developed in *CSD* that capitalism is not based primarily on competition in the market as this would not adequately explain growth and profit; he argued the driving force in capitalism is technical innovation, which makes possible growth and nourishes the entrepreneurial spirit. However, as an economist in the Austrian tradition he was in many respects close to the ideas of Friedrich von Hayek, who was also a critic of many of the assumptions of neoclassical economics (see Chapter 5).

Schumpeter begins his analysis with the argument that the apparent success of capitalism over the preceding half century or so does not warrant the conclusion that it will continue, even if the empirical facts suggest that capitalism will continue to enjoy much success, as in its total productive capacity. Capitalism, by introducing new mechanisms of production through technical innovation, progressively increases the standard of life of the masses, he argues; the increase in individual incomes leads to increased consumption of personal services and goods, diminishing poverty. He says the capitalist engine has the potential to repeat into the future its past performance, but historical reality can easily contradict this tendency that may be only short term. In short, Schumpeter thinks things have changed in the new era of monopolistic capitalism. He is not claiming there was once a golden age of perfect competition, which he thinks is a myth, and in fact capitalism prospered because circumstances favoured it, not because perfect competition existed, and its success has sown the seeds of its destruction.

The future of capitalism cannot be determined from its historical success. The fact that it may be performing well in the short term does not mean it will continue to do so in the long term. What is needed is an understanding of the nature and dynamics of capitalism, which he insists does not consist of perfect competition but of the relentless capacity for innovation. Drawing on Marx, he makes a major claim: 'The essential point to grasp is that in dealing with capitalism we are dealing with an evolutionary process' (p. 72). Capitalism, as noted earlier, cannot therefore be stationary. For this reason, the implication of Schumpeter's argument is that the notion of perfect competition, espoused by neoclassical economics, is false since it rests on some notion of a static system that achieves equilibrium between buyers and sellers. Capitalism is a dynamic system; it is not leading towards convergence or equilibrium; it is 'by its nature a form or method of economic change and not only never is but never can be stationary' (p. 72). The prime movers of capitalist evolution, he argues, do not come from the social and natural environment, which only conditions change. 'The fundamental impulse that sets the capitalist engine in motion comes from the new consumers' goods, the new methods of production or transportation, the new markets, the new forms of industrial organization that capitalist enterprise creates' (pp. 72/3). He insists on the importance 'for the capitalist process in general and for its competitive mechanism in particular of the intrusion of new commodities' (p. 80). This is a view of major change coming not from revolutionary movements, wars, rebellion etc. but from the productive capacity of capitalism, which is a powerful engine of growth.

The capitalist system is constantly revolutionized 'from within'. For Schumpeter, this has two sides: one is a positive fact about capitalism as a creative and dynamic system, and another is a negative one that generates crisis and ultimately self-destruction. There are in fact two notions of destruction at work here: 'creative destruction' and 'self-destruction' or as he also called it 'decomposition'. The first is Schumpeter's most famous concept, outlined in the short Chapter 7 of *CSD*. Capitalism is a system that incessantly destroys the old system and creates a new one: 'This process of Creative Destruction' is the essential fact about capitalism. 'It is what capitalism consists in and what every capitalist concern has got to live in' (p. 73). In essence, this is a positive feature of capitalism and allows it to deliver enormous results, principally large-scale commodities for the population: 'the capitalist engine is first and last an engine of mass production' (p. 58). But capitalism is caught up in a 'perennial gale of creative destruction' that unleashes negative tendencies. This situation leads not to perfect competition but competition between old and new systems of production, technology, organization and new commodities. Such challenges are best solved by monopolistic corporations and not by the private entrepreneur, who was the basis of the historical model of capitalism. The new capitalism thus generates anti-capitalist tendencies, as in the growth of bureaucracy and technocrats who increasingly dominate the new kind of monopolistic capitalism. In this situation, creative destruction ceases and capitalism becomes simply self-destructive. The era of decomposition begins.

There are then two notions of destruction at work. Creative destruction is the process by which capitalism evolves through creativity and productivity. It is driven by innovation, which is the real spirit of capitalism. In this sense, creative destruction is a positive force. But once it runs its course and other forces take over, capitalism becomes self-destructive. It is in essence a story of the decline of creativity and its decomposition into sterile forms. The notion of creative destruction is clearly inspired by Marx's theory of the permanent revolutionizing of the means of production, but includes a personality dimension in incorporating the figure of the entrepreneur.

Schumpeter places much emphasis on new commodities and on new technologies as a feature of the evolving face of capitalism and evidence of creative destruction. The condition of the possibility of capitalism and the driving force of its creative destruction is innovation, which makes possible 'the intrusion of new commodities' (p. 82). It is this that allows it to achieve its primary function, namely the large-scale production of commodities for mass markets. Capitalism is the first economic system based on innovation and it is innovation that makes capitalism possible. It allows the system of production to be linked to markets and consumption. Innovation is more than scientific and technical invention; it requires creative implementation and business sense. With this argument, Schumpeter shifts the focus away from the primacy of the market and competition to innovation. The nature of innovation is that it does not foster equilibrium, the axiom of faith in neoclassical economics, but turbulence, instability and crisis. Innovation, of course, is also the basis of renewal, but in the context of 'late capitalism', to use the term popularized by Ernst Mandel in 1972 (1999) but invented by Werner Sombart, it is overseen by, what James Burnham called in a classic work in 1941, *The Managerial Revolution*, a technocratic and managerial class rather than a capitalist elite. Schumpeter seems to hold to this argument: 'Technological progress is increasingly becoming the business of teams of trained specialists who turn out what is required and make it work in predictable ways'. The result is that 'economic progress tends to become depersonalized and automatized' (p. 117–8).

His argument goes beyond the idea that the new and increasingly important managerial and technocratic class does not share the same values and interests of the capitalist class, which it serves. So long as the figure of the entrepreneur, essentially the capitalist elite, is in charge, capitalism will thrive. But 'the modern corporation, although the product of the capitalist process, socializes the bourgeois mind; it relentlessly narrows the scope of capitalist motivation; not only that, it will eventually kill its roots' (p. 140). Capitalism is also 'civilizational' in that it creates a culture or mentality. In this respect, Schumpeter is in the footsteps of Weber. It is this perspective that also gives to his analysis of capitalism the character of what we call a conservative cultural critique, for capitalism was not ultimately able to sustain the civilization it created. It nurtures values that may be, if not antithetical to capitalism, counterproductive while at the same time being products of capitalist rationalism. These values shape not just our methods to attain ends but also the end themselves. For example, he claims feminism 'is an essentially capitalist phenomenon' (p. 113) in that it cultivates values that are compatible with the rationalistic requirements of capitalism. His reasoning is that feminism is capitalistic in the sense that it emerged in the context of the modern civilization of capitalism. The civilizational character of capitalism is clear from his remarks in the essay, 'The March into Socialism' [1949], his final word on capitalism. Capitalism 'is a scheme of values, an attitude toward life, a civilization – the civilization of inequality and of the family fortune. This civilization is rapidly passing away … ' (p. 379).

For Schumpeter, economy and society are entangled in each other, such that currents in one sphere spill over into the other. Modern society is shaped by capitalism but modern society is not controlled by capitalism and will rebel against it. This is because capitalism has created a non-static world. The prospect that all needs could be met leads to a situation that weakens the entrepreneurial motive to push production ahead; progress turns out to be mechanized and innovation is reduced to routine. The result is that the 'romance of the earlier commercial adventure is rapidly wearing away' simply now because so many things can be calculated (pp. 116–7). In contrast to Weber, who thought rationalization would reduce crisis tendencies by allowing everything to be managed through routinization, calculability and bureaucratization, Schumpeter sees in such processes the seeds of not creative destruction but of self-destruction. In fact, as discussed above, he held that Weber's substantive arguments can be easily accommodated within Marx's framework. The evolution of capitalism into the 'bureaucratized giant industrial unit' in the end 'ousts the entrepreneur and expropriates the bourgeoisie as a class', which loses not only its function but also its income in that much of the old bourgeoisie is transformed into a wage-earning class (p. 119). In this analysis, Weber's theory of capitalism would imply its stagnation, since the creative spirit of innovation is suffocated.

Schumpeter's analysis in the course of *CSD* unfolds from an economic to a sociological account of the destructive tendencies within capitalism.[2] Capitalism first destroyed the feudal world, the world of the artisan, lord and peasant. However, this was also creative destruction in that it removed obstacles in the path of capitalism; it was not, as Marx and Engels also wrote in the famous opening words of the *Communist Manifesto,* purely destructive, since it also removed forms of oppression that were in effect obstacles in the path of capitalism. But, the capitalist process also undermined its own institutional framework just as it undermined feudal society. What it did to the pre-capitalist strata, it also does to the small producer and trader. Schumpeter is convinced that capitalism is proceeding in a direction that undermines the capitalist class simply because that class no longer commands the process of technical innovation, which is taken over by 'teams of trained specialists': 'Innovation is being reduced to routine. .... The romance of earlier commercial adventure is rapidly wearing away, because so many more things can be strictly calculated that had of old to be visualized in a flash of genius' (pp. 117–8).

Capitalism thus becomes 'atrophic' as a result of automatization and de-personalization. It also 'creates a critical frame of mind which, after having destroyed the moral authority of so many other institutions, in the end turns against its own' (p. 128). 'Capitalism', he argues, 'inevitably by virtue of the very logic of its civilization creates, educates and subsidizes a vested interest in social unrest' (p. 131). Intellectuals are given a new significance by capitalism, which creates a large class of educated people who do not share the same values and interests of the capitalist class and who cannot be easily controlled through work and discipline. Schumpeter sees this class as generating 'growing hostility' to capitalism. In stark contrast to Weber's theory of rationalization in all spheres of life and his depiction of the disenchanted 'Iron Cage' of a world rationalized by capitalism, Schumpeter says the bureaucracies of Europe, which are of pre- and extra-capitalist origin, are open for conversion by the modern intellectual with whom they have much in common. The result is the 'decomposition' of capitalism:

> Faced by the increasing hostility of the environment and by the legislative, administrative and judicial practice born of that hostility, entrepreneurs and capitalists – in fact the whole stratum that accepts the bourgeois scheme of life – will eventually cease to function.
>
> (p. 139)

His account emphasizes the narrowing of the scope of capitalist motivation and the disintegration of the bourgeois family that was the bedrock of nineteenth-century capitalism.

So, capitalism will come to an end, just as Marx claimed, but not as a result of the reasons given by Marx, but due to the very success of capitalism as an economic system. The political challenge for an alternative system does not come from outside capitalism, but from within capitalism and not from deprivation but from prosperity. The relative wealth that capitalism generates for everyone does not saturate the critical mind, as Marcuse (1964) claimed in *One-Dimensional Man,* but nurtures it. Socialism thus will not arise due to its inherent appeal over a perfectly working capitalist system but because the capitalist system will crumble from within. He argued, interestingly but implausibly, that

> Capitalist evolution tends to weaken that motive for desiring wealth with all others. Socialism will hence, require not nearly as great a revaluation of the values of life in what now forms the uppermost stratum as it would have done a hundred years ago.
>
> (p. 185)

However, the idea that socialist values are prepared within capitalism is an interesting idea. There is a tension in this argument, which is never clearly stated between two positions. The first is that changes in the nature of capitalism are preparing the ground for the largely silent transformation into socialism, through for example the socialization of large parts of the economy and value-change. The latter process is not unlike Inglehart's theory of the 'silent revolution' through the advent of post-material values and a greater concern with quality-of-life issues over material values and security in western societies since the 1960s (Inglehart 1977). The second is the rejection of capitalism in favour of socialism in contrast to a gradual transformation whereby the transition occurs within capitalism. In the second case, socialism would be a new kind of society, as opposed to an evolution from within capitalism. However, the ground would be prepared for it within the late stage of capitalist development. Bottomore has pointed out that this argument is close to that of the Austro-Marxists, in particular Karl Renner and Rudolf Hilferding (Bottomore 1985: 443–4). It would seem that the logic and general direction of the argument of *CSD* is closer to the former. It may be the case that socialism was the wrong term to use, except perhaps in the sense of social democracy. Yet it is clear he thought that socialism and democracy are not incompatible (p. 252). However, it is also clear that he had something more radical in mind than social democracy, or anything that fell within the compass of democratic capitalism, as represented for example by his contemporary J. M. Keynes, whose ideas he was largely opposed to and which were becoming increasingly the orthodoxy at the time he was writing. Keynes, who was also born the same year as Schumpeter, argued for a stronger position of government over the economy than did Schumpeter, who adhered to liberal ideas in this regard.

Was Schumpeter Right?

Since the financial crash of 2009–10, there has been a new interest in Schumpeter's *CSD* and attempts to apply some of his ideas to the current situation (see for example Burlamaqui and Kattel 2019; Aghion et al 2021).

There are clearly many problems with Schumpeter's account of capitalism and its demise (see Coe and Wilbur 1985). Some of the problems are due to the lack of clarity in *CSD*.[3] As often noted, his somewhat persuasive style of writing involved rhetorical tricks, as in referring to a previous argument as a basis for a correct inference, or simply declaring his arguments to be true.

Especially today with the rise of precarious work in the gig economy, global inequality and austerity politics, it cannot be so easily argued that capitalism has generated prosperity for all citizens even in the advanced economies of the west. Widespread social discontent does not lead inexorably to a questioning of capitalism, but to support for autocratic populists, conspiracy theories and right-wing neo-nationalist parties. He was wrong to claim that the rise of a critical counter-culture will undermine capitalism. The counter-culture and new left that came did not bring about the end of capitalism, which adapted to the new styles of critique. Schumpeter lacked a perspective on how capitalism stabilizes itself not only with the help of the state but also through democratization.

Capitalism easily domesticates the potential dissatisfaction that the world of work produces, to follow the argument developed by Boltanski and Chiapello in *The New Spirit of Capitalism*, producing a new spirit of capitalism and not one that fosters a desire for an alternative social and political order (Boltanski and Chiapello 2006). In this view, to be discussed in Chapter 9, crises do not necessarily entail the self-destruction, or the 'decomposition of capitalism', but its structural transformation. In his account, only the heroic figure of the entrepreneur is really capable of agency. This is a too nostalgic view of the nineteenth century. But it is also a misreading of the new era of so-called monopoly capitalism. It is an entirely incorrect understanding of capitalism to think that innovation is possible only under the conditions of classic entrepreneurialism and the advent of the giant corporation kills it by standardization and bureaucratization. This argument has been clearly falsified by major developments in technical innovation as well as other kinds of innovation in economic organization. One has only to consider the revolutionary impact of digital technologies and the turn to green technology to see that contemporary capitalist societies are capable of tremendous creativity in economic organization.

There is also something unsatisfactory in his more or less rejection of the relevance of class analysis. In this respect, he went further than Weber who operated with a notion of 'social classes' and socio-economic groups. The key evolutionary agent for Schumpeter is the entrepreneur. The decline of the entrepreneur and the rise of the intellectual and the bureaucrat mark the point at which the march to socialism is supposed to begin. This conception of the first half of the twentieth century fails to account for class politics and other forms of collective action as well as democracy.

Schumpeter had no appreciation of the fact that capitalism is organized as a world system such that prosperity and growth for some is possible only because of poverty elsewhere. Western consumption is enabled by producers in Asia. Imperialism, arguably more significant than technological innovation for the rise of capitalism, is poorly theorized in his account, which implausibly sees capitalism as anti-imperialistic (Greene 1952). His work was a product of the age of monopoly capitalism in the era of the nation-state and cannot be easily applied to the post-Fordist economy of small-to-medium-sized firms and global systems of supply and rubbish disposal. In this context, it is not entirely convincing that technological innovation is a product of the giant corporation. Both before the era of monopoly capitalism and after it, scientific and technological innovations are more heterogeneous. His account was overly nostalgic of an authentic capitalist order that existed in the past but had become decadent. Despite having demolished the fable of a free-market economy that once existed, he adhered to the myth of the heroic entrepreneur who preceded the decadent bourgeois and rentier capitalist. His prediction of the victory of socialism clearly has to be revised in light of the demise of the socialist order that appeared to be a competing force in his time. Due to his obsession with innovation, he neglected the engine of profit maximization and the relentless drive for the accumulation of capital, which has clearly survived the demise of the old bourgeois capitalist class.

CSD is full of flaws. The theory of capitalist collapse borders on satire – the idea that those who benefit from capitalism will reject it for a system that makes them less well-off is not plausible – and may have been designed to scare the political elites of the liberal democracies of the West out of complacency and to force them to face up to the threat of socialism, which he characterized as less prone to collapse.

As a theorist of capitalist crisis, Schumpeter failed to take on board the significance of the Wall Street Crash and the Great Depression of the 1930s. The first major crisis of capitalism in the twentieth century is not easily accommodated in Schumpeter's framework. In this respect, he was overshadowed by Keynes, who proved to be more attuned to the reality of the world than Schumpeter with his backward-looking theory of the decomposition of what was just one model of capitalism (we discuss Keynes in Chapter 5). In the end, Schumpeter had no ideas for a better world, other than to make the case for innovation. As Schumpeter himself noted of Keynes, with whom he had some disagreements, he was always involved in projects for a better world, whereas he was not involved (see Minsky 1986: 114–5).

Despite these drawbacks – which after all only confirm the history of modern political thought as the history of error – Schumpeter's theory of capitalism has survived the test of time and is a classic work in theorizing capitalism that brings together macro-economic and sociological perspectives. While his main thesis has been disproven, capitalism has not collapsed but the version of socialism that triumphed in the USSR and the Warsaw Pact countries did, one of the legacies of this great work is the theorization it offers of capitalist crisis. It places at the centre of the logic of capitalism turbulence and instability: turmoil is an outcome of innovation and it is not compatible with the logic of equilibrium. Capitalism is not static but evolutionary in the sense that it is in perpetual transformation. This condition goes beyond market turbulence to something more deep-rooted and with cultural and political effects. Now, while this mostly involves structural transformation, it can also lead to systemic transformation whereby crises generated by the turmoil of technical innovation, which in turn is a response to the need for incessant production, are not domesticated by the capitalist system and as a result anti-systemic movements emerge. The capitalist system is not in fact a system but is composed of contradictory tendencies. It is the great merit of *CSD* that it draws attention to the crisis-ridden nature of capitalism and the prospect of an alternative cannot be excluded. While his account of socialism is in part farcical, not least for it to function it will need to emulate much of the capitalist system, it is possible to think of a more distant future in which an alternative social and political order might emerge. Schumpeter is also convincing in his emphasis on a civilizational shift in consciousness taking place, even if he sees this as generated by capitalism itself rather than by other sources of consciousness as well as democratization.

The crisis-prone nature of capitalism in *CSD* is as much cultural as it is economic in the emphasis given to shifts in mentality and in the decomposition of entrepreneurial capitalism. The hypothesis of capitalism's self-destruction, however, fails to do justice to the full range of countervailing movements in modern society, which are not all due to technical innovation. Even the digital revolution – clearly one of the most important examples of technical innovation – does not just lead in one direction, as for example simply extending and facilitating consumption or digital surveillance, but many, and not all are harnessed by capitalism. Democracy, the weak spot in his analysis, is reduced to the parliamentary process by which elites are selected. A more satisfactory account would give greater attention to the dialectical relation of capitalism and democracy. While Schumpeter is arguably correct in noting the transformations in consciousness that accompany the rise of the middle class and various kinds of knowledge producers – the intellectuals – the emergence of a critical frame of mind and political opposition is not simply a product of class positions. There is one sense in which he may have been correct. The attitudes of the middle class will increasingly be shaped by values other than capitalism. Now, while he says the relationship between democracy and capitalism is fairly stable, it is possible to see the process of the decomposition of capitalism being nurtured by democratization.

An alternative notion of crisis that gives greater emphasis to agency is needed to capture the emancipatory dynamics able to effect a radical transformation. Such an account will have to embrace a notion of democracy as a form of contestation, a perspective that does not figure at all in *CSD*, which sees democracy only as a mechanism for the selection of elites. This will require, too, a wider different treatment of crisis than one of turmoil, self-destruction, instability etc. that is generated as a necessary consequence of innovation. This is where other theories of capitalist crisis need to be drawn on to provide a more adequate picture of crisis tendencies. Karl Polanyi in the *Great Transformation* – the topic of the next chapter – offers one such corrective in theorizing relations between economy and society.

Perhaps, the ultimate weakness of *CSD* is that despite drawing on sociological arguments, it was written by an economist who did not fully appreciate the heterogeneity of society and the fact that democracy like capitalism also undergoes change. Even if its primary function is to compete to form a government, as he claims, this does not say enough about democracy and its relation to capitalism. Schumpeter overstated the case for the civilization of capitalism to the extent that he believed that capitalism would become coeval with modern society and that the transformation in the latter would necessarily entail the demise of capitalism and the formation of a new social order. From a wider sociological perspective, we have to see modern society as irreducible to capitalism, which, as argued earlier in relation to Marx, is best seen as a political economy. In this way, societal transformation does not entirely derive from the perpetual structural transformations within capitalism. Schumpeter certainly went beyond the analyses offered by orthodox economists who saw the supposedly natural tendencies in the economy, by which they mostly meant the market, as reaching equilibrium. But his correction of this model of how economies function did not go far enough as far as his social and political theory was concerned. In this respect, the work of Karl Polanyi offers an alternative, one that gives the social and political dimensions greater autonomy than being simply the responses to changes in the economy.

Notes

1 Published in the USA in 1942; in the UK in 1943.

2 Many of the central ideas in *CSD* were set forth in an essay in 1928 when he argued that the economic system of capitalism (characterized by private initiative, production for a market and credit) tends to threaten the institutional survival of the capitalist civilization by undermining the social positions on which the 'order' rests (Schumpeter 1989 [1928]).

3 Schumpeter provided a concise summary of his argument in a late essay based on a lecture, 'The March into Socialism', which has been published as an Appendix to most editions of *CSD*. See also Schumpeter's essay 'Capitalism' (1951 [1946]).

References

Aghion, P. Antonin, C., Bunel, S. 2021. *The Power of Creative Destruction: Economic Upheaval and the Wealth of Nations*. Cambridge, MASS.: Harvard University Press.

Boltanski, L. and Chiapello, E. 2006 [1999]. *The New Spirit of Capitalism*. London: Verso.

Bottomore, T. 1985. *Theories of Modern Capitalism*. London: Routledge.

Burlemarqui, L. and Kattel, R. (eds). 2019. *Schumpeter's Capitalism, Socialism and Democracy: A Twenty-First Century Agenda*. London: Routledge.

Coe, R. and Wilbur, C. 1985. *Capitalism and Democracy: Schumpeter Revisited*. Notre Dame: University of Notre Dame.

Collins, R. 1986. 'Weber and Schumpeter: Toward a General Sociology of Capitalism'. In: *Weberian Sociological Theory*. Cambridge: Cambridge University Press.

Dahms, H. 1995. 'From Creative Destruction to the Social Rationalization of the Economy: Joseph A. Schumpeter's Social Theory'. *Sociological Theory*, 13 (1): 1–13.

Dahms, H. 2011. 'Joseph A. Schumpeter'. In: *The Wiley-Blackwell Companion to Major Social Theorists*. Edited by G. Ritzer and J. Stepnisky. Oxford: Blackwell.

Elliott, J. 1980. 'Marx and Schumpeter on Capitalism's Creative Destruction: A Comparative Restatement'. *The Quarterly Journal of Economics*, 95 (1): 45–68.
Greene, M. 1952. 'Schumpeter's Imperialism: A Critical Note'. *Social Research*, 19 (4): 453–63.
Ingham, G. 2003. 'Schumpeter and Weber on the Institutions of Capitalism'. *Journal of Classical Sociology*, 3 (3): 297–309.
Inglehart, R. 1977. *The Silent Revolution: Changing Values and Political Styles among Western Publics*. Princeton: Princeton University Press.
Love, J. 2017. *Weber, Schumpeter and Modern Capitalism*. London: Routledge.
Mandel, E. 1999 [1972]. *Late Capitalism*. London: Verso.
Marcuse, H. 1964. *One-Dimensional Man: Studies in the Ideology of Advanced Industrial Society*. London: Routledge & Kegan Paul.
Minsky, H. 1986. 'Money and Crisis in Schumpeter and Keynes'. In: *The Economic Law of Motion of Modern Society: A Marx-Keynes-Schumpeter Centenary*. Edited by H.-J. Wagener and J.W. Drukker. Cambridge: Cambridge University Press.
Schumpeter, J. 1934. *Theory of Economic Development*. Cambridge: Harvard University Press.
Schumpeter, J. 1939. *Business Cycles: A Theoretical, Historical and Statistical Analysis of the Capitalist Process*, 2 vols. New York: McGraw-Hill.
Schumpeter, J. 1951 [1946]. 'Capitalism'. In: *Essays*. New York: Addison-Wesley.
Schumpeter, J. 1989 [1928]. 'The Instability of Capitalism.' *Economic Journal*, 38 (151: 361–86). Reprinted in *Essays: On Entrepreneurs, Innovations, Business Cycles, and the Evolution of Capitalism*, Edited by R.V. Clemence, pp. 47–72. New Brunswick: Transaction Publishers.
Schumpeter, J. 2010 [1942]. *Capitalism, Socialism and Democracy*. London: Routledge.
Shionoya, Y. 1997. *Schumpeter and the Idea of Social Science: A Metatheoretical Study*. Cambridge: Cambridge University Press.
Swedberg, R. 2002. 'The Economic Sociology of Capitalism: Weber and Schumpeter'. *The Journal of Classical Sociology*, 2 (3): 227–55.

4 Karl Polanyi and the Moral Critique of Capitalism

Karl Polanyi's *The Great Transformation: The Political Origins of Our Time* [1944] like Schumpeter's *Capitalism Socialism and Democracy* [1942] is one of the classic works of the mid-twentieth century on modern capitalism. Unlike Schumpeter, who attained fame in his lifetime, Polanyi did not. *The Great Transformation*, his major work, did not win widespread acclaim after its publication (Polanyi 2001 [1944]). The book received a mixed reaction from Marxist theorists and was criticized by historians in Britain who were not enamoured by his long-run historical analysis. The book however had a more positive reception in the USA where it was completed when Polanyi moved to Columbia University. There was a new interest in *The Great Transformation* in the 1980s and its appeal has not abated (Stanfield 1986). Polanyi was writing at a time when Marxist thought was dominated by orthodox theorists – figures such as Maurice Dobbs and the libertarian socialist G. D. H. Cole, a friend of Polanyi – who favoured a narrowly economic interpretation of Marx. Polanyi's emphasis on a wider framework that did not privilege the economy over other aspects of society was seen as a betrayal of what was then regarded to be Marx's legacy or lacking in political application. Historians, including the influential British Marxist historians, were not impressed by the historical evidence he provided to support his arguments, especially relating to the double movement.

Since the 1980s, with the rise of the New Left, greater interdisciplinary, and a more favourable context for theoretical analysis within the history profession in the English-speaking world, many of the earlier criticisms were less important. Polanyi's book became important in providing a theoretical framework for critical analysis across a range of disciplines, from anthropology to sociology and history to political science. The 1980s was a period that saw a new interest in theory across the human and social sciences, ranging from the critical theory of the Frankfurt School and neo-Marxism, as in Immanuel Wallerstein and Perry Anderson, E.P. Thompson, to French post-structuralism, Foucault and Bourdieu. Polanyi's book offered a far-reaching historical analysis of the idea of social transformation. It was read less as a work in economic history than an interpretation of the formation of the modern world. It remains one of the major works on understanding historical rupture. There is now a vast scholarship on his work (see Vail 2022). While the historical examples he discussed are difficult to generalize on, and the over-reliance on the history of England limited the analysis, his theoretical concepts – the idea of a great transformation, the double movement, fictitious commodities, embeddedness – have provided a new generation of scholars with the conceptual tools to address the very different circumstances of neoliberalism and globalization. In short, Polanyi's *The Great Transformation* is an essential text for the critique of the self-regulating market and for understanding the logics of counter-systemic movements as well as the processes by

DOI: 10.4324/9781351017671-5

which capitalism stabilizes itself. The questions he posed are still relevant, even if we find different answers. One of the challenges, which we consider in this chapter, is whether his core concepts can be separated from the specificity of his historical analysis.

The story of *The Great Transformation* was one of the rise of the self-regulating market in the nineteenth century and its decline with the rise of fascism and the decent into catastrophe with the Second World War. The book continues to attract readers today due to the new great transformation of neoliberalism and the prospects of a moral economy. The hegemony of self-regulating markets did not in the end collapse but returned in the 1980s, raising again the questions that Polanyi addressed in his book about an alternative and more embedded economy. The central problem that Polanyi sought to understand was how it came about that the economy became detached from the rest of society as a result of the belief in the self-regulating market. His argument was that it was never possible for the market to become free of the rest of society but the attempt to make it possible created societal upheaval and catastrophe. That basic idea has proven to be of enduring appeal.

The Moral Critique of Capitalism

At the time of writing *The Great Transformation,* Karl Polanyi was reassessing Marxism as a viable theoretical framework. He was a socialist and influenced by Marx and Marxism but sought to develop his own version of socialism, which drew on Marx but also on central European ideas of liberalism socialism and the British socialist tradition. He was also inspired by the work of the British anthropologist Bronislaw Malinowski and his fellow Hungarian, Lukács, with whom he corresponded. Another influence on his work was the German sociologist, also a guild socialist, Ferdinand Tönnies. It was probably through Lukács that Max Weber's ideas entered his work. Block and Somers argue that he broke from Marxism in the course of writing *The Great Transformation* when he aimed to offer an alternative socialist theory to the mainstream Marxist one (Block and Somers 1984, 2014).[1] Hegelian ideas remained, and it could be said that he continued to stand in the left-Hegelian tradition, but like many figures within western Marxism, he abandoned orthodox Marxism and became anti-communist after he moved to the USA. The conceptual language of the book does not fit easily into the Marxist framework, not least his preference for the idea of market-society rather than capitalism, whose origins precede the rise of market society, as scholars such as Immanuel Wallerstein (1983) have argued. It is clear, from a late lecture, that by the market he meant liberal capitalism, for in his view 'the production and distribution of goods is controlled by prices resulting from the functioning of markets' (Polanyi 2014: 215). Yet, he offered a far-reaching critique of capitalism, which in many ways was compatible with Marx's own ideas, especially his earlier and more explicitly humanist philosophy, which Polanyi retained with his emphasis on the human or the idea of the human personality. One of the central ideas of Hegelian-Marxism is also present in Polanyi, namely the importance of looking at society in terms of its totality (see Jay 1984). This requires a view of the economy as related to the wider societal context.

The particular kind of a critique of capitalism that Polanyi offered was a moral critique that drew on Marxist humanism. It was not a critique of political economy as such and it was different from what we characterized in the previous two chapters as a cultural critique, as represented in their different ways by Weber and Schumpeter. Tim Rogan in *The Moral Economists* has given a reconstruction of the idea of the moral economy in

British socialism. The notion of the moral economy was developed by E. P. Thompson in *The Making of the English Working Class* [1963], a work that was the culmination of a long history of what can be termed a moral critique of capitalism. In a much cited phrase, he wrote 'the final years of the eighteenth century saw a last desperate effort by the people to reimpose the older moral economy as against the economy of the free market' (Thompson 1991: 73)[2]. This moral critique draws on notions of social solidarity both before capitalism and forms of solidarity produced after the rise of capitalism. However, to refer to Polanyi only as offering a moral critique is inadequate, for it was more of a sociologically grounded moral critique. A distinctive feature of this critique, which marks it off from standard accounts of Marxism, is that the deprivations in material life do not account for class politics, which are rooted in social solidarities that make possible collective action. In the British socialist tradition, in which Polanyi inserted himself when he arrived in England in 1934 as a Jewish refugee from Vienna, the moral critique of capitalism was frequently cast as a spiritual critique that often took the form of Christian socialism and which in many ways was compatible with Victorian moral critique. It was also present in a stronger and more left-wing way in the British political tradition of Guild Socialism, as in the writings of its most prominent figure, G. D. H. Cole and was also influenced by the early Labour Party. In Rogan's reconstruction of this now almost forgotten tradition, Polanyi stood between Tawney and Thompson. What united these in fact quite very different thinkers and the tradition in which they stood was their anathema to utilitarianism and the reverence of the market. They all made the object of their analysis capitalism. Tawney was different from the Guild Socialists in his concern with morality. According to Rogan, Polanyi also read Adam Smith as the 'last humanist' before the turn to a naturalistic view of the market became dominant with the rise of utilitarianism (Rogan 2017: 91).

R. H. Tawney, in many ways Polanyi's mentor in the English-speaking world, found alternative forms of life in the working class communities in the north of England and which could be reduced neither to individualism nor collectivism. Tawney's *Religion and the Rise of Capitalism* [1926] set the terms of analysis for Polanyi, as did his other well-known work, *The Acquisitive Society* [1921] (Tawney 2015, 1982). Polanyi parted company from Tawney in that he did not share his Christian socialism and his reliance on what appeared to be a model of solidarity that was essentially pre-capitalist and insufficiently secular. Although from a family of assimilated Jews, Polanyi had life-long Christian leanings and converted to Protestantism; but he did not make religion central to the moral critique of capitalism that he was developing. He was also a disciple of G. D. H. Cole and regarded himself as a guild socialist even before he came to England. According to Rogan, the moral critique of capitalism that developed in Britain in the early twentieth century depended on the idea of human personality, which can be seen as a direct attack on the idea of liberal individualism. With its idea that fellowship was social it found a mid-way position between liberalism and collectivism: 'Under individualism, fellowship was lacking. Under collectivism, plurality was missing' (Rogan 2017: 73). This was not just an English preoccupation. It was also reflected in the writings of Marcel Mauss in France and central European liberal socialism. In the aftermath of the collapse of the central European empires, collectivism failed to provide a model for society, and it was also evident that liberal individualism was not going to offer an alternative.

Today, R. H. Tawney is a historical figure in the British socialist tradition. Polanyi in contrast reaches out from the mid-twentieth century to speak to us today in a way that Tawney does not. The past cannot redeem the present. Polanyi offered new insights into modernity that went beyond Tawney's preoccupation with the social solidarities of a world that is now vanished. Tawney was an influential and respected figure from within British academia, a professor of economic history at the London School of Economics. His critique of liberal individualism created an intellectual space for Polanyi to develop his particular version of the moral critique of capitalism and the dominant legitimating ideas of capitalism. While his work at first received a mixed reception, it was to enjoy major international success in its capacity to revision how the present was shaped by the past and what an alternative future might be.

We can also see Polanyi as a key figure in opening up the path to democratic socialism and to a different relationship between capitalism and socialism. We return to this in Chapter 6.

The Great Transformation and Its Aftermath

Polanyi's focus is on the 'great transformation' of the nineteenth century, which led to the dominance of liberal capitalism and its subsequent collapse. It is a story as much of collapse as it is of the victory of the market. From the vantage point of the present day, we are presented with a problem in that the market has clearly not collapsed. But a collapse did occur of, what he referred to in the opening words of *The Great Transformation*, as nineteenth-century civilization. This broader argument is presaged by Polanyi's introductory summary: 'Nineteenth-century civilization has collapsed. This book is concerned with the political and economic origins of this event, as well as with the great transformation which it ushered in' (p. 3).

Despite its ascendency, the great transformation was not in the end so great and led to a 'second transformation' as a result of its inability to reform itself and more importantly as a consequences of its basic logic of 'disembededness', that is the separation of economy from society. The essential point in Polanyi's analysis is that the great transformation did not work because it could not work, for markets ultimately cannot be disembedded from society. The price paid for the illusions of economic liberalism was the reactive transformation brought about by fascism – part of the second transformation – and the catastrophe of the world war that followed. The second transformation of course included other more progressive reactions, such as emerging regimes of the New Deal and the welfare state, developments endorsed by Polanyi. The end of the great transformation led to a plethora of political trajectories. For this reason, it is perhaps more accurate to speak of a plurality of transformations that followed in the wake of the first 'great transformation' in the nineteenth century: the emergence and consolidation of capitalism by the middle of the twentieth century led to a variety of paths based on different historical forms of capitalism.

The central idea in Polanyi's theory is that markets, and the economy more generally, are embedded in society. This is both an empirical and analytical argument. Economic activity is embedded in social institutions since it is based ultimately on social relations. The economy is a social institution. That is the normal condition of human societies, which he thinks was disturbed by the great transformation brought about in the nineteenth century with the rise of capitalism. A feature of the rise and dominance of the market that came with liberal capitalism was the commodification of areas of social life that were previously uncommodified. Labour markets replaced the older professions, such as the guilds and cooperative networks in which trust, reciprocity and redistribution were central, and machinery transformed the very nature of work and production. 'Instead of economy being embedded in social relations, social relations are embedded in the economic system' (p. 60). The great transformation was completed with the creation of 'fictitious' commodities. He singles out land, labour and money as key fictitious commodities in that these are not primarily commodities and never have been, but with capitalism they became commodities. They are not intrinsically commodities, since a commodity is something created for the purpose of being sold on the market, which is not the case with land, labour and money. The basic lines of his argument are obviously very close to Marx in terms of the transformative power of capitalism, alienation and commodification. However, his concern was less with commodity fetishism than with fictitious commodities.

Polanyi's analysis challenges the assumptions of liberal economic thought that sees the economy as a functionally autonomous domain separate from state and society. This was his legacy. He rejects the notion of the economy as a self-correcting system whereby economic agents, such as buyers and sellers, operate within a system that left to its own devices is able to achieve equilibrium. Like Schumpeter, he claims the free market is not a reality but a utopia and the drive to establish it as the basis of the economy results in doing the opposite; it requires the massive reshaping of state and economy. He is clear that the new laws set up to manage the great transformation, for example, the 1834 Poor Law in England required the state to implement it in the provisions of poorhouse etc. So, it came about that in order to make possible the free market of liberal capitalism major societal changes were needed. This was a political project; it did not come about on its own, but required political agency to put new ideas into practice. Polanyi emphasizes four such changes that were products of the nineteenth century and were the basis of 'nineteenth-century civilization': the balance of power system, the international gold standard, the liberal state and the self-regulating market. The first three institutions served the needs of the free market, which was never really free since it needed the state to implement it and sustain it. But Polanyi makes clear that the idea of a self-adjusting market could not exist for any length of time 'without annihilating the human and natural substance of society' (p. 3). Its conditions had to be secured by both national and international institutions. The costs of maintaining the self-regulating market were enormous, and in the end, the three pillars that were created to make it possible were sacrificed in a vain effort to save it.

The great transformation functioned for a time. The nineteenth century was a period of unprecedented peace in Europe. After 1815, the Concert of Europe system established peace in Europe so that modern capitalism could grow and, of course, it was a period in which the European powers pursued colonial wars. The Gold Standard made possible an economic system in which international finance was becoming more important and served to secure stable conditions for trade and investment. The liberal state secured the conditions necessary for the competitive labour market to operate and for capitalism to have unlimited access to markets at home and abroad. In England, for example, the Poor Law of 1834 established wage labour as the main source of income other than the workhouse, which was effectively designed to force people to accept low wages. The liberal state enforced *laissez-faire* policies. Polanyi's main thesis is that despite these measures, they did not in the end work and as a result the great transformation led to crisis, upheaval and turmoil when those institutions came to an end:

> the origins of the cataclysm lay in the utopian endeavour of economic liberalism to set up a self-regulating market system. Such a thesis seems to invest that system with almost mythical faculties; it implies no less than that the balance of power, the gold standard, and the liberal state, these fundamentals of the civilization of the nineteenth

century, were, in the last resort, shaped in one common matrix, the self-regulating market.

(p. 31)

The great transformation required major social dislocation to make possible the free market, and, when it finally failed, it produced catastrophe. The argument offered an economic analysis to the widely felt 'crisis of civilization', a crucial theme in the social and cultural thought of the period. But Polanyi went beyond the general diagnosis of the times literature, as in Freud's *Civilization its Discontents* [1930], Spengler's *The Decline of the West* [1918] and Adorno and Horkheimer's *Dialectic of Enlightenment* [1944], works which tended to remain on the level of a cultural critique of civilization. His work was more in keeping with the spirit of the work of the Fabians, Sydney Webb and Beatrice Webb, as in their book *The Decay of Capitalist Civilization* (Webb and Webb 1923).

The crisis and the end of liberal capitalism, which culminated in the Second World War, was not necessarily foretold. Despite the disembedding brought about by the great transformation, there were reactions to it that sought to reset the balance between economy and society. Since the goal could not be achieved, despite the stabilizing mechanisms of the international state system, which in many instances only made matters worse, the political and social struggles from the latter quarter of the nineteenth century can be seen as attempts to 're-embed' the economy in social institutions. So, disembedding provokes counter-hegemonic reactions that reassert social constraints on economic activity. This is the famous notion of the 'double movement', which can be characterized as a struggle between *laissez-faire* liberal capitalism and demands for social protections. The double movement began once the liberal project was in place – in England from c.1834 – but gained momentum by the 1870s. It began in the politics of fictitious commodities. 'Social history in the nineteenth century', he argues, was 'the result of a double movement: the extension of the market organization in respect to genuine commodities was accompanied by its restriction in respect to fictitious ones' (p. 79). The double movement opened up a range of counter-movements that led to the end of the great transformation. Not all of these were progressive movements. It should also be said that Polanyi's argument, which was not always clear, was that the end of the great transformation, that is the rise and dominance of unrestricted markets, came to an end because the pillars needed to keep it in place collapsed. Of these, the collapse of the gold standard was the first. Like much of the scaffolding of the self-regulating market, it required a tremendous belief to sustain it, in this case the belief that the value of money corresponded to a measurable quantity of gold deposited in central banks, such as the Bank of England or the Federal Reserve.

The double movement can be understood in different ways. In one sense, it is about the assertion of social demands against economic dictates; in another sense, it is about the search for stability and cohesion; but it may also be an attempt to return to the priority of an embedded economy. For Polanyi, it is not necessarily a zero-sum in that the free market is an illusion and cannot be created without destroying itself – what in effect happened – and the demand for social protection alone could easily morph into political authoritarianism, which is what effectively happened with the rise of fascism (which solved, however temporarily, some of the economic problems of liberal capitalism through state-directed economic policies). The double movement can also result in a political stalemate in so far as it expressed a conflict between two political systems, liberal democracy and political authoritarianism. Polanyi, deeply influenced by guild socialism and a proponent of democratic socialism, was clearly in favour of the socialist desire to reset the balance between the free market and social protection in a way that did not erode liberal democracy.

Polanyi's argument while being nuanced and subtle is also open to some interpretation. It is not entirely clear what the double movement achieves, whether it simply heralds the end of the great transformation or provokes alternative transformations. Clearly, there is not just one great transformation. The end of one presages movement to another. On the one side, the double movement recalls Marx's dialectical vision of class struggle but, on the other side, it does not necessarily lead to the creation of something new and thus is not essentially dialectical. If it simply keeps the free market in check, it is not really dialectical since nothing fundamentally changes and no new transformation ensues. He suggests that the two forces in it are two organizing principles in society. The double movement

> can be personified as the action of two organizing principles in society, each of them setting itself specific institutional aims, having the support of definite social forces and using its own distinctive methods. The one was the principle of economic liberalism....the other was the principle of social protection.
>
> (p. 138)

If capitalism worked well – with the stability mechanisms of the national and international state system, the gold standard etc. serving the needs of capitalism – it would embrace the double movement in preserving social protection for workers and setting limits to disembeddedness. In that case, the double movement would be part of the functioning of a social order that controlled capitalism. This would be in line with the notion of a Keynesian 'democratic capitalism', a social model of capitalism or social democracy, or the theories of the French Regulation School, and therefore not a counter-hegemonic movement. However, the double movement could also express a stronger critique of capitalism as in outright class conflict and open up major social transformations.

At the end of a discussion on Robert Owen, Polanyi appeared to hold to a strong notion of self-protection when he commented that Owen 'did not foresee that the self-protection of society for which he was calling would prove incompatible with the functioning of the economic system itself' (p. 135). Either way it is clear that the double movement did not achieve social cohesion and liberal capitalism embarked on self-destruction. This may be because the 'the self-protection of society', which is what the double movement aims to achieve, is not compatible with capitalism or because it did not go far enough. For Polanyi, it worked for a time but in the end it ceased to constrain capitalism:

> For a century the dynamics of modern society was governed by a double movement: the market expanded continuously but this movement was met by a countermovement checking the expansion in definite directions. Vital though such a double movement was for the protection of society, in the last analysis it was incompatible with the self-regulation of the market, and thus with the market system itself.
>
> (p. 136)

The turmoil produced in the nineteenth century by the great transformation did not in the end reach a point of equilibrium through the double movement. By the 1920s, and culminating in 1940, that order collapsed due in part to its internal contradictions and above all the failure to re-embed the economy. The price for the failure was very great. It led to a major crisis of capitalism in which two authoritarian orders competed between themselves and with liberal capitalism. For a time, the fascist solution got the upper-hand: 'The fascist solution of the impasse reached by liberal capitalism can be described as a reform of market economy achieved at the price of the extirpation of all democratic institutions, both in the industrial and in the political realm' (p. 245). Polanyi's position here is in line with that held by many historians that Second World War was the expression of the struggle between two models of capitalism represented by the USA and Germany.

While the great transformation came to end, capitalism itself did not and one model of capitalism triumphed, divested of nineteenth-century liberalism. In the post-1945 period, at least in western Europe and the developed world, a new social and political order arose that reflected the new orthodoxy of Keynesianism. In the three decades or so from the end of the war, western societies enjoyed a new era of prosperity and economic growth. In the terms of Polanyi's analysis, the double movement functioned to reset the balance between democracy and capitalism. Despite their shortcomings, the establishment of welfare states, democratization, the advancement of higher education, improvements in public health, the project of European integration, the consolidation of social democracy etc., they can all be seen in terms of attempts to re-embed the economy in social institutions. In a more long-term perspective, the crisis was simply postponed and new cultural and political currents came to the surface. Thus, from the early 1970s, a new period of capitalist crisis emerged with the so-called fiscal crisis of the state, rising inflation and unemployment. In Polanyian terms, the crisis was resolved by the rise of neoliberalism in a new era of accentuated globalization.

It is possible to see the emergence of neoliberalism from the 1980s onwards as a third great transformation – assuming that fascism counts as part of the failed second – in the relation of economy to society and the state, and society more generally. In the course of the previous four decades or so, neoliberalism has brought about a major transformation of society in ways different, to be sure, yet comparable to, the great transformation that Polanyi described in the nineteenth century. This is not to say that all aspects of neo-liberalism are incompatible with democratic capitalism, not least as neoliberalism is not a single or coherent order. However, the intensity and expansiveness of the neoliberal project does amount to a 'great' transformation in terms of disembedding processes. What was dismantled were the institutions established by the counter-movement that led to the short-lived era of democratic capitalism in the post-1945 period (see Streeck 2014). To this, we can add the transition from state socialism in central and eastern Europe to a neoliberal economic order. Neoliberalism can be seen as a project of disembedding that culminated in the crisis of 2007–10 with pervasive austerity politics and precarity. From our vantage point today, especially in the context of the Covid-19 pandemic, we can look back on this period in much the same way as Polanyi did in 1944, seeing it as the outcome of the crisis of neoliberalism. The great transformation of neoliberalism is not necessarily over, since neoliberalism is not a static movement having morphed into a variety of forms. However, there can be no doubt that neoliberalism as a project is in crisis and has set in play once again the double movement. But the question must be posed whether the Polanyian model is really adequate if, as seems to be the case, the double movement, shorn of dialectics, simply works to achieve a balance between the relentless push for unrestricted markets and protective counter-movements. The latter by definition in seeking protection is not necessarily the source of an alternative. The double movement did not succeed in returning fictitious commodities – land, labour and money – to their previous condition. Before looking more closely at how Polanyi might be used to view the current situation, a little more needs to be said about his other key concept, embeddedness and processes of disembedding.

Polanyi tended to assume too easily that pre-capitalist economies were embedded and that capitalist societies are not embedded. This has been the subject of considerable controversy since he introduced the terms. It is highly questionable that the market under the conditions of capitalism, whether self-regulating or not, is disembedded from social institutions. It is not enough to argue, as Polanyi did, that the dream was never possible without collapsing into catastrophe. It is simply difficult to conceive of a disembedded market (Granovetter 1985). The free market after all did work for a time. But could it ever be termed disembedded? Even neoliberal deregulation, an obvious candidate for a politics of disembedding, required considerable new forms of regulation, as the history of European integration reveals. The deregulation of the airlines in early 2000s was one side of the coin, the other side of which was new forms of regulation. It has been argued by Gemici (2015) that he too easily accepted the neo-classical notion of the self-regulating market, seeing only the need to be liberated from it. But what if it was a myth to begin with? To an extent, as Gareth Dale (2010) argues, Polanyi provided a critique of the power of ideas, since ultimately the self-regulating market was the product of a certain way of thinking. 'Born of a mere penchant for nonbureaucratic methods, it evolved into a veritable faith in man's secular salvation through a self-regulating market'. He refers to it as a 'fanaticism' imbued with 'evangelical fervor' (p. 141). In the end, *laissez-faire* was not a method to achieve a thing, it was the thing to be achieved (p. 145). But market fundamentalism was also a set of practices that led to considerable societal transformation. The great transformation, the product of an idea, was a historical reality.

There would appear to be a consensus amongst critics that the market under the conditions of capitalism is not entirely disembedded; if it were, it would simply not work (see Hann and Hart 2009; Harvey et al. 2007; Holmes 2012). If the market must be seen as somehow embedded, it is also not necessarily detrimental to society. Markets have also brought about considerable social improvement and prosperity, a claim that has been accepted by most Marxist theorists in relation to the so-called impoverishment thesis of Marx. Moreover, to the extent that capitalism is the cause of impoverishment, this is not necessarily entirely as a result of the existence of markets. In short, markets are necessarily social institutions and cannot be entirely disembedded and they also have to be regulated to function.

It has also been much discussed whether pre-capitalist or non-capitalist agrarian societies were embedded in the sense that they were not organized around markets. There is a vast literature on primitive markets to which Polanyi contributed, as in Polanyi et al. (1957). One of the most influential anthropologists of recent times, Marshall Sahlins, who was a contemporary of Polanyi at Columbia University, was taken by Polanyi's work and used his ideas in his research on primitive exchange in his famous book *Stone Age Economics* [1972] (Humphrey 1969: 177). While it can be plausibly argued that the economy in the pre-modern world before the rise of capitalism was more embedded, it is not the case that pre-modern society enjoyed greater solidarity or that markets were not important; nor is it obvious that before the rise of capitalism there was a greater range of social protections in place. Such a position would go against the argument of Marx and Engels in the *Communist Manifesto,* and accepted by their critics, that capitalism entailed emancipation from the old forms of oppression. His proposition 'that all economic systems known to us up to the end of feudalism in western Europe were organized either on the principle of reciprocity or redistribution, or householding, or some combination of the three' is highly contentious (p. 57). Polanyi tended to think the pre-capitalist past had a better integration of market and society. This also led him to a more positive view of early attempts to reset the balance, as in the somewhat confused debate around Speenhamland as a form of social protectionism, a chapter that earned Polanyi much criticism and is now generally regarded as a problematical interpretation. In this case, if it were a protective counter-movement, it was one that was the product of the rise of capitalism. This leads to the question whether there can be markets that are not disembedded and not just simply the product of protective counter-movements. To this question, Polanyi clearly thinks that is the case, even though the examples he provides appear to be simply attempts to domesticate capitalism. For this reason, adherents to Marxist theory have never been happy with Polanyi who ultimately did not demonstrate how modern societies could liberate themselves from the hegemony of the market. If there were to be a new great transformation, it would be very far in the future. But Polanyi did not see his task to deliver a future world but to understand the struggles of the present one.

As argued earlier, following Tim Rogan, Polanyi's critique of capitalism was essentially a moral critique, rooted in the guild socialist tradition and in other schools of liberal socialism that saw forms of solidarity that developed in the past destroyed by capitalism. Despite a latent nostalgia, it was not a backward looking critique; yet, it did not offer an adequate account of new forms of solidarity. His diagnosis was in many ways correct but he did not offer a viable alternative. His thought was characterized by the notion that what modernity needed was a regenerative moral order, above all, a moral economy based on reciprocity and redistribution, and this gave to his work a certain utopianism (Humphrey 1969: 172). A political remedy needs in the first instance a morality. The old morality was gone but a new one was not in sight.

A Contemporary Reappraisal

The question remains whether widespread demands for social protection actually amount to a durable double movement that might bring about progressive change or simply lead to a multiplicity of outcomes. The history of social democracy suggests that the double movement goes only so far. The rise of right-wing populist politics and neo-nationalism – as reflected in Brexit, Trump and the Alt-Right, Erdogan, Bolsonaro etc., have been widely seen as a response to the havoc produced by several decades of neo-liberalism (Brown 2019; Bornshier 2018). In that sense, it is a movement that reflects a similar logic to that of fascism in the period in which Polanyi was writing. It is clear that such movements do not achieve their stated aims and probably are best seen as dysfunctional responses to capitalist crises rather than genuine attempts to re-embed the economy in social institutions. If this is the case, signs of a progressive double movement must be found elsewhere.

It is not entirely clear what might be evidence of a double movement today. According to Nancy Fraser, 'our crisis seems to share a distinctive deep-structural logic with the one Polanyi analysed. Both appear to be rooted in a common dynamic, which he called "fictitious commodification"' (Fraser 2013: 119). However, it is difficult to disagree with Fraser that while the sense of crisis is similar, with similar structural contradictions, there is a fundamental difference in that today there is a plurality of political movements and there is no single fault-line that can be compared to the one that Polanyi discerned in the final stages of the great transformation. The post-1945 period when, as suggested, the double movement re-emerged and restored a new balance between economy and society, was perhaps the last time that such a large-scale counter-movement would be possible. But this led to the stability of capitalism, not its transformation. Fraser is correct to argue that progressive social movements tend to suffer from fragmentation and have not united in a coherent counter-project to neoliberalism, which still exists despite the crisis and – despite widespread questioning of unfettered markets – has not entirely come to an end in the way Polanyi claimed liberal capitalism came to an end. In contrast to the left, the diverse moments of the right tend to be less fragmented and have more easily accommodated neoliberalism at the same time as voicing demands for social protection. But more than this, the political struggles of the present do not quite so easily fit into the dualism of marketization versus protectionism. Demands for social protection against market forces can often be accommodated within neoliberalism, as in the example of third way politics. The full range of contemporary social struggles, in any case, includes conflicts that go far beyond issues of equality and protection (see also Azmanova 2020). Polanyi's model does not easily capture the social struggles of recognition, as opposed to struggles over distribution. Ecological politics also does not fit into his conceptualization of the double movement. One can easily substitute growth for the role Polanyi assigned to the market. For many people today, the real problem is not curbing the market as such, but controlling growth in the name of sustainability (we discuss this in Chapter 9).

Polanyi's interpretation of capitalist crisis remains of great relevance, despite the changed circumstances of our time. *The Great Transformation* continues to attract considerable interest. It is not without its flaws. Aside from the too simplistic account of liberal markets facing the reaction of demands for social protection, the global context is inadequately theorized. Even in the nineteenth century, markets were already global. While acknowledging colonialism, it did not figure sufficiently in his account of the rise of capitalism, as Sandra Halperin has argued, nor did class politics (Halperin 2003). Yet, his notion of the great transformation raised the prospect of future transformations and his work is an essential reference for theories of major social and political transformations.

In their different ways, Schumpeter and Polanyi offer insightful theories of capitalist crisis, though not ones that are entirely compatible. Schumpeter drew attention to the likely end of capitalism while Polanyi saw possibilities for a reformed capitalism to be re-embedded in society. Polanyi's account is compatible with Keynesianism, though his critique of liberal capitalism was more far-reaching in that he was more interested in the systemic transformation of capitalism than its domestication and management by government. Neither Schumpeter nor Polanyi saw capitalism as a stable system that had eliminated opposition and had achieved a high degree of conformity and functionality. In this respect, they differed from the assessment of the Frankfurt School thinkers, who tended to see capitalism as triumphant and stable. For those in search of a theory of crisis, there is much to be found in the writings of these authors. Notions of the 'decomposition' of capitalism, the double movement etc. capture the fluid nature of capitalism and, as David Harvey has written, the multiple ways in which crises can form in different historical and geographical situations (Harvey 2010: 117).

Missing from these accounts is an adequate perspective on human agency. This is especially the case with Schumpeter, for as we argued his account confines agency to the figure of the heroic entrepreneur embellished with creative powers. As we have seen, this is because his analysis is largely structural. Polanyi's account, in contrast, is more differentiated in this respect in seeing the main parties, the trade unions and the Catholic church join forces to protect society from the corrosive effects of the market, thus bringing about a radical transformation. However, his analysis, while giving a firmer position to agency, tends to see agents as primarily reactive to developments rather than being proactive and driven by ideals of justice. Moreover, his approach does not embrace the full spectrum of political revolts against marketization: race, gender, ecological politics etc. do not figure in the double movement. Especially for an understanding of social transformation today, a wider perspective of agency is needed, and perhaps embeddedness is not sufficiently robust to capture the spectrum of social and political struggles today. Polanyi, despite his differences with the Marxist left, did not quite fit into the New Cultural Left. However, with some liberty of interpretation, the double movement can be extended to embrace anti-globalization movements and the social and political struggles of the 'Global South' (Goodwin 2018; Munck 2006).

The structural transformation of capitalism and the prospect of catastrophic collapse that was very much their concern is of course still relevant today, whether as a result of climatic change or as a consequence of another major pandemic occurring in the near future. Anti-systemic movements are not only responses to objective circumstances, but also products of transformations in consciousness and of democratization. In that sense, a crisis is a turning point when social actors reinterpret social and political reality. As Jürgen Habermas argued in another important work on capitalist crisis, *Legitimation Crisis*, in 1973, a crisis is a turning point that also depends on how the subject reacts to the external situation: 'only subjects can be involved in crises. Thus, only when members of a society experience and feel their identity threatened can we speak of crises' (Habermas 1976: 3). This perspective on the response of social actors to capitalism is necessary in order to understand critical moments such as those that are now becoming more frequent. The end of capitalism or its transformation into a post-capitalist form will not occur simply as a result of the contradictions of capitalism or as a consequence of its systemic problems, but only as a result of the purposeful actions of social actors and transformations in consciousness. This brings us back to the argument that capitalism is best seen as a political economy formed through relations between economy, state, law and social institutions. It is through these relationships that social struggles are constituted. Capitalism is always politically constituted with the result that political modernity is embroiled in economic modernity (see Joerges 2005). With Polanyi we can see how capitalism relies on non-market institutions, even when they are transformed by capitalism, as in the thesis of fictitious commodities.

Notes

1 For an account of his life and work, see the prodigious studies of Gareth Dale, especially Dale (2010, 2017).

2 However, he did not develop the concept of the moral economy in this work with which it is normally associated. For a fuller development, see Thompson (1971).

References

Azmanova, A. 2020. *Capitalism on Edge: How Fighting Precarity Can Achieve Radical Change without Crisis or Utopia*. New York: Columbia University Press.

Block, F. and Somers, M. 1984. 'Beyond the Economistic Fallacy: The Holistic social Science of Karl Polanyi'. In: *Vision and Method in Historical Sociology*. Cambridge: Cambridge University Press.

Block, F. and Somers, F. 2014. *The Power of Market Fundamentalism: Karl Polanyi's Critique*. Cambridge: Harvard University Press.

Bornschier, S. 2018. *Globalization, Cleavages, and the Radical Right.* Oxford: Oxford University Press.
Brown, W. 2019. *In the Ruins of Neoliberalism: The Rise of Antidemocratic Politics in the West.* New York: Columbia University Press.
Dale, G. 2010. *Karl Polanyi: The Limits of the Market.* Cambridge: Polity Press.
Dale, G. 2017. *Karl Polanyi: A Life on the Left.* New York: Columbia University Press.
Fraser, N. 2013. 'A Triple Movement? Parsing the Politics of Crisis after Polanyi', *New Left Review,* 119: 119–32.
Gemici, K. 2015. 'The Neo-Classical Origins of Polanyi's Self-Regulating Market'. *Sociological Theory,* 33 (2): 125–47.
Goodwin, G. 2018. 'Rethinking the Double Movement: Expanding the Frontiers of Polanyian Analysis in the Global South.' *Development and Change,* 49 (5): 1268–90. https://doi.org/10.1111/dech.12419
Granovetter, M. 1985. 'Economic Action and Social Structure: The Problem of Embeddedness.' *American Journal of Sociology,* 91 (3): 481–510.
Habermas, J. 1976 [1973]. *Legitimation Crisis.* London: Heinemann.
Halperin, S. 2003. *War and Social Change in Modern Europe: The Great Transformation Revisited.* Cambridge: Cambridge University Press.
Hann, C. and Hart, K. (eds.) 2009. *Market and Society: The Great Transformation Today.* Cambridge: Cambridge University Press.
Harvey, M., Ramlogan, R. and Randles, S. (eds.) 2007. *Karl Polanyi: New Perspectives on the Place of the Economy in Society.* Manchester: Manchester University Press.
Holmes, C. 2012. 'Problems and Opportunities in Polanyian Analysis Today', *Economy and Society,* 41 (3): 468–84. DOI: 10.1080/03085147.2012.682004
Humphreys, S. 1969. 'History, Economics, and Anthropology: The Work of Karl Polanyi.' *History and Theory,* 8(2): 165–212.
Jay, M. 1984. *Marxism and Totality: The Adventures of a Concept from Lukacs to Habermas.* Berkeley: University of California Press.
Joerges, C., Strath, B., and Wagner, P. (eds). 2005. *The Economy as a Polity: The Political Constitution of Contemporary Capitalism.* London: UCL Press.
Munck, R. 2006. 'Globalization and Contestation: A Polanyian Problematic'. *Globalization,* 3 (2): 175–86. doi.org/10.1080/14747730600702956
Polayni, K. 2001 [1944]. *The Great Transformation.* Boston: Beacon Press.
Polanyi, K. 2014. *For a New West.* Cambridge: Polity Press.
Polanyi, K., Arensberg, C., and Pearson, H. (eds.) 1957. *Trade and Market in the Early Empires: Economies in History and Theory.* Glencoe: Free Press.
Rogan, T. 2017. *The Moral Economists: R. H. Tawney, Karl Polanyi, E. P. Thompson, and the Critique of Capitalism.* Princeton: Princeton University Press.
Schumpeter, J. 2010 [1942]. *Capitalism, Socialism and Democracy.* London: Routledge.
Stanfield, R. 1986. *The Economic Thought of Karl Polanyi.* London: Macmillan: Palgrave Macmillan.
Streeck, W. 2014. *Buying Time: The Delayed Crisis of Democratic Capitalism.* London: Verso.
Tawney, R. H. 1982 [1921]. *The Acquisitive Society.* Brighton: Wheatsheaf Books.
Tawney, R. H. 2015 [1922]. *Religion and the Rise of Capitalism.* London: Verso.
Thompson, E. P. 1971. 'The Moral Economy of the English Crowd'. *Past & Present,* 50: 76–136.
Thompson, E. P. 1991 [1963]. *The Making of the English Working Class.* London: Penguin.
Vail, J. 2022. *Karl Polanyi and the Paradoxes of the Double Movement.* London: Routledge.
Wallerstein, I. 1983. *Historical Capitalism.* London: Verso.
Webb S. and Webb, B. 1923. *The Decay of Capitalist Civilization.* New York: Harcourt Brace and Company.

5 F. A. Hayek and the Emergence of Neoliberalism

The previous chapters looked at some of the major critiques of capitalism since the middle of the nineteenth century. We have identified four major critiques of capitalism: Marx's critique of political economy that was kept alive by many of the major Marxist theorists of the first half of the twentieth century, such as Lukács, Rosa Luxemburg and the Austro-Marxists; Max Weber's theory of capitalism, which we characterized, with some qualifications, as a conservative cultural critique of capitalism; and Joseph Schumpeter's theory of capitalism, which was also cast in the terms of a conservative cultural critique, in this case one tinged with cynicism. We have also identified a third critique based on the idea of the moral economy, which is best exemplified by Karl Polanyi's *The Great Transformation* (Polanyi 2001 [1944]). In the next chapter, we consider a fourth and more technocratic critique of capitalism, which was linked to the idea of democratic capitalism but administered by experts. This was already anticipated by Polanyi, who helped to nurture post-1945 social democracy, even if his politics called for something closer to democratic socialism than the more conservative politics of John Maynard Keynes and the turn to macroeconomics.

In this chapter, we look at one of the most influential books of the twentieth century, *The Road to Serfdom* by Friedrich August von Hayek (normally referred to as F. A. Hayek after he anglicized his name). Published in 1944, it stands alongside Karl Polanyi's *The Great Transformation*, published the same year and Schumpeter's *Capitalism, Socialism and Democracy* [1942] as a work of considerable historical significance. It is striking how different were the visions of the two central European figures who came to Britain from Vienna in the early 1930s: one a defender of capitalism based on liberalism and the other a critic fleeing the Nazis and inspired by libertarian and Christian socialism. Hayek's book was written as a rebuttal of what was then the dominant view of government as responsible for the management of the economy. The Great Depression and the New Deal in the USA, along with the running of war economies, led to the final end of nineteenth-century liberalism as the dominant political force in the western world. This did not mean that liberals were not important or that liberalism vanished, but after 1918, the political landscape changed following the extension of the franchise and the steady rise of the socialist movement around organized labour. In Britain, a liberal social reformer, William Beveridge published a ground-breaking report in 1942, *Social Insurance and Allied Services*, which led to the post-war welfare state and the National Health Service, which was spearheaded by the Labour Party. This was the context that set the scene for Hayek to write what was intended as a philosophical onslaught against Beveridge and the political project of the post-war Labour government in Britain. Ironically, it was Beveridge who

DOI: 10.4324/9781351017671-6

earlier as the Director of the London School of Economics was responsible for hiring F.A. Hayek.

The Road to Serfdom is the foundational text of the school of thought that came to be known as neoliberalism. The title is said to have been inspired by Alexis de Tocqueville's term 'the road to servitude'. It was written at a time when classical liberal ideas about the role of government were generally abandoned in the favour of protectionism and a new concern with central planning. The circumstances of the war necessitated a new role for the state as did later post-war recovery.

F.A. Hayek was a critic of the new ideas about economy and state. His ideas gave neoliberalism an important philosophical foundation that made it possible to revive older notions of liberalism. He was in essence the prophet of the market fundamentalism that Polanyi criticized. He had a clarity of purpose and methodological and philosophical acumen that Polanyi lacked, though it is fair to say that both figures were writing for opposite sides and there was more or less no dialogue between them. Hayek was a philosophically inclined economist while Polanyi was a sociologically inclined economic historian. Schumpeter remained closer to Hayek, despite his differences, including on socialism as a viable project. The version of market liberalism that Hayek espoused did not allow for any accommodation of those in the socialist tradition. Keynes, a liberal reformer but no socialist, agreed with many of his ideas, while disagreeing with his philosophy, which he erroneously believed would have no practical consequences.

The Road to Serfdom

F. A. Hayek was the author of many important books on legal and political philosophy as well as on economics, from the early *Prices and Production* [1931] to *The Constitution of Liberty* [1960] and the later three volumes *Law, Legislation and Liberty* [1973, 1976, 1979]. Our main focus in this chapter is *The Road to Serfdom* and the intellectual foundations of what was to become neoliberalism. The arguments given in the book constitute the basic philosophical tenets of neoliberalism but are not systematically developed and neither the words capitalism nor neoliberalism occur in the text. The absence of the word capitalism is perhaps explained by the fact that the word has generally been used by the left in contrast to those, like Hayek, of the right, who preferred the term the market. However, Schumpeter used the term, as did Milton Friedman in a famous book published in 1962 that became the de facto bible of neoliberalism, *Capitalism and Freedom* (Friedman 2003). The unprepared reader, unfamiliar with Hayek's writings, will be surprised in a first reading of the book that many of the chapters are difficult to relate to what is today known as neoliberalism. It is true of course that neoliberalism did not spring alone from the pages of this book. Many other thinkers were involved in the shaping of the movement, especially the work of his early mentor Ludwig von Mises and the Chicago school of economists, especially Freedman, who all rejected Keynesianism in the favour of monetarism. But the book acquired a notoriety as a foundational philosophical text. It is said that in the late 1960s, Ronald Reagan read a condensed version in *Reader's Digest. The Constitution of Liberty* also had this icon status. According to an oft-told anecdote, Margaret Thatcher once had a copy of the book in her handbag which she slammed on a desk during a Conservative Party meeting some time in 1975 after she became party leader saying 'This is what we believe in'. It is not clear if she had actually read the thick book of 569 pages. If she had not read it, as was probably the case, she would have been in the company of most of its left-wing critics. In the following, we try to set forth Hayek's core ideas about capitalism and government.

Hayek stood in the tradition of neoclassical economics but set out to revise some of its core ideas. This was in line with his broader project as outlined in the later *The Constitution of Liberty*. While his main target was the political and economic ideas of the left, including the New Deal, his revision of neoclassical economics provides the basis of his objections to government intervention in the market. The main problem he found with neoclassical economics was the inbuilt assumption that people act on the basis of full and relevant information on the means to attain their desired ends. He aimed to correct this tendency in economics with a theory that gave more recognition to uncertainty. He accepted the basic rationale of neoclassical economics that people have preferences which they rationally pursue and that the outcomes, which can be identified, can be given values. People act on the basis of self-interest in so far as they seek to maximize their benefits and pursue ends through what they think are rational means. The problem for Hayek is that the means to ends are not always rational, for if they were, the actor would have complete knowledge. He argued that the knowledge or information that actors have about market outcomes is always necessarily limited. The market, he held, is a complex system that can never be fully known. It follows from this premise that it cannot be planned, since this would require what is not available, namely complete knowledge. As in the analogy of a game, the outcome cannot be decided and the winner must not be planned if the game is to be fair. He saw the market in similar terms as a game that cannot be mastered; it must be left to run its own course.

Underlying Hayek's economic and political philosophy was this epistemological thesis about the nature of complexity and its implications for knowledge. It can also be said that this thesis rested on an ontological claim concerning the nature of order. Order is not fixed and immutable but subject to change. Moreover, reason is limited, a strong Kantian position that was central to his thought and led to scepticism about what political will could achieve (see Kukathas 1989). He held to a strong view of the unpredictability of order and how this can easily encroach on chaos. A spontaneous order can emerge from market forces. These ideas he developed in his economics in relation to the price system, for which he was co-awarded the Nobel Prize for Economics in 1974.[1] The market is not seen as a perfect system but is a highly complex system that is not amenable to planning since the price system can make the necessary adjustments to produce an optimal equilibrium between supply and demand. The price system that the market generates is akin to the model of a language; it is a form of communication and cannot be known in advance. Prices constitute a form of order that is unpredictable and consequently unknowable. His complaint was that neoclassical economics was not sufficiently tuned into the nature of order and the fundamental problem of knowledge.

For Hayek, this seems to be less of a problem for neoclassical economics than for all varieties of socialism. Both assumed the availability of adequate information for the management of the market. In *The Road to Serfdom*, he set out to demolish the emerging project of social democracy and all varieties of socialism. Since his arrival in London in 1931, he had already engaged in a critical debate with J. M. Keynes, whose *Treatise on Money* was published in 1930 and two years later, *The General Theory of Employment, Interest and Money*. Although Keynes was broadly favourable to *The Road to Serfdom* and interested in Hayek's thinking, the latter was not in the favour of what Keynes stood for, though he did take on board some of Keynes' more technical economic arguments (see Wapshott 2012). Hayek's book was published at a time when, especially in Britain and the USA, central planning had been embraced by the liberal as well as by the conservative elites. It was of course also integral to the left, as we have seen with Polanyi and the British liberal socialist tradition, which was influential at the London School of Economics in the 1930s and 1940s. The war economy additionally made central planning necessary and gave to government a role that Hayek thought was detrimental to capitalism, which required unrestricted markets. Hayek was lamenting the end of the unrestricted market, which had also collapsed in much of Europe as a result of the rise of fascism in Italy, Spain and Germany and too in the USSR with its own more radical conception of the command economy.

The book was as much a critique of the Anglo-American abandonment of the free market as it was of continental political authoritarianism. A book published in the middle of the war would be inevitably addressed to fascism. The arguments however preceded the war and were formulated before fascism became a serious threat. The background of the Great Depression of the early 1930s does not seem to impinge on his thinking. While this receded in importance during the war, it was the context for almost all political and economic thinking in the 1930s when Hayek formulated his ideas. His critique was clearly directed against socialists – a term that had to be so all-encompassing that it included the liberal centre-ground. Hayek disagreed with the view common amongst the left and, central to Polanyi's argument, that fascism was a product of the transformation of capitalism in its exit from the unregulated market. Against this view, he saw fascism as a product of the planned state and was dismayed to see the western liberal democracies taking on the project of central state planning, including large-scale nationalization necessitated by the war. In one way, he shared the view of the Frankfurt School and Hannah Arendt in the 1940s that the models of political modernity embraced by Germany and the USSR were simply different versions of totalitarianism. But unlike Marcuse, Adorno and Horkheimer, he did not see an incipient authoritarianism developing in the west and nurtured by capitalism. It is true of course that he saw an authoritarianism developing under the cover of social democracy and what he called socialism in some general and unspecified sense and propagated by what he referred to as 'the totalitarians in our midst', singling out the British historian E. H. Carr.

There is obviously a huge difference between state socialism, as in the USSR, the market socialism that was broadly the position of the western social democratic left, the welfare state and the pathological phenomenon of National Socialism. Hayek's book, which had the dedication – written as he wrote to the 1956 American edition in 'the spirit of mockery' – 'To the socialists of all parties'. This angered, as it was intended to do so, many readers in not making clear what model of central planning he had in mind. As the preface announces, it was a political, even a polemical book, paradoxically to separate economics from politics in order that the former can guide governments. Although the book was written initially for a British readership, 'the socialist intelligentsia of England', the crude and all-encompassing notion of socialism in it made more sense to an American readership for whom the New Deal was an exercise in socialism that needed to be scaled back. Hayek did acknowledge, as in the preface to the 1976 edition, that he was wrong to have said that 'any movement in socialism would lead to totalitarianism'. He qualified the message of the book as containing 'a warning that unless we mend the principle of our policy, some very unpleasant consequences will follow, which most of those who advocate these policies do not want' (p. 55). *The Constitution of Liberty* in 1960 did not present the same caricature of socialism and was more nuanced on the welfare state. The concessions came too late. By 1976, new policies were about to be adopted, shaped in no small part by this book, which led to different unpleasant outcomes.

The argument of *The Road to Serfdom* begins with a strong claim that socialism has displaced liberalism. While socialism, he admits, did not at first foster freedom, it allied itself with the forces of freedom after 1848. He sees democracy as the main expression of freedom and this is at odds with socialism, since democracy he claims, following de Tocqueville, is individualist. But democracy in his narrative became co-opted by socialism and lost its true nature. Hayek was greatly influenced by de Tocqueville and saw himself following in his footsteps to the extent that he initially wanted the Mont Pèlerin Society to be named after him. The relation between democracy and socialism is an 'irreconcilable conflict' even if they both share one thing, namely equality. But these are very different forms of equality: 'while democracy seeks equality, socialism seeks equality in restraint and servitude' (p. 77). Socialism promised a greater freedom, but 'what was promised to us as the Road to Freedom was in fact the Road to Servitude' (p. 78). So, liberals were lured to the road to socialism by the promise of a greater freedom, a 'great utopia' that could not be delivered.

Many of the key ideas are set out in Chapter 3 on individualism and collectivism. By socialism, Hayek means 'the planned economy' in which the private entrepreneur working for profit is replaced by a central planning body. His thesis rests on a basic dichotomy between individualism and collectivism, which correspond to liberalism and socialism. Hayek's objection to socialism was not so much about the ends of socialist politics but the means. While he thinks some of the ends of socialism are not compatible, the problem boils down to the means to achieve goals that may be desirable but are unattainable. Planning is the means to achieve the ultimate goals of socialism. Hayek warns the reader that the kind of planning he is questioning in the book is 'planning against competition'. In some ways, he is questioning Weber's view of the inevitability of planning. He argues that the obsession with planning is not inevitable or beyond our control but the product of a deliberate political position. Despite his qualification, that the problem is not planning in general, but planning that undermines the competitive spirit, the general position advanced in the book is an attack on planning, even of co-ordination. Hayek falls back on his epistemological argument of planning always requiring knowledge that is not available. 'The economist is the last to claim that he has the knowledge which the coordinator would need' (p. 99). In this, Hayek is a prisoner of his Kantian philosophy of the limits of reason which he too readily applied to the sphere of politics. His abstract argument is also a reflection of the historical complexity of the division of labour:

> Far from being appropriate only to comparatively simple conditions, it is the very complexity of the division of labour under modern conditions which makes competition the only method by which such co-ordination can be adequately brought about. There would be no difficulty about efficient control or planning were conditions so simple that a single person or board could effectively survey all the relevant facts. It is only as the factors which have to be taken into account become so numerous that it is impossible to gain a synoptic view of them, that decentralisation becomes imperative. (p. 95)

Hayek attributes to all forms of collectivist politics goals that are cast in the language of 'common purpose', 'the common good' and the 'general welfare', which he claims have no content since they lack definitive meaning. These goals are more complicated than

Hayek allows for. They are in part general aspirations that do not prescribe specific courses of action; in some cases, they are collective policies, as in the so-called post-war consensus on the goal of full employment. A goal does not have to be achievable in full for it to be effective. He is correct in claiming that more people can agree to a common course of action than on a common goal. However, he does not consider that while the common good cannot be easily defined, it nonetheless exists as a general normative framework, which serves as a point of reference for different political positions and strategies, as Boltanski and Thévenot (2015) have argued from a different political theory.

The arguments concerning democracy and planning reduce democracy too much to a planning exercise, as perhaps represented by Karl Mannheim, a fellow academic at the LSE and Jewish émigré from Budapest, whose ideas for social and political reconstruction Hayek was strongly opposed to. He saw Mannheim's project as contrary to the essence of democracy, which 'is essentially a means, a utilitarian device for safeguarding internal peace and individual freedom. As such it is by no means infallible or certain' (p. 110). The reader cannot help being irritated by Hayek's reasoning that seems to entail straw man arguments and a disagreement with everyone he encountered at the LSE, though he was often in agreement with the economist Lionel Robbins. Even if planning were the central purpose of a democracy, it is not evident that this entails a politics of certainty or that planning inevitably leads to a dictatorship. In this regard, the book makes some very strong claims, as in the opening sentence of Chapter 7: 'Most planners who have seriously considered the practical aspects of their task have little doubt that a directed economy must be run on more or less dictatorial lines' (p. 124). Hayek criticizes the trend towards monopolies as a symptom of the obsession with planning that is contrary to the needs of the free market. But economic planning by government and monopolistic practices are very different kinds of planned operations and the latter is not necessarily a product of state planning.

Hayek in effect sought to reset the balance between economic freedom and political liberty. The latter is now to be based on economic freedom. The particular kind of liberalism that he espoused gave a greater role to market freedom as the best guarantor for other kinds of liberty. 'What our generation has forgotten is that the system of private property is the most important guaranty of freedom, not only for those who own property, but scarcely less for those who do not' (p. 136). While political freedom is endangered by the trend towards planning, it is not evident how if this were the case it was responsible for monopoly capitalism. Hayek seems to think that labour and capital are complicit:

> The recent growth of monopoly is largely the result of a deliberate collaboration of organised capital and organised labour where the privileged groups of labour share in the monopoly profits at the expense of the community and particularly at the expense of the poorest, those employed in the less well organised industries and the unemployed.
>
> (p. 207)

The planned society according to Hayek has been tempted too much by the goal of security over freedom, which is already undermined by the aspiration for equality. Security, equality and freedom may be incompatible. For Hayek, the pursuit of security beyond a certain level is too high a price to pay for the loss in freedom. In this respect, he clearly is opposed to the Polanyian argument for social protection as a normative goal for a progressive politics. However, he was not arguing that the state has no responsibilities for society.

The Road to Serfdom was a provocative book, written, as he somewhat laconically said in the preface, in his spare time to annoy socialists. Despite the philosophical arguments, the arguments were not designed for fellow philosophers or economists. It is hardly surprising that he had problems in getting the book published. But once published, it was extraordinarily successful as it appealed to a new readership, those with doubts about the steady rise of the big state. In many ways it was a political utopia for the right in the way the *Communist Manifesto* or Lenin's *State and Revolution* were for the left. The overall argument was simple and glossed over obvious objections: the decline of unregulated markets led to a loss in freedom. The allure of security that won many people to socialism and to the centrally planned state is a poor substitute for liberty. The big state and socialism were more or less equated. His aim was to undermine 'the moral basis of collectivism'. In the context of the time, written between 1941 and 1944, the horrors of National Socialism were there as a reminder of the danger of socialism. But Hayek was not claiming that the trend towards the centrally planned state in Britain was the equivalent of Nazi Germany. In any, National Socialism had very little to do with socialism.[2] It was 'the Germany of twenty or thirty years ago to which conditions in the democracies show an ever increasing resemblance' (p. 193). Hayek was probably correct in his claim that if Nazi Germany were simply a revolt against reason, it would not have been so dangerous, but his argument was that it was made possible by an intellectual current that began in the nineteenth century that undermined liberalism. However, neither socialism nor nationalism alone, or together, accounts for Nazism. Centuries of virulent anti-Semitism spouted from the pulpit, the disastrous Treaty of Versailles and its economic impacts, the writings of the Artaman League and Walther Darré, and the development of social Darwinist eugenics; many more complex factors must be included within such an analysis. It is evident that Hayek's thesis is therefore a partial view of the predicament of German liberalism and fails to account for other currents, including ones that built upon liberalism, such as cosmopolitanism, which were strong in pre-war Germany (see Mommsen 2011, Harrington 2016).

The Rise of Neoliberalism

Anyone in search of an argument against the big state will find much to convince themselves against the virtues of planning in *The Road to Serfdom*, which gave the nascent movement of neoliberalism its basic philosophical rationale. The book was more about what it was opposed to than what it stood for. Hayek made that clear in the conclusion when he wrote that the purpose of the book was not to sketch a detailed programme of 'desirable future order of society' (p. 237). While invoking the spirit of liberalism, it was a warning against the loss of freedom at a time when it was apparent that freedom was in grave danger. But once the threat of fascism was gone, the ideal of freedom could be given a new meaning. His basic understanding of freedom is freedom from coercion. In concrete political terms, this could be used to justify anything. From its basic meaning as freedom for the individual, its political, and especially its economic, dimensions could be given a new meaning for the world in the aftermath of the war. This proved to a highly attractive ideal for many intellectuals who were not aligned with the left.

In the formative period of Hayek's writing, in the 1930s and 1940s, but extending into the 1960s, the school of thought he represented was contra the mainstream, with the exception of the related but different school of *Ordoliberalism* in Germany in the 1950s.[3] In the USA, Lyndon Johnson in 1964 announced his 'Great Society' manifesto to expand federal spending to reduce poverty. These projects of state spending – from the New Deal to the Great Society – were anathema to Hayek's project, even though they had nothing to do with socialism. The period before the war saw the rise of the big state, largely as a response to the Great Depression. Even the British Conservative Party signed up to a programme that had originated within the liberal tradition that saw the need for social reform and accepted the programme taken forward by the Labour Party under Clement Atlee. After 1945, British politics was reshaped around a set of key policies that defined what became known as the post-war consensus. This was the view that government should provide certain social and economic functions for society, such as welfare provision for all, national insurance reform, full employment and the nationalization of important industries, such as coal, iron and steel, electricity and the railways. It included the extension of higher education with the creation of new state-financed universities since the early 1960s. This consensus, which had the support of the Conservative Party, collapsed in the course of the 1970s and it was the declared goal of the Thatcher government in 1979 to end such policies. This was also the period that saw the rise of the movement that led to European integration – championed by the British Conservative Party – and the growing power of the trade unions and national wage bargaining.

The neoliberal movement emerged and consolidated in this period.[4] The term was in usage in the German-speaking world in the 1920s and was given its first international meaning in a conference in Paris in 1938 that brought together many thinkers who went on to become the stalwarts of the movement. But it was the Mont Pèlerin Society since its first meeting on a mountain in Switzerland in 1947 that consolidated the movement that later became known as neoliberalism. Today it has acquired a negative connotation, like its main protégé, capitalism, but in the post-war period, it indicated a political stance critical of central planning. The Mont Pèlerin Society cultivated the view that the competitive spirit of capitalism and the liberal idea of freedom are linked. The early meetings chaired by Hayek included Karl Popper, Milton Friedman and Ludwig von Mises. The enemies of freedom are the centrally planned economy and monopolistic capitalism. Karl Popper was a supporter of Hayek's political project, though he disagreed with some of his more extreme positions on the role of the state. Popper's notion of the 'Open Society', as in the 1945 book, *The Open Society and its Enemies*, found common cause with the neoliberal advocacy of a free society. The political ideas of neoliberalism provided a backdrop for an economic theory of the free market and a programme for how private enterprise can take over areas of social and economic provision controlled by the central state.

Hayek led the offensive in his attack on central planning as a core function of government. The argument paid little attention to the different types of planning and the fact that like many terms it is ambiguous. It can include the Soviet command economy, for instance; a weak model of state socialism where the state manages large sectors of society; the model dominant in the western post-war democracies whereby the state controls key social and economic functions (railways, national airlines, telecommunications, healthcare and education for instance); the welfare state. It can include fiscal/budgetary planning and also embraces regulation. The extent to which neoliberalism in its formative period was opposed to all forms of planning is a matter of interpretation. No government, not even the ideal neoliberal model, can function without planning. In this context, Foucault's lectures in 1979 on neoliberalism are relevant. He argued that neoliberalism should not be identified exclusively with the free market as such. His key insight was that neoliberalism is not simply about, what it came to be identified as, deregulation and privatization, but surveillance and the extension of the market into all aspects of social and cultural life as well as the sphere of the state (Foucault 2008; see also Gane 2012). Despite Hayek's attempt to free the market from the state, the historical experience is that the opposite happened. As Foucault brilliantly showed, neoliberalism required the state to implement its project. The notion of the free market does not mean less state. It means whatever is needed to achieve market liberalization. In effect, it means more state not less state. The notion of the free market is therefore an illusion, since no market can be free and cannot be free of the state, which is what makes markets possible. Following Foucault's pioneering analysis, neoliberalism is best seen as a project for the maximization of the reach of the market.

It is difficult to look back on the formative period of neoliberalism without taking into account the later Marxist analysis that sees neoliberalism as the final victory of capital over labour. We discuss this in more detail in Chapter 11. At this time, Marxist theory was not specifically addressed to neoliberalism, since it had no real political influence until the late 1970s. Foucault was ahead of his time in this respect, but then he was not a Marxist and not specifically setting out to reject it. According to some accounts, he was infavour of certain aspects of neoliberalism (Zamora and Behrent 2016). Hayek's main interlocutors were figures not specifically associated with the socialist left. They were more likely to be liberal reformers, such as William Beveridge and J. M. Keynes, or the historian E. H. Carr.

Since he operated at a high level of abstraction and had expertise as an economist, his ideas at first did not seem radical. He sought to develop a moral and political philosophy of the just society. He has been undoubtedly much misunderstood (see Kley 1996). Many thinkers with less extreme views, such as Karl Popper and the conservative French sociologist Raymond Aron, could find common cause with his ideas. The latter agreed with market freedom but from a position that had a stronger adherence to democracy. Aron is an example of a divergent path within the neoliberal movement, which in its formative period was not foreclosed (Gane 2016). Hayek, who stood for a restricted understanding of democracy, was opposed to stronger notions of democracy, such as those that can be associated with the republican tradition and less anything that could be related to radical democracy (the latter in any case was not much of a threat in the 1940s and 1950s). Against the conservative neoliberalism of the influential French sociologist Raymond Aron, his project was a more radical one that sought to sever the strings that bound capitalism to democracy. But he was also vague on how his ideas might be politically realized. In this matter, the beacon was passed to others working within the field of economics to lead the way to more practical programmes of economic and political reform. Milton Friedman was a key figure in this respect. He made the transition from Hayek's political philosophy to the doctrine of *homo economicus* and a more explicitly developed economic theory that had policy implications. By the early 1970s, the period of philosophical consolidation gave way to a political project.

It is perhaps one of the greatest political ironies that the first implementation of neoliberalism was in Chile by the Pinochet military dictatorship. In Britain, Thatcher, a friend of the Chilean general as well as an admirer of Hayek, implemented her own brand of neoliberalism, which soon became a worldwide movement with different trajectories. The post-1973 context will be discussed in Chapter 11 around new critical literature, including the work of David Harvey, Nancy Fraser and Wendy Brown.

It will suffice to mention here that the emerging movement of neoliberalism was a project of market liberalization born of a time when the state controlled large sectors of the economy. The collapse of communism in the early 1990s increased the appeal of Hayek. It was therefore a political project against the status quo, or what had been, and hostile to labour politics in an era when western societies were still predominantly industrial. Its more concrete aims were to reverse the nationalization of those sectors under direct state control through privatization and deregulation. Often hailed as the return to the minimal state, in fact, as argued, the sphere of the state was not necessarily reduced, but restructured and expanded to serve the interests of market liberalization. This project was put in place by Margaret Thatcher and Ronald Reagan during the 1980s and in Latin American countries, such as Chile as the forerunner. The project then extended to the liberalization of trade through global markets and policies aimed at lower general taxation. A further feature of neoliberalism was the emphasis on monetarism as opposed to fiscal policy in order to combat inflation. It aimed at the rolling back of the welfare state, a project that arguably did not entirely succeed, at least in western Europe. In more recent times, neoliberalism became increasingly bound up with processes of financialization, a new style of managerialism often called the New Public Governance, securitization and the new ideology of individual as consumer, but that takes us beyond the formative phase of the movement.

Hayek and His Contested Legacy

F. A. Hayek was a significant figure in the rise of neoliberalism, which provided the right with a powerful ideology that reshaped the world since its adoption by governments in the 1980s. He provided the movement with a philosophical foundation that furnished the ideology with utopia, which once realized could be cast off. While today neoliberalism is a heterogeneous and deeply contested order of governance rooted in neither utopia nor ideology, Hayek and his disciples in the Mont Pèlerin Society gave it a unity of purpose. His work brought together political philosophy and economics. In doing so, he revived nineteenth-century liberalism and gave liberalism a new relevance that could claim the mantle of freedom and all in the name of value-free science. This rallying cry inevitably pitted itself against democracy.

Perhaps his hostility to anything more than a restricted model of democracy ensured his appeal in an era of growing discontent with projects of nationalization. In the marketplace of ideas, his philosophy found an audience willing to take it up as a political project at a time when the post-war consensus was breaking down along with the onset of a new economic crisis in the early 1970s. It was less the force of his philosophical ideas and economic theory that led to neoliberalism than an ensemble of different forces, including the support of the Chicago Economists and the Nobel Committee which endorsed neoliberalism,[5] and a historical moment of opportunity for the emerging new right. These factors along with the Mont Pèlerin Society produced the movement.

Hayek was an ambivalent figure for whom much could be justified if it could be deemed to fall within the scope of freedom. Hayek believed his normative political philosophy was supported by scientific foundations, but this is deeply questionable (see Kley 1996). His notion of the limits of reason provided a convenient cloak to justify opposition to anything that could be seen as a danger to liberty, which always fell outside the compass of reason. It is true that when Hayek defended competitive individualism rather than collectivism as the basis of society, he was not arguing for the extension of the market – or some notion of market fundamentalism – to everything. His position was rather the reverse, namely that non-market forces should not intrude into the domain of the market (see Shearmur 1996). The problem was that too much was included in this category, effectively much of the functions of the state. His neoliberalism reflected the liberal conception of negative as opposed to positive freedom, which might be seen as including a wider conception of social freedom. But the notion of freedom as in his concern with economic policy for a free society, shorn of any real link with democracy and justice, was in the end hollow.

His disciples such as Milton Friedman and Gary Becker certainly made a much stronger case for the superiority of *homo economicus* and the limited state than he did. Yet, by the time of his death in 1992, he never fundamentally disagreed with the aggressive neoliberalism that unfolded since the 1980s. His ambivalent relationship with Pinochet, who he visited in Chile in 1977 and again in 1981, remains controversial even if he did not explicitly approve of the dictatorship, which he also did not condemn. It is clear he was more hostile to Allende's programme of nationalization, which corresponded to his notion of totalitarianism, than he was to Pinochet's rule, which he saw as an acceptable dictatorship. It is difficult to take seriously his defence of what he called a 'transitional dictatorship'.[6]

In this chapter, we have concentrated on *The Road to Serfdom*, but a more complete appraisal of Hayek's thought would need to take into account a wider range of his work. A sympathetic reader might find in his writings a more favourable assessment than the dismissive response typical of the left to *The Road to Serfdom*, but those in search of a basis for progressive politics will struggle to find anything more than a weak defence of the negative conception of liberty as a basis for a just society. Yet, some of his philosophical premises are not to be entirely dismissed, especially those concerning the nature of knowledge, which for Hayek cannot be centralized.

A more charitable interpretation of his concept of a 'spontaneous order' will see that it resonates with non-Hayekian theories, including positions in progressive politics, as in the work of Hilary Wainwright (1994), that seek to address the fundamental problem of how societies should be co-ordinated. Hayek believed societies should be co-ordinated through the market not the state. This followed from his underlying epistemological position that knowledge is not concentrated in a specific site but is dispersed in the social and economic order. This insight is of fundamental importance to the progressive left in that a spontaneous order can open up opportunities for alternatives kinds of co-ordination to highly centralized ones. Both Hayek and the progressive left are opposed to centralized systems of control, as was Foucault, and see knowledge as essential open and contingent, but also as social and not as in Hayek as individual. While Hayek thought only the market left to its own devices through the pricing system was the appropriate response to the problem of co-ordination, democratic socialist politics emphasises de-centralized alternatives, as in co-operatives and various kinds of solidarity economies. Such forms of social and economic organization can use knowledge in more spontaneous and creative ways to advance human autonomy and freedom. In sum, Hayek posed the question how societies should be co-ordinated but failed to provide an adequate response. Neither the economy not the state is the solution.

Notes

1 The co-recipient was the Swedish social democratic thinker, economist and sociologist, Gunnar Myrdal, who represented an intellectual and political position that was the opposite to that of Hayek. He was a key figure in the development of the Swedish welfare state and advocated a

world welfare state. He protested, as many people did, about the Nobel Prize award being given to Hayek on the grounds of Hayek's association with the Chilean dictatorship.
2 Hitler clearly disliked socialism of any kind. The label socialism in National Socialism was probably due to its association with mass employment.
3 This was a German variant based on the idea of market liberalism but gave government a stronger role than in Anglo-American neoliberalism.
4 For general studies, see Campbell and Pedersen (2001), Duménil and Lévy (2004), Harvey (2005), Mirowski and Plehwe (2009) and Seidman Jones (2012).
5 See Offer and Söderberg (2016).
6 For a balanced analysis of Hayek's relationship with Pinochet, see Caudwell and Montes (2015) and Farrant et al (2012).

References

Boltanski, L. and Thévenot, L. 2015. *On Justification: Economies of Worth*. Princeton: Princeton University Press.
Campbell, J. L. and Pedersen, O. K. (eds.) 2001. *The Rise of Neoliberalism and Institutional Analysis*. Princeton: Princeton University Press.
Caudwell, B. and Montes, L. 2005. 'Friedrich Hayek and His Visits to Chile'. *LSE Research-Online*. http://eprints.lse.ac.uk/63318/1/__lse.ac.uk_storage_LIBRARY_Secondary_libfile_shared_repository_Content_Caldwell,%20B_Hayek%20and%20Chile_Cladwell_Hayek%20and%20Chile_2015.pdf
Duménil, G. and Lévy, D. 2004. *Capital Resurgent: Roots of the Neoliberal Revolution*. Cambridge: Harvard University Press.
Farrant, A., McPhail, E., and Berger, S. 2012. 'Preventing the "Abuses of Democracy: Hayek, the "Military Usurper" and Transitional Dictatorship in Chile'. *The American Journal of Economics and Sociology*, 71 (3): 513–38.
Foucault, M. 2008. *The Birth of Biopolitics: Lectures at the Collège de France, 1978–79*. London: Palgrave.
Friedman, M. 2003 [1962]. *Capitalism and Freedom*. Chicago: Chicago University Press.
Gane, N. 2012. 'The Governmentalities of Neoliberalism: Panopticism, Post-panopticism and Beyond'. *The Sociological Review*, 60 (4): 611–34
Gane, N. 2016. 'In and Out of Neoliberalism: Reconsidering the Sociology of Raymond Aron.' *Journal of Classical Sociology*, 16 (3): 261–79.
Harrington, A. 2016. *German Cosmopolitan Social Thought and the Idea of the West*. Cambridge: Cambridge University Press.
Harvey, D. 2005. *A Brief History of Neoliberalism*. Oxford: Oxford University Press.
Hayek, F.A. 1960. *The Constitution of Liberty*. London: Routledge & Kegan Paul.
Hayek, F.A. 2007 [1944]. *The Road to Serfdom*. Chicago: Chicago University Press.
Kley, R. 1996. *Hayek's Social and Political Thought*. Oxford: Oxford University Press.
Kukathas, C. 1989. *Hayek and Modern Liberalism*. Oxford: Oxford University Press.
Mirowski, P. and Plehwe, D. (eds.) 2009. *The Road from Mont Pèlerin: The Making of the Neoliberal Thought Collective*. Cambridge: Harvard University Press.
Mommsen, W. 2011. 'German Liberalism in the Nineteenth Century'. In: *The Cambridge History of Nineteenth-Century Political Thought*. Edited by G. Steadman Jones and G. Claeyss. Cambridge: Cambridge University Press.
Offer, A. and Söderberg, S. 2016. *The Nobel Factor: The Prize in Economics, Social Democracy, and The Market Turn*. Princeton: Princeton University Press.
Polanyi, K. 2001 [1944]. *The Great Transformation*. Boston: Beacon Press.
Shearmur, J. 1996. *Hayek and After: Hayekian Liberalism as a Research Programme*. London: Routledge.

Stedman Jones, D. (2012) *Masters of the Universe: Hayek, Friedman and the Birth of New Liberal Politics*. Princeton: Princeton University Press.

Wainwright, H. 1994. *Arguments for a New Left: Answering the Free Market Rise*. Oxford: Blackwell.

Wapshott, N. 2012. *Keynes Hayek: The Clash that Defined Modern Economics*. New York: W.W. Norton.

Zamora, D. and Behrent, M. (eds.) 2016. *Foucault and Neoliberalism*. Cambridge: Polity Press.

6 The Rise and Fall of Organized Capitalism

J. M. Keynes and Social Liberalism

This chapter deals with some of the most important theories and critiques of capitalism in its so-called Golden Age, the period from the late 1940s to the early 1970s. After 1945, the first major crisis of capitalism of the early 1930s receded into history and capitalism underwent a period of stability. The war changed everything and the period, especially from 1950 to 1970, saw rising prosperity and employment, growth in western societies and the advancement of the welfare state. The model of capitalism that consolidated has been referred to as 'organized capitalism', a term that was first used by the Austro-Marxist, Rudolf Hilferding, in the early twentieth century but revived in the early 1970s (Barkin 1975). The term referred to the shift towards an activist state in the management of the economy, which had become characterized by increased concentration and bureaucratization. Organized capitalism came to be adopted as the term to describe the state-managed economy that was a feature of most western countries in the period that followed the war, though its origins were pre-war. In this period, capitalism and democracy struck a new balance by which the former reconciled itself to certain aspects of a model of democracy that was characterized by a high degree of technocracy. Democratic capitalism was a technocratic form of democratic governance.

As we have seen, Karl Polanyi offered a powerful theory of capitalism generating a double movement whereby demands for social protection kick in, setting limits to the corrosive forces of the market in a new settlement. Depending on how the double movement plays out, democracy may be the winner. However, there is another story to be told to Polanyi's socialist narrative. In this chapter, we look at the most influential figure of the era, John Maynard Keynes. Keynes was not just a theorist of capitalism but in many ways its architect and savour. His ideas about economy and government were an expression of social liberalism tinged with technocratic leadership.

Since the 1930s, social liberalism was an important movement amongst British political intellectuals with major representatives, including Keynes and the Bloomsbury Group, but also important establishment figures such as Beveridge. As argued in the previous chapter, the ideas of F. A. Hayek were addressed to what had become the status quo, as far as big government is concerned. However, at this time, it was not socialists as his book suggested, but representatives of social liberalism that were influential along with the social democratic movement. It is not easy to separate the different movements within the left and of progressive politics more generally in this period, which ranged from democratic socialism (for example Polanyi, the radical left, including figures such as H. G. Wells and the short-lived experiment of Alexander Dubček in Prague in 1968), social democracy (the mainstream UK Labour Party, for example Anthony Crosland, who wrote *The*

DOI: 10.4324/9781351017671-7

Future of Socialism in 1956, and in Sweden with Gunnar Myrdal) and social liberalism (e.g. Keynes, William Beveridge, T. H. Marshall).[1]

The Era of Organized Capitalism

The Second World War provided the foundations for a period of unprecedented growth in western societies. It was a period of unbounded optimism about the future. The post-war boom was largely led by the USA where the war had brought more or less full employment in what had become a highly industrialized economy. Industrial society had finally arrived along with managerial capitalism. Japan and western Europe followed. Japan's industrial economy was more or less intact after the war and quickly made the transition, which was slower in Europe. Germany's industrial complex was shattered after the war and recovery took longer, but when it did from 1948, the so-called *Wirtschaftswunder*, or 'economic miracle', overtook Britain, due in part to being more technologically advanced and having a highly skilled labour force. The aftermath of the Second World War was very different from the aftermath of the First World War when the 'roaring twenties' gave way to the depression of the 1930s: economic recovery after 1945 was nothing short of a miracle throughout the western world and was sustained for almost three decades. In France, this was the somewhat exaggerated *Les Trente Glorieuses*, from 1945 to 1975. In Britain, in the 1950s, Harold Macmillan's election phrase in 'you've never had it so good' captured the new optimism of the post-war recovery. In reality, there were not quite 30 glorious years, as the period went into decline from the late 1960s. But a golden age there was (see Marglin and Schor, 1992).

In France, the economy was under strong state control, it was in effect a quasi-state-managed capitalism, while, in West Germany, a mixed economy emerged, the so-called Rhinish model (Albert 1991). In Britain, as discussed in the previous chapter, the post-war Labour government drove through new plans for nationalization and the creation of the welfare state. Western Europe's recovery would not have been possible without the Marshall Plan, from 1948 to 1951, which in effect tied the economies of western Europe, especially the emerging power-house of Germany, to the US economy. Post-war economic recovery was inevitably about Europe catching up with the USA, which itself was not in need of recovery.

The political context for the Golden Age of capitalism was the Cold War. The USA replaced the UK, for long in decline, as the major economic and political power in the western world. The Bretton Woods system, established in 1944, cemented US financial dominance as the major currencies of the world were tied to the US dollar, itself based on the gold standard. The context for the new era of organized capitalism was a major shift in the scales of world power between the two superpowers, the USA and USSR. But as E. P. Thompson argued in *Exterminism and Cold War*, the Cold War was a 'phoney war', in that both sides had reconciled themselves to each other and were in effect using the war to exert domination of their spheres of influence as well as to scramble for as much control over what was then known as the 'Third World' (Thompson 1982).

Unlike the present day, capitalism in these decades was relatively contained. It was contained within the confines of the West and at least until the 1980s by the strong arm of the corporatist state and the trade unions (Schmitter and Lehmbruch 1979). It was based not only on the organized labour and government cooperation but also on relations with the powerful agrarian sector, for in the period agriculture was powerful. Industrial capitalism was underpinned by agrarian capitalism. The post-war state has been termed the 'military industrial complex' – a term used by President Eisenhower in his farewell speech in 1961 warning the USA of its dangers – due to the fact that the era of enhanced industrialization was also a military economy in that the permanent preparation for war meant that a large part of industrial production was for defence. It was the other side of Keynesian, so-called military Keynesianism.

This was also the era of European integration, which began in 1951 with the Treaty of Paris establishing the European Coal and Steel Community. The treaty, which sought to integrate the coal and steel industries, was the first step in the project of European integration and what was to become the common market. The age was still that of the nation-state, but nationalism had receded making possible a period of international collaboration between the capitalistic liberal democracies. The ideology of capitalism and liberal democracy that they all shared provided in these decades the veneer of a consensus that had no significant challenges from within. The major political challenges were external.

The left was largely domesticated by institutionalized labour politics and the benefits of taxation. In western Europe, corporatism – a form of collectivist mobilization by organized groups such as trade unions but within the auspices of the state – evolved variously in many countries. Social democracy and the growth of trade unions, collective wage bargaining, the growth of the public sector all made possible increased wages, increased productivity and economic growth. Such was the power of the new ideas of planning and central government that in 1960 the conservative American sociologist Daniel Bell, writing about the USA, announced the 'end of ideology' following the exhaustion of all counter political currents in the 1950s, including the liberal belief in the free market (Bell 2000).

This rosy story of the golden age of capitalism as the victory of liberal democracy over totalitarianism was in part a myth. In Europe, dictatorships remained both East and West of the Iron Curtain. Salazar and the *Estado Novo* ruled Portugal until 1974 and Franco remained *Caudillo* in Spain until his death in 1975. Greece was under a military dictatorship between 1967 and 1974. In this period of peace, political stability and growing prosperity in western Europe, it should also be recalled that empire persisted: the old imperial powers were still running overseas empires until the 1970s. In France, the Algerian War (1954–62) cast a dark shadow across the period undermining the dominant narrative of European peace. In this period, racial discrimination was normal. The USA was a racially segregated democracy until progressive legislation was introduced since 1964. South Africa, with its apartheid system, was part of the West and one of the founding members of the UN (despite the UN being opposed to its apartheid policies, which it condemned).

The era of organized capitalism was the age of the middle class, affluence and the expansion of higher education for the baby boom generation. The period saw an increase in social mobility, social inclusion and living standards and a drop in inequality. This was within the limits of firm boundaries. Nation, state and class provided the substance of what Peter Wagner has termed 'organized modernity', which established a new context for collective identities and boundaries. An equilibrium was achieved in the 1960s between different forces, reducing the divisions and differences that beset an earlier modernity. Organized capitalism can be located in this wider context of organized modernity as the 'building of state-and-nation-wide conventionalizations of major sets of social practices in a relatively coherent, interlocking form' (Wagner 1994: 74). Organized modernity was built around social classes and the restructuring of allocative practices that can be characterized by the (a) second industrial revolution, (b) the emergence of oligopolistic managerial enterprise and (c) economic protectionism. The quest for certainty in modernity reaches its highest point in this period when progress in science and technology led to a new confidence in certainty and, as a result, social and political order and stability. This was also reflected in a new interest in social forecasting, futurism and in space exploration (see also Anderson 2018).

The emergence in this period of mass culture is a further feature of organized modernity. While this marks a shift from an earlier more divided society to one of greater cohesion and equality, it can also be seen in the terms of Marcuse's *One-Dimensional Man* as a false cohesion or what Adorno and Horkheimer called the 'culture industry', essentially the penetration of capitalism into the sphere of culture and consciousness (which we discuss in more detail in Chapter 7). Marcuse showed that the affluent society and its homogenized mass culture entailed deceptive liberties that led to the elimination of critical thinking and amounted to a new kind of domination in which the individual is enslaved by what appears to be freedom (Marcuse 1964). It can also be seen as a highly regulated kind of capitalism, as Aglietta (1979) argued in a classic book. In this view, capitalism does not rest only on manipulation or social control, as Marcuse claimed, but is embedded in social and political institutions that provide it with continuity and stability.

Sociological perspectives vary on the question of conflict and consensus. Ralf Dahrendorf in an influential book, *Class and Class Conflict in Industrial Society* in 1959, argued that the class structure had become more fluid to the point that a 'post-capitalist society' was emerging and class conflict was largely contained within the structure of capitalism. He disagreed with Marxism and with its main sociological alternative, structural functionalism. Class conflict had not disappeared as the latter argued, but industrial society, his preferred term, had brought about a high degree of cohesion and consensus. This account was in part reflected in the sociology of Pierre Bourdieu, whose major works on the class structure in France painted a picture of a fairly intact class structure despite increased opportunities. However, Bourdieu gave greater emphasis on the reproduction of inequality from generation to generation.

Weberian-influenced sociological approaches, popular in British sociology, such as David Lockwood's classic 1958 study, *The Black Coated Worker*, or the famous book by Westergaard and Resler on class in modern Britain, stressed a more plural concept of class as occupational groups shaped more by the market than by production. In these accounts, Weber's notion of status played an important part in the analysis of class. In *The Affluent Worker in the Class Structure*, Goldthrope (1969) along with other British sociologists, David Lockwood, Frank Beckhofer and Jennifer Platt, critiqued the Marxist notion of the 'embourgeoisement' of the working class who were allegedly adopting the class consciousness of the middle class. The working class may have become more affluent, they argued, but were different in their consciousness than the middle class in terms of lifestyle, aspirations and notions of status.

Despite the differences between these approaches to class and conflict, the overall picture is one of industrial society as a class society. It was not significantly transformed by migration, as migration was limited and often regarded to be temporary, as in the case of the 'Guest workers' from southern Europe to Germany. The welfare state was able to accommodate the new arrivals, whose numbers were relatively low and the virulent nationalism of the pre-war years had been drained of any real danger to destabilize the industrial order. The massive incorporation of women into the labour market had begun but the impact of feminism did not occur until the end of the period of organized capitalism, which was predominantly based on industrial male labour and gendered work. The counter-culture did not emerge until the second half of the 1960s, but by then organized modernity was beginning to unravel, as it did in May 1968 in Paris.

The post-industrial society was taking shape, as described in a famous work by Daniel Bell (1974) who coined the term. But western societies were still industrial societies throughout this era of organized modernity. Despite the rise of the middle class, the welfare state and the growth of suburbia, capitalism was organized along the lines of Fordism, large-scale industrial production based on the assembly line of largely standardized products from cars to house appliances. The term Fordism was coined by Antonio Gramsci in an essay 'Americanism and Fordism' in his *Prison Notebooks*, written between 1929 and 1935. Gramsci (2011) inspired a generation of critical scholarship on capitalism in the post-Second World War period with this notion and with his concept of cultural hegemony as the basis of capitalist domination. Critical sociologists, such as C. W. Mills and the more Marxist-oriented Frankfurt School (see Chapter 7) drew attention to new sources of power, such as an incipient technocracy that came with the instrumentalization of science and technology, as in Taylorism (see Braverman 1974). Fordism was enabled by the application of scientific management, which made possible labour discipline and the organization of the workplace giving a new meaning to Marx's notion of alienated labour. As Habermas wrote in a much-discussed essay in 1968, science and technology had become ideologies of capitalism (Habermas 1970). Organized capitalism was thus the culmination of what Weber had described as a process of instrumental rationalization incorporating technical and scientific rationality. Other critical Marxist-inspired works, such as James Burham's theory of the managerial revolution, as in his 1941 book, emphasized the rise of a new managerial elite, a theme also in the sociology of C.W. Mills, *The Power Elite* [1956] (Mills 2000), Paul Sweezy's *Theory of Capitalist Development* (Sweezy 1942) and, from a different but equally critical perspective, John Kenneth Galbraith's *New Industrial State,* based on his Reith lectures in 1966 (Galbraith 1972).

We conclude this brief sketch of organized capitalism with a discussion of the notion of democratic capitalism, which in the present day is widely seen to be in crisis. In western societies, the post-1945 period saw a general expansion of mass party electoral politics, generally organized on centre-left and centre-right lines. In this period, social democracy became entrenched along with the consolidation of health systems and mass vaccination programmes that saw the elimination of infectious diseases leading to greater longevity. To characterize these developments as a false inclusion or monolithic instrumental rationality is too one-sided. A fairer and more democratic society emerged. Capitalism was domesticated by democracy and regulated by the state. The price that had to be paid was that democracy had to be limited to the institutionalized channels of parliamentary democracy and mass-party politics. It was a democracy administered by a technocratic elite.

Democratic capitalism, despite its limitations, reset the balance between inequality in the class structure and the need for political equality. It led to relative political stability, at least until 1968. The corporatism of the period further diffused potential unrest through, for example, national wage bargaining and social insurance. The model of industrial capitalism based on growth and consumption in domestic markets as well as on full employment created the conditions for what can also be called social capitalism. The latter is more relevant to the historical experience of western Europe – in particular the German and Scandinavian varieties of capitalism – than North America, due to the stronger tradition of worker rights and trade unionism. According to Claus Offe (2003), the basis of social capitalism is the predominance of state-defined and state-protected status categories which are defined by rights and obligations that set limits to contractual economic transactions. For Offe, this means that capitalism, in the terms of Polanyi, was embedded in social norms, which limits to the expansion of markets and to exploitation.

The marriage of capitalism and democracy was precarious; it was not a lasting alliance and was destined to break up when either side changed course. It presupposed a docile model of democracy and a constrained form of capitalism. As Wolfgang Streeck (2014) has shown, the era of democratic capitalism came to an end in the aftermath of the 2008–10 crisis (see Chapter 11). It also rested on the material foundations of coal and steel production, which in time were replaced by oil and nuclear power and later by gas (see Mitchell 2011). These foundations provided relative stability for both capitalism and democracy, for coal and oil were in abundance and unquestioned in the decades following the end of the war.

Saving Capitalism: Social Liberalism

Social liberalism was a significant movement in social and political thought in the first half of the twentieth century. It was especially influential in Britain and in France. As noted in the previous chapter, it was dominant in Britain at the time Hayek initiated the neoliberal movement, which was an attack both on socialism in all its forms and on social liberalism (see Freeden 1986). Social liberalism was also more than an outcome of nineteenth-century liberalism; it was the social and political philosophy that lay behind the Keynesian revolution. It has been overshadowed by socialism and by social democracy, with which it is closely associated. However, it had a different background and trajectory. Social liberals saw capitalism, which they wanted to reform but not abolish, to serve the needs of the individual. In its endeavour to overcome the ill-effects of capitalism, social liberalism sought a reconstruction of economy and state that was gradualist rather than revolutionary. Social liberalism differs from socialism in not being primarily concerned with the problem of inequality. Social democracy, in contrast, was more addressed to social equality. A famous example is Anthony Crosland's book, *The Future of Socialism* [1965]. Crosland (2006) sought to revise the goals of the British Labour Party away from socialist ones, as in policies of nationalization, to a focus on social equality. He held that capitalism had changed and that it is now possible to realize social equality within the structures of capitalism. Perhaps not in theory but in practice, his managerial socialism was not far removed from the politics of social liberalism.

For social liberals in the first half of the twentieth century, capitalism needs to be placed under political control in order to solve the major problems of the day, poverty and unemployment. While advocating the advancement of democracy, social liberalism was an elite-led movement. It tended towards technocracy and fitted well into the emerging mould of organized capitalism after 1945.

Early figures in the tradition were Leonard Hobhouse, who reformulated the liberal legacy of J. S. Mill in *Liberalism* [1911] and, in France, Émile Durkheim. Durkheim's sociology was rooted in his theory of moral individualism. He held that modernity was in need of new kinds of solidarity to replace the old forms. Neither socialism nor liberalism offered the present what it was in need of: liberalism was too rooted in the individual and the collectivist goals of socialism would not cultivate sufficient resources for the individual. His moral individualism incorporated elements of both and also placed a strong emphasis on social cooperation among business, professional groups and the state. The cultivation of a civic culture based on solidarity and cooperation also required the advancement of education. However, Durkheim did not have a theory of capitalism as such, though his work is relevant to the critique of political economy (Steiner 2011). His concern was with the division of labour in the emergence of modernity.

In the USA, the movement known as pragmatism, as represented by John Dewey and William James, reflected the basic concerns of social liberalism as well as democratic socialism. In the influential writings of Dewey, modern society needed moral leadership and the cultivation of education in order to compensate for the ills of capitalism. Dewey, like Durkheim, had a social conception of the individual. Pragmatists accepted the application of socialist methods but with the aspiration to realize individualism. Roosevelt's New Deal reflected the spirit of social liberalism rather than socialism in that it did not derive from labour agitation but from government in conjunction with employers.

In Britain, two important figures in the tradition of social liberalism were William Beveridge and T. H. Marshall. The former, as discussed in the previous chapter, wrote the report, *Social Insurance and Allied Services* in 1942, which led to the post-war welfare state and the National Health Service. He also wrote *Full Employment in a Free Society* in 1944, which made an influential case for full employment as a goal of government (Beveridge 1944). In this view, which he shared with J. M. Keynes, full employment is necessary for the good of society for human flourishing, but it cannot be created by the economy alone. Beveridge stood in a long tradition of reformist thought that stood for social progress. His ideas reflected the orientation towards state control over society that came with organized modernity. He was, for instance, involved in the eugenics movement, which is also an illustration of the leanings towards technocracy and its broader limitations.

T. H. Marshall is best known for his 1949 essay, *Citizenship and Social Class* (Marshall 1950). His characterization of the emergence of social rights that followed from the earlier civic and political rights has been much discussed. In his outline of a trajectory of social progress modelled on British political history, the inequality that capitalism inevitably produces is alleviated by social rights which represent the progressive culmination of the rights of citizenship. This theory, which encapsulates social liberalism, but is also compatible with market socialism (i.e. a version of socialism that accepts the need for markets but not all aspects of capitalism) and social democracy (which is more forgiving of capitalism, as reflected in Crosland's book), basically accepted capitalism. The task of government is to alleviate social discontents and champion social reform. As in most of these accounts, there is a strong emphasis on the role of government led by intellectual and political elites. Marshall was blind to the facts of history, for example E. P. Thompson's argument in his *The Making of the English Working Class* that rights were not gifts of the state bestowed by a benevolent elite on pacified masses but won through social struggles (Thompson 1991 [1963]).

Social liberalism as a coherent political and social philosophy lost its direction since the 1960s. It can be related to the political theory of John Rawls who in *A Theory of Justice* in 1971 stood for a more egalitarian model of capitalism, but with the rise of the New Left, on the one side, and on the other neoliberalism, the critique of capitalism based on belief in central government lost its animus. In any case, Rawls's normative political philosophy did not engage with capitalism as reality. In the following, we consider one of its major champions, J.M. Keynes, whose legacy went beyond social liberalism to define an era.

John Maynard Keynes

To say J. M. Keynes is a figure of considerable significance is an understatement. He was undoubtedly the most influential economist of the previous century. Keynesianism shaped the post-1945 world in far-reaching ways. Since his first major publication, *The Economic Consequences of the Peace*, he became famous for his criticism of the economic conditions imposed on Germany after 1918. He was himself an advisor at the Paris 1919 conference that led to the Versailles Treaty. His position was a pragmatic one claiming that the war debts imposed on Germany would be an economic disaster for Europe because they undermined the German economic recovery, which was essential for the rest of Europe. On this, he was proven to be mostly correct, though it is debated whether it was the economic or the political blow to German national esteem that in the end was the greater. He disagreed with the view held for example by Polanyi that capitalism caused the Second World War. The drift to war in his view was due to avoidable measures and lack of foresight on the economic consequences. Keynes may have been too dismissive of long-term societal trends, but he proved to be remarkably prescient in his assessment of the terms of peace negotiated in 1919 and the need for governments to have greater control over their economies. In this respect, he recognized the importance even for protectionist economies, which were more or less the norm at this time, for international economic collaboration. Throughout his career, he was intensively involved in international economic and political affairs. In 1944, he represented the British Government in the creation of the Bretton Woods system, which formed the financial bedrock of organized capitalism after 1945. This aspect of Keynes's thought can be understood in the terms of John Ruggie's much-discussed essay on 'embedded liberalism' in international politics (Ruggie 1982).

Keynes's writings are relevant beyond the specialist field of macroeconomics, which he effectively founded in works such as the early *A Treatise on Money* [1921], *A Treatise on Probability* [1921] and *The Means to Prosperity* [1933].[2] His writings demonstrate the importance of a holistic view of the economy in relation to state and society. He showed how fiscal policy, including monetarism, must be located in the context of the economy as a whole. Since Smith and Marx, the economy has been seen as always more than the formal structures of the market and system of production. This too was a common trend in the different approaches of Weber, Schumpeter, Polanyi, as we have seen in the previous chapters. Hayek tried to sever that connection. Keynes provided an enduring counter-argument to the neoliberal argument for a disembedded economy. However, his target was not neoliberalism, which hardly existed in 1936 but neoclassical economics and its precursor, the so-called Classical Economists, i.e. the economic theory of early nineteenth-century theorists such as David Ricardo and Jean-Baptiste Say, of whom Marx, for different reasons, was also a critic. As he stated in the short opening chapter of his *magnum opus*, *The General Theory of Employment, Interest and Money*, the word 'general theory' in the title was to draw a contrast to 'classical theory': 'the postulates of the classical theory are applicable to a special case only and not to the general case' (p. 9). *The General Theory of Employment, Interest and Money* in 1936[3] was his major work and supplanted some of his earlier theories. It was an immediate success and changed in a very short time government economic policy in Britain and was taken up in many western countries. By the time of Keynes's untimely death in 1946, Keynesianism was the new orthodoxy. Central planning was of course already in place, but Keynes gave it a new rationale.

The 'Golden Age' of post-1945 capitalism was the era of Keynesianism. He provided the basic economic rationale that allowed 'organized capitalism' to make the leap from the immediate war context to a long period of sustained growth. Keynesianism is often taken as a byword for state intervention and state borrowing, but it is more than this. One of his key ideas was that the economy cannot be left to its own devices to produce general desirable social outcomes. The government must intervene to produce such ends as full employment and growth. These were the two most important goals of government to pursue. He disagreed with the old principles of neoclassical economics that the free market can bring about full employment and growth and also that it can prevent depressions. The book, written in the aftermath of the Great Depression, was a response to the crisis and the recognition that capitalism is inherently crisis prone but such major crises are avoidable. The government needs to kick-start the economy to get out of a recession or depression. The capitalist economy is inherently unstable and prone to downturns in business investment, which in turn generates a fall in consumption and as a result employment ensues. In effect, this meant that for the economy to remain stable and for growth to occur, something must ensure that consumption, i.e. demand remains buoyant. 'Consumption', he wrote, 'is the sole end and object of all economic activity' (p. 70). This pithy statement captured a truth that has escaped many economists, but of course it was a paraphrase of Adam Smith, who wrote in *The Wealth of Nations*: 'consumption' is the sole end and object of all production (Book 4, Chapter 8). In other words, supply does not automatically generate demand. For Keynes, it was the role of government to ensure that the conditions of demand were met by creating conditions favourable for private investment. He disagreed that supply generates demand. With this insight, Keynes changed the basic rationale of neoclassical economics. In order for demand to generate supply, the state must intervene. There is no natural tendency for the economy to produce an equilibrium between demand and supply. Once the state intervenes, the economy managed by the state will produce the necessary results, as in, for example, the Employment Multiplier effect, whereby for every job created another indirectly results. In this way, private enterprise also benefits, as in the example of government funding to build a road, other jobs supplied by private enterprise are created by supplying the materials.

Some qualifications are in order. Keynes was not setting out to reject neoclassical economics, but to correct it. The central role he gave to the state to intervene in the economy was, as the term suggests, to intervene when it is necessary for it to do so. He was aware that the special conditions of the war, which made possible full employment, would not last and that it would also not be desirable to have entirely state-managed economies. Private enterprise is the basis of the economy and the state should intervene – for example by measures for stimulating investment such as reducing interest rates – only when private investment is in short supply. So, state-funded employment will not alone provide the conditions for economic growth, which needs a thriving private section.

Keynes' economic theory was based on the fundamental insight that a fair and successful society needs to generate wealth. Wealth requires investment, which leads to employment ensuring the increase in demand for goods. It followed from this that saving is to the detriment of wealth creation. Keynes argued for the priority of spending, whether by private households or by government. 'Expenditure creates its income' was his motto and not that 'supply creates its own demand'. In this, he repudiated Jean-Baptiste Say's law that held the reverse. He was opposed to excessive savings, which he referred to as 'hoarding', for it led to poverty. These ideas were also reflected in this theory of money, which he saw not just as a medium of exchange but also as an indicator of wealth. In the huge shift from Marx's economics to Keynes's economics, capital is replaced by wealth creation. The modern economy is an engine for the creation and expansion of wealth. This he does not see as there primarily for private appropriation. A properly functioning economy is one based on private enterprise providing the basic drivers for growth and wealth creation.

The Keynesian revolution in macro-economic theory gave a new role to planning. Behind this concern with planning was also a philosophical idea that human societies need to cope with uncertainty, the reality of which he agreed with Hayek but not that it could not be managed. It is the task of government guided by an intellectual elite in possession of technical expertise to provide certainty in the sense of the reduction of risk. Without the right guidance, people seek certainty in the wrong things such as money, and its absence is detrimental to investment.

Neither monetarism, the policy of neoliberalism, nor fiscal policy (which includes monetary policy along with other instruments), the existing orthodoxy, would solve the systemic problems of capitalism. The state does not itself normally provide employment – except in non-normal times, such as war – but may need to supplement what is provided by private business. This gave a rationale for nationalization projects whereby the state provided major public goods, such as national transport (bus, rail and air), telecommunications, education and health, as well as other public works. Such a major role for the state in the economy reduces the capitalistic nature of the economy, since such ventures are not run as private profit-making. However, Keynesianism, as noted above, is not a vision of post-capitalism but of the mixed economy in which the private sector is the engine of growth.

A full view would have to conclude that Keynes was seeking to save capitalism from its destructive tendencies. The mixed economy that developed from 1945 in the western world where Keynesian economics was influential was still a capitalist one. After all, when the state borrows, it does so to stimulate investment not to create demand (Hayes 2020: 177). In other words, capitalism must be made to work. The price capitalism had to pay for its survival was to coexist with nationalization and central state management. Keynes demonstrated that the free market was not self-correcting and required state direction. In this respect, he was taking up Weber's notion of societal rationalization as the logic of capitalism and what allows it to overcome its inevitable problems.

There is a further question as to Keynes' ultimate political aims. James Crotty has presented a strong argument that questions the Marxist contention that Keynes was trying to save capitalism, even if that is what the end result was. Crotty (2019) makes the case for Keynes as a liberal socialist and there is much to support this view in that Keynes' policies came very close to socialism. However, this argument ultimately fails. He may have caused a revolution in economics, but it was to prevent a political revolution. Dunn (2021) makes the opposite case in a comparison between Keynes and Marx. Keynes was not a Marxist, even if he was born the year Marx died. Some of the methods Keynes advocated may resemble those of socialism – for example in giving the state a strong role to play in the organization and ownership of parts of the economy – but it does not follow that the ends that these methods served are socialist. The pursuit of full employment is not in itself a socialist goal; it was the aim of most western countries since the 1940s until it was abandoned in the 1970s. Keynes's ultimate political aims and predilections were those of an Edwardian social liberal. He had considerable sympathies for moderate socialism – as opposed to the version adopted by the USSR – but his cultural and political orientations went in a different direction and drew from other sources. He was a member of the Liberal Party, an important establishment figure in the British ruling elite and held to a political position similar to that of figures like William Beveridge. He was uncritical of imperialism and took for granted British world leadership. He had no inclinations towards collectivism, other than what was expedient in terms of the management of the economy. He stood for a technocratic capitalism run by experts within the structures of liberal democracy as opposed to an unrestrained individualism (see Freeden 1986). In that sense, he was a representative of a restricted democratic capitalism tempered by macro-economic planning. His concerns were more or less entirely short term as opposed to the long-term transformation of society. It is of course equally plausible to see him, as Robert Skidelsky does, as a proponent of social democracy, which flourished after his death in western Europe. But this political tradition is entirely compatible with technocratic management. His ideas provided a sound economic basis for social democracy, even if the political conditions had a different history. Yet, it is difficult to reconcile Keynes' obvious patrician elitism with the democratic currents that were forming in western societies in the period after his death when the older gulf of the masses and elites gave way to new formations.

There is little doubt that Keynes' attitude to capitalism was more typical of social liberalism. He certainly wanted greater egalitarianism and accepted the need for moderate redistribution, but he did not make a strong case for the welfare state as such. Poverty was to him a more serious problem as was its cause, unemployment, than equality. His aversion to huge income divides and the figure of the rentier was as much driven by what he thought was healthy for capitalism than about fairness. However, the dominant challenge in his eyes for his time was wealth creation. Socialists of all persuasions in his view had no real solution to the problem of how societies could achieve social progress. Only capitalism, which cultivates liberalism and freedom, could do this in his view if it were managed correctly. It is also clear that his main criticism of capitalism was in failures in planning. This is not to say that other more pessimistic currents about modern society were present in this work (Mann 2019).

Keynes was a champion of planning, but that does not make him a socialist. In the final summing-up chapter of the *General Theory*, he offers his assessment of the ills and advantages of capitalism, a term that he avoids in general but uses when alluding to the decadent aspects of capitalism, for example 'the rentier aspect of capitalism', which he deplores and he advocates lower interest rates to wipe it out. The main ill is unemployment. 'The outstanding fault of the economic society in which we live are its failure to provide for full employment and its arbitrary distribution of wealth and income' (p. 233). He argues for the conditions to be created for investment and the stimulation 'of the propensity to consume'. But the pursuit of full employment should be the major goal of government policy. For this reason, there is 'no obvious case made out for a system of State Socialism'. He comes close to market socialism in an argument that could have been written by Schumpeter in stating: 'the necessary measures of socialisation can be introduced gradually and without a break in the general traditions of society' (p. 236). But it is clear that is not market socialism. He qualifies his position with the claim: 'apart from the necessity of central controls to bring about an adjustment between the propensity to consume and the inducement to invest, there is no more reason to socialize economic life than there was before' (p. 237).

A distinction needs also to be made between Keynes and Keynesianism. Marx is reputed to have said he was not a Marxist. Keynes once said to a group of US economists that he was not Keynesian (Hayes 2020: 156). The point illustrates that Keynesianism, and neo-Keynesianism, came to mean many things that generally referred to the role of the state in the management of the economy. But, as Hayes (2020) has pointed out, Keynes' own economic views were much more in line with monetarist policies – controlling the supply of money, as in reducing interest rates to stimulate private investment – and he was generally not in favour of budget deficits.

There is nothing in the work of Keynes to reject *homo economicus*. He stood for a benign capitalism that was under the firm management of technocrats. He displayed a strong belief in the power of ideas with a view that effectively turned Marx on his head. The last lines of the *General Theory* are justly famous:

> the ideas of economists and political philosophers, both when they are right and when they wrong, are more powerful than is commonly understood. Indeed, the world is ruled by little else. Practical men, who believe themselves to be quite exempt from any intellectual influences, are usually the slaves of some defunct economist. Madmen in authority, who hear voices in the air, are distilling their frenzy from some academic scribbler of a few years back. I am sure that the power of vested interests is vastly exaggerated compared with gradual encroachment of ideas...But, soon, or late, it is ideas, not vested interests, which are dangerous for good or evil.
>
> (p. 239)

Disorganized Capitalism and End of the 'Golden Age'

Keynesianism, as adopted by western governments, in the three decades or so after 1945 took a variety of forms and has never lost its relevance, since in many ways his ideas were normalized. But it was nonetheless challenged by neoliberalism since the 1980s, when it failed to solve the problems in many western economies which arose as early as the late 1960s, when inflation and unemployment began to rise. In the USA, the high costs of the Vietnam War had a detrimental economic effect. After the financial crisis of 2008–10, there has been a new interest in Keynes, as reflected in neo-Keynesianism. But it is clear that the revival of Keynes is more of a revival and transformation of Keynesianism than Keynes's own theories. Keynes's own ideas were in many ways a product of his time. His main concern with employment is less relevant today and has also been given less emphasis by neo-Keynesian economists. Moreover, Keynes own ideas about employment are not without problems in that he held to a somewhat instrumental view of employment as a device to maximize spending to ensure economic growth through further investment. He saw no difference between work and employment, such that it was not important what kind of work people did (and it was mostly male industrial labour) so long as it was a form of employment. He did think that people could and should work less, as in a shorter working week, but this was because he saw work as purely instrumental and not intrinsically meaningful. In any case, in the present day, employment is structural and not easily solved by stimulating demand. Technological advancement has also fundamentally changed the nature of work and thus of employment.

Keynes's work was shaped by the great crisis of capitalism in the 1930s. As capitalism today enters a new stage after the failure of the neoliberal experiment and the subsequent crisis of 2008–10, it is not at all evident that Keynes' optimism in the power of government to intervene in the way his policies recommended. The basic axiom that governments should borrow during an economic downturn and payback in times of boom suffered from the obvious defect that there would be a boom time in which to pay back. It is plain today that the great boom of the post-1945 period has gone and will not return. Keynes had great faith in economic growth, but the general trend today is, if not stagnation, limited growth as well as a new questioning of growth with demands for de-growth.

The era of organized capitalism was in part not only the context but also the outcome of the economic and political thought of J. M. Keynes and other social liberals and social democrats. That era came to an end in the course of the 1970s. The social democratic left still looks back with nostalgia to the golden age of post-war capitalism but its political model is less relevant since the social and economic presuppositions no longer exist. The transition to the new times has been characterized by Claus Offe as a new era of 'disorganized capitalism' when the capitalistic democracies entered into a period of chaos and instability as a result of the failure of central planning to solve the problems of the economy (Offe 1985). Keynesianism did not in the end find a solution to the problems of capitalism, such as the so-called fiscal crisis of the state (O' Connor 2017 [1973]) and, what Habermas referred to as a legitimation crisis (Habermas 1975 [1973]). Organized capitalism and Keynesian economics were of an era that was more governable than the one that preceded it and the one that was to come about in the 1970s. In its modified form as neo-Keynesianism, some of the older ideas are relevant but they do not offer a political conception of an alternative nor a normative theory of society.

The 'Golden Age' of capitalism was golden for those who enjoyed it, but many did not. It was confined to the privileged societies of the west. It was premised on a high degree of social inclusion, which meant a high level of exclusion. Demands for greater inclusion could not be accommodated within that model, not least as the conditions of its possibility were in question by the early 1970s.

The political responses that ensued after the two great capitalist crises of late capitalism – the early 1970s and 2008–10 – were not cast in the terms of social liberalism, which seemed to have run its course having lost momentum in the mire of technocracy and the growing importance of globalization in politics and economy. Neoliberalism gained supremacy for a time having redefined the liberal heritage, while progressive politics drew on other ideas that came with the New Left.

Notes

1 See Mark Bevir's (2011) history of British socialism and Michael Freeden's account of the early history of British liberalism and Alan Ryan's (2012) study of modern liberalism.

2 The literature on Keynes' economic writings is vast. For an overview, see Hayes (2020), Skidelsky (2010) and Steward (1991). The definitive biography is Skidelsky's abridged version of three volumes (Skidelsky's 2010).

3 First published in 1936 by Palgrave Macmillan. In this chapter, citations are to a 2008 edition published by BN Publishing.

References

Aglietta, M. 1979. *A Theory of Capitalist Regulation: The US Experience*. London: New Left Books.

Albert, M. 1991. *Capitalism against Capitalism*. London: Whurr Publishers.

Anderson, J. 2018. *The Future of the World: Futurology, Futurists, and the Struggle for the Post-Cold War Imagination*. Oxford: Oxford University Press.

Barkin, H. 1975. 'Organized Capitalism'. *The Journal of Modern History*, 47 (1): 125–9.

Bell, D. 1974. *The Coming of Post-Industrial Society: A Venture in Social Forecasting*. New York: Harper Colophon Books.

Bell, D. 2000 [1960]. *The End of Ideology: On the Exhaustion of Political Ideas in the Fifties*. Cambridge: Harvard University Press.

Beveridge, W. 1944. *Full Employment in a Free Society*. London: Allen & Unwin.

Bevir, M. 2011. *The Making of British Socialism*. Princeton: Princeton University Press.

Braverman, M. 1974. *Labour and Monopoly Capitalism: The Degradation of Work in the Twentieth Century*. New York: Monthly Review.

Burnham, J. 1945 [1941]. *The Managerial Revolution*. London: Penguin.
Crosland, A. 2006 [1967]. *The Future of Socialism*. 50th Anniversary edition. London: Constable.
Crotty, J. 2019. *Keynes against Capitalism: His Economic Case for Liberal Socialism*. London: Routledge.
Dunn, B. 2021. *Keynes and Marx*. Manchester: Manchester University Press.
Freeden, M. 1986. *Liberalism Divided: A Study in Liberal Thought 1914–1939*. Oxford: Oxford University Press.
Galbraith, J.K. 1972. *The New Industrial State*. London: Penguin.
Goldthrope, J., Lockwood, D., Bechhofer, F., and Platt, J. 1969. *The Affluent Worker in the Class Structure*. Cambridge: Cambridge University Press.
Gramsci, A. 2011. *Prison Notebooks*. New York: Columbia University Press.
Habermas, J. 1970 [1968]. 'Science and Technology as "Ideology"' In: *Towards a Rational Society*. London: Heinemann.
Habermas, J. 1975 [1973]. *Legitimation Crisis*. Boston: Beacon Press.
Hayes, M. 2020. *John Maynard Keynes: The Art of Choosing the Right Model*. Cambridge: Policy Press.
Keynes, J. M. 2008 [1936]. *The General Theory of Employment Money and Interest*. BN Publishing.
Lockwood, D. 1958. *The Blackcoated Worker: A Study in Class Consciousness*. London: Allen & Unwin.
Mann, G. 2019. *In the Long Run We Are All Dead: Keynesianism, Political Economy and Revolution*. London: Verso.
Marcuse, H. 1964. *One-Dimensional Man: Studies in the Ideology of Advanced Industrial Society*. London: Routledge & Kegan Paul.
Marglin, S. and Schor, J. (eds.) 1992. *The Golden Age of Capitalism: Reinterpreting the Post-War Era*. Oxford: Oxford University Press.
Marshall, T. H. 1950 [1949]. *Citizenship and Social Class and Other Essays*. Cambridge: Cambridge University Press.
Marshall, T. H. 1987 [1950]. *Citizenship and Social Class*. London: Pluto Press.
Mills, C.W. 2000 [1956]. *The Power Elite*. Oxford: Oxford University Press.
Mitchell, T. 2011. *Carbon Democracy: Political Power in the Age of Oil*. London: Verso.
O'Conner, J. 2017 [1973]. *The Fiscal Crisis of the State*. London: Routledge.
Offe, C. 1985. *Disorganized Capitalism: Contemporary Transformations in Work and Politics*. Cambridge: Polity Press.
Offe, C. 2003. 'Can the European Model of "Social Capitalism" Survive European Integration?' *The Journal of Political Philosophy*, 11 (4): 437–69.
Ruggie, J. 1982. 'International Regimes, Transactions and Change: Embedded Liberalism in the Postwar Economic Order'. *International Organization*, 36 (2): 379–415.
Ryan, A. 2012. *The Making of Modern Liberalism*. Princeton: Princeton University Press.
Schmitter, P. and Lehmbruch, G. (eds.) 1979. *Trends Towards Corporatist Intermediation*. London: Sage.
Skidelsky, R. 2010. *Keynes: A Very Short Introduction*. Oxford: Oxford University Press.
Skidelsky, R. 2013. *John Maynard Keynes*. London: Penguin.
Steiner, P. 2011. *Durkheim and the Birth of Economic Sociology*. Princeton: Princeton University Press.
Stewart, M. 1991. *Keynes and After*. London: Penguin.
Streeck, W. 2014. *Buying Time: The Delayed Crisis of Democratic Capitalism*. London: Verso.
Sweezy, P. 1942. *The Theory of Capitalist Development*. Oxford: Oxford University Press.
Thompson, E. P. 1982. *Exterminism and the Cold War*. London: Verso.
Thompson, E. P. 1991 [1963]. *The Making of the English Working Class*. London: Penguin.
Wagner, P. 1994. *A Sociology of Modernity: Liberty and Discipline*. London: Routledge.
Westergaard, J. and Resler, H., 1975. *Class in a Capitalist Society: A Study of Contemporary Britain*. London: Heinemann.

7 The Frankfurt School

Capitalism, Reason, Desire

The 'Frankfurt School' was founded as the Institute for Social Research in 1923, initially affiliated with, but autonomous from, the Goethe University of Frankfurt. The history of the research institute, and its associated scholars, is a remarkable tale of persecution and resilience, of theoretical innovation and personal tragedy (see Jay 1973; Wiggershaus 1986; Jeffries 2016). The term 'critical theory' developed over time as a politically expedient proxy for the Institute's interdisciplinary Marxist studies. Originally the Frankfurt School was overwhelmingly comprised of orthodox Marxist economists; however, this was to change markedly with the appointment of Max Horkheimer as director of the Institute in 1930. Horkheimer initiated an innovative interdisciplinary research programme, fusing insights from psychoanalysis, sociology, political economy, aesthetics and Hegelian philosophy. This enabled the development of a remarkable conceptual arsenal, producing a new and original understanding of capitalism as a social totality. The key thinkers associated with this methodologically distinctive 'first generation' of Frankfurt School research are Theodor W. Adorno, Herbert Marcuse, Erich Fromm, Walter Benjamin and Horkheimer himself. Over time, the research focus of the Institute shifted, with a 'second generation' of scholars orbiting Jürgen Habermas, and a 'third generation' inspired by the work of Axel Honneth.[1] In this chapter, we focus on the 'first generation' of the Frankfurt School's analysis of capitalism, critically engaging with the work of its principal exponents.

While many of the theorists we discuss across the chapters of this book were politically active, the Frankfurt School were uniquely explicit in the relationship they saw existing between their theoretical contribution and (anti-capitalist) political praxis. As Max Horkheimer stated in his inaugural lecture to the Institute upon being appointed director, critical theory must make no false pretensions to 'objectivity' or 'neutrality' in its analysis of capitalist society. Rather, as all forms of labour, *including research*, sit within the broader system of production, the pursuit of scholarly 'objectivity' was futile. Instead, what was required was a critical reflexivity, and a self-awareness of their 'critical' transformative aspirations (see Horkheimer 2002). By the very process of exploring the 'pathologies' of the capitalist system,[2] Horkheimer (2018) argued, the forces which stabilized the exploitative and irrational social constellation could slowly be disclosed and neutralized. The Frankfurt School's expanding understanding of capitalism was presented as fusing theory and praxis; their theoretical analysis of the capitalist formation was presented as part of a self-conscious process of bringing about capitalism's downfall.

This concern with socialist transition animated first-generation Frankfurt School research. Karl Marx had written extensively of the contradictions of capitalism, describing with great foresight its volatility and its inherent propensity for worsening crises. While so many of Marx's predictions had been shown to be accurate, the central, teleological claim

DOI: 10.4324/9781351017671-8

of his meta-theory remained unfounded: capitalism, which was supposed to imminently collapse on the basis of its own contradictions, remained and appeared stronger than ever. Indeed, the Weimar Republic of the Frankfurt School's origin was a hotbed of nationalistic, regressive sentiments; communism did not appear to be on the horizon. As the horrors of fascism were displaced by advanced technical societies both sides of the Iron Curtain in the 1950s and 1960s, Frankfurt School scholars had an ever clearer research question guiding their programme: why had the socialist revolution failed to materialize? And reframed in more sociological terms: how were the structural contradictions of capitalism being stabilized in a manner that prevented their sublation?

To pursue these questions, Frankfurt School scholars drew far beyond the traditional Marxian corpus. Unlike Soviet Marxist economists, Frankfurt School researchers united insights from Max Weber and Sigmund Freud to embellish their analyses. More immediately, Adorno, Horkheimer and Marcuse were indebted to the work of György Lukács, a Hungarian Marxist, whose analysis of reification in *History and Class Consciousness* [1923] proved foundational for their later research. For Lukács (1972: 6), capitalism has led to the 'reification of all human relations', circumscribing the possibility for critical thought and inducing a form of technical and instrumental rationality. By combining the insights of Weber, Freud, Marx and Lukács, first-generation Frankfurt School theorists sought to understand capitalism as far more than a mere economic model. Rather, they presented a theory of capitalism as a totality, as an all-encompassing social system, which impacted on subjects' capacity for critical reason, shaped their deepest desires and created the necessary conditions for its own survival. In response to the question 'what did Marx fail to see?', critical theorists produced an answer: the possibility for capitalism to radically change how subjects think and what they desire in a manner conductive to capitalism's survival. In particular, Adorno and Horkheimer's engagement with this theme produced a wealth of stimulating, but darkly pessimistic, responses, which are often presented as indicative of first-generation scholarship more broadly.

Adorno and Horkheimer: Reification, Instrumental Rationality, the Culture Industry

While Marx, like Smith, saw his work as an extension of the Enlightenment project, Adorno and Horkheimer presented a deeply negative engagement with the development of rationality. Central to their work on capitalism was the idea that the market order furthered a destructive tendency within modernity. Rather than witnessing an inevitable teleological development towards a more 'Enlightened' and rational society, Adorno and Horkheimer charted the rise of barbarism and the ascendancy of a *rational irrationality*. Reason itself was held to have gone awry, with an instrumental form of thought displacing humanist critical inquiry. This posed a fundamental methodological problem for their research: how do you rationally present the argument that reason itself has been corrupted? For Adorno and Horkheimer, thought itself was victim to the deracinating effects of the capitalist system. How can you rationally explain to someone that their capacity for thought has been impeded? In this regard, Adorno and Horkheimer's critique of capitalism, in particular within their remarkable *Dialectic of Enlightenment* (1997 [1944]), is methodologically unorthodox, relying extensively on a 'disclosing' form of social criticism (Honneth 2000). The contradictions of capitalism, and the impeded forms of thought it induces, were presented through an aesthetic bricolage, through allegory, allusion and exaggeration, as much as through abstract Left-Hegelian philosophy (see

Van den Brink 1997). Works such as *Dialectic of Enlightenment* and *Minima Moralia* (1978 [1951]) are thus remarkable both for their synoptic, totalizing argument but are also striking in their unorthodox methodology.[3] As Felsch (2022: 16) wrote, *Minima Moralia* especially was more than theory, it 'catered for the poetic demand of the post-war period'.

For Adorno and Horkheimer, capitalism was characterized by the ascendancy of instrumental rationality and reified consciousness. While the co-authors saw these tendencies as present within all societies dating back to antiquity, the forms of equivalence which capitalism structurally encourages were held to enable instrumental rationality to run amok. The various forms of modern capitalism granted instrumental reason the conditions needed to colonize all thought processes. Reification and instrumental reason were held to have reached their apotheosis within the state capitalism of both fascistic and formally 'communistic' societies, and within more classical 'free market' societies. A totalizing, 'instrumental-efficiently' ordered society was held to have developed in equal measure in Soviet Russia and Nazi Germany, in the studios of Hollywood as much as in gas chambers of Auschwitz. Capitalist modernity, in its various iterations, saw that 'progress and barbarism' were systematically 'matted together' (Adorno 1978: 50). Central to Adorno and Horkheimer's critique of capitalism is the relationship they hold to exist between the totalizing nature of capitalist modernity and impeded cognitive capacity; the irrational rationality of capitalism had manifold social manifestations.

Reification is often presented as being the 'master-concept' of Frankfurt School Critical Theory and it certainly captures the research programme's fusion of Marxian, Hegelian and Weberian concepts. In *Negative Dialectics*, Adorno (1981 [1966]: 189–92) stressed that reification is an 'epiphenomenal' result of capitalist modernity; it is a result of socio-economic conditions, rather than a problem that can be ascribed to epistemology. Ironically, while the analysis of the impact of reification is heralded as being a key insight of critical theory, the primary Hegelian-Marxist work on reification was written by György Lukács, who was never actually part of the Institute for Social Research. His central analysis of reification, *History and Class Consciousness* [1923] was written decades before *Dialectic of Enlightenment* or *Minima Moralia*. It is important to stress how much Lukács' work influenced the Frankfurt School's critique of capitalism. It is better to understand Adorno and Horkheimer to be extending Lukács' insights and as bringing them into dialogue with a broader set of ideas. Crucially, also, Adorno and Horkheimer utilized Lukács' insights to perform an extended interdisciplinary-sociological analysis, something which Lukács had not pursued, his own work being more philosophical in nature (see Lukács 1962, 1972). For Lukács, reification derives from 'the fetish character of commodities' and is understood as being 'the subjective stance corresponding to it' (1972: 84). Lukács detailed how capitalism produces a 'phantom objectivity'. Capitalist economies lead to the general acceptance of 'false equivalences' between commodities, as 'exchange values' dominate over 'use values' (1972: 6). Put another way, the capitalist form of life induces a particular form of consciousness: reified consciousness, which is explicitly connected to market imperatives.

But what exactly is reification? Numerous conflicting definitions abound (see Honneth 2012; Dahms 1998; Feenberg 2013). Literally 'thingification', from the Latin 'res' for 'thing', reification traditionally refers to the processes by which modern subjects reduce the totality of their external world to discrete, static, objects, possessing calculable, quantifiable and exchangeable value. This necessarily leads to the loss of the subject's concern for all qualities, purposes and ontological differences. The reductive form of consciousness which reification induces serves to diminish the entire social world, reducing all social being and all social action to a 'thing-like' status, to easily exchangeable products. To the reified mind, human labour exists on the same plane as lifeless tangible commodities, such as the coats or wool. This can be seen as a direct return to, and extension of, Marx's analysis of the commodity in the very first chapter of Book One of *Capital*, where his analysis begins by citing 'old Barbon',[4] who stated that 'one sort of wares are as good as another' (Marx 1976: 127). Adorno and Horkheimer sociologically explore how exactly such a capitalistic logic induced a remarkable reification of consciousness within the modern subject, so that a radically distorted understanding of the social world gained hegemony. The co-authors seek to explore how, in the mind of the capitalist subject, 'one sort of wares' truly became ontologically equivalent to another. This can be understood as the triumph of the 'exchange value' of the market. Crucially, for Adorno and Horkheimer, 'exchange value' belongs in the marketplace; however, the form of consciousness which corresponds to it has colonized the subject's understanding of the social totality. The co-authors are explicit in *Dialectic of Enlightenment* that it is the logics of the capitalist economy which are central in perpetuating such an irrational rationality; advanced capitalism necessitates subjects reducing the particularities of both subject and object into mere units of equivalence in all spheres of social life (Adorno and Horkheimer 1997: 36). From such a perspective, reification serves to impede critical and humanist thinking and is the primary pathology endemic to the capitalist form of life.

In both *Dialectic of Enlightenment* and *Minima Moralia* the reification of consciousness is intimately connected to the distortion of social rationality. While consciousness is seen to have been pathologically 'reified' as a result of systemic capitalist imperatives, rationality is held to have been pathologically 'instrumentalised' (Adorno and Horkheimer 1997: 84–5). With the onset of reification, the subject increasingly sees the world as mere 'dead matter – a heap of things' (Horkheimer 1993: 81). This enables the enthronement of an instrumental form of reason, where subjects are able to unthinkingly proceed with their lives with a robotic single-mindedness of focus on achieving the efficient completion of their goals. The sole objective is efficiency: the capitalist subject utilizes the optimally efficient means to achieve their desired end.

Yet, despite the apparent blinkered focus on the 'end-goal' being achieved, ironically both the 'means' and the ultimate 'ends' of social action within capitalism are now reduced to quality-less, mathematical considerations. Capitalism sees the 'elimination of qualities' (Adorno and Horkheimer 1997: 39). The moral righteousness, indeed the actual 'purpose', of both 'ends' and 'means' is now functionally irrelevant to the instrumental calculation. The sole measure of expediency is efficiency. As such, it is instrumental rationality which was utilized when the victims of the Holocaust were loaded onto cattle trucks to enable their most efficient movement to the death camps. Likewise, it was instrumental rationality which mass produces inane products which are ideally situated between maximal profit margin and saleability. For the co-authors, it is crucial to understand that the Holocaust and Hollywood are precipitants of a similar, pathologically deformed, mode of reasoning. The actual specifics of the 'commodity' as matter, as Kantian 'thing in itself', are now entirely irrelevant. Hollywood and Birkenau are both products of this deformed species of rationality.

For Adorno and Horkheimer, the rise of instrumental rationality is tied to a foundational flaw within modernity, it is connected to capitalism but, at the same time, distinct from it. Crucially, it is the structural imperatives of industrial capitalism which have enabled instrumental rationality to run wild; however, the authors stress that instrumental rationality *preceded* capitalism. The particular intensity of the 'conversion into functions' of social relations (Adorno and Horkheimer 1997: 36) is a result of the perversion of the Enlightenment project, which capitalism has expedited, but not instigated. The total dominance of instrumental rationality, and the death of quality, purpose, animism and aura, is captured in the co-authors' framing of the Culture Industry.

Written as an excursuses within *Dialectic of Enlightenment*, the analysis of the 'Culture Industry' has since been developed far beyond critical theory (see Hesmondhalgh 2019). The central idea put forward by Adorno and Horkheimer is that, due to the systemic demands of capitalist economics, and the instrumental rationality and reified consciousness it precipitates, all culture has come to take on an identical form as a mundane commodity. The role of art as transformative social critique, as a reflection which pierces the veil of social irrationality, has been lost. With an increasingly pronounced sociological inflection, Adorno and Horkheimer comment that 'movies and radio no longer pretend to be art' in contemporary capitalism (Adorno and Horkheimer 1997: 121), they are honest and frank about their status as a commodity, boasting their box office blockbuster sales, proudly commenting on the return on investment they attain. The aim of culture with capitalism is not to stimulate reflection on the human condition, rather, the aim is to produce a profit. As such, cultural products become homogenous, the aesthetic dimension is corroded by instrumental rationality (see Adorno 2001). As Adorno bitingly wrote of Hollywood: '[every] visit to the cinema leaves me, against all my vigilance, stupider and worse' (Adorno 1978: 25).

The central theme which resonates through the analysis of the 'Culture Industry' is the totalizing nature of the capitalist system. The space outside of capitalism for reflection and critique has been lost. This is because the Culture Industry 'impresses the same stamp on everything' (Adorno and Horkheimer 1997: 120), subsuming all ideas, all opposition within its parameters. Even dissent, at its most raw and radical, becomes repurposed, co-opted and is sold back to the masses; everything is 'made to pass through the filter of the culture industry' (Adorno and Horkheimer 1997: 126). This is achieved by identifying the particular defining characteristics of the resistance as a particular commodity, as a distinguishing marketable unique sales point (USP). The Culture Industry thus thrives off 'realistic dissidence' (Adorno and Horkheimer 1997: 132); the lovable rogue draws in the crowds. Pink Floyd's deeply political critique of the black capitalist heart of the music industry, 'Welcome to the Machine', becomes a best seller. Bob Dylan packs out concert venues. As Adorno and Horkheimer write of the dissident, 'Once his particular brand of deviation from the norm has been noted by the industry, he belongs to it as does the land-reformer to capitalism' (Adorno and Horkheimer 1997: 132). As such, there is nothing 'innocuous left' (Adorno 1978: 25). This very book, despite its focus on critiques of capitalism, remains a commodity to be bought and sold, traded at the instrumentally determined optimal price point between profit margin and saleability. As Adorno wrote of philosophy itself, in his introduction to *Minimia Moralia*, the study of the good life, once central to a humane existence and the principal vector of scholarly inquiry, is now relegated to an object of 'mere consumption, dragged along as an appendage of the process of material reproduction' (Adorno 1978: 15). Adorno and Horkheimer's analysis of capitalism as a repressive totality, which impeded critical thought, was foundational for future theorists. Yet, the defiant negativity of Adorno's work, typified by the aphorism, 'the whole is the false' (Adorno 1978: 50), left scholars and activists little room for manoeuvre and foreclosed possibilities for immediate political praxis.

Adorno and Horkheimer provide a valuable and intimidatingly negative critique of capitalism as a totality. This is both their fundamental insight and the impotency of their legacy: when the 'whole is the false' scholars and activists are left wondering what to do next, unsure where resistance can be applied or where crises within capitalism may emerge. In part, this arises from the epistemic understanding of capitalism, as a totalizing system of thought, which Adorno and Horkheimer develop. It is a tremendously valuable insight to realize capitalism is more than just a market order, that it is also a form of consciousness, a form of social life. In this regard, Adorno and Horkheimer are undeniably right to suggest capitalist societies engender a pathologically reified form of thought. However, problems emerge when theorists forget that capitalism remains, at a very important level, also an economic system and that this economic order has distinct contradictions and crises tendencies inherent in its logics of production, distribution and consumption. While the form of consciousness which capitalism induces can rightly be framed as increasingly totalizing, capitalism, as an economic system, is far from stable. The capitalist economy is neither totalizing nor self-correcting, other modes of production remain, crises emerge constantly. Indeed, as Marx argued, and as we stress throughout this book, a central feature of capitalism has always been its instability and tendency towards *worsening* crises (see Mandel 1975, Habermas 1973, Hirsch 1976). There are contradictions at the core of the capitalism as an economic system. This is something which Adorno and Horkheimer never fully engaged with, perhaps because it sits so diametrically opposed to their totalizing Hegelian-Weberian understanding of capitalism as a form of rationality and a mode of rationalization. As a socio-economic system, crisis, as much as control, is a central feature of capitalist societies. On this reality, Adorno and Horkheimer are guilty of a certain myopia.

As a result, for Adorno, the 1960s was not the time for active revolution against capitalism, much to the disappointment of his radical students. Indeed, Adorno famously called the police on students who occupied his office (Richter and Adorno 2002: 11), leading to the activist chant: 'if Adorno is left in peace, capitalism will never cease!'. The question of the co-authors' ultimate legacy, and of how to optimally incorporate their insights into a broader theory of contemporary capitalism, remains unaddressed within today's scholarship. At the core of this challenge is finding a way of embedding an awareness of the totalizing tendencies of capitalist rationality within a broader examination of the crisis tendencies of the capitalist economy.

Marcuse and 'One Dimensionality'

While Adorno and Horkheimer were accused of producing a paralyzingly totalizing analysis and of inducing political inertia, Herbert Marcuse was a frontline political activist throughout the 1960s and 1970s. Famously, Marcuse had a standoff with the then governor of California, Ronald Reagan, which was sparked, in part, by the infamy in which Marcuse's critique of capitalism was held by the American right (see Katz 1982). It is worth stressing that, despite their differences, Marcuse was invested in many of the same concerns as Adorno and Horkheimer. He too was a Hegelian-Marxist and he wrote a famous study on Hegel and Marx, *Reason and Revolution* [1941]. Yet, where Adorno and Horkheimer focused on fusing Marx, Hegel and Weber, in their analysis of capitalism, Marcuse's conceptual arsenal drew also upon Freudian psychoanalysis and phenomenology. This resulted in a critical theory with both clear continuities and divergences from Adorno and Horkheimer's.

Central to Marcuse's work was his analysis of the 'One Dimensional' subject of capitalism, expressed in his landmark text, *One Dimensional Man* [1964]. Reminiscent of the analysis of the Culture Industry, above, Marcuse (1964: 3) argued that the social totality was coalescing into a 'comfortable, smooth, reasonable, democratic unfreedom' in which capitalism was increasingly unopposed. For Marcuse, one dimensionality was crucial to explaining the relative stability of capitalism, despite the market's continuing propensity for worsening crises. Where Adorno and Horkheimer focused on the spread of reified consciousness and of an instrumental form of rationality, Marcuse focused on how these were experienced by the subject, both phenomenologically and psychically.

One dimensionality is crucially a state to which the subject consents, this is part of its power. A one dimensional existence is embraced by, rather than forced upon, the exploited class. Yet, as Marcuse wrote, 'one dimensionality' is

> the pure form of servitude: [enabling the subject] ... to exist as an instrument, as a thing. And this mode of existence is not abrogated if the thing is animated and chooses its material intellectual food, it does not feel it's being a thing, if it is a pretty, clean, mobile thing.
>
> (Marcuse 1964: 36)

We identify two key components of 'one dimensionality' central to Marcuse's work which we discuss below: repressive desublimation and the technical a priori. While both can, and have been, studied in isolation (see Feenberg 2011, 2013) we argue that they are best understood as constituent parts of Marcuse's broader critique of capitalism.

In *Minimia Moralia* Adorno wrote that, despite the totalizing nature of the modern capitalist system, some 'dim awareness' remains that the capitalist form of life is false (Adorno 1978: 15). However, this did not lead Adorno to engage in a depth-psychological engagement with the particular source of the 'dim awareness'. Neither did Adorno seek to explore how this 'awareness' was repressed by the dynamics of the social totality. It was instead Marcuse and Fromm who sought to integrate Marxian and Freudian insights in their critical theories. While they both presented fiercely different readings of Freud, they were united in exploring how (often capitalist) social-structural imperatives interacted with the subject's libidinal drives. For Fromm, the drives themselves were malleable and were reshaped by capitalism. For Marcuse, this was a dangerous and ill-considered revision to Freud's work. Rather, for Marcuse, capitalist institutions should be understood as adaptive, reshaping themselves to respond to and disarm resistance to capitalist norms originating from their divergence from our fixed libidinal drives. Crucial to Marcuse's Freudian-Marxism is his account of repressive desublimation.

For Freudians, 'sublimation' is the process through which unacceptable urges are transformed into socially acceptable behaviours. For example, if someone has a bad argument with their partner, instead of punching them, they might go and tidy the house. Likewise, instead of murdering your annoying neighbour, you might go for a jog. In these scenarios, the sublimation is healthy, it enables peaceable co-existence and the subject ends up healthier (after a jog) or with a tidier house. For Marcuse, the consumptive logics of capitalist society present a vehicle, not for sublimation, but of 'desublimation'. This is a central feature of Marcuse's framing of 'one dimensionality'. When the worker is incredibly frustrated with their alienating and exploitative job, they may be minded to protest against the employer and seek fairer working conditions. Ultimately, popular dissatisfaction against capitalism, a mobilization built upon Adorno's 'dim awareness', might grow into a critical mass of people demanding qualitative social change. Instead, Marcuse argues, advanced industrial society serves to prescribe avenues for sublimation in the form of consumption. If the worker is angry after being forced to work in exploitative conditions, they can simply forget about their exploitation and alienation by purchasing commodity X. This may provide a temporary respite from their psychic torment. However, instead of enabling a healthy sublation, the worker's dissatisfaction with their working conditions does not abate. The same exploitative conditions will await them, day after day, only with minor variation. Further, the dopamine hit of consumption is temporary and ultimately unsatisfactory. The novelty of the purchase swiftly fades and the disgruntled worker quickly desires a new commodity, a new purchase, which traps them further into their exploitative employment. They cannot purchase the commodity to sublate their desire to hit their boss… until they are paid again by their boss.

The system is thus one of 'repressive desublimation'; socially prescribed behaviours are designed to facilitate trapping the worker within the system and to enforce obedience to mindless consumption and alienating labour. Rather than relying on primitive force or the carceral state, repressive desublimation is a 'new, more effective, and more pleasant form of social control and social cohesion' (Marcuse 1964: xlvi). Aware that the normal procedures of their working life are abhorrent at some deep level, workers learn to 'find their soul in their automobile, hifi set, split level home' (Marcuse 1964: 11). Yet, as stated, such products are a weak opiate, just as Marx wrote of religion as a stabilizing force which must ultimately be critiqued, so too was the case, Marcuse argued, with consumption. Ultimately, advanced industrial society has succeeded in obscuring the 'tangible source of exploitation', the market, 'behind the façade of objective rationality' (Marcuse 1964: 35). Yet, the socially prescribed desire to consume is precisely that: prescribed. The subjects of late capitalism are victim to false needs which have been 'superimposed' on the individual by capitalist interests, designed to ensure repression and the stability of capitalism (Marcuse 1964: 7). As Marcuse writes, while

> their satisfaction might be most gratifying to the individual, … this happiness is not a condition which has to be maintained and protected if it serves to arrest the developments of the ability (his own and others) to recognise the disease of the whole and grasp the chance of curing the disease. The result then is euphoria in unhappiness.
>
> (Marcuse 1964: 7)

The structural repatterning of the subject's desires through repressive desublimation is married to a fundamental change in how the subject experiences the world. To understand Marcuse's framing of 'one dimensionality' in full, repressive desublimation, mass acquiescence to a societally prescribed mass consumption, needs to be held in tandem with pathological changes which occur to the subject's phenomenology. For Marcuse, advanced technical societies represent a particular fusion of science, technology and capitalism. Taken together, they fuse into a 'political rationality' which has an attendant pathological way of viewing, and being, a subject within the lifeworld. It is this pathological phenomenology which is captured by the idea of the 'technical *a priori*' (see Feenberg 2013).

The technical *a priori* can be understood as a phenomenological partner to the Adornian understanding of reified consciousness. It represents another new 'form of social control' (Marcuse 1964: 149) through which the domination of the external world is naturalized within the subject. The subject experiences their world as existing solely of dead objects, which are of calculable, discrete worth. By drawing on Husserl and Heidegger, Marcuse offers an existentialist-inflection to critical theory, enabling an interrogation of the mode of existence which dominate within the capitalist lifeworld. The central idea is that the scientific and technical paradigms, which holds all matter to be valueless dead objects for experimentation and control, have become imbibed by the capitalist subject as a natural way of being within the world. There is no space left for projects of wonder, of incalculable beauty, of unqualifiable emotion. This space is lost, it has been 'invaded and whittled down by technological rationality' (Marcuse 1964: 12) which seeks to control and dominate. Just as Adorno and Horkheimer (1997: 5–7) wrote of the 'extirpation of animism' in the *Dialectic of Enlightenment*, for Marcuse, the 'music of the soul' has been lost too, displaced by the 'music of salesmanship' (1964: 61). Taken together, Adorno, Horkheimer and Marcuse teach that capitalism represents a distinct assault on the subject's epistemic and phenomenological capacities. Crucially, Marcuse's work stresses how capitalism has adapted such that the market order has become resilient to the depth-psychological drives which may precipitate social change.

Marcuse's account serves to complement Adorno and Horkheimer's, providing an additional Freudian and existential dimension to addressing the questions: 'what did Marx fail to see/how has the capitalist economy managed to survive, despite its contradictions?' That said, in his later work, Marcuse moved closer to providing a 'positive politics', investing not solely in the critique typical of Frankfurt School negativity, but working on a project to identify emancipatory potential in the aesthetic and erotic facets of human existence. Marcuse's *An Essay on Liberation* [1969] became a cornerstone for many counter-cultural and hippie activists of the late 1960s/1970s. While Marcuse is primarily studied as a canonical 'first generation' figure within critical theory, his work is increasingly being developed within Science and Technology Studies (STS). As digital affordances become increasingly integrated within our lives, in ever more intimate ways, the impact technology has on our phenomenology is increasingly a topic of contemporary concern (see Feenberg 2017). Thus, Marcuse's significance today, and the significance of his engagement with capitalism, is largely felt in terms of his analysis of the impeded phenomenology which advanced technologies can induce within capitalism. Interestingly, Marcuse's principal fusion of Freud and Marx, his analysis of repressive desublimation, has been largely ignored by contemporary theorists of capitalism and has been largely displaced by other developments with the critical theory of the Frankfurt School.

Fromm: Capitalism as 'Pathological Normalcy'

Until recently, Erich Fromm was a largely forgotten, fringe figure within critical theory. His distinctive fusion of Marx and Freud was too polemical to be embraced by either the Marxian or the psychoanalytic orthodoxy. In particular, his revisions to Freud's 'drive theory' alienated orthodox analysts and infuriated his Frankfurt School contemporaries. However, Fromm's work on capitalism is rapidly being reintegrated within contemporary scholarship as the value of his insights are increasingly appreciated (Durkin 2014). His analysis of capitalism focused on the primary question driving all critical theory: how has the unstable and contradictory capitalist order been stabilized? For Fromm, like Marcuse, addressing this question required a careful integration of sociological and depth-psychological research. As we discuss below, central to Fromm's work is his theory of 'pathological normalcy', where he engaged in depth with the questions of institutionalized alienation and the normalization of capitalist imperatives within the individual psyche.

Fromm's framing of 'pathological normalcy' was presented in his book *The Sane Society* [1955] and was expanded upon at length during his lectures at the New School in New York (see Fromm 2010 [1991]). The strength of 'pathological normalcy' is that it simultaneously offers an anchored critique of capitalism and a disclosing-critique of the means of its survival. This 'double-action' is crucial to Fromm's understanding of 'pathological normalcy' and both facets of his framing need to be grasped in unison. Crucially, for Fromm, it is *both* the standard operating procedures of capitalism, and the means through which it is normalized, which are 'pathological'.

Drawing on Freud, Fromm repeatedly returned to the aphorism '*mens sana in societate sana*', or 'a healthy mind is produced by a healthy society' (Fromm 2010: 86). Conversely, unhealthy minds, indicated by anxiety, paranoia, feelings of alienation, are produced by unhealthy societies. For Fromm, capitalist society evinces a pandemic of heterogenous social neuroses. This indicates foundational problems within the central structures steering social development. Chief amongst these was the capitalist system which needed to be urgently replaced with a more humane alternative. What was required was a more 'sane society', a more socialistic society. As Fromm argued in *Beyond the Chains of Illusion* [1962], this necessitated a 'complete change of the economic-social constellation' (Fromm 1983: 56). As a result, for Fromm, gradual reform and piecemeal change was fundamentally inadequate. Only revolutionary social change out of capitalism would suffice.

Fromm's humanism shines through in his critique of the 'insane' capitalist society. It is not the inefficiency of the capitalist market which he targets, although he was sensitive to its structural limitations. Nor was Fromm primarily concerned with the exploitative nature of capitalism. Rather, it was the alienating nature of capitalism which drove Fromm's critique. Marx's early work was repackaged as providing a normative ballast to Fromm's revised-Freudianism. For Fromm, alienation was '*the* sickness of man' (Fromm 1983: 45) and was inseparable from capitalism. The imperatives of the market order necessitated forms of abstraction and reification which induced a deformed psychology, so that 'life itself appears only as a *means of life*' (Fromm 1983: 44). Capitalism is thus presented as a 'sick' and 'insane' form of life as it induces a plague of psycho-pathologies, chief amongst these being alienation. Alienation derives explicitly from capitalism, it

> follow[s] from the fact that the worker is related to the *product of his labor* as to an *alien* object. For it is clear on this presupposition that the more the worker expends himself in work, the more powerful becomes the world of objects which he creates in face of himself, the poorer he becomes in his inner life and the less he belongs to himself....
> (Fromm 1983: 42–3)

Fromm's account of 'pathological normalcy' is thus anchored in the idea that the capitalist constellation is 'insane' as it fails to attend to the needs of humanity. Instead, as a direct result of its standard operating procedures, it induces psycho-pathologies. It is worth stressing that it was the 'normal', 'quotidian' operation of capitalism, which Fromm wished to target here. It was the 'everyday' normalcy of market behaviour that was pathological. In contrast to a more orthodox scientific division between 'normal' and 'pathological', with the 'pathological' defined as a departure from 'normalcy' (see the work of Canguilhem 1991 [1966]), for Fromm the 'norm' was *itself* pathological.

Crucially, the means of *normalization* were understood by Fromm as being an essential part of the pathology (see Harris 2019). Central to this process was a negative social dynamic which Fromm termed 'consensual validation' (Fromm 1963: 14). The central idea here is that 'it is naively assumed that the fact that the majority of people share certain ideas or feelings proves the validity of these ideas and feelings' (Fromm 1963: 14). For instance, the fact that everyone else around the social subject goes to work and accepts the logics of capitalist society exerts a remarkable socializing force. Capitalist subjects accept market logics: most people buy a smart phone, wear denim jeans, drink Coca Cola... The pressure to conform, and to assume that conformity equals 'rationality' or 'proper' behaviour, is immense. Crucially, however, just because all my acquaintances choose to do X, does not, in itself, make X rational or healthy. As Fromm stresses, 'consensual validation' is 'both truly deceptive' (Fromm 1963: 14) and remarkably powerful. The desire to 'fit in' is often unassailable.

For Fromm, there is a pathological negative dynamic at work here, the more people who ultimately acquiesce to the exploitative and alienating conditions of capitalism, the more likely it is additional people will follow suit. Once a critical mass of people embark on course X, it is incredibly difficult to induce a mass change in course. Capitalism has benefitted enormously from this foundational anthropological-psychological flaw; a flaw which is routinely utilized by capitalists. Advertisements show the most popular commodity, the Culture Industry presents the most consumed products as badges of pride. Proof of mass purchase is a rarely questioned proxy for proof of status. Tellingly, the badge 'best-seller' is held to be proof of an item meriting purchase in and of itself. Fromm argues that such dynamics of normalization have played a crucial role in protecting and sustaining the capitalist form of life. As Fromm writes, mass acquiescence to capitalism is interpreted by capitalist subjects as an indication of the rationality of the market. This ultimately does not proves the coherence of market logics, but that just 'as there is folie á deux, there is folie á millions' (Fromm 1963: 15).

Throughout *The Sane Society*, Fromm developed this insight further, arguing that 'consensual validation' can lead to the normalization of 'socially patterned defects' within the individual subject. For instance, subjects can become unaware of their own alienation or the irrationality of their particular form of work. As a result, the subject may feel neurotic or anxious, but the precise cause of their psychological disquiet can become obscured as the worker's capacity to critically analyse their working conditions is blunted. In keeping with Marcuse's analysis of 'repressive desublimation', alienated workers often take pride in their alienating labour and seek recourse, and pride, in constant consumption.

In summary, Fromm argues that exploited, alienated workers may be socially conditioned to lose their capacity to interrogate the alienating and exploitative nature of their working conditions. Instead, they are often accultured to seek solace within their identity as a worker and consumer, wearing both as badges of pride. Fromm (1983: 14) writes that, in such cases, people are complicit in deluding themselves so they may forget their 'slavery to the economy'. Ultimately, the pathological normalcy of capitalism is reinforced through the subject's self-deception. In the words of Fromm's biographer Rainer Funk (2000: 11), '[the] fact that we do not experience the emptying and devaluation of the subject, as well as the dependency on the market as something abnormal anymore is a central indication for what Fromm calls "the pathology of normalcy"'. Fromm's framing of pathological normalcy serves to unite a critique of the objective 'insanity' of the capitalist constellation with a simultaneous attack on the equally pathological mechanisms which stabilize the economic order. Fromm argues that the very normalcy capitalism has achieved is a central part of its pathology.

The Limits and Contemporary Relevance of First-Generation Critical Theory

Many of the insights of the early Frankfurt School remain central to contemporary critiques of capitalism. The work of Marcuse and Adorno informs much of the literature within today's STS, as illustrated by the extensive and impactful writings of Andrew Feenberg (2011, 2013, 2017). Similarly, James Bridle (2018), David Berry (2014) and Shoshana Zuboff (2018) are all conceptually indebted to first-generation Frankfurt School social research. Further, as discussed above, the framing of the 'Culture Industry' has been adopted and adapted far beyond the Frankfurt School. It would therefore be foolish to dismiss the work of first-generation Frankfurt School theorists as an irrelevance, or as no longer pertaining to the today's world. That stated, there are crucial areas of divergence between early Frankfurt School scholarship and the dominant literature on capitalism today (see Delanty and Harris 2021). We turn to two particular limitations of early critical theory below: the relative lack of scholarship on gender and imperialism. These lacunas are found across all first-generation theories into capitalism, and are not contingent 'blind spots' to particular theorists. Many contemporary Frankfurt School scholars, such as Fraser and Jaeggi (2018), have worked to bridge these gaps, explicitly seeking to bring the 'hidden abodes' of capitalism (see Fraser 2014) to the fore (see Chapter 9).

While contemporary critical theorists acknowledge the crucial role gender relations play in stabilizing capitalism (Fraser and Jaeggi 2018), for first-generation critical theorists, gender was not a topic meriting extended discussion. On the rare occasions where the founding critical theorists did discuss gender, such as Marcuse's (1974) lectures on 'Marxism and Feminism', their work is uncharacteristically unsophisticated and cursory. From today's perspective, Wendy Brown writes, early Frankfurt School writings on gender are 'vulnerable to emerging postfoundational critiques of the humanist subject, progressive historiography, and their entailments: essentialized identities, totalizing identities, undeconstructed binary oppositions, faith in emancipation, and revolution' (2015: 1). This stinging indictment is fair and representative: the failure of early critical theorists to engage with gender as a stabilizing force within capitalism is a significant weakness of their output. As Brown writes, gender is 'impressed in thought' (Brown 2015: 4) and has much in keeping with the broader epistemic and phenomenological considerations of wider Frankfurt Scholarship. Yet, in the 'canonical' Frankfurt School texts, women are either conspicuously absent or simply evil. On the rare occasions women are discussed, it is as murderers (consider the sections on de Sade's Madame de Clairwill, in *Dialectic of Enlightenment*) or as deadly seductresses, who are a threat to otherwise rational men (recall Odysseus and the sirens). In light of the development of gender studies and the increasing reach of intersectional research, the scant treatment afforded to gender by early Frankfurt School theorists appears an obvious limitation. While this is unjustifiable theoretically, it is explicable historically. When one reflects on the period in which first-generation Frankfurt Scholars were writing, in light of the emerging horrors of the Holocaust and the threat of nuclear annihilation, the lack of focus on gender is much less surprising. That said, contemporary theorists of capitalism, who seek to draw on the work of the first-generation theorists, need to be mindful of this limitation. A satisfactory critique of capitalism must be sensitive to the role gender relations play within the social totality.

As we will discuss in Chapters 9 and 10, capitalism is increasingly interpreted as a global system, with the particular relationship between centre and periphery often framed as one of imperialism or as neo-imperialism. There is a growing demand within the academy to 'decolonise' traditions of thought and to question epistemic privilege (see Fricker 1999). The Frankfurt School, and particularly its earliest iterations, are often held to be deficiently Eurocentric and disengaged with the realities and experiences of colonialism, slavery and imperialism. This is perhaps an exaggerated and hackneyed criticism; the Frankfurt School were deeply invested in exploring racism, the experience of the Holocaust being central to the canon of first-generation texts. As with the relative absence of the discussion on gender, the first-generation theorists were understandably primarily focusing on the horrors of the Holocaust when they were engaging with questions of race *and* slavery; recall the forced-labour campus many victims of the Nazi horror were forced to work in. Forced servitude, domination, the loss of identity, racism... these were central concerns for Frankfurt School theorists, just not with the focus on the global South which rightly proliferates today. Baum (2015) has also convincingly argued that there is more engagement with race within the work of the Frankfurt School than many of its decolonial critics acknowledge. These caveats aside, it does undeniably remain the case that first-generation Frankfurt School scholarship does not provide an adequate theorization of capitalism as a global system in which the domination of non-white peoples has always been an essential structural function. This omission is particularly stark in light of contemporary academic currents. The role of the slave trade, 'scientific racism' and the broader realities of colonial and neo-coloniality need to be integrated within any satisfactory contemporary theory of capitalism.

There is more to the decolonial critique of first-generation Frankfurt School research. In addition to identifying the lack of focus on coloniality and race (at least beyond Europe), Bhambra (2021) and Allen (2016) argue that the conceptual foundations of critical theory themselves require 'decolonising'. For Bhambra (2021), the Hegelian conception of history which critical theory is built upon is problematic and reflects racist, imperialist and colonial rationalities. Amy Allen (2016) also presses this point, arguing that the normative foundations of critical theory require decolonizing. Allen and Bhambra are of course correct that any contemporary theory of capitalism must be able to critically interrogate the logics of racism and neo-imperialism. However, the argument that critical theory is fundamentally predicated upon a racist normative foundation which requires decolonizing is exaggerated. The fact that Adorno et al. were largely concerned with European history and myopic about colonialism opens them to the possible charge of Eurocentrism, but not to racism. Even if one were to allow, but not concede, that the normative foundations of Frankfurt School research were irrecoverably tarnished, the explanatory utility of the concepts developed by critical theorists to explore capitalism remains unblemished: they can be simply extricated from the broader (alleged) theoretical toxicity. The analytical utility of the framings of 'repressive desublimation', 'the Culture Industry' and 'instrumental rationality' etc. are not dependent on the viability of the caricatured teleology narratives that many decolonial theorists present. Contemporary critical theorists can (and do) meaningfully utilize the framings of the 'Culture Industry', and 'technical a priori', for example, to critique contemporary capitalism, without the need to offer extensive historicizing propitiations.

Conclusion

It is, however, undeniable that the substantive content of the early Frankfurt School has aged, and so too has its critique of capitalism. This is somewhat ironic as low-grade contemporary neoliberal commentators, especially online, seek to attack the dominance of 'cultural Marxism', which is often incorrectly elided with 'woke-ism', 'liberalism' and 'political correctness'. The manifold limitations of this should be apparent from our above engagement with critical theory's critique of capitalism. The Frankfurt School offers an interdisciplinary critique of capitalism, predicated upon, and much broader than, typical Marxian scholarship. While the substantive content of the first generation's critique of capitalism, and the idiosyncratic manner of its presentation, may seem a legacy of a bygone era, the fundamental conceptual and methodological insights remain valid today. The awareness that social-structural forms of power, rooted in capitalist economic imperatives, serve to impact upon forms of thought and desire has been embraced across traditions. This fundamental Frankfurt School insight has been expanded, repackaged and reformulated, at times beyond all recognition of the intentions and politics of first-generation scholars.

While this chapter has focused on the critique of capitalism advanced by the first generation of the Frankfurt School, the research programme developed in remarkable ways as new methodologies and political sensitivities rose to the fore. An analysis of Habermas' 'second generation' critical theory, and his particular understanding of capitalism, forms part of the next chapter. While the critical theory of the first generation reached its zenith with the 1960s, the 1970s saw a proliferation of divergent theoretical approaches. However, as we discuss, central insights from the Frankfurt School held such potency that their impact can be identified across a wide range of theoretical persuasions.

Notes

1 There is even discussion of a 'fourth-generation' of Critical Theory led by scholars such as Hartmut Rosa and Rahel Jaeggi (see Fuchs 2016: 154).
2 For a broader discussion of the Critical Theoretical term 'social pathology' see Harris (2022).
3 It is also worth noting that neither *Dialectic of Enlightenment* nor *Minima Moralia* is explicitly about theories of capitalism. Rather, instrumental rationality and reified consciousness are the primary objects of analysis; capitalism enters the discussion to the extent to which it is linked to these twin-concerns.
4 Nicholas Barbon (c.1640–c.1700) was one of the very first advocates of a 'free market' economic system. He was both an economist and an active financier and proto-businessman; he was an active property developer and helped to popularize a variety of revolutionary new "commodities" such as an early form of insurance.

References

Adorno T.W. 1978 [1951]. *Minima Moralia: Reflections from Damaged Life.* Translated by E. Jephcott. London: Verso.
Adorno, T.W. 1981 [1966]. *Negative Dialectics.* Translated by E. Ashton. London: Continuum.
Adorno, T.W. 2001. *The Culture Industry: Selected Essays on Mass Culture.* Abingdon: Routledge.
Adorno, T.W. and Horkheimer, M. 1997 [1944]. *Dialectic of Enlightenment.* Translated by J. Cumming. London: Verso.
Allen, A. 2016. *The End of Progress: Decolonizing the Normative Foundations of Critical Theory.* New York City: Columbia University Press.
Baum, B. 2015. Decolonizing Critical Theory. *Constellations,* 22 (3): 420–34.
Berry, D. 2014. *Critical Theory and the Digital.* London: Bloomsbury.
Bhambra, G.K. 2021. 'Decolonizing Critical Theory?: Epistemological Justice, Progress, Reparations'. *Critical Times,* 4 (1): 73–89.
Bridle, J. 2018. *New Dark Age: Technology and the End of the Future.* London: Verso.

Brown, W. 2015. 'Feminist Theory and the Frankfurt School: Introduction', *Differences,* 17 (1): 1–5.

Canguilhem, G. 1991 [1966]. *The Normal and the Pathological.* Translated by Carolyn R. Fawcett & Robert S. Cohen. New York: Zone Books.

Dahms, H. 1998. '"Beyond the Carousel of Reification": Critical Social Theory after Lukács, Adorno, and Habermas'. *Current Perspectives in Social Theory*, 18 (1): 3–62.

Delanty, G. and Harris, N. 2021. 'Critical Theory and the Question of Technology: The Frankfurt School Revisited'. *Thesis Eleven*, 166 (1): 88–108.

Durkin, K. 2014. *The Radical Humanism of Erich Fromm.* New York: Palgrave Macmillan.

Feenberg, A. 2011 'Rethinking Reification'. In: *Georg Lukács: The Fundamental Dissonance of Existence.* Edited by T. Bews and T. Hall. New York: Continuum, 101–20.

Feenberg, A. 2013. 'Marcuse's Phenomenology: Reading Chapter Six of One Dimensional Man'. *Constellations*, 20 (4): 604–14.

Feenberg, A. 2017. 'Critical Theory of Technology and STS'. *Thesis Eleven*, 138 (1): 3–12.

Felsch, P. 2022. *The Summer of Theory: History of A Rebellion 1960–1990.* Translated by T. Crawford. Cambridge: Polity.

Fraser, N. 2014. 'Behind Marx's Hidden Abode: For An Expanded Conception of Capitalism'. *New Left Review*, 86: 55–72.

Fraser, N. and Jaeggi, R. 2018. *Capitalism: A Conversation in Critical Theory.* Cambridge: Polity.

Fricker, M. 1999. 'Epistemic Oppression and Epistemic Privilege'. *Canadian Journal of Philosophy Supplementary Volume*, 25: 191–210. Civilisation and Oppression.

Fromm, E. 1963 [1956]. *The Sane Society.* London: Routledge & Kegan and Paul.

Fromm, E. 1983 [1962]. *Beyond the Chains of Illusion: My Encounter with Marx and Freud.* London: Abacus.

Fromm, E. 2010 [1991]. *The Pathology of Normalcy.* Riverdale: AMHF.

Fuchs, C. 2016. *Critical Theory of Communication: New Readings of Lukacs, Adorno, Marcuse, Honneth and Habermas in the Age of the Internet.* London: University of Westminster Press.

Funk, R. 2000 [1999]. *Erich Fromm: His Life and Ideas.* New York: Continuum.

Habermas, J. 1976 [1973]. *Legitimation Crisis.* Translated by T. McCarthy. Cambridge: Polity Press.

Harris, N. 2019. 'Reconstructing Erich Fromm's 'Pathology of Normalcy': Transcending the Recognition-Cognitive Paradigm in the Diagnosis of Social Pathologies'. *Social Science Information*, 58 (4): 714–33.

Harris, N. 2022. *Critical Theory and Social Pathology: The Frankfurt School Beyond Recognition.* Manchester: Manchester University Press.

Hesmondhalgh, D. 2019. *The Cultural Industries, 4th edition.* London: Sage.

Hirsch, F. 1977 [1976]. *Social Limits to Growth.* London: Routledge and Kegan Paul.

Honneth, A. 2000. 'The Possibility of a Disclosing Critique of Society: The Dialectic of Enlightenment in Light of Current Debates in Social Criticism'. *Constellations*, 7 (1): 116–27.

Honneth, A. 2012. *Reification: A New Look at an Old Idea,* Oxford: Oxford University Press.

Horkheimer, M. 1993. 'Reason Against Itself: Some Remarks on Enlightenment'. *Theory, Culture and Society*, 10 (2): 79–88.

Horkheimer, M. 2002 [1937]. 'Traditional and Critical Theory'. In *Critical Theory: Selected Essays.* Translated by J. O'Connell. New York: Continuum, pp. 188–244.

Horkheimer, M. 2018 [1931]. 'The State of Contemporary Social Philosophy and the Tasks of an Institute for Social Research', *Journal for Cultural Research*, 22 (2): 113–21.

Jay, M. 1973. *The Dialectical Imagination: A History of the Frankfurt School and the Institute of Social Research, 1923–1950.* Oakland: University of California Press.

Jeffries, S. 2016. *Grand Hotel Abyss: The Lives of the Frankfurt School.* London: Verso.

Katz, B. 1982. *Herbert Marcuse and the Art of Liberation: An Intellectual Biography.* London: Verso.

Lukács, G. 1962. *The Destruction of Reason.* Translated by P. R. Palmer. London: Merlin Press.

Lukács, G. 1972 [1923]. *History and Class Consciousness: Studies in Marxist Dialectics.* Translated by R. Livingstone. Cambridge: The MIT Press.

Lukács, G. 1974 [1916]. *The Theory of the Novel: A Historico-Philosophical Essay on the Forms of Great Epic Literature*. Translated by A. Bostock. Cambridge: The MIT Press.

Mandel, E. 1975 [1972]. *Late Capitalism*. Translated by J. De Bres. London: New Left Books.

Marcuse, H. 1964. *One Dimensional Man*. Boston: Beacon Press.

Marcuse, H. 1969 [1941]. *Reason and Revolution: Hegel and the Rise of Social Theory*. London: Routledge and Kegan Paul.

Marcuse, H. 1974. 'Marxism and Feminism'. *Women's Studies*, 2 (3): 279–88.

Marx, K. 1976 [1867]. *Capital: Volume 1: A Critique of Political Economy*. Translated by Ben Fowkes. London: Penguin.

Richter, G. and Adorno, T. W. 2002. 'Who's Afraid of the Ivory Tower? A Conversation with Theodor W. Adorno'. *Monatshefte*, 94 (1): 10–23.

Thompson, M. J. 2017. 'Normative Humanism as Redemptive Critique'. In: *Reclaiming the Sane Society*. Edited by S. J. Miri, R. Lake and T. Kress. Boston: Sense. pp. 37–58.

Van den Brink, B. 1997. 'Social Theory and the Art of Exaggeration'. *Neue Rundschau*. 1.

Wiggershaus, R. 1986. *The Frankfurt School: Its History, Theories, and Political Significance*. Cambridge: Polity Press.

Zuboff, S. 2018. *The Age of Surveillance Capitalism: The Fight for a Human Future at the New Frontier of Power*. London: Profile Books.

8 Late Capitalism and Capitalist Crises

From 1945 to 1973 the Global North enjoyed remarkable economic prosperity. Amongst intellectuals and statesman alike, there was a widespread belief that capitalism had finally been controlled. History has proven this tendency to repeat through nearly all cycles of boom; capitalist technocrats consider 'busts' to be consigned to an economic pre-history, when less competent hands held the tiller. In 2002, Gordon Brown declared that he had achieved the end of boom and bust economic cycles in the UK (see Summers 2008). Like the post-2008 financial crash, which demonstrated Brown's naïve hubris, the 1970s were also characterized by multiple crises. Indeed, the very word 'crisis' dominated public discourse throughout the decade. *The Sun* newspaper memorably paraphrased UK Prime Minister 'Sunny Jim' Callaghan as saying 'Crisis? What Crisis?' during the so-called winter of discontent (1978–9). Callaghan's symbolic denial of the nature and extent of the crisis ultimately destroyed his political credibility, contributing to his election defeat shortly after. While the crises of the 1970s were particularly severe in the UK, they impacted all nations in the Global North. In many countries, mortgage rates spiralled to over 20%, manufacturing industries were crippled, inflation hit double digits and unemployment rose exponentially, before stabilizing at over 10% (see Shepherd 2015).

A significant challenge for capitalism in this period was the 1973 Oil Crisis. Following Israel's victory in the Yom Kippur War (October 1973), the Arab members of OPEC responded by introducing an oil embargo. While initially intended to target states which had supported American foreign policy (America had resupplied Israeli military forces during the conflict), the result of the embargo was that the oil price quickly rose globally. The rate of the price rise was remarkable: in September 1973, oil was trading worldwide at around $3 a barrel; by spring 1974, it had risen to nearly $12, with prices even higher in North America. The shock to global markets that this induced was not a one-off event; the 'second oil crisis' occurred six years later with the Iranian revolution of 1979. The oil crises contributed to a further economic challenge of the 1970s: 'stagflation', where low or no economic growth was accompanied by unacceptably high inflation (see Venn 2002).

Seemingly every year in the 1970s brought new and unpredicted crises. The USA left the Bretton Woods system in 1971; their unilateral withdrawal from the gold standard for currency exchange created complicated shockwaves. At the time, the USA's withdrawal was linked to their humiliating defeat in Vietnam, which itself put manifold pressures on the American economy. Today, scholars increasingly acknowledge how crises in western Europe also contributed to the collapse of the Bretton Woods system (De Groot 2019). Throughout the decade, there were also unsustainable pressures on heavy industry, with the global steel trade suffering repeated crises (see Rhodes and Wright 1988). The period

DOI: 10.4324/9781351017671-9

was also marked by a growing awareness of the environmental damage caused by capitalism (Carson 1962, Schumacher 1973, *inter alia*), which we discuss in detail in the next chapter.

These historical developments were reflected in the changing theories of capitalism which emerged in these years. As we charted in the preceding chapter, 'first-generation' critical theorists understood capitalism as a stable totality which induced pathological forms of consciousness and desire. Their totalizing framing of capitalism reflected the socio-economic conditions of the post-war consensus. Predictably, the critiques of capitalism which emerged in the 1970s focused on crisis rather than stability. Perhaps the most important weakness of the Frankfurt School's theory of capitalism, as reflected for example in Marcuse *One-Dimensional Man* in 1964, was that it lacked a satisfactory engagement with the crisis prone nature of what was now seen as 'disorganized capitalism' (see O'Conner 1973, Offe 1985).

In direct contrast to the work of the early Frankfurt School, one trend which emerged in the 1970s was a return to a more orthodox Marxist economic analysis which centred crisis as a fundamental characteristic of capitalism. Such an approach was typified by Ernest Mandel. Mandel sought to demonstrate how orthodox Marxist economics could explain both the relative stability of *les trente glorieuses* and its inevitable collapse into crises. We start this chapter by interrogating Mandel's particular fusion of economic theory and history and his analysis of cycles of capitalist development in *Late Capitalism* [1972]. For Mandel, capitalism's crisis tendencies could never be 'managed out' by state bureaucrats. While approaching capitalism from a very different perspective to Mandel, this belief in the endemic nature of capitalist crisis was shared by Fred Hirsch. We turn to Hirsch's *Social Limits to Growth* [1976] to show how critiques of capitalism in this period identified 'social' as well as economic and environmental crisis tendencies.

In this new terrain, with crisis, rather than stability being the dominant concern, Frankfurt School scholarship performed something of a metamorphosis. Rather than reverting to an orthodox Marxism, in the style of Mandel, critical theorists chose to part company with some fundamentals of Marxist theory. Jürgen Habermas' work in this period, especially *Legitimation Crisis* [1973], invested in divergent philosophical traditions, previously absent in the first generation's critique of capitalism. As we discuss, Habermas' critique of capitalism in this period actually sits closer to systems theory rather than to historical materialism.

The 1970s were marked by a flourishing of heterogenous critiques of capitalism, arising from both the political left and right. Reflecting contemporary developments in French philosophy and insights from linguistics, semiotics and psychoanalysis, post-structuralist and post-modern engagements of capitalism sought to provide a 'deeper' critique to that provided by earlier theorists. We discuss Baudrillard's post-modern critique of capitalism, *For a Critique of the Political Economy of the Sign* [1972], which typifies this elision of disciplines. We then turn our attention to the work of Michel Foucault, who we argue provides a more complicated engagement with neo-liberalism than many of his contemporary devotees acknowledge. By turning to *The Birth of Biopolitics* [1978–9], we read Foucault as presenting a guarded support for neo-liberalism, while demonstrating his awareness of its disciplinary tendencies. Finally, we turn to Daniel Bell's *The Cultural Contradictions of Capitalism* [1976]. In this striking conservative cultural critique of capitalism, Bell argued that the aggressive form of contemporary capitalism has served to attack the protestant ethic which enabled its very development.

Throughout this chapter, we draw attention to the centrality of crises within the period. The 1970s marked a qualitatively distinct socio-economic epoch to the social democratic consensus which preceded it. The changing critiques of capitalism we engage with here reflect these developments within the global economy and the economies of the Global North in particular.

The Inevitability of Crises in Late Capitalism: Ernest Mandel and Fred Hirsch

Belgian economist Ernest Mandel wrote what is undoubtedly the finest work on the collapse of the post-war boom from an orthodox Marxist perspective. Mandel was a remarkable figure: he was a Holocaust survivor and had been an active resistance fighter and underground journalist during the Nazi occupation (see Stutje 2009). In later life, he was famously denied entry into the USA on the basis of his anti-capitalist views, resulting in a much publicized Supreme Court case (see Löwy 2009). While Mandel was a prolific author, with over 30 books to his name, he is today best remembered for *Late Capitalism*.[1] This work served to popularize the framing 'late capitalism' and today Mandel is nearly synonymous with the term. This is somewhat ironic as Mandel was neither the first to use the phrase, nor was his use of it in keeping with how it is predominantly mobilized today.[2] Mandel is today largely remembered for his insightful and dedicated application of Marxist theory as well as for his strident and articulate anti-Stalinism (see Mandel 2022).

As Michel Husson (1999: 75) stresses, 'Mandel's work must … be situated in the context of the time'. While many non-Marxist economists in the 1960s considered the economic growth of the period to be potentially never-ending, and part of a qualitative change in economic formation, maybe even out of capitalism altogether, Mandel was adamant that capitalism remained. For Mandel, the same fundamental economic forces described by Marx remained dominant: the *dirigiste* turn did not mark the end of capitalism's inherent propensity for crises. Accordingly, a longer historical view was needed on economic development (Albarracin and Montes 1999: 38). Mandel was defiant against repeated criticisms (see Althusser et al. 1970): the expansive growth of the post-war period needed to be grasped as part of longer waves within capitalism, only then could it be critically interrogated and understood.

Mandel's work was driven by two central beliefs: that 'late capitalism' was not a qualitatively new kind of economy, it was definitely still capitalism, and that the same fundamental economic laws, as detailed by Marx, applied. For Mandel, Marx was the most venerable guide to economic development and needed to be respected, almost doctrinally. Throughout Mandel's work, there is a remarkable fidelity to Marx's concepts, with Mandel seeking to analyse the interplay of *all* the laws which Marx discovered. Indeed, the reader of *Late Capitalism* may come to think that Mandel's ultimate challenge was more to perfectly honour Marx's system than to optimally analyse the economy. Tellingly, much of the secondary literature on Mandel consists of Marxist scholars seeking to identify the potential areas of 'deviation' from Marx's method which Mandel inevitably slipped into (see Krätke 2007: 125). This is problematic, as Krätke (2007) notes, as Marx had not completed his economic analysis by the time of his death; Marx did not leave a complete system which could be mobilized by later scholars. In this regard, Mandel's desire to retain total fidelity to Marx's economic laws seems misguided.

If Mandel is to be understood as a devotee of Marx, he settled on one of the most coherent and persuasive parts of Marxist economic analysis as his foundation. Mandel argued that the fundamental crisis tendency of Marx's analysis remained valid: the *tendency of the rate of profit to fall*, which would inevitably induce crises. In *Late Capitalism,* Mandel persuasively demonstrated how the post-war boom was as vulnerable to this tendency as any other period of capitalist development. This conclusion was not only reached through a complex analysis of the interplay of the basic laws discovered by Marx, but also through a strictly *historical*, rather than merely abstracted economic analysis.

Mandel saw the particular historical conditions to be crucial in understanding the development of *Late Capitalism*. Historical specificity had to be respected in keeping with Marx's work. As Mandel wrote in an earlier text, *Marxist Economic Theory* [1962], what was required was a 'dynamic conjunction between economic history and economic theory' (Mandel 1968: 17). He sought to do two intricate tasks in concert: to chart the development of post-war economic development and to locate this within the meta-history of capitalism, stretching back centuries (see Krätke 2007: 124). Mandel's particular form of historico-economic analyses was therefore highly distinctive; most non-Marxist economists of the period had little interest in historical economics.[3] Even some contemporary Marxist scholars thought Mandel's historical focus was problematic, a view notably held by Althusser and his followers (see Althusser et al. 1970). However, Mandel stuck to his idiosyncratic historical-economic methodology and presented the 'late capitalist era' as one of three distinctive periods of recent capitalist development.

For Mandel, the period from 1700 to 1870 was typified by freely competitive productive capitalism, with a focus on industrial capital, while the years 1870–1940 were dominated by monopoly capitalism typified by imperialism, colonialism and market expansion. In contrast, the Late Capitalist era, emerging out of Second World War , was characterized by the ascendancy of multinational companies, globalized markets, mass consumption and international capital flows. Crucially, late capitalism was typified by ever increasing commodification and the industrialization of ever more areas of society as multinational companies competed for profits. The transition from one period of capitalism to the next was explained by Mandel (1975: 442) through strict adherence to Marxist categories:

> Two decisive factors … explains the long wave with an undertone of expansion which lasted from 1940 to 1966. In the first place the historical defeats of the working class enabled fascism and war to raise the rate of surplus value. In the second place the resultant increase in the accumulation of capital (investment activity), together with an accelerated rhythm of technological innovation, and a reduced turnover time of fixed capital led in the third technological revolution to a long-term expansion of the market for the extended reproduction of capital on an international scale, despite its geographic limitations.

For a short period, totalling less than half a century, the pace of technological evolution had managed to temporarily stave off crises and had brought spectacular economic growth. However, in keeping with Marxist theory, this was not to last: technological innovation could not indefinitely keep pace with the capitalists' need for constant compound growth in profits. As Harman (1978) writes,

> … eventually, the 'wave' of innovations begins to falter. At the same time, full employment leads to workers gaining new confidence. The classic pressure on profit rates begins to be felt. The well spring of expansion begins to dry up, and a new period of crises and stagnation begins.

Mandel's *Late Capitalism* presents an explanation for the onset of the crises of the 1970s, which was explicitly drawn from Marxist laws. His work demonstrated the inevitability of crises and the impossibility of perpetual growth. *Late Capitalism* also led to a resurgence of interest in 'long waves' of capitalist development, leading to critical engagements with the work of Nikolai Kondratieff.[4] Yet, the extent to which *Late Capitalism* served to successfully combine Marx's foundational laws of motion of capital into a coherent whole connected to an abstracted economic history is questioned. Therefore, the degree to which he achieved his ultimate objective, of determining the inevitability of the crises of the 1970s through recourse solely to Marx economics, is contested (see Wolfe 1986).

While emerging from a different school of thought entirely to Mandel, Fred Hirsch similarly offered insights on the inherent crisis tendencies of capitalism. Hirsch was not a doctrinaire Marxist, nor was he a career academic, having spent decades working in journalism. His critique of capitalism was grounded in an analysis of economic policy and international trade. Tellingly, the title of his most famous work is itself a *clin d'œil* to a Club of Rome Report. Before his move to academia, he had worked as chief financial editor for *The Economist* and as a senior adviser for the *International Monetary Fund*, a very different backstory to the underground resistance fighter and Trotskyist activist, Mandel. Hirsch's life was cut tragically short; he worked as an academic for just three years as he died prematurely from motor neurone disease. However, Hirsch (1977) still managed to produce one of the most important works on capitalism in the 1970s, *Social Limits to Growth*.

Many professional economists during the boom years of the social-democratic consensus thought that economic growth could continue indefinitely. For Whitehall mandarins, growth was the ultimate indicator of economic functioning, a proxy for 'successful' socio-economic development. There was a widely held belief that increased growth led to increased well-being across society. In *Social Limits to Growth*, Hirsch demonstrated the manifold weaknesses of this elision of 'economic growth' and 'positive economic development'. This, in itself, was an important contribution, and one which chimed with the emerging environmental critiques of capitalism, such as E. F. Schumacher's *The Small is Beautiful* [1973], which we turn to in the next chapter. Despite the significance of Hirsch's critique of growth as a catch-all indicator, he is primarily remembered for his other insights.

For many, the name Fred Hirsch will be synonymous with the concept of 'positional goods'. It is through this framing that Hirsch demonstrated the very real *social constraints* which limit economic growth. The title of Hirsch's book, *Social Limits to Growth,* was a direct reference to a recently published report by the Club of Rome, *The Limits to Growth* [1972], which, in itself, was highly significant. Importantly, the Club of Rome was neither the fifth international nor the Mont Pellerin Society. It was, nominally a pragmatic, politically 'neutral' organization, comprised primarily of current and former statesmen, UN administrations and politicians. Their work was viewed as 'reasonable' by centrists and was taken with a degree of gravity by professional economists and bureaucrats. Using newly developed computer technology, in particular the modelling of pioneering computer engineer Jay W. Forester (see Bardi 2016), the Club of Rome's report offered a warning: if growth continues unchecked on the current trajectory, the world will soon reach a point of over-population and of resource depletion. There were, in short, environmental and demographic limits to growth. Indefinite growth, as per the current model, was not tenable. This was in itself was a remarkable admission from the liberal capitalist elite.

For Hirsch, these limits needed to be taken seriously; the Club of Rome had sounded a very significant wakeup call and mainstream economic theorists needed to realize that limits existed on capitalist consumption. Yet, Hirsch was mindful that these significant computer simulations failed to account for a key factor: human psychology. Market actors consume products for various reasons. Some products are bought for their obvious *material* use value to fulfil a material human need: for example basic groceries and toilet paper. Hirsch realized that there was also another logic governing contemporary consumption patterns: consumption to demonstrate your *position* within society. There was thus a 'positional economy' which existed in addition to the more obvious 'material economy' (Hirsch 1977: 27–54). Many products are consumed not for their use in themselves, but to enable people to demonstrate their relative superiority to others. Hirsch argued that this socio-psychological feature of consumption needed to be accounted for and it too posed serious challenges and had an inbuilt propensity to trigger crises. In short, there were also fundamental *social* limits to growth, connected to the consumption logics of 'positional goods'.

Hirsch argued that the recent period of sustained growth had led to an increased 'demand for positional goods, a demand that can be satisfied for some only by frustrating the demand by others' (Hirsch 1977: 67). You cannot demonstrate your 'elite' status by consuming the same products as the masses; superiority can only be shown by consuming luxuries which are beyond the reach of the multitude. A product's luxury status does not derive from its use value, but from its inaccessibility. This idea harks back to one of the earliest critiques of the proto-capitalist economy put forward by Jean-Jacques Rousseau in his *Discourse on the Origins of Inequality* [1755] and *Emile* [1762]. In *Emile,* Rousseau explains that the 'rich think so much of ... their possessions ... not because they are useful, but because they are beyond the reach of the poor' (1911: 149). For Rousseau, the desire to demonstrate superior status, and to be explicitly acknowledged as superior, precipitates deeply pathological socio-economic dynamics.

For Hirsch, this was exactly what the recent period of economic growth had achieved: pathological economic development. Rather than growth leading to the coherent evolution of the economy so that all people could live a happier, more content life, the capitalist economy simply responded to demand. Industries frantically rushed to provide for the exclusive tastes of the most opulent, who sought extravagancies to demonstrate their distinction. As Hirsch (1977: 67) wrote, in 'the positional sector, individual's chase each other's tails'. In the positional economy, two dangerous uncontrolled forces collide: the intoxicating desire for status from the elite and the instrumental pursuit of profit from the capitalist. The result is an economy structured around high-end luxury items for the super-rich, which remain unavailable for the masses (see Veblen 1899). Hirsch's argument was based on solid factual analysis: increasingly, economic growth and material affluence had led to a smaller and smaller elite providing economic demand for an ever more inaccessible products to demonstrate their superiority. For example, the 1970s saw exponential growth in the production of private jets and supercars. The upwardly mobile middle class aspired to be flown to New York on the new Concorde supersonic airliner, while sipping champagne in first class. Perhaps the ultimate status symbol of the period was the new Learjet, which memorably featured in a chart hit of 1972, 'You're So Vain' by Carly Simon. The song's nameless protagonist encapsulates the phenomena Hirsch described.

Crucially, for Hirsch, the problem is one of 'positional goods'; as such they cannot be democratized, they cannot be socially distributed. The 'positional economy' which thrives in boomtimes means that economic growth does not lead to a fairer, more rationally organized economy, rather it leads to a tapering pyramid. To achieve distinction as part of the elite in an increasing affluent society, absurd positional goods are demanded and the capitalist economy is structured to comply: a supply emerges to meet the demand. While this reality may first seem to be limited to ostentatious commodities: flashy cars and yachts, for instance, Hirsch was keen to argue the positional economy is not just about brash excess. Hirsch spends a considerable section of *The Social Limits to Growth* reflecting on positional educational qualifications. There are two main reasons for attending a prestigious university: not only (a) for the quality of the education, but also (b) as a marker of distinction, to demonstrate your comparative greater 'employability' relative to other candidates. In this regard, a Harvard Education is as much a positional good as a speedboat or a private jet. A problematic dynamic arises in the affluent society: when increasing numbers of people have an undergraduate degree, a post-graduate qualification becomes an essential marker of distinction, and so on, *ad infinitum*. As Hirsch (1977: 49) argued, 'more education for all leaves everyone in the same place'; as such, these industries boom and then bust, no longer able to provide a positional bolstering.

The positional economy exacerbates capitalism's crises tendencies as 'it intensifies the distributional struggle to a potentially dangerous point. In short, it threatens to displace Smithian harmony by Hobbesian strife and is thereby a dangerous element to leave in the Smithian sector of individualistic optimalization' (Hirsch 1977: 185). As such, 'positional competition' is a 'hole in the affluent society' (Hirsch 1977: 102), one which needs to be analysed as a fundamental crisis tendency within the economic system. Growth has limits, and when they are reached, be it social-psychological, demographic or environmental, crises will inevitably occur. Both Mandel and Hirsch demonstrate the fundamental instability of capitalism, its continuing propensity for crises and the naivety of the belief in perpetual economic growth.

Habermas and Legitimation Crises

The early Frankfurt School's view of capitalism as a self-stabilizing totality, advanced by Adorno, Fromm and Marcuse, was displaced by Jürgen Habermas' work throughout the 1970s. While the first generation of critical theorists fused Marx, Freud and Weber to explore capitalism's stability, Habermas drew on an even broader palate of thinkers to theorize capitalist crises. Habermas departed from many of the central features of early critical theory, yet he still saw his overall project as a reconstruction of historical materialism encompassing a wider spectrum of theoretical approaches. Ultimately, Habermas sought a critical theory of society with normative content which did not require a foundation in metaphysics. In this regard, Habermas is best known today for his two-volume *Theory of Communicative Action* [1981] in which he identified an emancipatory potential existing within intersubjective communication practices.

Habermas' key work in the 1970s focused explicitly on crises. It was published in English with 'crisis' in the very title: *Legitimation Crisis* [1973].[5] In this text, which emerged out of a research programme at the Max Planck Institute of which he was Director, Habermas provided an extensive engagement with the crisis tendencies of capitalism, fixing a serious lacuna within first generation scholarship. Habermas' book marked not just a change in topic but a remarkable adoption of a new set of conceptual tools. Although central Marxist themes remained, not least the endemic nature of crisis within capitalism, *Legitimation Crisis* represented a significant departure from both his own, and the Frankfurt School's, previous research.

While *Legitimation Crisis* was innovative, Habermas was far from the first sociologist to engage with crises of legitimacy; the idea that leaders, institutions, bureaucracies, even armed forces, could lose legitimacy had been considered for centuries.[6] What made Habermas' account of a 'legitimation crisis' distinctive was that he sought to marry analyses of the 'social' and the 'systemic' crisis tendencies within society. In this regard, *Legitimation Crisis* can be read as an extension of the systems theoretical understanding of 'legitimacy', linking the dynamics of two distinct social systems: the 'subjective' and the 'objective'. Social integration and the 'subjective' dimension relates to the intersubjective forms of consensual validation, communicative rationality, popular support, consent. Systemic integration, in contrast, referred to the 'objective', calculable, quantifiable ability for the state to control and distribute resources and opportunities. While the social and subjective dimension could be impacted by charismatic leadership and affective ties, the systemic/objective realm could be impacted by environmental or structural-economic realities. For Habermas, a legitimation crisis occurs when there is no longer public belief in the social formation to provide for the demos at the level they demand. For Habermas, this is exactly what occurred at the end of the post-war boom.

Before the social-democratic consensus crises primarily arose out of systemic, 'objective', economic conditions. For instance, there may be a demand crisis, a recession or hyper-inflation. State management had briefly succeeded in mitigating these 'objective' systemic crises. Key to this alliance among state, industry and demos was the demand that the state delivered far more services than was the case pre-war. While in 1900, the state was primarily responsible for maintaining low inflation and keeping the borders of the country secure, by 1970, the state needed to maintain a sense of legitimacy over a much larger list of functions: the capacity to provide employment, pensions, lifelong learning, social healthcare, vocational training programmes, etc. This expanded list of obligations created crisis tendencies in the socio-cultural as well as the political and economic domains. What if people stopped having confidence in the state to deliver these provisions? What if the existing capitalist formation no longer appeared optimal at delivering the goods due to increased costs?

Habermas argued that the advanced capitalist model after the Second World War had served to 'depoliticise' the economy. The provision of services was increasingly seen as a technical problem rather than a political compromise. However, as Mandel argued, profits started to fall for industry as technical innovation slowed and labour unions gained strength. It rapidly became clear that the state was being pushed in two opposite directions: to manage the economy to maintain low inflation while ensuring large profits for industry and to maintain the standard of social services the public had come to expect. As this unravelled, the legitimacy of the socio-economic system was increasingly questioned and the 'apolitical' nature on the economy began to be doubted.

The failed delivery of expected socio-cultural goods served to 'repoliticise the relations of production' which led to the system having an 'increased need for legitimation' (Habermas 1976: 36) at exactly the moment it was losing control. As a result, late capitalism was left in a precarious position, unable to simultaneously solve systemic demands (in the capitalist economy) and maintain its subjective legitimacy. The conflict between welfare and the demands of the private sector deteriorated as free marketeers grew increasingly unhappy about *any* state constraint on their profits, while the public vocally expected an ever higher degree of state provision. As a result, as Habermas argued, the legitimacy of the entire system was in crisis. Governments were suddenly swamped by demands from their population which were directly at odds with the demands of industry.

As a result, Habermas argued, the 1970s demonstrated a spectacular legitimation crisis for the capitalist system.

Habermas was also clear that other crises tendencies remained. As well as 'legitimacy crises' the tendency towards 'rationality crises' persisted, in which the system was no longer able to produce and distribute goods. This could lead to scarcity or to an unacceptable rise in prices. A rationality crisis is thus an 'output crisis' which can occur in varying forms. Output crises remained a serious threat to capitalism's stability. This was in addition to the legitimation crisis, which was instead framed as an 'input crisis', in which the public did not invest the capitalist system with sufficient legitimacy. A legitimacy crisis is thus the result of the public no longer holding 'the requisite level of mass loyalty' (Habermas 1976: 46) to enable the state to facilitate the smooth running of the capitalist economy.

Habermas' work provides an important meditation on the crisis tendencies of capitalism and on the particularities of the crises of the period. The expanded conceptual arsenal Habermas created bears both important continuities and divergences from the critique of capitalism put forward by first generation theorists. In keeping with Mandel and Hirsch, Habermas retains the Marxist insight that capitalism is a system which is marked by endemic crisis tendencies. *Legitimation Crisis* demonstrates not just the explicable nature of the crises of the 1970s, but also the plurality of alternative species of crisis which capitalism is structurally predisposed to.

That said, there are also several important limitations to Habermas' framing which need to be acknowledged. With hindsight, it is apparent that he fundamentally failed to identify key trends emerging within the social order: his analysis did not afford primacy to globalization or the move towards financialization. Both are not only crucial developments within capitalism but also changes which served to impact the legitimacy of the market order (Raulet 2011). As we discuss in Chapter 12, for Wolfgang Streeck (2016), the rise of an unaccountable international coterie of neoliberal technocrats, the so-called *marketvolk*, serves to threaten not merely the legitimacy of capitalism and produce 'legitimation crises', but may even be a central feature in the end of capitalism altogether. In time, Streeck and Habermas would come to clash extensively on this question and on the role of the state in particular (see Habermas 2015; Šumonja 2019). While Habermas' failure to grasp the significance of the move to globalization and financialization can be forgiven as no theorist of capitalism should be expected to have the gift of foresight, there is a more serious criticism which can be directed at Habermas' basic argument within *Legitimation Crisis.* There is an unstated presupposition that the democratic critique of capitalism has the ability to control and restrain market forces. Again, Streeck (2016) demonstrates the flaw in this idea: increasingly neoliberalism serves to capture and erode all democratic vehicles of resistance to market imperatives. In short, Habermas failed to account for the idea that capitalism may actually collapse as a result of its internal dynamics, that the manifold pressures of constant growth and profit accumulation would destroy the social preconditions required for capitalism's survival. Habermas may be fundamentally mistaken in his belief that democratic checks and balance can serve to manage and restrain capitalism.

Post-structuralist and Post-modern Critiques of Capitalism

Throughout the 1970s, a radical critique of western philosophy emerged, rooted in linguistics, semiotics and psychoanalysis. In place of the fixed categories and universal claims of the Enlightenment, theorists increasingly rejected binary oppositions, coherent narratives, even the notion of 'progress'. While many of the critiques of capitalism discussed in this book have their origins in German Idealism or the Scottish Enlightenment, many of the insights of this era emerged from a cocktail of French thinkers (see Felsch 2022). While the period saw a rapidly eliding mix of perspectives, today it is often taught that the emerging insights divided into two similar, but distinct, strands of thought: 'post-modernism' and 'post-structuralism'. Advocates of both perspectives produced innovative critiques of capitalism, explicitly challenging the preceding understandings of political economy. It is worth noting that the leading scholars of both camps consciously eschewed labels and classifications. While Jean Baudrillard is today associated with post-modernism and Michel Foucault with post-structuralism, neither embraced such terms, indeed, both explicitly rejected them. Today, the legacy of these theorists is increasingly in flux. To Baudrillard's admirers, he produced the masterwork of postmodernism; yet to his detractors, most famously Alan Sokal and Jean Bricmont (1997), he typified a form of irrational gibberish. While Foucault, and his particular form of post-structuralism, remains associated with the political and economic left, we engage with the emerging literature which suggests that Foucault's work needs to be seen as presenting a more ambivalent engagement with capitalism (Zamora and Behrent 2016).

The roots of the bloom in 'French Theory' lay in a rejection of the structural linguistics of Ferdinand de Saussure. de Saussure argued that language operates on the basis of there being 'signifiers' (words or phrases), 'signifieds' (meanings) and 'referents' (the object pointed to by the signifier). For de Saussure and his followers, this model explicated the stability of language and of thought itself. Through Saussure's model, it was possible to see a knowable external world due to the existence of collectively accepted fixed correlating terms and referents. In the 1970s, the ideas of theorists as diverse as Roland Barthes, Jacques Lacan and Jacques Derrida were developed and elided to challenge de Saussure's account. In contrast to the stable relationship between 'signifier', 'signified' and 'referent', or more simply 'language' and 'world', a new understanding emerged in which dynamic instability dominated. The stable 'signifier'–'signified'–'referent' relationship was problematized as the socio-temporal specificity of language and knowledge was stressed. The relationship between the 'signifier' and the 'signified' and the 'referent' was now understood as being contingent on opaque power relationships which constitute subjecthood and which shape the unconscious.

By the end of the 1970s, the structural linguistic model was displaced by a new paradigm in which the external world was no longer dominant. In the work of Jean Baudrillard, an increasingly closed circuit of 'signifiers' ('signs') emerged, in which the external world of 'things' is absent. Meaning becomes an internal, self-referential plane, in which there is no direct correlate within the objective world. Signifiers increasingly get their meaning from their relationship to other signifiers. As a result, there are no 'universal truths' which people can access because the means of their comprehension and communication are constantly shifting. For Baudrillard, we are left with a relationship of 'signs' to 'signs', of unfixed, self-referential signifiers. In this dynamic and uncertain maze of signs, there is no possibility of a 'grand narrative', as Lyotard framed it in *The Postmodern Condition* [1979]. There is no accessible bird's eye view of society and no perspective from which to present a universal history or teleology. Stable foundations of knowledge became increasingly illusive. Post-modernism embraced this complexity to discredit the claims to eternal truths, or superior forms of theoretically grounded wisdom (i.e. Marxism). The new world of multiple, internally referential and socio-temporally specific 'signs' was a maze. There was no singular truth, no grand answer. Post-modernists meditated on the uncertainty and complexity of the socio-cultural domain, including the specifics of capitalism. In contrast, while typically embracing some form of the critique of Saussure's linguistic model outlined above, post-structuralist thinkers reflected on the instability of knowledge in this new framing, and focused more on the relationship between knowledge and power.

In this heady theoretical landscape, Baudrillard wrote a remarkable critique of capitalism, *For a Critique of the Political Economy of the Sign* [1972]. He could not have been better placed to engage in the debates of the period; his doctoral thesis was supervised by a remarkable trio: Roland Barthes, Henri Lefebvre and Pierre Bourdieu, all of whom influenced his mature work. Baudrillard's political economy is perhaps best understood as the development of a semiotic critique of Marx, drawing on the critique of de Saussure. For Baudrillard, Marx's engagement with capitalism was nowhere near critical enough as he remained trapped within the fundamental symbolic order of liberal political economy in which production was paramount. As a result, Baudrillard argued, Marx is tied to the 'phantasm' of labour as the defining factor of human nature. This myth was built into the language of classical political economy. Marx's entire critique of capitalism can be understood as being predicated on accepting this error: that human essence is fundamentally productive and that this productive capacity can, and must, be emancipated. Marx identified the exploitative nature of capitalism, through his theory of surplus value; humanity's productive abilities were being exploited and used against them, engendering alienation. Baudrillard, particular in his early work, admired Marx and respected this insight. But, Baudrillard argued, why did Marx focus so narrowly on production when it is the primary concern of the political-economy he despised?[7] As a result, he unintentionally embraced this fundamental concern of liberal political economy. Baudrillard argued, *pace* Marx, that people are more than their mere labour power. What about the meanings people invest their actions with? What about the symbolic order of capitalism itself? For Baudrillard, Marx was trapped within the semiotic-linguistic constellation of classical political economy. Baudrillard argued that this semiotic order needed to be urgently transcended before any meaningful critique of capitalism could emerge.

Baudrillard's criticism of Marx here is simple: Marx remained problematically invested in the terms, values and concerns, of classical political economy. Baudrillard's critique of capitalism pointed to something far deeper than the exploitation of labour. Rather, advanced capitalism had wrought and thrives upon the fundamental disintegration of the symbolic order. In *For a Critique of the Political Economy of the Sign*, the foundation of capitalist political economy is not the structurally exploited productive capacity of labour, rather it is the disintegration of the stable relationship between signifier, signified and referent. In late capitalism, signifiers have become detached from what they signify. In their place, a world of 'signs' emerge, which are 'at once signifier and signified' (Baudrillard 2019: 145). This is the central property of capitalism in Baudrillard's analysis, and is at the core of his broader engagement with the economy.

Commodification, from such a view, is radically recast as just one example of a hyper-abstract resignification, a move towards a broader 'hyper-reality' (Baudrillard 1994 [1981]). The dominance of 'exchange value' over 'use value' is just one case of the distortion of meaning which is induced by capitalism. In late capitalism

> … the signified and the referent and now abolished to the sole profit of the play of the signifiers, of a generalized formalization where the code no longer refers back

> to any subjective or objective 'reality', but to its own logic. The signifier becomes its own referent and the use value of the sign disappears to the profit only of its commutation and exchange value. The sign no longer designates anything at all.
>
> (Baudrillard 1975: 127–8)

This is clearly a more wide-ranging critique than Marx's; the world of Smith and Ricardo has been left far behind. Instead of a reticulated system of exploitative production, we see the ascent of a 'code', of a self-referential system of signs that dominate human action. This self-referential code is in a constant process of reproduction and adaptation. Crises tendences emerge as this code struggles to repeat itself seamlessly. The meaninglessness of the signifier enables the new form of late industrial capitalism. The 'precision nuclear weapon', the 'war on carbohydrates', the 'battle against plaque', the 'revolution in underarm deodorants' can only have meaning within this self-defining code (Poster 1975: 8). Ultimately, the code is now the dominant force of social reproduction. This is a remarkable analysis and a total reversal of Marx's critique of political economy. In Baudrillard's system, the code is dominant and production is a result of the functional necessities of the code's evolution. This is no longer a form of historical materialism, but a radically new critique of capitalism.

To substantiate his claims, Baudrillard analysed consumption patterns. This is a further inversion of Marxism; for Baudrillard the semiotic code determines production, but it is consumption, rather than production, which is the optimal entry point for social research. As Baudrillard's translator, Poster (1975: 8–9) frames it,

> ... in consumption there is an active appropriation of signs, not the simple destruction of an object. What is consumed is not simply a material object that satisfied an all too rational need, but a symbolic meaning in which the consumer places himself in a communication structure where an exchange occurs which is profoundly tied to the whole system of political economy.

There is a systemic necessity for constant consumption as this enables the justification, modification and reproduction of the semiotic-code, which is performatively enacted through consumption. Under capitalist economics all social interaction is reduced from a reciprocal transfer of symbols to the 'terrorism of the code' (see McLaverty-Robinson 2012). Marx has been left far behind by this stage of Baudrillard's analysis; the commodity is now an object of consumption invested with meaning far more than it is the fetishized manifestation of abstracted labour. This, bizarrely, is now too objective a referent, too 'real' even in its fundamental abstraction. Rather, the commodity has no objective referent at all, not even in abstract labour time; the consumer can invest the commodity with whatever meaning the code permits, which itself is constantly adapting. The golden arches of McDonalds have a constantly shifting meaning, which is far more than a mere epiphenomena of processes within the economic base (Ritzer 1993). The commodity is no longer understood as a product of labour which emerged from humans working on the natural world, rather it is a part of dynamic and illusive code which lacks any stable referent. This is because,

> ... *the structure of the sign is at the heart of the commodity form* that the commodity can take on, immediately, the effect of signification – not epiphenomenally, in excess of

> itself, as "message" or connotation – but because its very form establishes it as a total *medium*, as a *system of communication* administering all social exchange.
>
> (Baudrillard 2019: 149)

While Baudrillard's critique of political economy is a cornerstone of post-modern thought, his particular relationship to Marx and to post-structuralism demonstrates a constant revisionism. In *For a Critique of the Political Economy of the Sign* Baudrillard presents himself as working within, but substantially developing Marx's work. Yet, in *The Mirror of Production* there is a more definitive break from Marx's critique of capitalism. Ultimately, Baudrillard served to inspire a further generation of thinkers (see Poster 2002). In places, Baudrillard's critique of capitalism reads like science fiction with 'the code' ruling not just the market, but all humanity. Adam Gopnik (2003) of the *New Yorker* even joked that Baudrillard's critique of capitalism was so essential to the plot of the 1999 movie *The Matrix* that he should sue for a screen credit. Remarkably, contemporary readings of Foucault's work are even more polarized than readings of Baudrillard. For his left-leaning devotees, Foucault offered a paradigm shift in the critique of power. To his supporters, his insights extend to the critique of capitalism, enabling the disciplinary forces of the market to be optimally understood and resisted. Foucault's admirers often reflect the zeal of dogmatic Marxists, with Halperin (1997) offering an unashamedly hagiographic inflection to his work, titling one of his replies to Foucault's critics *Saint Foucault*. Yet, Foucault's profane conduct is increasingly subject to justifiable and important scrutiny (Campbell 2021). Over the past decade, his work has increasingly been read as possessing a more ambivalent relationship with neoliberalism (Zamora and Behrent 2016).

Foucault was never far from controversy. He rose to fame as a result of his attack on Marxism and humanism and has been accused of being both a KGB agent and a CIA stooge (Foucault 1984: 376, see Kelly 2021). In an interview towards the end of his life, he wryly commented that he had 'been situated in most squares of the political checkerboard.... as anarchist, leftist, ostentatious or disguised Marxist, nihilist, or secret Anti-Marxist, technocrat in the service of Gaullism, new liberal [sic] etc' (Foucault 1984: 383–4). Considering such passionate verdicts were passed on Foucault on the basis of his alleged economic preferences, it is worth stressing that the bulk of Foucault's writing side-lined capitalism as an object of study. He was neither an economists nor an economic sociologist. When pressed, he preferred to consider his methodology to be an 'archaeology of knowledge' (Foucault 1969). However, throughout his work, Foucault provided a radical new understanding of power, which has had a sustained impact on the critique of capitalism.

In Foucault's *Discipline and Punish* [1975], the gruesome fate of Robert-Francois Damiens is detailed. Damiens' assassination attempt on Louis XV was foiled and he was put to death in a macabre public spectacle. Foucault details the horrific increments of his dismemberment, the ritual form of execution reserved for regicides in France. The carnivalesque spectacle of Damiens' death and torture is then contrasted with the new forms of punishment reserved for prisoners in modern society. In contrast to a baying crowd and horses pulling (or failing to pull) limbs off a condemned man, Foucault details the new disciplinary practices of the prison, typified by the panopticon. The idea of the panopticon is that a guard can be positioned in such a way so that all prisoners can be observed and their conduct monitored. Rather than the frenzy and chaos of Damiens' last moments, the modern prison is a system of control, with clear rules, timetables and constant surveillance. It is a regimented, rationalized, disciplined operation, the antithesis of the spectacle of Damiens' execution. Foucault argues this mirrors a broader transition in society: a turn from the state ritualistically exerting the power of life and death over deviants, instead, increasingly the state seeks to control how the living behaves. In short, Foucault details the ascent of a form of 'biopower': disciplinary control which the state exerts over people's lives.

By reflecting on the relationship between 'power' and 'knowledge' in society, Foucault argued that a complex series of 'discourses' exist which designate 'normal conduct' and 'normal behaviour'. Indeed, Foucault's entire corpus is built around understanding and resisting the shifting definitions of 'normalcy', demonstrating how conduct is policed, and why such power must be resisted. For Foucault, those on the edge of society are particularly vulnerable to the normalizing, disciplinary power of discourse: prisoners, the mentally ill, children, those who have non-normative sexualities. As a result, his wider study concentrated on such marginalized social subjects. Foucault's work, up until the late 1970s, was largely focused on developing this particular understanding of power, based on the normalizing power of discourse, the states' biopolitical control of its subjects and the impact on the most marginalized in society: capitalism was certainly not his central concern.

Foucault turned his attention to capitalism, and to neoliberalism in particular, in the late 1970s, when neoliberal ideas was starting to proliferate. To understand Foucault's more 'ambiguous relationship with neoliberalism' (Zamora 2016: 2) one must return to the context of the period through which Foucault was writing. As with Mandel, Hirsch, Habermas and Baudrillard, the specific historical moment is essential to understanding Foucault's engagement with capitalism. Foucault lived and wrote in an intellectual climate where authoritarian governments were a central feature of debate and discussion. In France, the Communist Party (PCF) offered a dogmatic support of the USSR, denouncing the Hungarian uprising and rejecting the 1968 demonstrations. In contrast, the PCF fetishized the working class and deferred to the Soviet leadership. As a result, Foucault viewed Marxism through a highly critical lens, dismissing it as a nineteenth century philosophy, unsuited to the conditions of the day. In *The Order of Things* [1966] he provocatively presented his Marxist contemporaries are living like fish out of water (1973: 261).

A further important contextualization, as discussed by Habermas in *Legitimation Crisis*, was the rapid expansion in the role and scope of the state following the post-war settlement. For Foucault, Marxism and the creeping expansion of the state both posed credible, imminent threats to liberty. There was something of an inevitability to the rise of authoritarianism and the biopolitical control it yielded with an expanding state: the technocratic economy of Keynesian was not a road to a socialism and to the eventual 'withering away' of the state. In this vein, Foucault memorably endorsed the 'new philosophy' of the period, typified by Andre Glucksmann's *The Master Thinkers* [1977]. This so-called new philosophy held that Marxism and revolutionary politics more broadly led inexorably to the gulag, a position Foucault came to vocally support (Christofferson 2016: 6, 18–20).[8] When one locates Foucault's work within this broader context, it is easier to see how he could have been 'seduced by neoliberalism' (Zamora 2016: 3).

As a result, as part of his lectures at the Collège de France, later published as *The Birth of Biopolitics* [1979], Foucault provided an ambivalent engagement with neoliberalism. It is evident that this in part sprung from his deepening frustration with the enduring power of Marxism within French academia and politics. As stagflation threw France into economic turmoil and the Keynesian axioms were systematically discarded throughout the 1970s, the French media turned on Keynes himself (Behrent 2016: 33). President Valéry Giscard d'Estaing then embraced a wide ranging set of economic reforms, including, symbolically, deregulating the price of bread. Compared to the economic demands from the new right in England and the USA, France's turn towards economic liberalism was hardly a radical embrace of the free market; however, it opened the floodgates to economists who sat closer to the neoliberal imagination. Most notable here was Henri Lapage (1978), who both praised marketization and decried the purported totalitarian tendences of even the mildest state intervention. Crucially, this anti-statism was embraced by a swathe of socialist-anarchists, the so-called French 'Second Left', who found common cause with Lapage's anti-authoritarian politics.[9] It is through his engagement with this 'Second Left' that Foucault engaged with neoliberalism; as a politics devoid of Marxist dogma, capable of reducing the scope of the state. It is this combination of factors which presaged Foucault's *The Birth of Biopolitics*: his hatred of Marxism, his anti-statism, the increasingly vocal economic right in light of the crises of the French economy and the ascendant 'Second Left' and 'New Philosophy'. As Behrent (2016: 39) argues, this context is vital to understanding why Foucault lectured on neoliberalism, and with such a degree of ambivalence, in what was originally intended to be a lecture series, not on capitalism, but on biopolitics.

The tension in Foucault's lecture series lies in the fact that, while he opposed both biopolitics and neoliberalism, he sought to utilize neoliberalism to demonstrate the problems embedded within Marxism. Crucially, he sought to provide a critique of neoliberalism as being based on unstable philosophical foundations and as possessing an inbuilt structural tendency to governmentality. Yet, he also saw neoliberalism as some kind of theoretical ethanol, capable of cleansing discussions of stale Marxist dogma, yet it remained fundamentally corrosive and dangerous. Central to his critique of liberalism was the role of law and its relationship to power. While classical liberal theorists held that law was derived from the natural self-interest of subjects, mutually consenting to government by surrendering a portion of their natural rights, the 'social contract' tradition, for Foucault, this abstraction was incoherent and problematic. Sitting ironically close to Bentham on this issue, who had argued 'rights' were 'nonsense on stilts', Foucault argued that liberalism, as a broader philosophy, had an undue attachment to law, which served no theoretical purpose and which risked embedding governmentality. Rather, a more utilitarian-inflected liberalism would see power as a sufficiently expansive concept in and of itself and would enable the statist investment in law to be discarded. 'Where there is power, there is resistance', wrote Foucault (1978: 95–6), but power is the dominant factor, not the fictive anthropological 'social contract' which gives legitimacy to the juridical mechanisms of the state. The problem with liberalism is that, through its reliance on law, it creates the preconditions for juridically grounded disciplinary biopower. These are preconditions, Foucault argues, which are in contradiction to the philosophy's fundamental aims. Liberalism, defined by its prioritization of liberty, ends up swinging closer to an excess of government, rather than to an excess of freedom. Liberty is thus understood as being a 'side effect of power' (Behrent 2016: 47), rather than a result of some social contract which invokes and legitimates juridical restrictions on freedom. The market, in economic liberalism, had no need for *juridical* justification – it could, in and of itself, serve to comprehensively 'cut off the king's head', to dramatically remove the power of the state.

From this position, Foucault saw in neoliberalism the possibility for a reduction in governmentality, a decline in the power of the state, and an alternative to Marxist dogma, at exactly the time where economic tides were changing. However, Foucault argued that the tendency to statism remained latent within neoliberalism. While today Foucault's work is increasingly used to study neoliberal forms of subjecthood (see Brown 2015), and to study the specifics of a 'neoliberal governmentality' (see Kipnis 2008, *inter alia*), ironically Foucault's explicit work on neoliberalism itself is rarely used in this endeavour. This is perhaps because the emancipatory possibilities Foucault saw within neoliberalism never came to fruition. In direct contrast, it is increasingly argued that we live in a period of 'authoritarian neoliberalism' (Bruff 2013) and 'surveillance capitalism' (Zuboff 2018), developments which Foucault would have likely despised. In this regard, there is a curious parallel with the Marxists which Foucault found most contemptible: both Foucault and Marx provide fascinating concepts which inform today's critiques of capitalism; however, both decisively failed as fortune tellers of capitalism's future development. To a lesser extent, the same can be said of Daniel Bell's conservative critique of capitalism.

Daniel Bell: The Cultural Contradictions of Late Capitalism

We turn now to Daniel Bell's *The Cultural Contradictions of Late Capitalism* [1976]. While the previous works discussed have a progressive inflection, Daniel Bell's work is distinctly conservative in nature, at least on cultural issues.[10] Bell was one of the most important sociologists in the USA in the post-war era and an influential public figure. He described himself in a famous phrase as a socialist in economics, a liberal in politics and a conservative in culture. His most famous works were *The End of Ideology* [1960] and *The Coming of the Post-Industrial Society: A Venture in Social Forecasting* [1973]. He coined the term the post-industrial society and, as reflected by the title of his work, he was interested in forecasting the future of American society. Part of this endeavour, which was an expression of modernization theories and supported by the RAND organization, was an attempt to understand what societal trends could provide stability for a desirable future. By the time he came to write *The Cultural Contradictions of Late Capitalism*, he had become more sceptical of his earlier announcement of 'the end of ideology' and the smooth path of modernization.

Indicatively, on only the second page of the text, Bell aims an intellectual dig at Foucault's work for elevating 'madness' as a form of 'truth' (Bell 1996: 34), arguing that Foucault's work will be 'remembered, if at all, as a footnote to cultural history' (Bell 1996: 52). This is representative of Bell's broader attack on contemporary relativist, sensuous, culture: both intellectual and popular. For Bell, as a result of this cultural demise, capitalism was dramatically unravelling and might well collapse before the end of the twentieth century. This cultural crisis extended far beyond his native America. His work is a melange of conservative socio-cultural criticism, sweeping and synoptic in style, taking in the beats, Salinger, hippies, Byron, modernism, secularism. The primary argument Bell presented is that the demands of the economy, and the new cultural mores, are vastly at odds.

Bell presented a tripartite model of society, compromising the cultural, the political and the economic realms. The importance of culture, and culture's relationship with socio-economic structure, is central in his analysis. While crude Marxists present the capitalist economic 'base' as determining all cultural forms, Bell argues that culture changes far faster, and often far more dramatically, than the economy. Indeed, even technology is held to be slumberous in comparison to changing cultural currents. For Bell, there exists a fundamental tension between the cultural attitudes and values required for the prime functioning of the socio-economic domain and those existing in the present day. Bell (1996: 37) makes this point explicitly,

> ... what I find striking today is the radical disjunction between the social structure (the techno-economic order) and the culture. The former is ruled by an economic principle defined in terms of efficiency and functional rationality, the organization of production through the ordering of things, including men as things, The latter is prodigal, promiscuous, dominated by an anti-rational, anti-intellectual temper in which the self is taken as the touchstone of cultural judgements, and the effect on the self is the measure of the aesthetic worth of experience.

What Weber described as the 'Protestant ethic', with its asceticism, self-control and the fetishization of hard work, enabled the growth of capitalism. For Bell, these ethical values remained relevant for the marketplace of late capitalism, the socio-economic structure required workers who placed value on 'self-discipline, delayed gratification, and restraint' (1996: 37). Yet, paradoxically, the capitalist system, and the consumer society it spawned, induced a total rejection of these values, promoting materialism, excess, hedonism, luxury. Even worse, from Bell's perspective, was the rise of the counter-cultural groups, such as the Beats and Hippies, who rejected conservative morals regarding drug taking and sexual permissiveness. The sensibility of the sixties, for Bell, saw 'a preoccupation with the sexually perverse', an 'anti-cognitive and anti-intellectual move' and the elevation of the hallucinatory experience (Bell 1996: 121). In characteristically acerbic style, Bell attacked what he famously framed as the move from 'the protestant ethic to the psychedelic bazaar' (Bell 1996: 54).

Accordingly, the crisis tendency Bell identified in late capitalism lay in the disjunction between the demands of the techno-structural economic system and the character types and ethical values that it produced. For conservatives like Bell, this was only exaggerated by the growth of social security systems throughout the West; states were increasingly expected to provide the capital for citizens to engage in culturally normalized irresponsible hedonism. The 'over-reliance' on welfare served to put further pressure on the state to ensure steady economic growth and predictable economic forecasting, exaggerating this contradiction. William Beveridge, who famously took a cold bath each morning, then spent hours poring over statistics, could not be further from William Burroughs, a repeated source of Bell's contempt. For Bell, the late capitalist economy desperately needed more Beveridges; however, it kept producing Burroughses. Towards the end of his first essay in *The Cultural Contradictions of Capitalism* Bell wrote, 'it is this disjunction which is the historic cultural crisis of all western bourgeois society. This cultural contradiction is, in the longer run, the most fateful division in the society' (1996: 84).

Conclusion

The 1970s saw a proliferation of critiques of capitalism, with conceptual innovations abounding. Yet, similarities can be traced across all the critiques we discussed here. Bell's work is in keeping with the other theorists of this period in that he identified fundamental crises tendencies within capitalism. For Mandel, these crises arise from the cyclic nature of long waves of capitalist development. For Hirsch, crises arise out of the inability for equal access to positional goods. Habermas identified a plurality of crisis tendencies, with the period dominated by legitimation crises. For Baudrillard, crises emerge as the code struggles to seamlessly reproduce, threatening the stability of referent-less hyperreality. For Foucault, crises emerged from inevitably resistance to the authoritarian tendencies of both liberalism and Marxism. The centrality of the analysis of 'crises' and of 'contradictions' in the critiques of capitalism in this period reflects the socio-economic climate.

Notes

1 The text was originally published in German as *Der Spätkapitalismus* in 1972. The English translation appeared in 1975, which contained some revisions and updates from the original German.
2 The term 'late capitalism' was actually first used by Werner Sombart in his *Modern Capitalism* [1902].
3 A notable exception being Walt Whitman Rostow, see *The Stages of Economic Growth: A Non-Communist Manifesto* [1960].
4 Indeed, some contemporary scholars consider the revival Mandel sparked in 'long wave' analyses to be 'his main contribution' to the critique of capitalism (Albarracin and Montes 1999: 52, *inter alia*).
5 The original German title translates to *Legitimation Problems in Late Capitalism*.
6 For example, Rousseau's notion of the 'general will' in *The Social Contract* [1762] can be understood as an extensive meditation on this theme.
7 As we argued in Chapter One, Marx was influenced by the work of Smith and his contemporaries.
8 It has been suggested that Foucault's support for 'the new philosophy' was more a political rather than a theoretical endorsement. Indeed, much of Foucault's work clashed with Glucksmann's even when the latter was attempting to mobilize Foucault's own ideas (see Christofferson, 2016: 13).
9 This bizarre coalition of economic left and right is a continuing feature in French politics, which is manifest today with the gilet jaune, for instance, or the anti-vax movement.
10 While written two decades after Bell's *The Cultural Contradictions of Capitalism,* Peter Berger's *The Capitalist Revolution* [1988] is an important, similar work offering a conservative critique of capitalism.

References

Albarracin, J. and Montes P. 1999. 'Late Capitalism: Mandel's Interpretation of Contemporary Capitalism'. *The Legacy of Ernest Mandel.* Edited by G. Achcar. London: Verso. pp. 38–74.

Althusser, L. Balibar, E. Establet, R. Rancière, J. and Macherey, P. 1970 [1965]. *Reading Capital.* London: New Left Books.

Bardi, U. 2016. 'Jay Wright Forrester (1918–2016): His Contribution to the Concept of Overshoot in Socioeconomic Systems'. *BioPhysical Economics and Resource Quality,* 1 (12): 9–12.

Baudrillard, J. 2019 [1972]. *For a Critique of the Political Economy of the Sign.* Translated by Levin, C. London: Verso.

Baudrillard, J. 1975 [1973]. *The Mirror of Production.* Translated by Poster, M. St. Louis: Telos Press.

Baudrillard, J. 1994 [1981]. *Simulacra and Simulation.* Translated by Glaser, S. F. Ann Arbor: The University of Michigan Press.

Bell, D. 1996 [1976]. *The Cultural Contradictions of Capitalism.* New York: Basic Books.

Berger, P. 1987 [1986]. *The Capitalist Revolution: Fifty Propositions about Prosperity, Equality, and Liberty.* Aldershot: Wildwood House.

Brown, W. 2015. *Undoing the Demos: Neoliberalism's Stealth Revolution.* New York City: Zone Books.
Bruff, I. 2013. 'The Rise of Authoritarian Neoliberalism'. *Rethinking Marxism,* 26 (1): 113–29.
Campbell, M. 2021. 'French Philosopher Michel Foucault "Abused Boys in Tunisia"'. *The Times.* 28 March 2021. www.thetimes.co.uk/article/french-philosopher-michel-foucault-abused-boys-in-tunisia-6t5sj7jvw
Carson, R. 1962. *Silent Spring.* Boston: Houghton Mifflin Harcourt.
Christofferson, M. S. 2016 [2014]. 'Foucault and the New Philosophy: Why Foucault Endorsed Andre Glucksmann's *The Master Thinkers*'. In: *Foucault and Neoliberalism.* Edited by D. Zamora and M.C. Behrent. Cambridge: Polity. pp. 6–23.
De Groot, M. 2019. 'Western Europe and the Collapse of Bretton Woods'. *International Journal: Canada's Journal of Global Policy Analyses,* 74 (2): 282–300.
Felsch, P. 2022. *The Summer of Theory: History of A Rebellion 1960–1990.* Translated by T. Crawford. Cambridge: Polity.
Foucault, M. 1969. *L'archéologie du savoir.* Paris: Éditions Gallimard.
Foucault, M. 1973 [1966] *The Order of Things: An Archaeology of the Human Sciences.* New York: Vintage.
Foucault, M. 1977 [1975] *Discipline and Punish: The Birth of the Prison.* Translated by A. Sheridan. New York: Pantheon Books.
Foucault, M. 1978. *The History of Sexuality: Vol. 1: An Introduction.* New York: Random House.
Foucault, M. 1984. *The Foucault Reader.* New York: Pantheon.
Fourastié, J. 1979. *Les Trente Glorieuses, ou la révolution invisible de 1946 à 1975.* Paris: Fayard.
Glucksmann, A. 1977 *The Master Thinkers.* Translated by B. Pearce. New York: Harper and Row.
Gopnik, A. 2003. 'The Unreal Thing: What's Wrong with the Matrix?' *The New Yorker.* 11 May 2003. www.newyorker.com/magazine/2003/05/19/the-unreal-thing
Habermas, J. 1976 [1973]. *Legitimation Crisis.* Translated by T. McCarthy. Cambridge: Polity Press.
Habermas J. 1986 [1981]. *The Theory of Communicative Action, Vol. 1: Reason and the Rationalization of Society.* London: Polity Press.
Habermas, J. 1988 [1981]. *The Theory of Communicative Action, Vol. 2: Critique of Functionalist Reason.* London: Polity Press.
Habermas, J. 2015. *The Lure of Technocracy.* Cambridge: Polity Press.
Halperin, D. 1997. *Saint Foucault: Towards a Gay Hagiography.* Oxford: Oxford University Press.
Harman, C. 1978. 'Mandel's Late Capitalism'. *International Socialism.* 2(1). www.marxists.org/archive/harman/1978/07/mandel.html (accessed 15 February 2022).
Hirsch, F. 1977 [1976]. *Social Limits to Growth.* London: Routledge and Kegan Paul.
Husson, M. 1999. 'After the Golden Age: On Late Capitalism'. In: *The Legacy of Ernest Mandel.* Edited by G. Achcar. London: Verso. pp. 75–103.
Kelly, M. 2021. 'Must We Cancel Foucault?' *Telos.* www.telospress.com/must-we-cancel-foucault/#notes
Kipnis, A. 2008. 'Audit Cultures: Neoliberal Governmentality, Socialist Legacy, or Technologies of Governing'. *American Ethnologist,* 35.2: 275–89.
Krätke, M. 2007. 'On the History and Logic of Modern Capitalism: The Legacy of Ernest Mandel'. *Historical Materialism,* 15 (1): 109–43.
Lapage, H. 1978 *Tomorrow Capitalism: The Economics of Economic Freedom.* Translated by C. S. Ogilvie. Chicago: Open Court.
Löwy, M. 2009. 'A Systematic Biography of Ernest Mandel'. *International Viewpoint.* 10 October 2009. https://internationalviewpoint.org/spip.php?article1729
Lyotard, J-F. 1984 [1979]. *The Postmodern Condition: A Report on Knowledge.* Translated by G. Bennington and B. Massumi. Minneapolis: University of Minnesota Press.
Mandel, E. 1968 [1962]. *Marxist Economic Theory.* Translated by B. Pearce. New York: Monthly Review Press.
Mandel, E. 1975 [1972]. *Cultural Contradictions of Capitalism: Late Capitalism.* Translated by J. De Bres. London: New Left Books.

Mandel, E. 2022. *Marxists against Stalinism*. London: Resistance Books.

McLaverty-Robinson, A. 2012. 'Jean Baudrillard: The Code'. *Ceasefire*. 27 April 2012. https://ceasefiremagazine.co.uk/in-theory-baudrillard-5/

Meadows, D. H., Meadows, D. L., Randers, J. and Behrens, W. 1972. *The Limits to Growth: A Report for the Club of Rome's Project on the Predicament of Mankind*. New York: Universe Books.

Müller-Doohm, S. 2016. *Habermas: A Biography*. Cambridge: Polity.

O'Connor, J. 1973. *The Fiscal Crisis of the State*. Abingdon: Routledge.

Offe, C. 1985. *Disorganized Capitalism*. Cambridge: MIT Press.

Poster, M. 1975 [1973]. 'Translator's Introduction'. In: *The Mirror of Production*. Edited by J. Baudrillard. Translated by Poster, M., St. Louis: Telos Press.

Poster, M. 2002. 'Introduction'. In: Edited by M. Poster *Jean Baudrillard: Selected Writings*, 2nd edition. Edited by M. Poster. Redwood: Stanford University Press. pp. 1–12.

Raulet, G. 2011. 'Legitimacy and globalization'. *Philosophy and Social Criticism,* 37 (3): 318–23.

Rhodes, M. and Wright, V. 1988. 'The European Steel Unions and the Steel Crisis, 1974–84: A Study in the Demise of Traditional Unionism'. *British Journal of Political Science,* 18 (2), 171–95.

Ritzer, G. 1993. *The McDonalidization of Society*. London and New Delhi: Thousand Oaks.

Rostow, W. W. 2017 [1960]. *The Stages of Economic Growth: A Non-Communist Manifesto*. Eastford: Martino Fine Books.

Rousseau, J. J. 1911 [1762]. *Emile, or On Education*. Translated by B. Foxley. London: Everyman's Library.

Rousseau, J. J. 1968 [1762]. *The Social Contract*. Translated by M. Cranston. London: Penguin.

Rousseau, J. J. 1984 [1755]. *A Discourse on the Origins of Inequality*. Translated by M. Cranston. London: Penguin.

Shepherd, J. 2015. *Crisis? What Crisis? The Callaghan Government and the British 'Winter of Discontent'*. Manchester: Manchester University Press.

Sokal A and Bricmont J 1997. *Impostures Intellectuelles*. Paris: Éditions Odile Jacob.

Sombart, W. 1902. *Der Moderne Kapitalismus*. Berlin: Duncker and Humblot.

Streeck, W. 2016. *How Will Capitalism End?* London: Verso.

Stutje, J. W. 2009. *Ernest Mandel: A Rebel's Dream Deferred*. London: Verso.

Summers, D. 2008. 'No Return to Boom and Bust: What Brown Said When He Was Chancellor'. *The Guardian*. 11 September 2008. www.theguardian.com/politics/2008/sep/11/gordonbrown.economy

Šumonja, M. 2019. 'The Habermas-Streeck Debate Revisited: Syriza and the Illusions of the Left-Europeanism'. *Capital and Class,* 43 (3): 437–58.

Veblen, T. 2009 [1899] *The Theory of the Leisure Class*. Oxford: Oxford University Press.

Venn, F. 2002. *The Oil Crisis*. Abingdon: Routledge.

Wolfe, D. A. 1986. 'Capitalist Crisis and Marxist Theory'. *Labour,* 17: 225–54.

Zamora, D. 2016 [2014]. 'Foucault, the Left, and the 1980s'. In: *Foucault and Neoliberalism*. Edited by D. Zamora and C. Behrent. Cambridge: Polity. pp. 1–5.

Zamora, D. and Behrent, M. C. (eds.) 2016 [2014]. *Foucault and Neoliberalism*. Cambridge: Polity.

Zuboff, S. 2018. *The Age of Surveillance Capitalism: The Fight for a Human Future at the New Frontier of Power*. London: Profile Books.

9 The Hidden Abodes of Capitalism

Environment, Gender, 'Race'

In this chapter, we discuss the critiques of capitalism which centre the economy's 'hidden abodes'. This literature developed slowly from the 1970s and today occupies an important place in broader discussions on capitalism. The term 'hidden abode' arises from the first volume of Marx's *Capital*, where he writes that economists must venture into the 'hidden abode of production' (1976: 279). While for Marx the 'hidden', unexplored abode of capitalism was located within the specificities of the waged-labour dynamic, for subsequent scholars, such as Nancy Fraser (2014), other crucial sites of extraction were hidden by classical political economy. For ecological, gender and critical race theorists, capitalism's 'hidden realms' stretch far beyond the immediate site of production. In this chapter, we attend in turn to three of the most discussed areas of capitalism's 'back-story'.

While we defined capitalism in Chapter 1, following Marx, as a socio-economic system which transforms the world into commodities to facilitate the extraction of surplus value, and we continue to present this as a working definition, this framing does not capture the totality of capitalism. It could be argued that this definition focuses myopically on capitalism's 'front-story'. Scholars are increasingly conscious that capitalism is predicated on the exploitation of 'back-story' domains which are treated as exploitable commodities without ever being allocated a market value (see Fraser and Jaeggi 2018). This is in contradiction with the terms through which 'front-story' capitalism purportedly operates. Be it care labour, the extraction of natural resources, the ability to pollute the environment or the exploitation of 'raced'[1] communities, capitalism's 'front-story' is dependent on these hidden abodes. There is thus a clear contradiction immanent within capitalism: the system which seeks to transform everything into commodities of quantifiable values is predicated on the extraction and exploitation of resources which are *not* allocated a market value. This contradiction leads to various crisis tendencies: be it of the environment, of race-relations, crises of care etc. Recently, theorists such as Nancy Fraser (2014) and Fraser and Jaeggi (2018) have argued that these back-stories do not sit in isolation. Rather, the crises tendencies inherent in the unsustainable and contradictory exploitation of capitalism's hidden abodes intersect, both with other 'hidden domains' and with capitalism's 'front-story'. Thus, when legitimation crises combine with crises of care, for example, the potentials for more permanent transformation can be identified. Through an examination of the contradictions present within capitalism's back-story, we argue that the fragility of the entire system becomes apparent.

While in this chapter we examine three areas of capitalism's hidden 'back-stories': the extractive relationships linked to the environment, gender and 'race', this is far from an exhaustive analysis. The literature on each of these areas is vast and multifaceted.

DOI: 10.4324/9781351017671-10

Scholarship on 'race' and gender is difficult to chart and delimits and stretches far beyond the critique of capitalism, while offering an important contribution to it. Equally, the literature on the environment, while comparatively more focused on capitalism, is extensive and highly differentiated. Further, it is important to note that capitalism does not simply have just three 'hidden abodes'; other sites of extraction and exploitation upon which 'front-story' capitalism depends require study, domains which also fall outside the purview of market value. For example, in India, caste remains in an important vector in capitalist reproduction. Indeed, there is a growing critique of a 'racial-caste' capitalist system which extends beyond South Asia (see Wilkerston 2020).

We start this chapter by charting the literature that targets capitalism's unsustainable relationship with the natural environment. An important contribution here was E.F. Schumacher's *The Small is Beautiful* [1973] in which he argued for a fundamental paradigm shift in 'meta-economics', necessitating a rejection of most central capitalist imperatives: growth, 'gigantism', limitless profit accumulation. While Schumacher's work informed future ecological critiques of capitalism, subsequent scholarship has developed in multiple directions. We turn next to the work of Peter Newell and Matthew Patterson (2006) who adopt a markedly different approach to Schumacher, supporting a reluctant reconciliation with capitalist economics. For the co-authors, decarbonizing the economy is the focus, and capitalist imperatives have a role in helping to facilitate this. However, as we show, Newell and Patterson are extensively criticized by the ecological left. For example, we turn next to Jason Moore (2015, 2016) who provides a Marxist-ecological critique of capitalism. For Moore (2016), the ecological footprint of capitalism has been so pronounced that the entire era should be considered a form of 'capitalocene'. No coalition between capitalist imperatives and environmental activists is tenable. For Moore, in direct contrast to Newell and Patterson, capitalism is a meta-socio-ecological process, which will inevitably collapse into worsening crises until a qualitative transformation occurs. But Moore, too, has his critics: we explore the opposing view of Dipesh Chakrabarty (2014), who has argued that, when approached from a longer view, such talk of a 'capitalocene' is indicative of an anthropocentric short-sightedness. The most contemporary ecological critiques of capitalism reflect the growing frustration of environmental activists. Andreas Malm's (2020) *How to Blow Up a Pipeline* captures the rising activist and academic critique of capitalism that the system no longer holds the possibilities for peaceful decarbonization. We return the discussion to Fraser and suggest that capitalism's environmental back-story is a crucial feature for any contemporary critique of capitalism as the impending climactic crises demonstrates the untenability of the extractive logics which determine capitalist economies.

Next, we engage with the critiques of capitalism that centre gender. Again, the 1970s and 1980s marked a radical growth in this literature, reflecting changing socio-economic realities. While the social democratic period was amenable to a traditional patriarchal division of labour, typified by a nuclear family with a man working for a wage and a woman providing care labour, the move to neoliberalism made this model financially unviable for most families. Two regular incomes were increasingly required for basic material survival, even within the Global North. As a result, the question of care labour became increasingly pronounced: if both partners were employed in paid work, who was taking care of dependents? Arlie Hochschild's (1989) work, especially *The Second Shift,* provided valuable critical insights in this regard. Capitalism was increasingly normalizing a system where women were coerced to provide free care labour in addition to now working demanding and demeaning waged-labour jobs. As Fraser (2013) argued in *Fortunes of Feminism,* this was an unintended consequence of demands for female liberation from the tedium of the immanent drudgery of care labour. Neoliberalism ostensibly liberated women from the shackles of domesticity, only to actually typically add additional mundane labour to their lives on top of their existing care labour. This has typically left women as multiply marginalized subjects, trapped in low paid waged labour and unpaid care labour. However, we stress that the feminist engagement with capitalism is far from homogenous. We discuss the debate between Ann Cudd and Nancy Holmstrom (2010), *Capitalism For and Against*, which typifies this plurality of thought. We conclude this discussion by returning to Fraser, to demonstrate how gendered labour patterns are a crisis prone 'hidden abode' of capitalism, requiring attentive research.

The final 'hidden abode' discussed here is 'race'. While traditional liberal scholars have considered racism to be a separate, distinct concern to capitalism (see Sunkara 2021), an important body of work rejects this distinction. As with the environment and gender, Critical race theorists argue that capitalism relies on the exploitation of non-white subjects who are simultaneously crucial for capitalism's functioning yet who are exploited in domains beyond market logics. For Cedric Robinson (1983), what is required is not a critique of 'racism' and a critique of 'capitalism'. Rather, the problem is 'racial capitalism': a system in which racism fundamentally serves to stabilize and maintain the capitalist economy. For example, for Robinson, class differentiations are enabled and perpetuated through racialized stereotypes. The literature on 'race' and capitalism is vast and we make no claims to provide a total engagement. While scholars such as Walter Rodney (1972) have argued that capitalism has been predicated on imperialism and the extraction of resources from colonies, other pools of literature focus more on the present importance of racism for capitalism's operation 'at home', within the core, as much as within the periphery and within processes of 'peripheralization'. For example, Angela Davis (1981) has written on the importance of prison abolitionism as a means of resistance to racist patriarchal capitalism. For critical race theorists, no critique of capitalism would be complete without considering racial exploitation a crucial feature of capitalism's 'back-story'.

We argue throughout this chapter, in accord with Fraser (2014), that capitalism is dependent on its 'hidden abodes'. These are the extractable resources which have long fallen outside market logics, but upon which capitalism depends. While the literature on these 'hidden abodes' is vast and heterogenous, in this chapter we seek to demonstrate the importance of the scholarship on 'race', gender and the environment for contemporary critiques of capitalism. We also stress the continuing evolution and topicality of this literature. With Extinction Rebellion (XR), Black Lives Matter (BLM) and #MeToo, much of the possibilities for qualitative transformations of capitalism today appear to lie within the immanent contradictions of its back-stories.

Environmental Critiques of Capitalism

Unregulated capitalism has caused devastating environmental damage (Klein 2014). As Fraser and Jaeggi (2018) argue, this is a result of capitalism's failure to account for the environment as a meaningful resource, it is an exploited abode, hidden in plain sight. Capitalism has engorged upon natural resources, polluted streams, decimated ecosystems (Carson 1962), depleted the ozone layer, raised global temperatures … and never had to pay a penny for it (Klein 2014); the environment is simply not a factor within neoclassical economics. Pollution can be dismissed as an incidental 'externality'. This relationship is clearly no longer sustainable and since the 1970s, critiques of capitalism have placed increasing emphasis on capitalism's extractive relationship with the natural world.

One of the most significant texts in this regard was E. F. Schumacher's *Small is Beautiful: A Study of Economics as if People Mattered* [1973]. Ernest Friedrich Schumacher had a remarkable life and kept equally remarkable company, which influenced his critique of capitalism. His brother-in-law was the theoretical physicist Werner Heisenberg and he was himself the protegee of John Maynard Keynes, who rescued Schumacher from a British internment camp during the Second World War, where he had been placed on the basis of his German nationality. Schumacher worked for the British Control Commission (responsible for rebuilding the post-war German economy), and the National Coal Board (NCB). He travelled extensively in the global South, delved into Buddhism, Christian mysticism and studied the writings of Gandhi and Kumarappa. It is thus unsurprising that his critique of capitalism was idiosyncratic, urging nothing less than a paradigm shift in economics.

Having worked for two decades for the NCB, Schumacher was sensitive to the importance natural resources held within the economy. He was explicit in his central claim: humanity cannot keep consuming and producing at the same rate: coal, oil and natural gas are non-renewable resources: when they are gone, they are gone. While economic growth continued, many economists and Whitehall mandarins believed that '"the problem of production" had been solved' (Schumacher 1980 [1973]: 10). For Schumacher, this was 'one of most fateful errors of the age' (1980: 10): infinite consumption of finite resources is self-evidently unsustainable.

Schumacher's work consistently focused on both the environment and people. Rather than suggesting people must suffer lower standards of living to enable sustainability, Schumacher argued that the current economic model was actually devastating for both the natural world and for humankind. Just as the environment is destroyed and polluted by the push for perpetual growth, people suffer panic attacks, stress, anxiety and alienation as a result of capitalist dynamics. For Schumacher, market dogmas hurt people and the environment. What was required was an economics 'as if people mattered' (the subtitle of *Small is Beautiful*), rather than mere obeisance to the imperatives of the market. The current approach, of infinitely maximizing production and consumption, or what Schumacher termed 'gigantism', was full of 'inherent dangers', both to the environment and 'to the integrity of the individual' (Schumacher 1980 [1973]: 225). Schumacher was clear: capitalism did not function to promote either human or environmental well-being. The environment was not sacrificed on the altar of human self-realization: it was sacrificed solely for market imperatives to be met. As Schumacher argued, the belief in the primary importance of 'bigger is better', of growth, 'efficiency', 'vastness', was accepted 'by virtually all experts' (Schumacher 1980 [1973]: 10; 225). In direct contrast, Schumacher argued that 'vastness' did not lead to happiness. Rather, 'small is beautiful'; the challenge is not for perpetual expansion and vastness. Instead, 'the fundamental task is to achieve smallness *within* large organisation' (Schumacher 1980 [1973]: 226).

In *Small is Beautiful*, Schumacher argued that the capitalist world was dehumanizing, alienating and unsustainable. Central to this pathological status quo was '*western* man's attitude to nature' (Schumacher 1980 [1973]: 11). In capitalism, 'modern man does not experience himself as part of nature but as an outside force destined to dominate and conquer it' (Schumacher 1980 [1973]: 11). Sharing sentiments, Fraser would later echo, Schumacher argued that coal and other natural resources needed to be understood not as some limitless resource, but as a form of 'irreplaceable capital', without which capitalists 'can do nothing' (Schumacher 1980 [1973]: 11). The current model of resource extraction was simply unviable. Capitalist economics serves to obscure 'man's dependence on the natural world' (Schumacher 1980 [1973]: 39). As Schumacher argued:

> A businessman would not consider a firm to have solved its problems of production and to have achieved viability if he saw that it was rapidly consuming its capital. How, then, could we overlook this vital fact when it comes to that very big firm, the economy of Spaceship Earth.
>
> (Schumacher 1980 [1973]: 11)

What was required was a fundamental paradigm shift, to see the end of 'giantism'. Instead of a world where 'biggest is best' what is needed was a society in which what is 'actually needed' is best (Schumacher 1980 [1973]: 59). For this change to occur, capitalist economics requires a sustained ecological critique of its foundational tenets. What was required was a deeper analysis than capitalism could allow within its dominant paradigm. In Fraser's terms, one needed to venture into capitalism's 'hidden abodes' and explore the back-story preconditions upon which capitalism depends. For Schumacher, this exploration was termed 'meta-economic' study, a form of economic analysis which finally probed 'into the depths of things' (Schumacher 1980 [1973]: 40), where the sole concern was not merely 'to obtain the best value for money' (Schumacher 1980 [1973]: 39).

As Schumacher argued, economics 'does not stand on its own feet', it is derived from a set of unspoken assumptions and values which he deemed 'meta-economics' (Schumacher 1980 [1973]: 42). Schumacher's ecological critique of capitalism can be summarized as the demand for a new meta-economics, a fundamental revision of capitalism's foundational axioms. Schumacher introduces meta-economics thus:

> As economics deals with man in his environment, we may expect that meta-economics consists of two parts -one dealing with man and the other dealing with the environment. In other words we must expect that economics must derive its aims and objectives from a study of man, and that it must derive at least a large part of its methodology from a study of nature.
>
> (Schumacher 1980 [1973]: 42)

As is clear from this definition, a crucial part of meta-economics, missing from capitalism, was the need to create economic axioms 'derived from a study of nature' (Schumacher 1980 [1973]: 42). It is simply absurd to 'ignore man's dependence on the natural world' (Schumacher 1980 [1973]: 43); however, this is exactly what capitalism does, capitalist 'economics, as currently constituted and practised, acts as a most effective barrier against the understanding of these problems, owing to its addiction to purely quantitative analysis and is timorous refusal to look into the real nature of things' (Schumacher 1980 [1973]: 43). At present, growth is an unqualified good in the eyes of economists. Growth of Gross National Product (GNP) must 'be a good thing' (Schumacher 1980 [1973]: 44). The very idea 'that there could be pathological growth' is seen as 'perverse' (Schumacher 1980 [1973]: 44). In capitalist economics, only quantitative analysis is allowed, qualities are displaced. But, as Schumacher argues, things are not identical, qualitative differences matter. There needs to be a distinction in any economic model between finite and infinite resources: free market capitalism does not permit this (Schumacher 1980 [1973]: 45). The marketplace simply cannot accommodate this; however, there could 'hardly be a more important distinction' (Schumacher 1980 [1973]: 45). The market is simply unable to operate with this degree of qualitative complexity, there is, in short, a 'basic incommensurability; between market logics and the ontological difference between different goods' (Schumacher 1980 [1973]: 46).

For Schumacher, capitalism is unable to acknowledge these differences due to its deficient 'meta-economics'. Market dynamics are only suited to enable the exchange of infinite secondary goods, not finite primary goods (Schumacher 1980 [1973]: 45). This is compounded by the fundamentally extractive nature of capitalism's back-story; that crucial factors upon which capitalism depends are not legible to its current meta-economic foundations. Air, water, the soil, for instance, never appear as market items (Schumacher 1980 [1973]: 46). They 'cannot be, or have not been privately appropriated' (Schumacher 1980 [1973]: 46). On the existing meta-economic foundations, 'economists have felt entitled ... to treat the entire framework within which economic activity takes place as *given*, that is to say, as permanent and indestructible' (Schumacher 1980 [1973]: 46). It was simply 'not part of their job' to do otherwise (Schumacher 1980 [1973]: 46). As Schumacher witheringly worded it, with mainstream economists at the helm of capitalism, society was victim to 'the bland leading the blind' (Schumacher 1980 [1973]: 13). What was required was a meta-economic shift; this is the core tenet of Schumacher's critique of capitalism. Schumacher was explicit about the depth and breadth of his critique: arguing that 'the entire outlook and methodology of economics [needs to be] ... called into question' (Schumacher 1980 [1973]: 47).

While Schumacher demanded a radical paradigm shift and a new 'meta-economics', Newell and Patterson's more recent *Climate Capitalism* is a more measured and pragmatic engagement with capitalism and the environment. While the co-authors retain an unease with capitalism, and are certainly not enthusiastic free marketeers, they both argue for the need to work within the confines of the given circumstances and to view capitalism as potentially possessing the means to rescue itself. What is required, the co-authors argue, is the rapid 'decarbonising' of the market and they contend that, despite its limitations, some system of 'carbon credits' could enable this. It is worth stressing that this is not the co-authors' preferred option; however, they underscore the need for realism and clear, manageable objectives: decarbonizing now and decarbonizing hard. The goal is to keep fossil fuels in the ground, or as the phrase goes, the aim is to 'leave the oil in the soil' and 'the coal in the hole'.

For Newell and Patterson, carbon markets can support decarbonization and have multiple advantages which show the continuing adaptability and resilience of capitalist imperatives. For example, a system based on carbon credits can be flexible and adaptive, as the circumstances and science change, the system can adapt. The carbon market can be monitored by prudent governance: state bodies can increase duties on particular forms of consumption. Crucially, the government is able to respond to both the dynamics of the carbon market but also to democratic interventions. Mass mobilizations against a certain form of consumption can persuade governments to intervene in the carbon market to incentivize/disincentivize accordingly. If the public starts to mobilize against the damage done to the environment by four-by-four drivers, for instance, the government could implement a targeted increase in carbon taxes accordingly. As such, Newell and Patterson argue that a form of capitalism could exist that is capable of capturing the optimal fusion of prudent state intervention with responsiveness to democratic action. There remains a space for peaceful resistance within the co-authors' carbon capitalist formation. In their model, there is space for the state, business and green activists, as well as the electorate, who can support parties based on their proposed carbon-market policies. The adaptiveness of the model lies in the ability of market mechanisms to influence behaviour: capitalism has the potential to save capitalism. What is required is for the captains of industry to realize that decarbonization is in their interests and that growing democratic pressure for environmental action is not inevitably the death knell for their profits. Newell and Patterson argue that what is needed is to enlist capitalists in the goal of decarbonization as vital partners alongside the state and the public. Such a coalition, they claim, has the power to bring forth a greener, more sustainable future.

Newell and Patterson's position has been strongly rejected by a range of environmental activists and scholars. Larry Lohmann (2012) has argued that Newell and Patterson base their entire argument on a false premise: that the adoption of carbon markets leads to the reduction of overall fossil fuel use. This, states Lohmann, is the central principle for all carbon capitalist arguments. However, as Lohmann powerfully asserts, carbon markets simply do not do this. Rather, they 'help the most fossil-dependent parts of the industrial structure avoid decarbonization, while interfering with other measures that could foster it' (2012: 1117). Further, the process of 'marketizing' carbon is highly controversial as it serves to reinforce the commodifying logics of capitalism at exactly the moment when a broad coalition seeks to a paradigm change away from commodification and marketization. Perhaps most damaging for Newell and Patterson's argument is the fact that the captains of industry themselves consider carbon markets to be flawed and unviable. As Lohmann argues, the fact that Per Lakender of UBS and Johannes Teyssen of EDF consider carbon markets 'a joke' and 'dead', respectively, (c.f. Lohmann 2012: 1179) leaves the prospects for Newell and Patterson's state-public-industry coalition seeming very bleak.

Jason Moore's (2015, 2016) work provides an important counterpoint to Newell and Patterson's. In *Capitalism in the Web of Life* [2015], Moore stresses the need for critiques of capitalism to embrace what he deems a 'double internality': that nature works through capitalism and that capitalism works through nature. Past attempts to theorize a binary 'capitalism/nature' are held to be conceptually limited and politically problematic. Rather, in light of the unravelling of the relationship between capitalism and the environment what is required is a new understanding of capitalism as an *ecology*. Indeed, for Moore, the binary between 'nature/society is directly implicated in the colossal violence' of the present, it is a serious part of the problem (Moore 2015: 2). The understanding of nature as some 'externality', distinct from capitalism, must be overcome. Indeed, the 'view of nature as external' is itself a 'fundamental condition of capital accumulation' which Moore seeks to destabilize (Moore 2015: 2). As Moore argues, capitalism is the problem, not simply as 'an economic system' but as 'a social system' as a way of '*organizing nature*' (Moore 2015: 2). This framing is the key to Moore's work: capitalism needs to be subject to a critique as a faulty basis for organizing nature. Moore (2015: 2–3) expands on this in a manner which chimes with both Fraser and Schumacher:

> Capitalism's governing conceit is that it may do with Nature as it pleases, that Nature is external and may be coded, quantified, and rationalized to serve economic growth, social development, or some other higher good. This is capitalism *as a project*. The reality – the *historical process* – is radically different. While the manifold projects of capital, empire, and science are busy making Nature with a capital 'N' – external, controllable, reducible – the web of life is busy shuffling about the biological and geological conditions of capitalism's process. This 'web of life' is nature as a whole: *nature*

> with an emphatically lower can 'n'. This is nature as inside us, as around us. It is nature as a flow of flows. Put simply, humans make environments and environments make humans – and human organizations.

As such, Moore argues that we should understand capitalism as a 'world-historical process', a form of 'humanity in nature' (Moore 2015: 3). The liberal Cartesian subject needs to be displaced by the more nuanced picture which Moore suggests of capitalism as a 'co-constitutive ... world ecology' (Moore 2015: 3). Instead of viewing the 'environmental crisis' as something produced by capitalism, Moore's work suggests we need to view today's crises as one of 'modernity-*in*-nature' (Moore 2015: 4). This modernity is 'capitalist world-ecology' (Moore 2015: 4). From this position, it is absurd to imagine a world in which capitalist subjects abuse nature and then nature wreaks some inevitable quasi-karmic revenge. Rather, there exists a simple totality, a 'double internality', as Moore repeatedly frames it, which captures this crisis tendency: 'humanity in nature/ nature in humanity' (Moore, 2015: 5). 'In this double internality, everything that humans do is *already* joined with extra-human nature *and* the web of life: nature as a whole that includes humans' (Moore 2015: 5). In this regard, 'capitalism as *world ecology* is therefore not the ecology of the world, but a patterned history of power, capital, and nature, dialectically joined' (Moore 2015: 8). For Moore, Capitalism has created a false construct of an othered nature, distinct from the market. This 'false nature' is held to be independent of humans and the economy. We contend that this is very similar to the idea forwarded by Fraser as a 'hidden abode' and by Schumacher as a faulty 'meta-economics'. As Moore argues, this myth can no longer be perpetuated by capitalism. What is required is a new framing, a new language, devoid of false binaries; capitalism must be critiqued as a 'world ecology' predicated on an expanded framing of *oikeios.*

Moore's awareness that capitalism and nature need to be held in a 'double internality', as a form of ecology, is captured by the growing discussion and debate over yet further neologisms: the 'Capitalocene-Anthropocene' debate (see Moore 2016; see Delanty and Mota 2017). Increasingly, natural scientists and social scientists agree that the previous environmental epoch, the Holocene, has come to an end. It has been replaced by a new geological epoch, in which human activity is a substantial factor. Paul Crutzen is credited with coining the term Anthropocene which captures this new era of planetary history – a combination of the Greek for 'human' [Anthropos] with the suffix used to denote a geological epoch '-cene'. While the term 'Anthropocene' focuses on human activity, the term 'capitalocene' is preferred by Moore and many left-ecologists as it enables a more precise focus on the cause of the geological transition: capitalism (2016). As supporters of the 'capitalocene' framing argue, it is not *all* humans who are equally changing the environment. It is not isolated tribes in the Amazon, rather it is the societies which engage in capitalistic overconsumption. In short, it is capitalism's extractive relationship with the environment which is destroying the planet, not 'people' more generally. The preference of neologism, be it 'Capitalocene' or 'Anthropocene', reflects the varying centrality afforded to capitalism within this new epoch by different scholars. In a series of papers in *The Journal of Peasant Studies,* Moore (2017: 594) argued that humanity's ecological footprint correlates with the rise of capitalism and that it would be 'fruitless to explain these transformations without identifying how they fit into patterns of power, capital and nature'. Linking to his *Capitalism and the Web of Life,* Moore argues that the production of a 'cheap Nature' outside the cash nexus was crucial to the development of the capitalocene.

An important differing voice to Moore is Dipesh Chakrabarty (2014). While Chakrabarty notes that the term 'Anthropocene' is problematic in that climate change has not been equally induced by all humans (see also Agarwal and Narain 2019), he is also sceptical of the utility of the term 'capitalocene'. While Chakrabarty accepts it is important to reflect on the role capitalism has had in environmental processes, he considers it is 'insufficient' to reduce *all* environmental change to capitalism (Chakrabarty 2014: 4). As a result, Chakrabarty is keen not to advance a framing that 'puts capitalism in the driver's seat'. Rather, modernity itself need to centred in this discussion. This is in direct opposition to Malm (2016) and Žižek (2021). When one engages with geological epochs, quotidian language and conceptions of liminality fail us. According to Chakrabarty, we must move beyond 'human scales' and recentre our imagination; we must think beyond capital and climate, beyond our commonplace referents, when contemplating geological epochs (Chakrabarty 2014: 21). Part of the challenge, Chakrabarty argues, is to embrace the 'planet's otherness' (2014: 23). In this regard, from a longer perspective, the coal and oil which Schumacher was concerned with are not actually 'non-renewable', they will return, just on a scale far beyond the human life-cycle. Likewise, plants and animals may become extinct, humans included. The planet existed before humanity and will likely continue to exist after. As such, the risk of adopting the language of 'capitalocene' when conducting ecological critiques of capitalism is that it may normalize an anthropocentric short-termism. When one operates within geological timescales, capitalism is no longer central.

Chakrabarty, however, is not primarily a theorist of capitalism, nor of the environment, and his work is not indicative of the broader academic-activist consensus. Most ecological scholarship places capitalism firmly within its crosshairs. This literature is growing rapidly and growing in anger. This is typified by the energetic work of Andreas Malm (2016, 2017, 2020) who has a broad appeal with both activists and academics, and who advances an important ecological-Marxist critique of capitalism. In his most recent work, *How to Blow Up a Pipeline* (2020), Malm argues that capitalism has failed to provide a vehicle for peaceful decarbonization and that the growing visible impacts of climate change necessitates more immediate direct action. For Malm sabotage is now required and climate fatalism and liberal pacificism are both equally problematic. Malm (2020) argues that the choice is increasingly evident: capitalism or survival. It is time to 'blow stuff up' as capitalism can no longer be trusted to guarantee the conditions required for human survival.

We can unite these varied ecological critiques of capitalism by returning to the understanding of the environment as a 'hidden abode' of capitalist exploitation, a domain upon which capitalism depends, but one which falls outside its limited conception of value. As the theorists discussed above agree, this is unsustainable in its current form and has obvious crisis tendencies. Clearly no critique of capitalism can be complete without an engagement with the environmental crisis.

Feminist Critiques of Capitalism

While the pollution of the environment and the relentless extraction of natural resources have always elicited a conscious disquiet in most people when forced to confront its reality, feminist critiques of capitalism have additional ideological complications to deal with. The idea that a mother lovingly comforting her infant resembles, at some level, a manifestation of the same extractive logic which drives the deforestation of the Amazon is counter-intuitive. Yet, for generations of feminist scholars, capitalism is predicated on a similarly extractive relationship to care labour, which mirrors many of the dynamics of capitalism's other 'hidden abodes' (see Davis 1981, Vogel 1983, Bhattacharya 2017, Fraser 2014, Fraser and Jaeggi 2018). This is fundamental to the relationship which exists between capitalism and patriarchy: care labour is viewed by neoclassical economics as a limitless resource, which does not require reward in the form of a market wage, and, as such, can be infinitely exploited. As such, the relationship between mother and child in patriarchal-capitalism has been subject to extensive feminist scrutiny (Chodorow 1978). Like capitalism's reliance on the endless supply of natural resources which are not afforded a market value at point of extraction, care labour is a fundamental prerequisite for capitalist reproduction which lies outside the broader value-system of the market itself (Fraser and Jaeggi 2018).[2]

Marxist feminists have long been aware of this. Friedrich Engels's *The Origin of the Family, Private Property, and the State* [1884] located the unequal distribution of care labour as the original 'class' divide. For Engels, the rise of capitalism was predicated on the 'world historic defeat of the female sex' as the elevated status of women within pagan mysticism was replaced by the misogynistic dogmas of the emergent monotheisms. This, argued Engels, was essential to the development of a system of capitalism, as the reproductive capacities of women were constrained to enable a system of male–male inheritance which supported the growth of unconstrained profits, as ends in themselves. The exploitation of gendered care labour remained a concern for feminist critiques of capitalism, with Charlotte Perkins Gilman [1898] demanding compensation for women's housework and Angela Davis writing in *Women, Race, and Class* [1981], that women existed within a form of 'domestic slavery'. However, despite the contradictions and inequities of capitalism's relationship with gender and care previously, the situation was to rapidly deteriorate further throughout the 1980s, sparking a wave of new feminist critiques of capitalism. As a result, for many Marxist feminists, Eleanor Marx's (Marx and Aveling, 1987 [1887]) foundational insight became even more valid as neoliberalism progressed: women will never be free under capitalism.

While the social-democratic consensus enabled the continuation of the patriarchal family structure, with the male typically earning a wage and the female typically performing unpaid care labour, the ascent of neoliberalism made this model untenable. The co-ordinated attack on the welfare state, combined with the move from progressive to indirect taxation and a real-term reduction in wages, made the one-earner household financially unviable. To achieve even basic survival families in the Global North began to require multiple wage-earners, which was incompatible with the previous 'public'–'private' divide between the sexes. Quite simply, women were financially compelled to enter the marketplace, whether they desired to, or not. This produced an obvious crisis of care: if women, who had been overwhelmingly been providing unpaid care work, were now required to move to market jobs, where would the care labour come from?

For Arlie Hochschild in *The Second Shift* [1980], the answer was depressingly simple: women were increasingly faced with a 'double burden', required to now perform *both* unpaid care labour *and* paid market labour. The patriarchal norms that 'kept women in their place' served to maintain a male aversion to care labour. As Hochschild worded it in her opening to *The Second Shift*, typically while women exhaust themselves looking after infants and other dependents, men had been socialized to expect constant praise for merely looking after the dog. This created a fundamental crisis tendency within capitalism: women are expected to work two jobs at once. For Hochschild, the result is a gendered 'leisure gap' as men have been socialized to expect a paid work/relaxing home-life divide. In contrast, women experience a 'double burden', or 'second shift', which has become central to many contemporary feminist critiques of capitalism. The challenge of providing care labour represents a clear crisis tendency within neoliberalism. There exists a much discussed 'crisis of care': marketized care is prohibitively expensive for the median earner; however, dual incomes are increasingly essential for social reproduction. This is only exacerbated by an ageing population, in which additional demands for care work are placed on the younger generation.

For Hochschild, and subsequent feminist theorists (see Hartley 2018), there is a further 'third shift' which falls disproportionately on the backs of women: 'emotional work'. Hochschild (1983) differentiates between 'emotional labour', where managing people's emotions is financially rewarded as part of a waged-labour job, for example being an airhostess and soothing scared passengers, and 'emotional work': where managing other's emotions is demanded without financial recompense. In contemporary feminist critiques of capitalism, this 'third shift' of 'emotional work' is an additional burden that is placed on women, which is typically varied, unrewarding and emotionally demanding. As Berhau, Lareau and Press argue (2011: 48), this often involves 'blending cheerleading and coercion' of both children and partner. The duty of supporting children's homework, talking to in-laws, supporting the male partner's work anxieties, encouraging children to continue with musical instrument classes etc., all fall on the female partner, who struggles to present themselves as emotionally stable. For Fahs and Swank (2016), an important feature of this third-shift, which is a crucial result of the crisis of care of capitalism, is a defeatist yet pragmatic self-denial of women's own pleasure. This includes, but is not limited to, tolerating sexual pain, faking sexual pleasure and defining sexual satisfaction based on their partner's pleasure (Fahs and Swank 2016: 46). This is further complicated by the contradictions of the ascendant 'Lean In' form of feminism (see Scovell and Sandberg 2013), as discussed in Katherine Angel's (2021) *Tomorrow Sex Will be Good Again.*

The resulting crisis of care has been an important concern in Nancy Fraser's work, especially her *Fortunes of Feminism*. As she argues, the crisis points of both global warming and of care labour are real and pose existential challenges to the form of financialized capitalism. She argued that

> neither nature nor social reproductive capacities are infinite; both of them can be stretched to the breaking point. Many people already appreciate this in the case of nature, and we are starting to understanding it as well in the case of 'care'.
>
> (Fraser and Leonard 2016)

The demand for women to perform the three-shifts discussed above is unsustainable, as witnessed by the epidemic of mental health conditions. As Fraser argues, capitalism is rapidly 'depleting the very capacities on which it depends', 'financialized … capitalism is systematically consuming our capacities to sustain social bonds, like a tiger that eats its own tail' (Fraser and Leonard 2016).

Fraser consistently argues that capitalism's 'back-stories' need to be carefully unpacked, that they are as worthy of attentive study as capitalism's 'front-story' (Fraser 2014; Fraser and Jaeggi 2018). In *Fortunes of Feminism* Fraser charts the origins of the current crisis, demonstrating that capitalism's relationship with care has rapidly transitioned through several stages, each with distinct norms and dynamics. Liberal capitalism, as per Victorian sensitivities, served to strictly demarcate care labour from waged labour. Care labour was a private matter, to occur strictly behind closed doors, on pain of crippling social embarrassment and ostracision. The community-run creches which sustained the care labour of earlier eras were closed and care became hyper-individualized. In contrast, the period of state managed capitalism, of social democracy, served to partially re-socialize care, with welfare payments and sophisticated healthcare provision offering not merely the 'cradle to grave' care it claimed, but further, with developing ante-natal provision, families were supported from 'womb to tomb'.

For Fraser, the origins of the current crisis of care lay in the misfortune of feminism to rally for an end to the patriarchal control of the 'family wage', a single earning (usually male) family member who can earn enough to support the entire family, at exactly the moment when capital was ascendant over labour with the rise of neoliberalism. As Fraser words it:

> Feminists rejected the ideal of the family wage as an institutionalization of female dependency—and rightly so. But we did so at just the moment when the relocation of manufacturing kicked the bucket out from under the idea economically. In another world, feminism and shifts in industry might not have reinforced one another, but in this world they did. As a result, even though feminist movements did not in any way *cause* that economic shift, we ended up unwittingly supplying some legitimation for it. We provided some charisma, some ideological ballast to others' agendas.
>
> (Fraser and Leonard 2016)

As a result, feminist critiques of the 'family wage' served to 'unwittingly' legitimate the neoliberal 'dual earner' model. Fraser is clear, the crisis of care is a direct result of economic structural changes. It is 'by no means contingent or accidental, it is the expression, under current conditions, of a tendency to social-reproductive crisis that is inherent in capitalist society, but that takes an especially acute form in the present regime of financialized capitalism' (Fraser and Leonard 2016). As Fraser argues in *Fortunes of Feminism*, the feminist movement was co-opted, the cultural turn of feminist identity politics fitted optimally with neoliberalism and in particular with the neoliberal rejection of the need for economic redistribution.

On the one hand, struggles for recognition have exploded everywhere – witness battles over multiculturalism, human rights and national autonomy. On the other hand, struggles for egalitarian redistribution are in relative decline – witness the weakening of trade unions and the co-optation of labour and socialist parties in 'the third way'. The result is a tragic historical irony. The shift from redistribution to recognition has occurred just as an aggressively globalizing US-led capitalism is exacerbating economic inequality (Fraser 2013: 160).

Fraser's argument is clear: feminist critiques of capitalism need to centre both demands for economic redistribution as well as calls for recognition. However, it is important to stress that feminist engagements with capitalism are far from homogenous. This is aptly demonstrated by Cudd and Holmstrom's (2010) *Capitalism: For and Against: A Feminist Debate.* There are many nominal feminists who are explicit advocates, or reluctant apologists, for neoliberal capitalism. In their provocative dialogue, Cudd and Holmstrom illustrate these tensions within contemporary feminist theory and politics. Cudd argues that capitalism is good for most women, it is connected to the fundamental liberal idea of equality, which has enabled many women to escape a life of drudgery. Holmstrom, in contrast, argues that the logics of capitalism fundamentally favour men: women are more reliant on state handouts, especially single women. As Holmstrom argues, such welfare support has been eroded by neoliberal reforms. Crucially, however, both Cudd and Holmstrom agree that the question 'is capitalism good for women?' is incomplete. What must be asked is 'for which women?' and 'compared to what alternative?' For Holmstrom, in keeping with the dominant trend within contemporary feminist scholarship, women simply fare very badly under capitalism. Neoliberal capitalism is clearly reliant on the extraction of care labour, while destroying the conditions which enable its stable delivery. This is the central reason for the 'crisis of care' and demonstrates another 'back-story' or 'hidden abode' of capitalism in which crisis tendencies are worsening (Fraser and Jaeggi 2018).

Racial Capitalism

Just as there has been an increased recent interest in capitalism's exploitation of care labour and the natural environment, there has also been a rapidly expanding literature on 'racial capitalism', both within the academy (see Bhattacharyya 2018, *inter alia*) and more broadly (Lemann 2020, *inter alia*). As with the 'hidden abodes' discussed above, theorists of racial capitalism argue that capitalism is reliant upon exploiting 'raced' communities in a manner which structurally excludes them from the very market rules it aggressively enforces. Racialized communities are essential to capitalism's reproduction but are treated as expendable and infinitely exploitable. It should be stressed that the literature on 'race' and capitalism is vast and varied, and our engagement here is far from exhaustive. We focus on the unifying themes across the literature, while mindful of the heterogeneity of the existing and emerging scholarship.

At its most simple, scholars of 'racial capitalism' argue that capitalism needs to be critiqued as a system which is predicated upon racial exploitation (Robinson 2020 [1983]). To many liberal theorists, 'capitalism' and 'racism' are fundamentally divergent areas of study. For theorists of racial capitalism, the liberal error is to believe that capitalism is 'economic', while racism is 'cultural'; that there may be links between them, but these are contingent and inessential. In contrast, for advocates of a theory of 'racial capitalism', most notably Cedric Robinson, capitalism is fundamentally racist, and cannot be extricated from racializing dynamics and exploitative processes. Crucial to the understanding of 'racial capitalism' is thus this fusion of 'race' and 'capitalism' within a singular explanandum. Racism is understood as being a central feature of capitalism.

The term 'racial capitalism' first achieved resonance with the work of two Marxist scholars' writing on South Africa, Legassick and Hemson (1976). The co-authors argued that liberal anti-racist reform could never solve the economic inequities of the rainbow nation because racism was fundamentally 'baked in' to the economic system itself. As such, racism could not be independently excised while capitalism remained. Their insight catalysed extensive further study and Robinson's work, particularly *Black Marxism* [1983], developed these ideas substantially. Importantly for Robinson, capitalism was not a totalizing, modernizing force which magically swept away feudalism and instituted the 'proletariat' as the new universal underclass. Rather, capitalism existed alongside other modes of production and other forms of stratification, which was true to Marx's own analysis. As a result, the emergence of the working class occurred alongside other socializing forces, such as narratives of race which existed within the residual forms of feudalism. As Robinson wrote:

> the dialectic of proletarianization disciplined the working classes to the importance of distinctions: between ethnics and nationalities; between skilled and unskilled workers … and between races. The persistence and creation of such oppositions within the working classes were a critical aspect of the triumph of capitalism in the nineteenth century.
>
> (Robinson 2020: 42)

Despite his acceptance of much Marxist theory, Robinson's work was primarily intended as a criticism of the Eurocentrism of Marxism and its failure to engage adequately with race. In *Black Marxism,* Robinson argued that racism enabled both the development of class divisions and the perpetuation of non-marketized forms of economic extraction. Capitalism needed racism: it enabled the continuing pillaging and 'primitive accumulation' of colonialism. 'Racialized' others were not considered equal market actors, they were 'savages' incapable of rational action and requiring 'civilising'. As such, in Robinson's analysis, both the birth and the stabilization of capitalism required a critique of the normalization of racist ideologies. It should be noted that there have been various notable criticisms of Robinson's work.[3] Theorists such as Walzer (2020) and Go (2020) have argued that Robinson's attempt to collapse 'race' and 'capitalism' into a singular system fails to grasp the distinctive and often contradictory dynamics intrinsic to each.

The importance of 'race' in legitimizing brutal primitive accumulation in the development of capitalism, as stressed by Robinson, was also a primary concern for Guyanese historian and activist Walter Rodney. The violence which Rodney discussed in his foundational *How Europe Underdeveloped Africa* was reflected in his own life; he was assassinated in 1980 by a bomb likely planted on the orders of Guyana's president Burnham (Harding, Hill, and Strickland 2012: xv). For Rodney, capitalism and modernity were based on racism. Crucially, too, the development of Europe and 'the West' could be tied to the systematic 'underdevelopment' of Africa.

For much of the twentieth century, narratives on Africa's underdevelopment reflected the racist tropes of the period. Africa was poor because of isolated, contingent factors, entirely unrelated to European intervention. Africa was poor because it was a continent of genetically inferior, violent, over-sexualized, savages. Africa was poor because the climate was inhospitable, natural resources were supposedly lacking, Christian 'civilisation' was absent and the demonical 'tribalist' religions led to peoples who had a predilection for violent civil war and conflict, incompatible with the calculated restraint of modernity. Europeans were humbled to perform 'the white man's burden', to instil order and moral righteousness on this troubled land. Rodney's *How Europe Underdeveloped Africa* systematically dismantled these interlocking racist narratives. Rodney argued that African underdevelopment was a direct result of capitalism. The capitalist economic system was responsible for Africa's economic inequities, not some climatic, genetic, 'racial' or other cultural factor. Rodney argued that colonial subjects must unite and rise up against the capitalist colonialists.

Throughout his work, Rodney is careful to avoid the term 'developing nation'. Africa should not be considered a continent of 'developing' countries, because this obscures the historical reality. Rather, Africa had been explicitly 'underdeveloped' by European colonialism. The development of Europe explicitly occurred on the basis of the underdevelopment of Africa. Rodney argued that Africa was no more or less 'developed' than Europe before colonialism. Rather, the process of colonial extraction served to develop Europe at the precise cost of African development. This idea that capitalism must be understood as a broader 'world system' in which the development of X was related to the underdevelopment of Y was further explored by Immanuel Wallerstein, in a manner sensitive to, and directly crediting, Rodney's scholarship. In *World-Systems Analysis: An Introduction* (2004), Wallerstein argued that the development of the global 'core' was explicitly connected to the exploitation of 'periphery' and 'semi-periphery' regions. As such, contemporary critiques of capitalism must be mindful of how capitalist development remains predicated on the systematic exploitation of 'hidden abodes' which are obscured by their peripheralization.

Yet, theorists of race and capitalism do not solely focus on empire and colonialism. Rather, Angela Davis (2003) and Ruth Wilson Gilmore (2007) have both written extensively on the importance of the racial-carceral system in perpetuating capitalism within the global core, most notably within the heart of capitalism, California. Davis writes of the 'prison industrial complex', a system where growing prison populations have far less to do with rising crime rates, or more effective policing techniques, but are instead a direct result of the imperatives of contemporary racialized-capitalism. As Davis and Shaylor (2001: 2) argue, 'vast numbers of corporations … rely on prisons as an important source of profit and have thus acquired clandestine stakes in the continued expansion of the prison system'. Since the 1980s, the number of inmates within US prisons has increased by over 450% despite crime falling year on year (Davis and Shaylor 2001: 2). Race enters the discussion on prison abolitionism as a crucial factor, as Davis and Shaylor explain, 'because the overwhelming majority of U.S. prisoners are from racially marginalized communities'; as a result, the 'corporate stakes in an expanding apparatus of punishment necessarily rely on and promote old as well as new structures of racism' (Davis and Shaylor 2001: 2). Racism is perpetuated to enable the extraction of profit from non-white bodies. The figures bare out the extent of the racial inequity, an African-American female is over 7 times more likely to go to prison than a white woman (Davis and Shaylor 2001: 6). The process of expanding imprisonment of people of colour is a process of transforming racialized minorities 'into consumers and/or producers of an immense range of commodities' (Davis and Shaylor 2001: 3). Inmates are coerced to consume and produce. They are forced to work in demeaning conditions for scant or no wages, wages which are substantially below the market rate, as, in keeping with all capitalism's hidden abodes, they are not subject to market forces, despite being an integral factor in their stability.

In *Are Prisons Obsolete,* Angela Davis (2003) demonstrates why the tenets of 'abolition democracy' must be incorporated in any contemporary critique of capitalism. She powerfully argues that black people have moved from the prison of slavery to the slavery of mass imprisonment. Notably, the 13th amendment to the US Constitution, which abolished slavery, had an exception: slavery could still be permitted 'as punishment for crime' (see Benns 2015). For Dorothy Roberts (2019: 7–8) contemporary campaigns for prison abolitionism are an explicit continuation of Robinson's critique of racial capitalism because racialized imprisonment serves to socially justify irrational class stratification. As a result, BLM campaigners increasingly focus on abolitionism and place it as a central tenet within their critique of capitalism. 'Race' appears a further 'hidden abode', with extractive dynamics reproducing slavery conditions beyond capitalism's 'front-story' in periphery colonies and in Supermax prisons.

Conclusion

Despite the particularities of the specific 'hidden abodes' discussed, their fundamental relationship to capitalism remains the same. Capitalism is dependent upon forms of exploitation that exist outside the confines of the market: be it forced prison labour, care labour, the ability to pollute streams or the extraction of oil. The 'hidden abodes' discussed in this chapter are far from the full extent of capitalism's 'back-story'. Equally, the literatures on each of the abodes discussed are vast and heterogenous and our engagement is, at best, indicative. That said, we argue that there are fundamental commonalities across these 'hidden abodes', both in the manner of capitalism's exploitation of certain people and resources, but also in the inevitable crisis tensions these contradictory relationships engender. Just as infinite consumption of finite resources will inexorably induce crises, so will the escalating contradiction of formal legal equality with the reality of institutionalized system of racialized slave labour. So too, with care labour: as the inaccessibility of marketized care combines with the necessity for ever additional income for basic survival, health outcomes, as much as systemic legitimacy, suffer.

In accord with Fraser (2014) and Fraser and Jaeggi (2018), we contend that no critique of capitalism can ignore the 'hidden abodes' of the economy. We have identified some of the complex dynamics that serve to obscure capitalism's reliance on non-marketized resources. We contend these commonalities unites Schumacher's analysis of capitalism's 'false meta-economics', Moore analysis of capitalism's 'false nature' and Fraser's work on capitalism's 'hidden abodes'. Simply put: capitalism is predicated upon the unsustainable extraction of limited resources which are excluded from market valuation in a manner that threatens the very conditions of its survival. This presents yet another fundamental crisis tendency within capitalism, in keeping with the multiple crises discussed in the preceding chapter.

Notes

1 The use of the quotation marks for the word 'race' is common practice within the wider contemporary literature to designate the artificiality of the construct.

2 When attempts are made to place a monetary value on unpaid care work (UCW) figures typically sit close to $10 trillion per annum, which equates to 13% of global GDP (Dhar 2019: 31). This is clearly a startling figure.

3 It is vital to stress these do not arise from not sharing Robinson's abhorrence of racism and the need to urgently examine it as a central area of investigation.

References

Agarwal, A. and Narain, S. 2019. *Global Warming in an Unequal World*. Oxford: Oxford University Press.

Angel, K. 2021. *Tomorrow Sex Will Be Good Again: Women and Desire in the Age of Consent*. London: Verso.

Benns, W. 2015. 'American Slavery, Reconsidered'. *The Atlantic*. 21 September 2015. www.theatlantic.com/business/archive/2015/09/prison-labor-in-america/406177/

Berhau, B. Lareau, A. and Press, J. E. 2011. 'Where Families and Children's Activities Meet: Gender, Meshing Work, and Family Myths'. In: *At the Heart of Work and Family: Engaging the Ideas of Arlie Hochschild*. Edited by A. Garey and K. Hansen New Brunswick: Rutgers University Press, pp. 43–60.

Bhattacharya, T. (ed.) 2017. *Social Reproduction Theory: Remapping Class, Recentering Oppression*. London: Pluto Press.

Bhattacharyya, G. 2018. *Rethinking Racial Capitalism: Questions of Reproduction and Survival*. London: Rowman and Littlefield.

Carson, R. 1962. *Silent Spring*. Boston: Houghton Miffin Harcourt.

Chakrabarty, D. 2014. 'Climate and Capital: On Conjoined Histories'. *Critical Inquiry*, 41 (1): 1–23.

Chodorow, N. 1978. *The Reproduction of Mothering: Psychoanalysis and the Sociology of Gender.* Oakland: University of California Press.

Cudd, A. and Holmstrom, N. 2010. *Capitalism, for and against: A Feminist Debate.* Cambridge: Cambridge University Press.

Davis, A.Y. 2003. *Are Prisons Obsolete?* New York: Seven Stories Press.

Davis, A.Y. 2019 [1981]. *Women, Race and Class.* London: Penguin.

Davis, A.Y. and Shaylor, C. 2001. 'Race, Gender, and the Prison Industrial Complex: California and Beyond'. *Meridians*, 2 (1): 1–25.

Delanty, G. and Mota, A. 2017. 'Governing the Anthropocene: Agency, Governance, Knowledge'. *European Journal of Social Theory*, 20 (1): 9–38.

Dhar, D. 2019. 'Women's Unpaid Care Work Has Been Unmeasured and Undervalued for Too Long'. In: *Essays on Equality.* Edited by G. I. W. L. London: KCL, pp. 30–33.

Fahs, B. and Swank, E. 2016. 'The Other Third Shift?: Women's Emotional Work in Their Sexual Relationships'. *Feminist Formations*, 28 (3): 46–69.

Fraser, N. 2013. *Fortunes of Feminism: From State-Managed Capitalism to Neoliberal Crisis.* London: Verso.

Fraser, N. 2014. 'Behind Marx's Hidden Abode'. *New Left Review*, 86: 55–72.

Fraser, N. and Jaeggi, R. 2018. *Capitalism: A Conversation in Critical Theory.* Cambridge: Polity.

Fraser, N. and Leonard, S. 2016. 'Capitalism's Crisis of Care'. *Dissent Magazine.* www.dissentmagazine.org/article/nancy-fraser-interview-capitalism-crisis-of-care

Gilmore, R.W. 2007. *Golden Gulag: Prisons, Surplus, Crisis, and Opposition in Globalizing California.* Oakland: UC Press.

Go, J. 2020. 'Three Tensions in the Theory of Racial Capitalism'. *Sociological Theory*, 39 (1): 38–47.

Harding, V., Hill, R. and Strickland, W. 2012 [1981]. 'Introduction'. In: *How Europe Underdeveloped Africa.* Edited by W. Rodney. Dakar: Pambazuka Press.

Hartley, G. 2018. *Fed Up: Emotional Labour, Women, and the Way Forward.* San Francisco: Harperone.

Hochschild, A. 1983. *The Managed Heart: Commercialization of Human Feeling.* Berkeley: University of California Press.

Hochschild, A. and Machung, A. 1989. *The Second Shift: Working Families and the Revolution at Home.* New York: Viking Press.

Klein, N. 2014. *This Changes Everything: Capitalism vs. The Climate.* New York: Simon and Schuster.

Legassick, M. and Hemson, D., 1976. *Foreign Investment and the Reproduction of Racial Capitalism in South Africa.* London: AAM.

Lemann, N. 2020. 'Is Capitalism Racist?' *The New Yorker.* 18 May 2020. www.newyorker.com/magazine/2020/05/25/is-capitalism-racist

Lohmann, L. 2012. 'A Rejoinder to Matthew Patterson and Peter Newell'. *Development and Change*, 43 (5): 1177–84.

Malm, A. 2016. *Fossil Power: The Rise of Steam Power and the Roots of Global Warming.* London: Verso.

Malm, A. 2017. *The Progress of this Storm: Nature and Society in a Warming World.* London: Verso.

Malm, A. 2020. *How to Blow Up a Pipeline: Learning to Fight in a World on Fire.* London: Verso.

Marx, E. and Aveling, E. 1987 [1887]. *The Woman Question.* New York: International Publishers.

Marx, K. 1976. *Capital: A Critique of Political Economy.* Vol. 1. Translated by B. Fowkes. London: Penguin.

Moore, J. 2015. *Capitalism in the Web of Life: Ecology and the Accumulation of Capital.* London: Verso.

Moore, J. (ed.) 2016. *Anthropocene or Capitalocene? Nature, History, and the Crisis of Capitalism.* Oakland: PM Press.

Moore, J. 2017. 'The Capitalocene, Part I: On the Nature and Origins of Our Ecological Crisis'. *The Journal of Peasant Studies.* 44 (3): 594–630.

Patterson, M. and Newell, P. 2006. *Climate Capitalism: Global Warming and the Transformation of the Global Economy.* Cambridge: Cambridge University Press.

Roberts, D. E. 2019. 'Abolition Constitutionalism'. *Harvard Law Review*, 133 (1): 1–122.

Robinson, C. 2020 [1983]. *Black Marxism: The Making of the Black Radical Tradition*. London: Penguin Classics.

Rodney, W. 1972 [2012]. *How Europe Underdeveloped Africa*. Dakar: Pambazuka Press.

Schumacher, E. F. 1980 [1973]. *Small is Beautiful: A Study of Economics as if People Mattered*. London: Blond and Briggs.

Scovell, N. and Sandberg, S. 2013. *Lean In: Women, Work, and the Will to Lead*. New York: Alfred A. Knopf.

Sunkara, B. 2021. 'What if Liberal Anti-racists Aren't Advancing the Cause of Equality?' *The Guardian*. 6 March 2021. www.theguardian.com/commentisfree/2021/mar/06/racial-equality-working-class-americans-advocacy

Vogel, L. 1983. *Marxism and the Oppression of Women*. Leiden: Brill.

Wallerstein, I. 2004. *World-Systems Analysis: An Introduction*. Durham: Duke University Press.

Walzer, M. 2020. 'A Note on Racial Capitalism'. *Dissent*. 29 July 2020. www.dissentmagazine.org/online_articles/a-note-on-racial-capitalism

Wilkerston, I. 2020. *Caste: The Origins of Our Discontents*. New York: Random House.

Žižek, S. 2021. 'Last Exit to Socialism'. *Jacobin*. 21 July 2021. https://jacobinmag.com/2021/07/slavoj-zizek-climate-change-global-warming-nature-ecological-crises-socialism-final-exit

10 Neoliberalism Triumphant

The New Spirit of Capitalism, Networks, Globalization

With Thatcherism in the UK and Reaganomics in the USA, it was not merely free-market capitalism which dominated from the 1980s until the 2008 crash, but an aggressive form of neoliberalism. With the fall of the Berlin Wall in 1989, free-market capitalism appeared so hegemonic that Francis Fukuyama (1992) argued that the world was bearing witness to the 'End of History' itself. With neoliberalism ascendant, capitalism was held to be the final reconciliation of societal organization and human reason. While Fukuyama's thesis was controversial, the malleability of the market was increasingly beyond doubt. For Manuel Castells (1996, 1997, 1998), capitalism's dynamism was demonstrated by its embrace of technical innovation, with markets becoming amorphous and extra-territorial, developing in harmony with advances in computing and telecommunications.

This 'new' capitalism was held to be significantly distinct from the preceding Fordist model (Castells 1996, 1997, 1998; Boltanski and Chiapello 2018 [1999]). Informational, globalized capitalism had a 'new spirit' and produced a new ideal-typical social subject (Boltanski and Chiapello 2018). Stable jobs and incremental career progression were displaced by entrepreneur-employees, engaging in liminal 'projects', forever seeking to expand their 'employability' in the frenetic marketplace. As we underscore below, for Boltanski and Chiapello, this loss of stability was ironically legitimated by a contortion of the demands emanating from progressive voices. Trade unions responded to their members' desire for greater autonomy and more rewarding work; this served to lubricate the shift from stable, if dull, permanent jobs, to the 'flexible' but precarious employment regimes which predominate today. This totalizing picture, with capitalism co-opting progressive criticism, is replicated across much of the literature of the period, with echoes of the inescapable false capitalist 'whole' described by Adorno (1978 [1951]) reverberating throughout Boltanski and Chiapello's *The New Spirit of Capitalism* [1999], Hardt and Negri's *Empire* [2000] and Naomi Klein's *Shock Doctrine* [2007].

Another influential account from this period is Hall and Soskice's *Varieties of Capitalism* [2001]. Their approach has been widely embraced by orthodox economists and by scholars of comparative political economy in particular. Perhaps more than any other text of this period, Hall and Soskice's intervention reflects the dominance of capitalism during their time of writing. Their work is somewhat out of keeping with the overall concern of our book, in that, as Wolfgang Streeck (2010) argued, Hall and Soskice neither focus strictly on 'capitalism' nor offer much by way of a critique. However, due to the sustained impact of their work (see Hay 2020: 302) and the wider interest in varieties of capitalism, we engage with it here. We argue that the fact that *Varieties of Capitalism*, despite its manifold methodological and theoretical weaknesses, achieved such impact reflects the ideological saturation of capitalist thought at this historical juncture.

DOI: 10.4324/9781351017671-11

Globalization was also a central concern for theorists of capitalism within this period and two rival approaches to its study emerged. Manuel Castells' imposing 1500-page trilogy, *The Information Age* [1996–98], offered a prosaic and measured engagement with the new global capitalist formation. For Castells, while consciously eschewing technological determinism, the rise of information technology was crucial to comprehending the latest socio-economic developments. The 'information age' would, Castells presciently declared, lead to a new cast of 'winners' and 'losers', with those excluded from the global network regressing to identarian and reactionary politics. However, despite this remarkable foresight, we argue that Castells' work also reflects a timidity in terms of critique. Castells was suspicious of any attempt to fuse critique and praxis as he feared it may lead again to Leninist terror (1998: 358). The exact opposite tone and politics is adopted by Michael Hardt and Antonio Negri in their equally significant text on globalization, *Empire* in 2000.

For Hardt and Negri, capitalism requires remorseless and excoriating critique; the globalized economy is not one of amicable, measured self-interest, but of a totalizing neo-imperialism. For the co-authors, capitalism, in accord with the work of Castells, is increasingly complicated; it is networked, global, amorphous and dynamic. But, to use a term from one of Klein's anecdotes in the *Shock Doctrine,* for Hardt and Negri, neoliberal complexity is no less 'evil' (Klein 2007: 4). As we discuss, Hardt and Negri's fusion of post-structuralism and post-Marxism offers a critique of the globalized economy that retains the dissenting spirit of earlier authors. Nominally liberal institutions, such as the World Bank and IMF, are shown to be deeply complicit in the practice of Empire. In keeping with Adorno, Hardt and Negri stress the totality of 'Empire' and the limited possibilities for emancipation. There exists only one viable form of resistance, a negatively framed 'dissent'. While possibilities exist for the 'Multitude' to agitate (Hardt and Negri 2006), it is an agitation 'against' Empire from within, one which offers bleak and unspecified prospects.

A similarly near-totalizing, extractive and neo-imperialist theorization of capitalism is present in Naomi Klein's *Shock Doctrine*. Writing just before the 2008 financial crisis, Klein demonstrated how neoliberalism thrives, and embeds itself, in periods of tragedy and conflict. Through a wide-ranging study, encompassing the aftermath of hurricane Katrina, the forced 'shock therapy' of South Africa, post-Soviet nations, Central and Southern America and the permanent war footing of Israel, Klein argued that capitalism is able to thrive in adversity: real, induced or staged. Klein's work perfectly presages our discussion in Chapter 11, in which we attend to the critiques of capitalism influenced by, and emanating out of, the 2008–2010 financial crisis.

The New Spirit of Capitalism

Luc Boltanski and Eve Chiapello's *The New Spirit of Capitalism* [1999] was one of the most significant works on capitalism in the 1990s. The intellectual background to this book was a broader move away from Pierre Bourdieu's sociology to an approach that stressed the critical capacities of actors rather than the reproduction of the class structure and the different forms of capital. This was developed by Luc Boltanski and Laurent Thévenot in a major work that became the hallmark of French post-Bourdieu sociology, *On Justification: Economies of Worth*. This work advanced what was to become an influential 'pragmatic sociology', which gives a central place to the way people engage in action and the justifications they give to their action (2006 [1991]). Boltanski and Chiapello applied this approach to justifications of capitalism.

The challenge they set themselves was to understand the '*ideological changes that have accompanied recent transformations in capitalism*' (Boltanski and Chiapello 2018: 3, their italics). Their framing of 'ideology' is important. They do not use the term in the manner of crude Soviet Marxists, rather they understand ideology as a 'set of shared beliefs, inscribed in institutions, bound up with actions, and … anchored in reality' (Boltanski and Chiapello 2018: 3). Ideology in this sense sits closer to Weber's notion of a 'spirit' which legitimated each particular stage of capitalism. Capitalism needs a 'spirit' in the sense of reasons or justifications. Through a methodologically rigorous analysis of primary data, they argued that a fundamental change within this 'spirit' of capitalism had occurred, one which led to the domestication of 'critique'.

The relationship between the 'critique' of capitalism and the 'spirit' of capitalism is a central concern throughout their book. Critique was presented as 'a motor in changes in the spirit of capitalism' (Boltanski and Chiapello 2018: 27). As critique grows, the spirit of capitalism adapts and reforms. For Boltanski and Chiapello, the fundamental challenge was to understand the present 'waning of critique at a time when capitalism was undergoing significant restructuring whose social impact could not go unnoticed' (Boltanski and Chiapello 2018: 4). To explore how and why critique had withered, they investigated the specificities of the new 'spirit' which had emerged. To do so, they conducted a comparative analysis of the management texts of the preceding Taylorist period and the dominant management texts of the neoliberal era. Management books present themselves as being the 'normative literature' of capitalism offering an accessible and explicit legitimating 'discourse' for the co-authors to interrogate. The contemporary management literature thus demonstrated how neoliberalism was 'supposed' to work, detailing why and how employees were expected to 'buy into' the system. The authors thus sought to distil the new spirit of capitalism from an analysis of the management literature of the day.

As the pressures of work increased under neoliberalism, pay alone was increasingly 'insufficient to induce commitment and stimulate enthusiasm' for most forms of employment (Boltanski and Chiapello 2018: 8). While a typical worker cannot survive for long without employment, they can still resign from any particular job if they deem its demands overbearing and/or its rewards too slim. The worker's flexibility is central to free-market capitalism, this is one of the fundamental distinctions between even the most aggressive neoliberalism and slave economies. The 'spirit' of capitalism thus matters as it facilitates the 'voluntary subjection' of the worker; it is the 'ideology that justifies engagement in capitalism' (Boltanski and Chiapello 2018: 7–8) despite the hardships and limited rewards most employment provides. This 'spirit' thus becomes ever more important as the inequities and exploitative practices intrinsic to capitalism become increasingly visible to the populace.

To situate the 'new spirit of capitalism' historically, the two authors outlined three distinct 'spirits' which reflect different stages of capitalism's development. The first spirit legitimated the capitalism of the nineteenth and early twentieth centuries, ennobling the bourgeois entrepreneur as a gifted genius, who sought enlightened self-betterment. The ideological foundation for early free-market enterprise was that gambles, speculation and risk were to be applauded as they enabled the next generation to transcend the circumstances of their birth. Innovation and genius were celebrated as part of the broader valorization of enlightenment 'progress'. The disruptive, revolutionary spirit of innovation was balanced by the bourgeois morality of the period, typified by conservative social values.

The second 'spirit' identified by the authors captured the stable large-firm set-up of the 1930–70s. In contrast to buccaneering entrepreneurs, this spirit was connected to large, established companies, which were to be socially valued on the basis of the stability and security they provided. Societal valorization of professionally run, secure organizations, backed by responsible share-holders, typified this shift from the spirit of the heroic individual capitalist to the secure capitalist organization. This second spirit acclimatized workers to capitalist imperatives on the basis of the security provided for 'long-term planning' and predictable 'career management' (Boltanski and Chiapello 2018: 18, 25). In contrast, with the ascent of neoliberalism, a new, third spirit of capitalism was required to provide ideological stability in a dynamic and globalized market, which was increasingly reliant on emerging and complicated technologies. It is this third spirit of capitalism which is the titular new spirit of capitalism.

Boltanski and Chiapello contend that these historical spirits of capitalism occur partly in response to developing critiques of capitalism. Four distinct critiques of capitalism are described in *The New Spirit of Capitalism*, these are critiques of capitalism that are forms of indignation and expressed as: (a) disenchantment/inauthenticity, (b) oppression, (c) poverty/inequality and (d) egoism/opportunism. Boltanski and Chiapello suggest that these can be further simplified into two groups: critiques of capitalism which focus on social structure and inequality ('social' critiques) and those which focus on the impact of capitalism on the individual's experience of the world ('artistic' critiques). While artistic and social critiques can be fused into a singular analysis of capitalism,[1] typically social and artistic critiques are advanced in isolation.

For Boltanski and Chiapello, the neoliberal period represented a fundamentally new spirit of capitalism, bringing forth the dominance of artistic critique and a new relationship between critique and spirit. Central to their argument was the idea that the new spirit had managed to substantially co-opt critique as a stabilizing force that *legitimated* neoliberal imperatives. Both the new spirit of capitalism and the artistic form of critique reflected a transition away from the starchy, hierarchical tedium of the corporate world of the 1950s and 1960s. The ironed newspapers and taut breaches of the 1950s were replaced by the socially libertarian 'cool capitalists' of neoliberalism, typified by the T-shirt wearing Ben and Jerry (see Žižek 2009: 56). The new spirit of capitalism was about creativity, passion, enthusiasm, self-motivation. This married perfectly with the shifting focus of critique and the ascendant post-modern sensitivity (Jeffries 2021). No longer were unions focusing on class, or the irrationality and inefficiency of the market, but on workers' demands to end boredom, alienation and tedium. Social critique had been comprehensively displaced by artistic critique and the new spirit was perfectly equipped to co-opt this. Indeed, social critique was increasingly seen as dull and antiquated. The new neoliberal subject would be more likely to be self-ironically enjoying a 'Cherry Guevara' ice cream than to be found on a picket line (Žižek 2009: 57). As the authors argued, drawing on a comparative analysis of management texts from both the period of the second spirit and from the contemporary third spirit of capitalism, neoliberalism has managed to co-opt the dominant artistic critique by framing precarious employment as exciting projects, offering individuality, creativity and variety.

Boltanski and Chiapello outlined a whole raft of new practices which typify the new spirit of capitalism. At its most simple, employment norms were rapidly changing. Gradual and stable progression within large firms was being replaced by new 'autonomous teams' which were judged as being 'wholly responsible' for some delimited output. While this theoretically offered greater ownership for workers of their labour, it primarily served to replace managerial control with a 'market type of control' (Boltanski and Chiapello 2018: 82). In this new era, those who performed poorly in terms of quantifiable, targeted outputs (sales figures, production line efficiency etc.) were to be fired, there was no need for the paid surveillance of a manager. To offset these increased demands on productivity, the new literature focused on having the trust of a team and the importance of learning to exist in a network. If the capitalism of the 1960s was legitimated by a 'spirit' which promoted 'the exhilaration of progress … [and] of job security', the new spirit of capitalism championed 'personal fulfilment through a multitude of projects' (Boltanski and Chiapello 2018: 86, 90) and thriving in complex networked associations. A modicum of autonomy was offered in response to acquiescing to market control.

This was far from the only substantial change in employment practices brought about by neoliberalism which the management literature sought to normalize. Rather than a slow apprenticeship to tailored skills, and a stable, secure job, as offered by the second period of capitalism, neoliberalism offered workers curated 'enrichment' of their resumes, tied to an individualist 'employability' discourse. Workers were no longer to view themselves as having a job for life as part of a stable team, rather they were encouraged to invest in themselves and increasingly were expected to change 'team' constantly to progress. Company loyalty and jobs for life were replaced by investment in the individual who now skips between short-term contracts. This employability agenda has proliferated and remains central to neoliberal capitalism today, increasingly stretching into education (Pal 2022). Workers and students are encouraged to 'self-skill' by management, they are told they are enriching their prospects by investing in themselves. This spirit discursively legitimated the erasure of stable contracts and secure employment prospects. Increasingly, firms were seen as fulfiling their moral obligations on the basis of enriching employees' prospects for speculative further work in future years with limitless alternative employers.

A central argument advanced by Boltanski and Chiapello is that the particular combination of the new spirit of capitalism and the dominance of artistic critique served to displace social critique when it was most needed. Neoliberal capitalism maintains hegemony by co-opting the artistic critique of the preceding Taylorist workplace within its contemporary spirit. The dominance of the artistic critique was a result of the rebellious spirit of 1968, of a new generation who deplored rigid hierarchy. The children of 1968 were not prepared to accept the discipline of the old order and close supervision by management. The libertarian sentiments of progressive activists were repackaged as features of the new economic model: freedom, authenticity, creativity (see Žižek 2009: 59). The keywords of the neoliberal management manuals were thus 'taken directly from the repertoire of May 1968' (Boltanski and Chiapello 2018: 97). For theorists such as Nancy Fraser, such changes can be understood as being part of a broader problematic displacement of 'the social left' by 'the cultural left' (see Jallon et al. 2000).

The decentring of 'social critique' was a hammer blow to forces opposing capitalist imperatives. Artistic critique harmonized perfectly with the new spirit of capitalism. As a result, the referents of social irrationality, oppression and exploitation were largely discarded from the progressive lexicon. The new era of capitalism witnessed the 'quasi-obliteration of reference to social class' exactly when capital achieved a stranglehold over labour (Boltanski and Chiapello 2018: 167–8). Ironically, the embrace of the artistic critique by trade unions served to further legitimate this move away from social critique, especially within France, which was the overwhelming focus of the study. The new demands emanating from the main trade unions were for 'relaxing hierarchical control and taking account of individual *potential*' (Boltanski and Chiapello 2018: 190, italics in the original). As Boltanski and Chiapello frame it, the French Unions unintentionally exchanged economic security for a faux-sense of autonomy. This autonomy was symbolic rather than real: workers were policed by more pervasive market mechanisms, they had to monitor and manage themselves as poor performances led to quicker dismissal than before. Not only was such self-management required, but increasingly workers were expected to be striving to find meaning in these projects, to achieve what Axel Honneth (2004) called a form of 'organized self-realization'. Accordingly, the previous injunction to smile at customers was replaced with an even more corrosive superficiality: the worker is expected to be smiling at themselves, the onus becomes on them to see meaning and purpose in their labour. As Boltanski and Chiapello powerfully argue, not for the first time, forces opposing capitalism had unintentionally provided ample fodder for legitimating, rather than resisting, market imperatives.

The New Spirit of Capitalism was certainly not without its critics (see Gay and Morgan 2013; Taupin 2013). A criticism which has been levelled repeatedly is that Boltanski and Chiapello's theoretical framework is unstable. According to Gay (2013), their work is based on a misunderstanding of Weber which led to their adoption of an unnuanced understanding of agency. For Weber, Gay argues, subjects who adapt to bureaucratic norms are not simply surrendering their agency, rather such accommodations are more sophisticated in nature, agency remains; concessions are offered from subjects, not merely extracted from passive robots. For Willmott (2013), there are concerns with the empirics presented; for example, there is a lack of engagement with ideas emerging from Critical Management Studies (CMS). A repeated concern is the attempt to make internationally generalizable observations from a narrow case study: France is the sole focus of their empirical analysis (see Gay and Morgan 2013). In response to this last claim, Boltanski (2013: 50) and Chiapello (2013: 61) rightly reply that they are conscious *not* to make generalizing claims and convincingly claim that their text is best understood as a located engagement with the processes through which the demands from the protestors of the 1960s and 1970s (in France in particular) were co-opted.

Limitations aside, the prescience of their analysis is shown by the increasing ubiquity of zero-hour contracts, the rise of the 'gig economy', the increasing dependences on 'side hustles' and the new vulnerable 'underclass', theorized as 'the precariat' (Standing 2011). Boltanski and Chiapello provided a powerful explanation of the embedding of neoliberalism as a result of a changed spirit of capitalism which was capable of co-opting critique.

Varieties of Capitalism

Peter Hall and David Soskice's co-edited volume, *Varieties of Capitalism* [2001], presented an influential new typology of capitalist economies, although one limited to the Organization for Economic Cooperation and Development (OECD) world. We do not engage with this work on the basis of its merits (or even its explicit relevance) to the *critique* of capitalism (the focus of our book more broadly). Rather, we examine the core tenets of the co-author's framing as an artefact to demonstrate the crisis of critique, which Boltanski and Chiapello lamented. As Wolfgang Streeck (2010) argued, despite its title, *Varieties of Capitalism* does not really engage with 'capitalism' but focuses far more on 'the market economy'. While the term 'capitalism' captures the broader socio-political constellation and therefore offers ample possibilities for critique, the narrower focus of the 'market economy' serves to restrict critical analysis. Their book does not offer a definition of capitalism. Indeed, Hall and Soskice do not even provide a sustained critique of the 'market economy', rather they purport to offer a 'neutral' explanatory typology, which they contend supports economic analysis. This reflects the dominant strain of thought within mainstream economics at the time: the world was a naturalized market economy, with minor 'variations' existing thereof. As a result, while the study of markets remained important, the critique of capitalism was increasingly *dépassé*. Yet, as Hancké (2009) and Hay (2020) have argued, the 'varieties of capitalism' approach was influential in both comparative political economy as well as in mainstream economic thought. The idea that varieties of capitalism exist, as per Hall and Soskice's model, remains an 'almost foundational claim' for 'contemporary comparative political economy' today (Hay 2020: 302).

The varieties of capitalism approach adopts a 'firm-centric' perspective, which places the 'firm' as the central object of analysis. The variants of capitalism discussed are typified by the different ways in which firms adapt to solve problems of co-ordination and to secure their profits. The focus of the co-authors was researching how firms 'coordinate with other actors in the economy' (Hall and Soskice 2001: vi). The aim is to understand institutional variation across a variety of countries. Two ideal-typical models are presented: CMEs, co-ordinated market economies, and LMEs, liberal market economies. CMEs demonstrate a high degree of coordination between firms. Exemplar CMEs are Germany, Japan, Sweden and Austria. LMEs, in contrast, are organized more along market lines, where firms adopt a more hierarchical and self-interested approach. LMEs are typified by the UK and the USA.

Hall and Soskice stress that both models have distinct advantages and that they are 'not arguing … that one is superior to another' (Hall and Soskice 2001: 21). However, important differences are still held to exist. For example, they argued that CMEs and LMEs present different opportunities for technical innovation. CMEs are superior at providing steady, incremental progression in technologies. In contrast, LMEs are presented as offering fewer, but more substantial 'leaps' in technical development (Hall and Soskice 2001: 41). Both models, they claim, can provide social and economic stability and fertile soil for innovation. To support this analysis, Germany was taken as the ideal-typical CME, while the USA was presented as being the ideal-typical LME (Hall and Soskice 2001: 41).

Varieties of Capitalism focuses on exploring the particular ways LMEs and CMEs operate to enable firms to solve the problems which they encounter. Five key areas are explored, with LMEs and CMEs shown to offer different responses in how they manage: (a) industrial relations, (b) vocational training, (c) corporate governance, (d) inter-firm relations and (e) relations with their own employees. According to Hall and Soskice, this focus offers an important way of identifying similarities and differences between capitalist countries. In CMEs, co-ordination between firms and other actors leads to a heavier reliance on non-market relationships. In contrast, in LMEs, firms largely organize their activities via hierarchies and market arrangements. To thrive, Hall and Soskice argue, economies need to adopt a clear choice of either model: either embrace being a CME or an LME. Both formations have strengths, while favouring a middle ground tends to offer the worst of both worlds. The challenge is co-ordination in problem-solving, enabling firms to adopt a sustained CME or LME approach. The Varieties of Capitalism approach thus sits in clear opposition to the view that capitalism is moving towards a singular, homogenous neoliberalism (see Baccaro and Howell 2017). For Hall and Soskice, while CMEs can succeed in maintaining co-ordinated responses to the problems which firms face across the five areas discussed, neoliberalism will not emerge as the unchallenged form of market order.

One important outcome of the Varieties of Capitalism approach was a critique of some of the assumptions underlying the received notion of economic globalization. The analysis calls into question the notion of a homogeneous top-down process of globalization, claiming that especially in CMEs the move to deregulation will be slower and less extensive. So, for example, it claims that firms will not automatically offshore to benefit from cheaper supplies of labour because of the competitive advantage of staying at home. In contrast, LMEs are more likely to pressure governments for deregulation. Hall and Soskice imply that nations prosper not by becoming more similar but by building on their institutional advantages.

The limitations of the Varieties of Capitalism approach are extensive. As Streeck (2010) argued, Hall and Soskice do not actually offer a framework to explore varieties of capitalism as their focus is simply 'the market economy'. Conflating capitalism with the market economy is highly problematic as it erodes the critical power of the idea of capitalism by erasing its socio-political character. As Streeck argued, the

> very problems of distribution and exploitation that are centrally emphasized when a socioeconomic formation is referred to as capitalist are thereby submerged in, or redefined as, problems of efficient production. As a consequence, the fundamental ambivalence inherent in the concept of capitalism as a system of both economic progress and private appropriation is eliminated.
>
> (Streeck 2010: 27)

A further problem is that they make too much of institutional advantages. No connection is made among CMEs, more or less the European norm and social capitalism.

Today, critical voices have attacked almost every tenet of Hall and Soskice's framing. For example, they are often criticized for failing to allow space for agency in their approach (Crouch 2005a: 3). Subjects do not simply act in the manner which best abets firms in solving their problems; people have many complex, and at times contradictory and conflictual, motivations. As a result, both ideology and class conflict must be included within any theory of capitalism's varieties, something which Hall and Soskice fail to consider. Assessing everything on the basis of firms' abilities to solve co-ordination problems leaves no room to factor in class conflict, agency, crisis tendencies or history (Fast 2016). As a result of its 'firm-centric' methodology, the varieties of capitalism model has thus been criticized for being overly reductive and economistic (Fast 2016). Further, the framing's foundational methodology is not merely 'firm-centric', lumbering the approach with the problems this entails, but it is also based upon an outmoded methodological nationalism. While this may have been unremarkable in the 1950s, the underlying methodological nationalism seems sharply at odds with developments in the wider contemporary literature of the early 2000s, which stressed the primacy of international markets and emerging telecommunication technologies.

Perhaps most controversially, Hall and Soskice argued that despite 'some variation over specific periods, both liberal and coordinated market economies seem capable of providing satisfactory levels of long-run economic performance' (2001: 21). Critics argue that this is demonstrably not the case: LMEs are simply less equitable and more unstable. For example, for Hall and Soskice, the fact that it was the Boeing aircraft company in the USA which suffered a series of catastrophic accidents in recent times should not be linked to the USA's LME model, which systematically eroded regulation (see Raso 2019). The relative stability and superior flight safety record of recent Airbus aircraft (an international co-ordinated project of largely CMEs) would be seen as a sheer coincidence. This would seem to be an absurd position to take; clearly CMEs offer a structurally superior approach to LMEs on all meaningful metrics, something the co-authors implicitly point out themselves (2001: 21). Further, the empirical claim that LMEs are capable of enabling leaps of technological innovation has been challenged: the USA's technical development is usually a result of state-based military-industrial innovation, which sits closer to a state-corporation model than an LME (Crouch 2005b: 442). Further, the LME-CME binary has itself been challenged, with the co-authors' own work presenting 'Mediterranean economies' as existing within an unclear third position. Also, Hall and Soskice state that the USA and the UK are typical LMEs; however, the US and the British economies are fundamentally different in important regards. A framing which considers the US and the UK economy to both *typify* (not merely fall into) the same 'variety of capitalism' seems insufficiently refined (see Ahlquist and Breunig 2009). Seemingly innumerable further challenges have been levelled at the approach, with Hay even targeting the fundamental idea that varieties of capitalism exist. For Hay, the idea that '*capitalisms vary*' is not the same as saying that '*capitalism comes in varieties*' (Hay 2020: 302 – italics in original).

In summary, the Varieties of Capitalism approach leaves little space for agency, fails to engage with, let alone critique, 'capitalism' as a socio-political constellation, and remains vulnerable to a raft of methodological, empirical and theoretical criticisms. The fact that the perspective still achieved such dominance, becoming 'foundational' in comparative economic study (Hay 2020: 302), indicates far more about the state of the socio-political landscape than it does about capitalism itself.

The Information Age: Economy, Society, Culture

The work of Manuel Castells sits at odds with Hall and Soskice's in many important regards. Where the Varieties of Capitalism approach was presented in an introductory chapter to an edited volume, Castells' *The Information Age* is an imposing 1500-page trilogy. Where Hall and Soskice have been accused of over-simplification and reliance on outmoded binaries, Castells' entire corpus is an embrace of complexity and emergent technologies. While Hall and Soskice apply a methodological nationalism, Castells is one the principal theorists of globalization. Likewise, where Hall and Soskice show signs of being economistic and deterministic, Castells is at pains to pre-empt and avoid charges of technological determinism (Castells 1998: 358). Yet, as our examination of Castells' work demonstrates, for all his theoretical, empirical and methodological sophistication, this is yet another study that avoids making a sustained critique of capitalism. Castells was self-consciously opposed to any fusion of critique and praxis and had publicly renounced his earlier Marxism in the 1980s (Castells and Rantanen 2005: 137). As such, *The Rise of the Network Society* [1996], *The Power of Identity* [1997] and *End of Millennium* [1998] reflect the dominance of capitalism within this intellectual climate. We argue that for all the commendable analysis of *The Information Age*, Castells fails to skewer the contradictions of the emergent form of capitalism he describes.

The three texts that comprise *The Information Age* are united by Castells' goal of demonstrating the shift which occurred from an 'industrial' to an 'informational' form of society. To draw out this transformation, Castells utilized various methodological approaches and drew on extensive and varied empirical examples. The work is a daunting read and his methodological commitments and justifications require some extended consideration from the reader. This is a result of Castells seeking to make universal claims from some quite specific examples. While there is no space to detail such specifics here, it is worth noting that the second edition of *The Information Age* was heavily revised, with some methodological innovations reworked and extended. Ultimately, throughout both editions, Castells argued that 'informationalism' and globalization dominated the new 'information age'. In this new era, companies succeed or fail based on their ability to utilize data, new technologies, and to network. While technology is central to understanding Castells' work, he stresses that technology is a manifestation of society, rather than being an external force which dominates or determines it. As Wilenius (1998: 269–70) writes, for Castells, 'technology does not determine society: it only represents it'. However, technology, especially information and telecommunication technologies, such as the internet, are crucial to understanding this new society, which sprang forth out of the crises of the 1970s.

One of Castells' most significant claims throughout *The Information Age* was to stress that the new economic model was typified by a different spatial-temporal configuration. Where the old industrial era was largely fixed in space as (working) time progressed, the new informational age is one where data can be existing in multiple locations, and where connections can be instantaneous. Castells framed this transition as the move away from a world of 'places' to a new network of 'flows'. This was a new reality, which facilitated synchronous polycentric interactions. As a result of this shift, Castells argued, there was an emerging new cast of 'winners' and 'losers', based on the extent to how well actors are tapped into the new network. For those who were attuned to this new world of flows, the prospects were bright. For those trapped within the dying remains of the industrial world and unable to connect to the new 'information age' networks, the future was bleak. While *The Rise of the Network Society* [1996] charted the ascent of this new formation, *The Power of Identity* [1997] and *End of Millennium* [1998] focused on the new 'post-spatial' actors, social movements and institutions which facilitated and operated within these 'flows'.

While he was not in the business of presenting grandiose predictions, reading Castells' work 30 years on, one is struck by his prescience. Many of the socio-political challenges of today can be traced to developments which Castells identifies in their inception. Most obvious in this regard is the increasing cleavage between those who benefitted from globalization and those who resent it and offer an identarian pushback. This is clearly the case on both a global and a local scale. In this regard, Castells explicitly discussed the likelihood of an ascendant political Islamism, nearly half a decade before the attacks of September 11, 2001. For Castells, such radical religious movements would probably refuse 'to bend to the network' and would likely build 'self-contained cultural communes' (Castells 2000: 19). Likewise, the divides experienced in the UK between 'core' areas of high wealth created by financial service industries (London and the South East) and impoverished post-industrial heartlands (Wales, the Midlands, the North). Regions and networks which failed to transition from the industrial economy to the new informational economy responded with a strident introspective cultural resurgence. This can be seen as manifesting in the Brexit vote in the UK, or the Trump vote in the USA. Indeed, Castells explicitly makes such parallels with reference to *The Information Age* in his latest work, *Rupture* (Castells, 2018).

Yet, despite the complexity and foresightedness of Castells' work, he consciously shied away from offering a critique of capitalism. This is particularly clear when one considers his relative silence on the environmental impacts of the new globalized society he was identifying. As Wilenius (1998: 275) writes, Castells 'does not consider at any length the massive number of critical trends inducing global change on the biosphere. In other words … Castells … does not appreciate the economic and political manifestations of wasteful and resource intensive economies'. Further, the most economically significant development in the immediate aftermath of his book, the 2008 financial crisis, was not considered a possibility, despite Castells' foresight in other areas.[2] Ultimately the fundamental *irrationality* of the networked, globalized informational capitalist system was not the focus of Castells' work. He was not significantly invested in the critique of capitalism, as was the case with many of the authors within this period. His primary concern was with the implications of information technology on the world and the opportunities the new age of hyper globalization offers for progressive politics.

Empire

Michael Hardt and Antonio Negri, however, proved an important exception in this regard. In their *Empire,* globalized capitalism is most certainly subjected to critique. Some commentators have gone as far as to call Hardt and Negri the 'Marx and Engels of the Internet Age' (see Thompson 2005: 73). This has some truth to it as the neutrality and innate reason of liberal institutions is subjected to concerted criticism by the co-authors. Yet, as we argue here, a sense of capitalism's dominance remains within Hardt and Negri's Deleuze-inspired work. Unlike the *Communist Manifesto, Empire* does not suggest the imminent decline of capitalism. Far from it, within this new, complex globalized world, there is no obvious escape route. 'Empire' is presented as being totalizing and all-pervasive. As such, we argue that Hardt and Negri represent a significant critique of the globalized informational age which still reflects the spirit of the period.

In keeping with the work of Castells, Hardt and Negri argue that the new capitalist formation is a post-national, 'deterritorialized', order. There is not a singular state, nor even a discrete coalition of nameable states, which benefit from the global economy at the expense of a discrete list of others. Rather, the old framings of 'imperialism', and even 'neo-imperialism', fail to fully capture the complexity of the current globalized system. The new conjuncture is one of Multi National Companies (MNCs) and Trans National Companies (TNCs), international treaties, unelected international bodies and instantaneous and intercontinental capital flows. There is no 'winner' that extracts from clear 'Others'. Likewise, there is no meaningful 'Core' and 'Periphery', as per Immanuel Wallerstein's (2004) 'World Systems Theory'; rather the picture offered by Hardt and Negri sits closer to 'a pandemonium of interacting agents with no central authority' (Žižek 2009: 56). For the co-authors, there is thus no clear structure, merely a singular state of Empire in which all actors, states, companies are unwittingly located. There is no escape from the totality of the Empire which Hardt and Negri present. One cannot simply enact a war of resistance to McDonalds, for example, despite Jose Bove's remarkable symbolic attempt (see Henley 2000). As the co-authors put it, in today's globalized world, 'no nation state can today … form the center of an imperialist project' (Hardt and Negri 2000: xiv). This does not mean that the global capitalist system is any less extractive or brutal, rather 'a new imperial form of sovereignty has emerged' (Hardt and Negri 2000: xiii). The attendant new 'complex regimes of differentiation and homogenization, deterritorialization and reterritorialization' cannot be captured by the old terms of reference (Hardt and Negri 2000: xiii). A new, post-Marxian and post-structural account influenced by Deleuze is presented, one purportedly capable of capturing these dynamics and the accompanying deterritorialized flows of power.

Importantly, the new cast of imperial actors are not explicitly 'imperialistic', they position themselves as liberal champions of freedom, democracy, even of equality and human rights. Consider the IMF, the World Bank and much of the European Union; the executives of these institutions are arguably the most powerful unelected figures in world history. The global network is more fluid, more complicated, even, to quote Deleuze and Guattari (1977 [1972]), 'rhizomatic' in shape. However, despite this increase in complexity, the reality is quite unambiguous: imposed 'structural adjustment' and forced austerity by unelected agents of capital. This is no less of an aggressive and colonializing form of international order. Simply, the form of extraction has changed, it is deterritorialized. The hard-power of 'gunboat' democracy has been replaced by what Foucauldians refer to as 'biopower'. The language of 'prudence' and of 'sound financial management' is utilized to enable rapid and inequitable capital movement.

It is perhaps best to frame Hardt and Negri's critique of capitalism as a post-Marxism which embraces post-structuralism, while stridently rejecting post-modernism. Post-modernism is typically understood as the embrace of multiple narratives and the rejection of singular truths. Its supporters rejoice in the plural meanings of signs and the emancipatory promises of cultural and aesthetic hybridity (see Jeffries 2021). Hardt and Negri's work serves to disclose the lie of this intellectual trajectory. In this regard, they offer an explicit rejection of Homi Bhabha's postcolonial account of hybridity. For Bhabha, diasporic communities have access to multiple forms of knowledge which provides a powerful transcendent critical perspective and enriched hermeneutic position. However, hybridity and post-modernity, for Hardt and Negri, is not primarily reflected by intercultural aesthetic exchanges, or sophisticated intersubjective praxis. These, if existing, are incidental footnotes. Rather, a world of hybridity is typified by migrant boats sinking in the English Channel, of brain drains, capital flight and anomie. The fluidity of both meaning and of human movement is crucial to the functioning of 'Empire'. The imposition of 'fluidity' and 'hybridity' by Empire leads to tragic migration crises, rather than to virtuoso hermeneutic exegeses.

For Hardt and Negri, the possibilities for resistance are bleak. While in later work, such as *Multitude,* there is an extended discussion of the possibilities for mass 'refusal' (Hardt and Negri 2000: 203), the challenge faced is vast. The possibilities for 'reappropriation' and global citizenship are discussed, but without much hope. The 'armed globalization' of neoliberal capitalism is not going to surrender to 'democracy on a global scale' (Hardt and Negri 2006: xi) without a fight. The authors, here sitting closer to Castells, are wary of prescription, stating that only 'the multitude through its practical experimentation will offer the models and determine when and how the possible becomes real' (Hardt and Negri 2000: 411). Echoes with Adorno's philosophical negativity resonate (Hardt and Negri 2000: 203). Despite divergent politics to Castells, there remain clear similarities in this narrative: the significance of globalization, the complexity of the current conjuncture, the unwillingness to prescribe precise political actions.

Hardt and Negri, too, are most certainly not without critics. Perhaps the most repeated criticism of *Empire* is that it simply does not reflect the empirical reality: that there is one country which benefits from the current global order: America. To speak of a polyvalent, dynamic, capitalism, in which no singular 'imperial' power can be identified seems frankly absurd. When one considers the course of the past 100 years of world history, the rise of neoliberalism can be considered to be inextricably linked with the dominance of American Foreign Policy. There are clear winners and losers in globalized capitalism, and this is an important reality which needs to be captured by any satisfactory critical engagement with capitalism.[3]

As it stands, it also remains unclear precisely what does the 'totalizing' within *Empire*. If ultimately Hardt and Negri are arguing for a rejection of an economic model, or capitalistic dynamic, their work is substantially lacking in economic theorization and economic empirics. This is perhaps a result of their embrace of a Deleuze-inflected *post*-Marxism. If *Empire* is read as a critique of the global capitalist system, the most obvious criticism is that their analysis lacks rigorous economic foundations. Nevertheless, *Empire* became the bible for the anti-globalization movement and continues to be an essential text for contemporary scholars of globalization.

The Shock Doctrine

Naomi Klein's *The Shock Doctrine* [2007] is an equally significant text from the period of hyper globalization. In keeping with the other works discussed, Klein demonstrates neoliberalism's ability to thrive in adversity and to adapt quickly to changing conditions. Klein's central concern was to demonstrate the means through which neoliberal mechanisms are embedded. Her argument has had a sustained impact across disciplines and was even converted into a documentary film directed by Michael Winterbottom and Mat Whitecross (2009). She demonstrated that the free-market capitalism associated with Milton Friedman has typically taken root within periods of crisis and disaster, be they economic, environmental or military. Such crises can even be induced or prolonged as a means to aid transition to deregulated markets. The *Shock Doctrine* is thus another text which demonstrates the power and complexity of neoliberal capitalism, it is presented as a system which can feed off all kinds of human adversity.

The central idea of the 'shock doctrine' is that free-market policies are typically opposed to the interests of ordinary people. As such, neoliberal reforms need to be implemented when the democratic process is suspended or otherwise distracted by some 'shock', be it a natural disaster, terrorism, or full-scale war. The 'shock' aspect is twofold: consisting of both the presence of some exceptional circumstance, but also a 'shock' in terms of the rapid speed through which neoliberal reforms are implemented. The public are distracted, unable to resist and have no time to mobilize in opposition.

The book starts with a discussion of this 'shock doctrine' in effect in the aftermath of Hurricane Katrina. Republican figures were immediately presenting the hurricane as an opportunity to privatize community provisions and rebuild upon market lines. Klein quotes Richard Baker, a senior Republican politician and lobbyist, as stating '[w]e finally cleared up public housing in New Orleans. We couldn't do it, but God did' (c.f. Klein 2007: 4). In the immediate aftershock of the destruction, while communities were reeling and the dead were being counted, neoliberal interests were loudly speaking of 'very big opportunities' for business (Klein 2007: 4). This tone was entirely out of keeping with the grief and suffering of the populace. As Klein wrote, '[h]earing all the talk of "fresh starts" and "clean sheets", you could almost forget the toxic stew of rubble, chemical outflows and human remains just a few miles down the highway' (Klein 2007: 4). This, however, was exactly the moment neoliberal advocates needed, a chance to auction off New Orleans' public assets while attention was elsewhere. Ultimately said auction 'took place with military speed and precision' (Klein 2007: 5), in sharp contrast to the sclerotic pace of development which had occurred pre hurricane. As Klein sharply captured the dynamic at work in an exchange between two residents. An older man expressed '"What is wrong with these people in Baton Rouge? This isn't an opportunity. It's a goddamned tragedy. Are they blind?" to which a "mother with two kids chimed in". "No they're not blind, they're evil. They see just fine"' (Klein 2007: 4). Sure enough, Klein wrote, no new community schools were built, rather vouchers were distributed to the new for-profit academies.

As Klein argued, the relationship between neoliberal reform and crisis demonstrated by the aftermath of Katrina was not an aberration, it was the norm. The ultimate ally of neoliberal reform was 'fear and disorder' (Klein 2007: 9). Neoliberal interests learned to either capitalize on natural crises or manufacture them to precipitate free-market reforms. A key example of this was the horrors of the 'shock therapy' in Chile (see also Hitchens, 2001: 55–76). Klein quotes Eduardo Galeano (1978) from *Days and Nights of Love and War*, while 'the theories of Milton Friedman gave him the Nobel Prize; they gave Chile General Pinochet' (Klein 2007: 73). The imposition of a dictatorship and the erasure of democracy was a necessary precondition for the neoliberal reforms of the 'Chicago Boys' in South America.

Klein details how such horrific socio-political realities enabled neoliberal reform across the globe, discussing the 'scandalous' results of the rushed implementation of neoliberalism in South Africa (Klein 2007: 215) and in the post-Soviet states. Of particular interest to Klein is the 'standing disaster Apartheid state of Israel' (Klein 2007: 428). Klein notes how the state of induced perpetual crises of the ongoing illegal occupation of Palestinian territories enabled a thriving neoliberal economy built on 'selling expertise and devices related to counter-terrorism' (Klein 2007: 430). Israel became a neoliberal laboratory for the permanent crisis economy, where arms could be packaged as tried and tested on a 'expendable' nearby populace (see Halper, 2015). This shift 'in the nature of the economy' to 'guns and caviar' is presented as a 'stark warning' (Klein 2007: 428). Crises, be they environmental, socio-political, unavoidable or artificially induced, can aid neoliberalism. The free market seems able to feed off tragedy and disaster, with vested interests stalking peaceable social democratic states, waiting for the moment to strike.

The ability for neoliberal agents to turn apparent human tragedy and adversity to their interests was demonstrated most memorably with the 2008 financial crisis, a central theme of our next chapter. Despite the financial crisis being an explicit result of a failed financial model – neoliberalism – this too became a reason for further *neoliberal* reforms. This is a remarkable ability to co-opt critique, a vast extension of the capacities already outlined by Boltanski and Chiapello. More recently still, the Covid-19 pandemic, which caused tremendous harm to the global economy, actually served the interests of many neoliberal actors. Klein has recently written of a pandemic shock doctrine, a 'Screen New Deal', in which big-tech and big-pharma managed to oust social economic models and thrive during the collective suffering (Klein 2020). Klein's thesis is supported by ample data (see Neate 2020). In keeping with the literature of the period, in *The Shock Doctrine,* neoliberalism appears as a formidable and dynamic force.

Conclusion

Throughout the 1980s until the 2008 financial crash, capitalism adopted a new global form, based increasingly upon technologies, networks and data. The industrial age was replaced by the information age as the economy became increasingly complex and intangible. This complexity partially masked a radical shift in wealth from the poor to the rich, from the public to the private purse; however, its effects were still widely felt. Harold

Macmillan, a Conservative Prime Minister in the UK from 1957 to 1963, and a staunch enemy of communism, famously attacked neoliberal policy in this period as 'selling off the family silver'.[4] Even many Conservative supporters of capitalist economics were appalled by the neoliberal revolution. And 'revolution' is no hyperbole, for the ascent of neoliberal policy was rapid and aggressive, with 'shock therapy' applied across the globe. This was aided by a widespread erasure of social critique, with the artistic critique of the day easily co-opted by the new spirit of capitalism. Neoliberalism was reigning supreme, with even environmental and socio-political crises serving to strengthen the free-market formation. Understandably, then, the literature in this period reflected a sense of capitalism as a totalizing force, with little possibilities for immediate transition. In Hall and Soskice, capitalism is implicitly presented as an inescapable, rational and sustainable form of socio-economic organization. In Castells, there is an explicit fear of the dangers of fusing critique and praxis. Even within the explicitly critical texts of the era, capitalism is presented as a totalizing force with an unspecified form of 'dissent' as the best critical response.

As we show in the next chapter, this scepticism of the likelihood of any immediate transition away from capitalism was well founded. Despite a financial crisis entirely of neoliberalism's making, free-market institutions remarkably managed to further embed themselves after 2008. However, as we shall discuss in the next chapter, the 2008–10 crisis demonstrated the continued instability of capitalism. The crisis tendencies within neoliberalism were clearly even more pronounced than those within the preceding capitalist formations. A propensity for worsening crises was thus married with the continuing scepticism of post-capitalist transition. The legacy of these authors was thus central to the theorists of the post-2008 period.

Notes

1. As demonstrated by many of the contributions to *Les Temps Modernes* (Boltanski and Chiapello 2018: 39).
2. He did, however, produce a notable meditation on the crash in its aftermath which is worthy of comment, *Another Economy is Possible* (2017).
3. As Ayelet Shachar (2009) argues, one needs to be aware that globalized capitalism retains a 'birthright lottery' in which one's citizenship remains the primary determinant of their predicted future standard of living.
4. Although this quotation from Macmillan is well known, it is actually a paraphrase of his comments.

References

Adorno, T.W. 1978 [1951]. *Minima Moralia: Reflections from Damaged Life.* Translated by E. Jephcott. London: Verso.

Ahlquist, J. S. and Breunig, C. 2009. *Country Clustering in Comparative Political Economy. MPIfG Discussion Paper, No. 09/5.* Cologne: Max Planck Institute for the Study of Societies.

Baccaro, L. and Howell, C. 2017. *Trajectories of Neoliberal Transformation.* Cambridge: Cambridge University Press.

Boltanski, L. 2013. 'A Journey through French-Style Critique'. In: *New Spirits of Capitalism? Crises, Justifications and Dynamics.* Edited by P. Gay and G. Morgan. Oxford: Oxford University Press. pp. 43–59.

Boltanski, L. and Chiapello, E. 2018 [1999]. *The New Spirit of Capitalism*. Translated by G. Elliott. London: Verso.

Boltanski, L. and Thévenot, L. 2006 [1991]. *On Justification: Economies of Worth*. Princeton: Princeton University Press.

Castells, M. 1996. 'The Information Age: Economy, Society and Culture'. *The Network Society*. Vol. 1. Oxford: Blackwell.

Castells, M. 1997. 'The Information Age: Economy, Society and Culture'. *The Power of Identity*. Vol. 2. Blackwell: Blackwell.

Castells, M. 1998. 'The Information Age: Economy, Society and Culture'. *End of Millennium*. Vol. 3. Oxford: Blackwell.

Castells, M. 2000. 'Materials for an Exploratory Theory of the Network Society'. *British Journal of Sociology*, 51 (1): 5–24.

Castells, M. 2017. *Another Economy is Possible: Culture and Economy in a Time of Crisis*. Oxford: Wiley.

Castells, M. 2018. *Rupture: The Crisis of Liberal Democracy*. Cambridge: Polity Press.

Castells, M. and Rantanen, T. 2005. 'The Message Is the Medium: An Interview with Manuel Castells'. *Global Media and Communication*, 1 (2): 135–47.

Chiapello, E. 2013. 'Capitalism and Its Critics'. In: *New Spirits of Capitalism? Crises, Justifications and Dynamics*. Edited by P. Gay and G. Morgan. Oxford: Oxford University Press, pp. 60–81.

Crouch, C. 2005a *Capitalist Diversity and Change: Recombinant Governance and Institutional Entrepreneurs*. Oxford: Oxford University Press.

Crouch, C. 2005b. 'Models of Capitalism'. *New Political Economy*, 10 (4): 439–56.

Deleuze, F. and Guattari, F. 1977 [1972]. *Anti-Oedipus: Capitalism and Schizophrenia*. Translated by R. Hurley. Minneapolis: University of Minnesota Press.

Fast, T. W. 2016. 'Varieties of Capitalism: A Critique'. *Industrial Relations*, 71 (1): 133–55.

Fukuyama, F. 1992. *The End of History and the Last Man*. New York City: Free Press.

Galeano, E. 1982 [1978]. *Days and Nights of Love and War*. Translated by J. Brister. New York City: Monthly Review Press.

Gay, P. 2013. 'Notes on Aspects of the Conceptual Architecture of the New Spirit: Weber and Hirschman'. In: *New Spirits of Capitalism? Crises, Justifications and Dynamics*. Edited by P. Gay and G. Morgan. Oxford: Oxford University Press, pp. 82–97.

Gay, P. and Morgan, G. (eds.) 2013. *New Spirits of Capitalism? Crises, Justifications and Dynamics*. Oxford: Oxford University Press.

Hall, P.A. and Soskice, D. (eds.) 2001. *Varieties of Capitalism: The Institutional Foundations of Comparative Advantage*. Oxford: Oxford University Press.

Halper, J. 2015. *War against the People: Israel, the Palestinians and Global Pacification*. London: Pluto Press.

Hancké, B. (ed.) 2009. *Debating Varieties of Capitalism: A Reader*. Oxford: Oxford University Press.

Hardt, M. and Negri, A. 2000. *Empire*. Cambridge: Harvard University Press.

Hardt, M. and Negri, A. 2006 [2004]. *Multitude*. London: Penguin.

Hay, C. 2020. 'Does Capitalism (Still) Come in Varieties?'. *Review of International Political Economy*, 27 (2): 302–19.

Henley, J. 2000. 'Carnival Greets French Farmer Who Took on McDonald's'. *The Guardian*, 1 July 2000. www.theguardian.com/world/2000/jul/01/jonhenley

Hitchens, C. 2001. *The Trial of Henry Kissinger*. London: Verso.

Honneth, A. 2004. 'Organized Self-Realization: Some Paradoxes of Individualization'. *European Journal of Social Theory*, 7 (4): 463–78.

Jallon, H., Sintomer, Y., and Wright, S. 2000. 'Linking the Cultural Left and the Social Left: Interview with Nancy Fraser'. *Soundings*, 15: 12–26.

Jeffries, S. 2021. *Everything, All the Time, Everywhere: How We Became Postmodern*. London: Verso.

Klein, N. 2007. *The Shock Doctrine: The Rise of Disaster Capitalism*. London: Allen Lane.

Klein, N. 2020. 'Screen New Deal'. *The Intercept*, 8 May 2020. https://theintercept.com/2020/05/08/andrew-cuomo-eric-schmidt-coronavirus-tech-shock-doctrine/

Neate, R. 2020. 'Billionaire's Wealth Rises to $10.2 Trillion amid Covid Crisis'. *The Guardian*, 7 October 2020. www.theguardian.com/business/2020/oct/07/covid-19-crisis-boosts-the-fortunes-of-worlds-billionaires

Pal, M. 2022. 'Employability as Exploitability: A Marxist Critical Pedagogy'. In: *Thinking Beyond Neoliberalism*. Edited by N. Harris and O. Acaroglu. New York City: Palgrave Macmillan, pp. 197–219.

Raso, C. 2019. 'Boeing Crisis Illustrates Risk of Delegated Regulatory Authority'. *Brooking*, 18 December 2019. www.brookings.edu/research/boeing-crisis-illustrates-risks-of-delegated-regulatory-authority/

Shachar, A. 2009. *The Birthright Lottery: Citizenship and Global Inequality*. Cambridge: Harvard University Press.

Standing, G. 2011. *The Precariat: The New Dangerous Class*. London: Bloomsbury.

Streeck, W. 2010. 'E pluribus unum? Varieties and Commonalities of Capitalism'. *MPIfG Discussion Paper, No. 10/12*. Cologne: Max Planck Institute for the Study of Societies.

Taupin, B. 2013. 'Paul DU GAY & Glenn MORGAN (2013) New Spirits of Capitalism? Crises, Justifications and Dynamics' [review]. *M@n@gement*, 16 (4): 505–14.

Thompson, P. 2005. 'Foundation and Empire: A Critique of Hardt and Negri'. *Capital and Class*, 86: 73–98.

Wallerstein, I. 2004. *World-Systems Analysis: An Introduction*. Durham: Duke University Press.

Whitecross, M. and Winterbottom, M. 2009 [Film]. *The Shock Doctrine*. dir. Renegade Pictures, Revolution Films, and Channel Four.

Wilenius, M. 1998. 'A New Globe in the Making: Manuel Castells on the Information Age'. *Acta Sociologica*, 41 (3): 269–76.

Willmott, H. 2013. 'Spirited Away: When Political Economy Becomes Culturalized'. In: *New Spirits of Capitalism? Crises, Justifications and Dynamics*. Edited by P. Gay and G. Morgan. Oxford: Oxford University Press, pp. 98–123.

Žižek, S. 2009. *First as Tragedy, Then as Farce*. London: Verso.

11 The Financial Crisis and Austerity Capitalism

Responses from Thomas Piketty and David Harvey

The neoliberal revolution of the 1980s tore through existing regulatory constraints. Paraphrasing Gordon Gekko, greed was now seen as being good for the economy. Such an attitude persisted into the 1990s and the early 2000s. In the UK, Gordon Brown, the New Labour Chancellor of the Exchequer, reduced capital gains tax and granted operational independence to the Bank of England. Labour Party grandee Peter Mandelson captured the zeitgeist when he said he was 'intensely relaxed about people getting filthy rich' (see Moody 2019). Likewise, in the USA, Democratic President Bill Clinton drew a scythe through financial regulations, with frequent speeches about the need to liberate the market. However, while the market was largely set free, the power of labour was crippled. Predictably, workers' incomes fell and inequality rocketed. As such, these economies became increasingly reliant on private debt to artificially induce demand. In an absurd twist, this debt itself became a source of profit (through its complicated repackaging and resale) in an increasingly financialized economy. Indeed, by the mid-2000s, the economies of the Global North were dominated by nebulous 'financial services', which were subject to minimal regulation (Blakeley 2019). In this low-regulation environment, profits boomed. The precarity of this model is all too evident in hindsight: the economy was dominated by financial speculation and enabled by low to no regulation.

The first portents of the crash are now acknowledged to be a spiralling increase of foreclosures on so-called sub-prime mortgages in the USA. These omens went unnoticed by many financial observers as they predominantly impacted poor and disproportionately black Americans in a society which remained riven by racial and class divides. Even as bailiffs tore people from their homes, financiers continued to profit, with newspaper spreads juxtaposing eye-watering bankers' bonuses with photographs of mass evictions (see Story and Dash 2009). At the roots to the international financial crisis was the toxicity of complicated debt packages based on 'sub-prime' debts. In the pre-crash environment, companies were incentivized to offer extensive credit to prospective house-buyers, even those who could patently never afford to repay (Cowen 2008). Such mortgages were obviously risky investments for the lender. As a result, in a piece of what (at the time) seemed financial magic, these 'toxic' debts were combined with 'good debts' in a process known as 'securitisation'. A tranche of mortgages, including both 'good' and 'bad' (sub-prime) debts were parcelled up together and offered on the market as a commodity for purchase: a 'collateralised debt obligation' (CDO). While the 'sub-prime' mortgage tranches were risky investments, these CDOs were typically given an ultra-safe rating of AAA. These 'safe' tranches were then exchanged and modified repeatedly in ever more complicated chains of debt repackaging, known as Credit Default Swaps (CDSs). At the peak of financialization, billions of dollars of CDSs were being exchanged within the

DOI: 10.4324/9781351017671-12

global economy, with CDOs functioning as an anchor for further layers of even more abstract financial instruments (Tett 2009: 48–67). Ultimately, the crash spread as financial institutions were confronted with the undeniable reality that this entire exchange system was built upon bad debt which could never be repaid. Gradually, every institution touched by such toxicity felt the damage. First, mortgage finance businesses (such as Countrywide) were hit, followed by the investment banks who held these securities (such as Bear Sterns), all the way up to the companies that insured them (such as AIG). While it was the collapse of Lehman Brothers in the autumn of 2008 that truly sparked global financial cataclysm, the origins of the crash lay in the 'sub-prime' mortgages offered to people who could never afford to repay them.

A strict neoliberal response to the crash would have been to let the market take its course, failed businesses would ultimately have to face bankruptcy. Yet, this was not perceived to be a viable option. In the period of neoliberal reform, the economies of much of the Global North had become increasingly reliant upon financial services (Blakeley 2019). As a result, neoliberalism was suddenly thrown into an existential crisis. Should the market truly be free? Should failing banks be left to collapse? Ultimately, they were 'bailed out' at great expense to the tax payer. The free market was put on hold. Across both sides of the Atlantic both nominally socialist and proudly neoliberal governments supported 'bailing out' the banks. This led to the ironic situation in which the prime beneficiaries and political advocates of neoliberalism enjoyed the clemency of the state-aid they had spent decades admonishing as inefficient and even tyrannical (see Hayek 2001: 59–74).[1] Ultimately, the financial crisis resulted in an unprecedented movement of public money into private hands.

This could, and perhaps should, have been the end of the story. The state *could* have introduced much needed regulation while swathes of the banking sector were effectively semi-nationalized. The banks could slowly return to profit, paying off the public's generous charity, while they weaned themselves off their addiction to untenable speculation. The debt which existed, while high, was no higher as a proportion of GDP than it was after the Second World War. The economies of the Global North could have artificially induced demand and a more stable economy could have emerged. Such a Keynesian response, however, was not to be. As Klein argued in *The Shock Doctrine*, neoliberalism thrives in crises, even crises of its own making. In a remarkable twist of fate, the catastrophic crisis induced by neoliberal deregulation led to the widespread imposition of further *neoliberal* reforms (Klein 2007). The Keynesian orthodoxy that the state 'builds its way out of recession' was emphatically rejected throughout the Global North.[2] In a remarkable feat of propaganda, a surreal spin was placed on the financial crisis. The problem was not greed, speculation, deregulation, neoliberalism. Rather, much of the media presented the crisis as being a result of the state over-extending itself. 'Prudence' was required, not in the form of tighter regulation of the sector responsible for the crash, but prudence in terms of financial austerity. The crisis was counter-intuitively presented as emerging as a result of *excessive* rather than *insufficient* state action. A mass austerity drive was demanded by the agents of capital in a breathtaking counter-attack and ultimately this narrative achieved hegemony (Mullen 2018).

The austerity programmes which were introduced are now largely accepted to be politically motivated and economically untenable. Even self-identifying 'modern liberal' economists, such as Nobel Prize winner Paul Krugman (2015), stated that the idea that austerity was the best course to adopt was a clear 'delusion'. Krugman conclusively stated that 'all of the economic research that allegedly supported the austerity push has been discredited'. Yet the 'delusion' that austerity was an essential and prudent response to the financial crisis was widespread, even as it violated all axioms of economic theory. A new breed of economist emerged, the 'austerian', who attempted to do the impossible: to justify how growth can be supported by policies which cripple demand (see Maatsch 2013).

Rob Parenteau (2015) found such 'austerian' hegemony terrifying, writing that it reflected a 'Goebbelnomics', the product of a neoliberal propaganda war which normalized policies which defied logic. The irrationality of austerity campaigns was matched by their scale and ambition. Between 2010 and 2019, over £30 billion in public spending was cut in the UK, with key public services impacted (see Mueller 2019). Neoliberal institutions and norms were embedded under the cover of fiscal crisis, entirely true to Klein's work. In the UK, university tuition fees, which a government coalition partner had promised to abolish, were in fact tripled. NHS funding was drastically cut, regressive taxes, such as VAT, rose, social care budgets were cut. Between 2010 and 2019, the number of children relying on 'food banks' in the UK trebled (Mueller 2019) as the poorest suffered disproportionately. For Toynbee and Walker (2020), the financial crash was followed by a 'lost decade' of needless suffering. More bitingly, Chris Grover (2018) has argued that the austerity regimes were simply state-sanctioned 'social murder'.

In the global south, the strain of such neoliberal austerity had long been felt before the financial crash of 2008 (Connell and Dados 2014).[3] The transition to such an aggressive form of neoliberalism was largely driven by Wall Street and manifested in the form of so-called structural adjustment programmes. Structural adjustment was effectively the imposed transition to neoliberalism forced upon neo-colonial and post-colonial nations, held to ransom by the global capitalist elite and forced to embrace the free market or face the withholding of aid (see Harris and Acaroğlu 2022: 10–2). Developing nations were increasingly given access to vital development funding only if they agreed to the total dominance of market logics: food subsidies were to be abolished, progressive taxation systems revoked, wages cut, privatizations enforced. Such conditions were imposed by what Richard Peet (2009) calls the 'unholy trinity' of the IMF, WTO and WB (see also Gil and Cutler 2015). In many ways the reality of such 'structural adjustments' imposed on the global south foreshadowed the changes experienced in response to the 2008 crisis within the Global North (Oxfam 2013). The consequences in both scenarios were tragic and led to spiralling inequalities with the poorest in both contexts being hit hardest (Forster et al. 2010; Palast 2001).

The literature produced in this period reflected the overwhelming sense that something was deeply wrong with capitalism; that the system worked to protect the interests of the 'elite' at the expense of the '99%'. In this chapter, we turn to the work of Thomas Piketty, David Harvey, Richard Sennett and Guy Standing, all authors highly critical of neoliberalism. This literature also reflects a renewal of interest in broadly Marxian ideas. This can be seen both in works which targeted the structural contradictions of the capitalist model, as per the studies of Harvey and Piketty, but also by scholars who focused on the socio-psychological impact of capitalism. In this regard, echoes of the humanist ideas of the 'young Marx' can be found in the writings of Sennett and Standing.

Yet, while Marx believed that the proletariat would attain class consciousness to further the revolutionary overthrow of capitalism, such optimism is far from evident today amongst progressive theorists. There is even a certain weariness, an activist exhaustion and post-modern cynicism. What Mark Fisher (2009) called a 'Capitalist Realism' was juxtaposed with the intellectual awareness of the instability and irrationality of neoliberalism. Critics of capitalism were left in a bind: it was easier to imagine the end of the world than to imagine the end of capitalism; equally, it was undeniable that neo-liberalism was ever more incoherent and self-destructive. There was thus more of an interest in Marx, rather than in 'Marxism', and there was an interest in 'critique', yet no belief in revolution. There also remained a weariness of metanarratives and an air of political defeatism. Even amongst many of the leading critiques of capitalism which emerged in this period, authors who were certain that capitalism was broken, it was unclear what practically could be done differently.

Capital in the Twenty-First Century

Piketty's *Capital in the Twenty-First Century* (2014 [2013]) encapsulated this marriage of systemic critique and political impotency. While Marx wrote to draw proletarians to the barricades, Piketty's aims were far more measured, seeking to influence policymakers to consider imposing wealth taxes (Godin 2020). Despite this being Piketty's ultimate policy recommendation, he surreally acknowledged that such a policy would likely never come to pass. Indeed, the closer one looks at *Capital in the Twenty-First Century* the more the differences emerge with Marx's *Capital*. Yet, like the original *Capital*, Piketty's book came to symbolize something more than its content. It became a fashionable accessory, a shorthand signifier to express a contempt for capitalism and austerity. Piketty's work achieved this status despite the fact that the content of the book was fundamentally reformist in nature. Ultimately, the nod to Marx with the title is disingenuous: Piketty is most definitely not a neo-Marxist. Indeed, Piketty later boasted in an interview with *The New Republic* of having not been overly influenced by Marx; he implied he had read very little of Marx's actual work, which he considered dull and unsubstantiated (Chotiner and Piketty 2014). Ironically, a similar fate befell Piketty: his book sits atop many shelves, largely unread (see Flanders 2014). However unlike Marx, Piketty's work represents a cry for radical economic change which it does not actually possess. Rather, Piketty piggybacked on the broader Marxian revival and won the badge of iconoclast, while remaining comparatively unremarkable, at least in comparison to his nineteenth century forebearer.

But this orthodoxy was also key to Piketty's success. His fundamental claim was measured, simple, comprehensible. His methodology and analysis were presented in terms that mainstream economists accepted and understood. Ultimately, Piketty offered a clear, methodologically sound critique of the distributional laws of capitalism. As such, he was able to demonstrate that the ascent of an elite owning the vast majority of wealth, opposed to the interests of the 99%, was systematically built into capitalism. The rise of the elite was not an accident, an error or a contingent freak event: rather it was fundamental to the standard operating procedures of capitalism. Piketty demonstrated this with the most basic of economic statistics: consistently the rate of return on capital is greater than the rate of economic growth. As such, as the old saying goes, 'money goes to money'. Those who have inherited assets which they are able to invest will see a far greater return than those who labour. As such, inequality will inevitably grow: free market economics does not lead to an equitable distribution of social goods, based on effort. Rather, the market's dynamics privilege those with existing wealth over those who wish to work to earn their fortune. Central to Piketty's argument is thus the systematic rejection of a key claim made to justify free market economics: the so called Kuznets Curve.

Simon Kuznets was a Russian-American economist and statistician. He was awarded the Nobel Prize for economics in 1971 and was central to providing 'hard' quantitative normative foundations for capitalist economics. The eponymous law, a key tenet of the moral justification of the market, is that while free market reforms will initially lead to increased inequality, over time, as society adjusts to the new market structure, the economy will become more equal and the distribution of goods will become fairer (Kuznets 1955). In short, the Kuznets curve is the statistical justification that free market capitalism was capable of producing a fair and stable distribution of wealth, that the system is not a form of feudalism in which inherited wealth overpowers all else. The Kuznets curve was particularly significant for justifying 'structural adjustment' policies. The initial 'shock therapy' of early rising inequalities would, purportedly, inevitably be offset by the superior efficiency and distributional equity of market mechanisms. Piketty's *Capital in the Twenty-First Century* can be primarily read as an extended, methodologically rigorous, rejection of the Kuznets Curve.[4]

Drawing on substantial data, Piketty argued that the Kuznets Curve simply did not apply to the realities of the post-war period. The benefits of working for the common labourer (measured by the extent of economic growth) consistently lagged behind the benefits of investing capital. In simple terms: the rich will forever get richer as investing money gives far greater returns than working by selling one's labour. Piketty is not alone in criticizing the Kuznets Curve, nor was *Capital in the Twenty-First Century* the first publication in which he made such a rejection (see Piketty 2006; Toyama 2012).

While Marx's *Capital* concluded that capitalism was so contradictory, unstable, exploitative and alienating that the necessary response was its revolutionary overthrow, Piketty's proposal is rather less combative. In contrast, Piketty argued for an immediate wealth tax and the imposition of a permanent high-income tax level. All individuals who earn over 500,000 USD per annum should be paying 80% tax above that threshold. Interestingly, Piketty states that there would not be a political will to introduce such reforms. This is worthy of comment: it is unusual to advocate for a modest proposal and simultaneously argue for its infeasibility. On both the count of the reformist nature of his 'solution', and his claims that even these proposals are unviable politically, commentators have presented Piketty's work as one of 'mainstream economics rather than a form of "Soft Marxism"' (see Mason 2014).

Yet, while this led to Piketty's work being criticized by some on the left, Piketty's moderation and temperance led to his work being taken seriously by many commentators who would typically be alienated by more radical critiques of the market. As such, Mason claimed, Piketty 'placed an unexploded bomb within mainstream, classical economics', he had managed to offer a critique of the system from within. Piketty spoke the language of mainstream economists; he couched his claims carefully with meticulous statistical evidence and provided a transparent, clear methodology. While this enabled Piketty to become a so-called rockstar economist of international renown (Anthony 2020), his fame saw him highly criticized by both the left and right.

For many on the left, Piketty offered a vital critique of capitalism as he showed in hard statistics that capitalism worked for the few and not for the many. Piketty exploded the myth that capitalism 'worked', as such, for Trade Union leader Len McCluskey (2014), Piketty's intervention was 'manna from heaven'. Piketty was held to provide institutional credibility to activist demands for 'something new and bold and radical' (McCluskey 2014). Mason (2014) praised the lucidity of Piketty's argument, commenting that the work is undeniably internally coherent. Yet for others who opposed capitalism, Piketty's insights were neither new nor radical. For David Harvey, Piketty's work was unashamedly reductive, focusing excessively on distribution and was predicated on a problematic definition of capital. As Harvey argued, capital must be understood as a process, it is a social relation, a constant movement. The possibilities for rupture and conflict arise from blockages to this flow of capital. As such, Piketty's distributional statistical account was superficial as it will fail to engage with the complex undercurrents of this flow. Echoing Marx, Harvey argued that the challenge was to get at the reality of capitalism as a system of exploitative social relationships, to do so required a philosophical as well as political-economic analysis of the commodity, of capital, of social relations. Piketty's work made no such engagement with the 'mystical kernel' of capitalism, there was no investment in Hegelian dialectics, or the rationality of social institutions. Indeed, Piketty's lack of focus on the role of institutions was something which united both Piketty's left and right leaning critics.[5]

Piketty had a range of vocal critics from the right, who adopted varying degrees of academic rigour in this response (see Geier 2014). Some, such as Reihan Salam (2014), writing in the *National Review*, considered *Capital in the Twenty-First Century* too pessimistic, painting Piketty's claims as implicitly suggesting we are on the route to some dystopian science fiction plutocracy. Daniel Shuchman (2014) framed Piketty's work as a full-on revival of 'Marx for the 21st century', full of supposed economic inaccuracies precipitated by his evil 'ideological' views. This is a rather absurd criticism of a painfully methodical economic-statistical analysis, as various liberal commentators drew out (especially Branko Milanovic, see Geier 2014). Others, such as Kevin Hasser and Alan Auerbach (2015) suggested Piketty was wrong to focus on distributions of 'income', rather if Piketty had analysed relative distributions of consumption (i.e. expenditure), he would have seen that the standard of living has increased similarly across all income gradients. Such claims, however, are themselves the subject of debate, with the overwhelming evidence suggesting 'consumption inequality' has also increased markedly, roughly mirroring income inequality (Aguiar and Bils 2015).

Piketty's work piqued those who advocated for capitalism as a rational, equitable distributional mechanism, in a way which few preceding works had in recent decades. There is an edited collection, published by the CATO Institute, titled *Anti-Piketty: Capital for the 21st Century* which sought to unite arguments against Piketty's work (Delsol et al. 2017). The volume sought to challenge the empirical strength of Piketty's analysis, the pessimism of his 'apocalyptic vision', and the wisdom of his policy proposals. In contrast to the hysterical right-wing journalistic responses to Piketty's book, the interventions gathered by the editors are certainly more academic in tone, if not necessarily more coherent in substance. Ultimately, however, the central claim of *Capital in the Twenty-First Century* that returns on capital have exceeded the rate of growth is hard to dispute (Solow 2017). The evidence marshalled by Piketty is simply overwhelming. The Kuznets Curve has been substantially discredited, this is the most significant legacy of Piketty's work for scholars of capitalism today.

David Harvey: The Enigma of Capital

If Thomas Piketty was the new pretender, the 'rockstar economist' who captured the post-crash zeitgeist, David Harvey was a comparative stalwart of the left. Where Piketty brashly declared his disinterest in the tedious details of Marxian theory, Harvey had written one of the leading reading guides to *Capital* (Harvey 2018). Harvey's analysis of the financial crash and his accompanying critique of capitalism are thus predictably Marxian in tone. There is a further distinguishing feature of Harvey's account, by discipline he is a political geographer, rather than a political economist, philosopher, or sociologist, as per many of the other authors we engage with in this book. As such, his work, especially *The Enigma of*

Capital [2010], *Seventeen Contradictions and the End of Capitalism* [2014] and *A Brief History of Neoliberalism* [2005] reflect this idiosyncratic marriage of Marxism and political geography, which provides Harvey with a distinctive entry point to the study of capitalism.[6] We focus here on Harvey's much-read *The Enigma of Capital*, which presents a Marxian analysis of the financial crash as an entry point to a broader critique of capitalism.

While Piketty's analysis concentrated on the distribution of wealth within capitalism, Harvey was more concerned with the circulation of capital, not as a 'thing' but as a 'process'. Crucially, for Harvey, this 'process' is not limited to the distribution of wealth: rather capitalism is at core a 'flow' of capital throughout the economy. Harvey reminds his reader repeatedly that 'capital' is not synonymous with 'money'. Rather 'capital' is money which is invested in order to make more money. Central to understanding how capitalism works, both in theory and in practice, is learning the eddies and rivulets of this flow of capital. Equally significantly, particularly for the critique of capitalism, is understanding the various reasons why this 'flow' can be impeded. When the flow of capital gets suppressed, the capitalist system grinds to a halt in a financial crash. In the preamble to *The Enigma of Capital*, Harvey vividly compared the flow of capital in the economy to the flow of blood throughout the human body. He stresses this analogy, even referring to the original scientist who discovered this mainstay of human anatomy; his namesake, William Harvey. When blood flow is impeded, drastic interventions are required or catastrophe ensues. For Harvey, this is exactly what happened in 2008: the capital flow dried up and the economy suffered a convulsion and collapsed.

In the opening chapter of *The Enigma of Capital*, Harvey explained how the financial crash can be understood as both resulting from, and something which caused further, blockages in the flow of capital. For many commentators, the collapse of Lehmann Brothers was the flash point of the crisis; it represented the epicentre of the crisis. This is because the collapse led to the freezing of the global credit system. When Lehmann Brothers folded, the availability of credit vanished and as a result the supply of capital was drastically reduced. The flow of capital rapidly stagnated, debt dependent purchases, of all kinds, were radically curtailed and the global demand slumped. The world economy contracted. Export economies were hit as the months of impeded demand dragged by. In Harvey's analysis, these are all predictable consequences of the denial of credit: when the flow of capital is impeded, the capitalist system grinds to a halt. With the flow of capital reduced to a trickle, drastic measures had to be implemented by capitalists: a form of 'emergency transfusion' of capital into the economic body was needed (2010: vii). Capital also had to be rationed: staff had to be made redundant, wages had to be slashed, full scale restructurings had to be hastily implemented. The economic body is unable to survive without the coursing lifeblood of capital.

In our discussion of the crash above, the realities of the financial crash and the means of its resolution were consciously detailed in isolation, enabling us to underscore the contingency of the austerity drive and its economic irrationality. The financial crash did not necessitate an austerity response. Harvey's analysis sought to maintain this awareness; however, he rightly also stressed its fundamental connection to the reasons for the financial crash to start with: the emergence of a 'state-finance nexus' (2011: 48) which both orchestrated and benefitted from neoliberal deregulation and which retained hegemony of the narrative during the crisis itself. The obvious Keynesian response to the crash, of injecting more capital into the economic body, an 'emergency transfusion', was rejected in the USA because it would have initiated a return to a more equal balance between the power of labour and the power of capital. This was simply unthinkable to the state-financial elite and was rejected without consideration. As a result, the entire capitalist system in the USA teetered on the brink, lurching from crisis to crisis, exaggerated by the impotence of a partisan political infrastructure that made the passing of legislation granting an emergency capital injection impossible.

In contrast, as Harvey wrote is his afterword to *The Enigma of Capital*, the Chinese state was not burdened by such political impotence. The Chinese economy was potentially gravely at risk in the financial crisis, being largely export-based. However, the Chinese authorities took quick and decisive action. Where the USA offered politically motivated tax cuts to the ultra-rich, in a nod to a reheated trickledown economics, which proved entirely unsuccessful at growing the wider economy, the Chinese state spent furiously. Huge infrastructure projects were approved for rapid delivery. Further, where the flow of credit emanating from American banks had dried up and showed no rapid sign of returning, Chinese bankers did not inhabit the same political environment as their American counterparts. The authoritarianism of Chinese capitalism enabled the state simply to order its banks to turn the taps back on: to restart the flow of capital by making credit available again. The combination of these strategies: the forced return of credit and the mass roll-out of infrastructure projects led to the rapid return of demand within the Chinese economy. China succeeded in leaving the crash far quicker and much faster than nearly all other countries.

While grounded in an analysis of the financial crash, Harvey's *The Enigma of Capital* located the 2008 crisis within a broader critique of capitalism. Harvey segued from the financial crash to the broader contradictions of capitalism via an anecdote involving residual feudal power embarrassing neoliberal ignorance. Harvey tells how Queen Elizabeth II asked the economists at LSE at the peak of the crisis why nobody had seen the financial crisis approaching. In response, a British Academy group spent half a year ruminating on this very question: why had none of the key players seen the crisis coming? In response, the gathered policymakers and (largely neoliberal) economists stated that there was insufficient focus and study upon 'systemic risks'. For Harvey, this remains a fundamental weakness of mainstream university economics departments, they 'continue to promote the same useless courses on neoclassical economics or rational choice political theory' (2010: 239); what is desperately required is an urgent analysis of the systemic contradictions which are integral to the capitalist system. For Harvey, Marx is the obvious place to turn to study such 'systemic risks'.

While capitalism is sustained by the healthy, regular flow of capital throughout the economy, Harvey argued that there are various contradictions inherent within the market, which systematically increase the likelihood of 'blockages'. While in a later work Harvey (2014) examined 17 such contradictions, in *The Enigma of Capital* he limited his analysis to a central six. Harvey (2010: 47) presented these in detail, drawing to a great extent on Marx's *Grundrisse*. These are: (a) insufficient initial money capital; (b) scarcities of, or political difficulties with, labour supply; (c) inadequate means of production, including so-called natural limits; (d) inappropriate technologies and organisational forms; (e) resistance or inefficiencies in the labour process; and (f) lack of demand backed by money to pay in the market. While there is not space for us to discuss these all in detail here, Harvey is clear that blockages in the flow of capital can occur at any of these points in the capitalist system and inevitably such blockages lead to crises.

This propensity towards crisis is further exaggerated by the reality that capitalism today requires 3% of continual growth to function 'healthily' or else it will lead to an even bigger problem: a recession. A blockage caused by any of these routine obstacles can immediately impact growth, as a result capital has to keep flowing constantly. However, the ability to consistently achieve 3% minimum growth is becoming ever more challenging. Just where is this growth going to come from? More challengingly still, the required rate of growth is compound: as a result the expansion required gets ever larger in real terms. There is thus a constant need for capital to flow, to always be moving. Stagnation cannot be tolerated, for whatever reason. Hence, in the UK during the Covid-19 crisis, the government implored consumers to go out and spend money in restaurants, while it was clearly increasing the risk of spreading the disease (see Hern 2020). The so-called Eat Out to Help Out scheme was crucial, when the flow of capital dried up, when capital stopped circulating, capitalism desperately needed help. Harvey drew a similar parallel to Rudy Giuliani urging shoppers back out into malls in New York City after the 9/11 attacks.

Capitalism is an incredibly crisis-prone system and requires a constant life blood of capital to flow. The clarity with which Harvey expresses this insight awarded him substantial praise, even from reviewers nestled deep within the neoliberal apparatus, such as the in-house journal of the International Monetary Fund (see Ghosh 2010: 55). Ultimately, Harvey's critique of capitalism is inspired by Marx, and like Marx's work, he demonstrates the remarkable fragility of capitalism. For many progressive activists, infuriated by the neoliberal hegemony which dominated post-crash, Harvey's calm and systematic analysis positioned him as an avuncular heir to Marx. Today, Harvey is perhaps best known for his idiosyncratic bimonthly podcast, 'David Harvey's Anti-Capitalist Chronicles', through which he has introduced a diverse international audience to Marxist theory and analysis. Harvey thus sits as one of the best known popularizers of the critique of capitalism today and he continues to explore the same themes in his current work: the contradictions of capitalism, the flows of capitals, and the differentiated geographical experiences of neoliberal irrationality.

Precarity and Alienation

The austerity regimes enforced across the Global North post-crash expedited the transition to a more aggressive form of neoliberalism in which market diktats acquired ever greater control over social life. Work systems were further 'rationalised', departments restructured, employment terms casualized. While this was partly a continuation and embedding of an existing dynamic, a qualitatively distinct class of worker was also beginning to emerge. Guy Standing (2011) famously called this new 'dangerous class' the 'precariat', a portmanteau term uniting 'precarious' and 'proletariat'. Such workers were a product of both the further dominance of capital over labour, with the precariat typically employed on so-called zero-hours contracts and therefore ineligible for sick or holiday pay. Yet, the precariat was also a product of technological advances, with many precariat jobs connected to digital technologies and the so-called gig economy: Uber drivers, Deliveroo drivers etc. Yet, the 'precariat' did not solely work on the road, rather, companies such as Sports Direct in the UK increasingly moved to employ staff on such 'Zero-Hour' contracts (see Butler 2017). It was notably not only 'lower status' industries which transitioned to casualized forms of employment, in the UK the higher education sector has become increasingly reliant upon 'fractional' or 'associate' lecturers.

As Standing argued, the 'precariat' was different from the proletariat in important regards. The industrial proletariat pre-neoliberalism typically had a guaranteed secure form of labour and a shared cultural horizon. While such labour was typically dull, exploitative, alienating and depressing, it remained constant and formed part of the labourer's individual and collective identity. They were a miner, a welder, a waiter. Today's precariat do not even have the luxury of a guarantee of being exploited, let alone the knowledge of what form the exploitation will take. An Uber driver in the morning may well be a bar worker in the evening. Many precariously employed workers have to accept multiple jobs simultaneously, with hours and roles constantly shifting. Standing noted that the precariat experiences crippling alienation and holds a repressed anger as a result. Whereas the industrial proletariat were unionized and had close social bonds, shared symbols, common pubs and working men's clubs, today's precariat are increasingly atomized, isolated, anomic. Not knowing where your next gig will come from does not predispose one to build roots in a community, even if such community spaces (pubs, working men's clubs) still existed. As such, the precariat is in part defined by its shared experience of individualized anomie. In place of the pub, there are Netflix and Tinder and rants on online forums. There is thus less chance of a class consciousness emerging in the traditional Marxian sense. But, as Standing stressed, this does not preclude the possibility of spontaneous, revolutionary, violent upheaval. The precariat are dangerous as they are hard to predict.

Yet this 'precariat' is currently divided and as such has failed to live up to its progressive transformative potential. Standing argued that the precariat comprised three particular subsets: those who had fallen from stable working class jobs into precarious employment; those of migrant and minority labourers; and the educated youth, unable to find, or unwilling to accept, mainstream employment. As such the precariat underclass is inchoate, defined by cultural and generational division as much as the individual's experience of atomization. Socially conservative old white men share Uber's platform with unemployed liberal postgraduates. Yet, Standing retains an optimism that the educated precariat wishes to unite with all precarious workers to effect radical social transformation. There remains hope for progressive praxis as a result; Standing's narrative is more optimistic than Piketty's.

While aspects of Standing's work remain speculative and controversial, his claims as to the living conditions of such an underclass are widely accepted. The word 'precariat' has certainly entered both academic and popular discourse and has captured the imagination of various artists (see Scott 2015). This interest in the precariat also reflects a broader resurgence of study in the humanist writings of the early Marx. The precariat is simply one group amongst many who are suffering from a broader epidemic of alienation. It is not merely those with casualized and precarious employment who are experiencing psychic suffering as a result of post-crash neoliberal retrenchment (see also Azmanova 2020).

While written before the financial crash, Richard Sennett's *The Corrosion of Character* captured many of the alienating, psychologically damaging tendencies resulting from the neoliberal re-engineering of society. Sennett sought to address 'the personal consequences of work in the new capitalism', to explore how work impacted the psychic lives of individuals. Earlier in 1972, Sennett co-authored a classic study with Jonathan Cobb, *The Hidden Injuries of Class*. This work focused on the life and experiences of labourers towards the latter end of the social democratic consensus, focusing in particular on the life of a caretaker, pseudonymized as 'Enrico'. In contrast, *The Corrosion of Character* focused on the challenges faced by the following generation through a series of interviews, sketches and ideal-typical subjects. One such abstracted character is presented as being Enrico's son, 'Rico'. Sennett admits his methodology requires a degree of trust from the reader;

however, his narrative style is persuasive and fulfils a secondary purpose. The point of presenting such a fractured analysis, of drawing on such disparate characters, with their incomplete stories, is designed to mirror the fact that coherence is lacking in people's lives as a result of the new 'flexible' capitalism.

However, it is not reductively suggested that '1970s life' was good and that 'today's world' is bad; that Enrico had it easy and Rico was unlucky to be born decades later. Rather, the more 'flexible' neoliberal workplace is held to have clear material advantages. Enrico was a janitor, who cleaned toilets, while Rico is a picture of sartorial elegance, a corporate jetsetter. Yet, such advantages come at a cost in the harm inflicted by the rootlessness and dynamism of the modern workplace. While Enrico was a janitor, in a low-status occupation, he had a form of job security, a clear role, a plan for the future and his daily toil gave his life meaning and enabled him to develop a sense of self-respect. He laboured for his family so they could prosper and achieve more than he had. Enrico's objective was upward mobility for his family, a clear vision, which was potentially achievable. He had a fixity of purpose and of place. In many ways, Enrico lived out the textbook American-immigrant dream. Come to America, work hard so your children can have a better life, and Rico certainly did, at least financially.

Yet, as per the precariat Standing would describe a decade and a half later, Rico's life was complicated, and his relation to self, and to his family, was substantially distinct from his father's. While Enrico slaved away, with a clear narrative, a stable goal, self-respect and certainty, Rico was a product of the flexible neoliberal marketplace. While Enrico's toilets were there to clean, however disgusting them may be, his job was stable and secure. In contrast, Rico was taught to despise 'time-servers' (Sennett 1998: 18) and to take-risks, to gamble, to seek a quick profit, rather than stable toil. As a result, Rico prospered, but the story, as Sennett charted, is a complicated, and often unhappy one.

Rico's generation were rootless, required to move house constantly, to seek new opportunities. They had to balance child care and career requirements in a world where conjugal expectations were fast evolving. While Enrico had a stable network of friends and family, Rico's generation had no such kinship network, no such relation to place. Indeed, Rico has little stability in any aspect of his life. One company he moved to work for downsized, leaving him adrift. As a result, Rico opted to start his own consultancy, a move which required him to become entirely flexible to the schedules of potential clients, to charm, to network, to travel, to build relationships. There was also a constant fear that, despite their high salaries, the family would collapse, with no safety net. There was a continual threat of catastrophe. Sennett captured this sentiment with his discussion of ATT's motto 'no long term', which encapsulated the new marketplace in which the whole concept of a workforce becomes contingent upon liminal projects.

For Sennett, these new conditions had a deleterious impact on Enrico's psyche, damaging the features of his character which connect people as sociable, amiable beings. There is a 'meeting mindset', a short-termism, a lack of commitment which is induced by this new form of flexible capitalism (see also Sennett 2008). While Enrico had a fixed set of values, of sentiments, which were reflected in the attention and detail he gave to his work, despite its lowly status, Rico was caught in a contradiction of values. On the one hand, he retains a fixity of character: he seeks out a permanence of identity, of 'the good'. He seeks an ethical code, which retains a characterful permanence, of truth to self and to the community. Yet, this is constantly being challenged by the flexibility of the new capitalism, he is unable to live out his moral code. The contemporary buzzword, Sennett argues, 'teamwork' and of building a 'team player mentality', equates in reality to group processes of reified, hypocritical superficiality. As Sennett worded it, as a result of this bind between a desire for permanent values and the corrosive flexibility of market diktats, Rico's 'will has become static; he is trapped in the sheer assertion of values' (Sennett 1998: 30). He is tortured inwardly by this contradiction, a contradiction which Sennett presents as being that of the everyman within neoliberalism. Rico seeks to embody socially conservative values of permanence, commitment, loyalty, authenticity; while conditioned by his economic environment to embrace flexibility, superficiality and pragmatism. As Sennett framed it, 'it is against … severed ties at work, wilful amnesia of his neighbours, and the specter of his children as mall rats that he asserts the *idea* of lasting values' (Sennett 1998: 28). This tension is hard to deny.

Conclusion

The financial crash and the austerity regimes which followed in its wake served to expedite trends already present within the economies of the Global North. Growing inequalities between the rich and poor further augmented, public services were chiselled away, and market logics entered ever more spheres of social life. As Sennett argued, this created a fundamental psychic tension between people's desires to retain stable ethical and communal foundations, with the ever dominant diktats of market flexibility. New social cleavages emerged in this hyper-competitive neoliberal environment, with the rise of 'zero-hour' contracts, the gig economy and the birth of what Standing called the 'precariat'. Such tendencies continued a decade later, despite limited pushback: zero-hour contracts and the gig economy remain important components of contemporary capitalism. In part, this reflects Standing's argument that the political affinities of the precariat are varied, their social values contradictory. The Marxist belief in a class in itself, for itself, was not to be conjured out of the financial crash. There existed a frustrated tension between increasing dissatisfaction with the economic system but total discord over what remedial or transitional action could be taken.

There was thus a strong spirit of critique in the air, with Piketty's *Capital in the Twenty-First Century* capturing this popular sentiment. Portraits of Marx were suddenly on billboards, on magazines. While Piketty is the author most associated with this period, and his work served to destabilize the Kuznets Curve, we argue that David Harvey provides a more rounded analysis. Harvey also envisaged a possibility for revolutionary social change, a 'co-evolutionary theory', through which multiple social domains transition beyond capitalism, a concern we discuss in more detail in the following chapter.

It must be stated that in the decade following the crash there was a delayed but notably minority public opposition to capitalism as an economic order. Jeremy Corbyn in the UK, Bernie Sanders in the USA, Podemos in Spain and Syriza in Greece, all presented the rejection of neoliberalism as being central to their political visions. Ultimately, however, some of these movements faded away: Biden won over Sanders, Corbyn was replaced by Starmer and Tsipras agreed to a crippling austerity regime. Neoliberalism retained hegemony, establishing itself again as the inevitable, natural order. Naomi's Klein's (2007) thesis, that neoliberalism thrives on crises, even crises of its own making, was vindicated. Neoliberalism survived the financial crisis and emerged more certain than ever. Yet, as we discuss in the next chapter, its fundamental contradictions remained unresolved, contradictions which cannot be ignored.

Notes

1 There has been much written on what ardent neoliberal economists, such as Hayek and Friedman, would have deemed the best policy to adopt (see Elliott 2011).

2 With an absurd symbolism, Cameron's government at one point suggested the public should build themselves out of recession by carrying out home improvements (Kirkup 2012).

3 It is increasingly agreed that such non-European experiences has not been afforded due attention by the formal academy (see Kangas and Salmenniemi 2016). This is only now starting to be addressed (see Quijano 2000). This is important for the study of neoliberal crises in particular as some of the earliest studies on the impact of neoliberalism were about Latin America (see Silva 1987, 1988), yet these were later largely ignored in subsequent works which prioritized the experience of the Global North (see Connell and Dados 2014: 121).

4 It should be noted that Kuznets (1955) himself was more circumspect in his commentary. He admitted the data he drew on was limited and should not be viewed as an ardent neoliberal as his personal politics and academic conclusions are more nuanced than one may initially conclude.

5 Piketty explicitly remedied this gap in a later work, *Capital and Ideology* (2020).

6 For further works showcasing Harvey's Marxist Critical Geography, see *Spaces of Hope* (2000) and *Spaces of Capital: Towards a* Critical Geography (2001).

References

Aguiar, M. and Bils, M. 2015. 'Has Consumption Inequality Mirrored Income Inequality'. *American Economic Review*, 105 (9): 2725–56.

Anthony, A. 2020. 'Thomas Piketty: Why France's 'Rock Star Economist' Still Wants to Squeeze the Rich'. *The Guardian*, 23 February 2020. www.theguardian.com/books/2020/feb/23/thomas-piketty-why-frances-rock-star-economist-still-wants-to-squeeze-the rich

Azmanova, A. 2020. *Capitalism On Edge: How Fighting Precarity Can Achieve Radical Change without Crisis or Utopia*. New York: Columbia University Press.

Blakeley, G. 2019. *Stolen: How to Save the World from Financialisation*. London: Verso.

Butler, S. 2017. 'Sports Direct Fails to Meet 2016 Pledge on Working Conditions'. *The Guardian*, 5 September 2017. www.theguardian.com/business/2017/sep/05/sports-direct-fails-2016-pledge-zero-hours-shirebrook-mike-ashley

Chotiner, I. and Piketty, T. 2014. 'Thomas Piketty: I Don't Care for Marx'. *The New Republic*, 6 May 2014. https://newrepublic.com/article/117655/thomas-piketty-interview-economist-discusses-his-distaste-marx

Connell, R. and Dados, N. 2014. 'Where in the World Does Neoliberalism Come from?: The Market Agenda in Southern Perspective'. *Theory and Society*, 43 (2): 117–38.

Cowen, T. 2008. 'So We Thought. But Then Again …'. *The New York Times*, 13 January 2008. www.nytimes.com/2008/01/13/business/13view.html?_r=2&scp=1&sq=Tyler+Cowen&oref=login&oref=slogin

Delsol, J., Lecaussin, N., and Martin, E. 2017. *Anti-Piketty: Capital for the 21st Century*. Washington: Cato Institute.

Elliott, L. 2011. 'Welcome to the Living Dead Economy'. *The Guardian*, 4 December 2011. www.theguardian.com/business/economics-blog/2011/dec/04/global-economy-eurozone-debt-crisis

Fisher, M. 2009. *Capitalist Realism: Is There No Alternative?* London: Zero Books.

Flanders, S. 2014. 'Capital in the Twenty-First Century by Thomas Piketty – Review'. *The Guardian*, 17 July 2014. www.theguardian.com/books/2014/jul/17/capital-twenty-first-century-thomas-piketty-review

Forster, T., Kentikelenis, A., Stubbs, T., and King, L. 2010. 'Globalisation and Health Equity: The Impact of Structural Adjustment Programs on Developing Countries'. *Social Science and Medicine*, 267: 112496.

Geier, K. 2014. 'What Piketty's Conservative Critics Get Wrong'. *The Baffler*, 28 April 2014. https://thebaffler.com/latest/what-pikettys-conservative-critics-get-wrong

Ghosh, A. 2010. 'Mysterious Money'. *Finance & Development*, 47 (3): 55.

Gill, S. and Cutler, C. (eds.) 2015. *New Constitutionalism and World Order.* Cambridge: Cambridge University Press.

Godin, R. 2020. 'How Thomas Piketty Ignores Class Struggle'. Translated by N. French. *Jacobin*, 10 January 2020. https://jacobinmag.com/2020/10/thomas-piketty-class-struggle-book-review

Grover, C. 2018. 'Violent Proletarianisation: Social Murder, the Reserve Army of Labour and Social Security 'Austerity' in Britain'. *Critical Social Policy*, 39 (3): 335–55.

Harris, N. and Acaroğlu, O. 2022. 'Thinking beyond Neoliberalism: Theorising the Future in the Present'. In: *Thinking beyond Neoliberalism: Alternative Societies, Transition, and Resistance.* Edited by N. Harris and O. Acaroğlu. New York: Palgrave Macmillan, pp. 1–28.

Harvey, D. 2001. *Spaces of Capital: Towards a Critical Geography.* Abingdon: Routledge.

Harvey, D. 2005. *A Brief History of Neoliberalism.* Oxford: Oxford University Press.

Harvey, D. 2010. *The Enigma of Capital.* London: Profile Books.

Harvey, D. 2014. *Seventeen Contradictions and the End of Capitalism.* London: Profile Books.

Harvey, D. 2018 [2010]. *A Companion to Marx's Capital: The Complete Edition.* London: Verso.

Hasser, K and Auerbach, A. 2015. 'Capital Taxation in the Twenty-First Century'. *American Economic Review*, 105 (5): 38–42.

Hayek, F. A. 2001 [1944]. *The Road to Serfdom.* London: Routledge.

Hern, A. 2020. '"Eat Out to Help Out" May Have Caused Sixth of Covid Clusters over Summer'. *The Guardian*, 30 October 2020. www.theguardian.com/business/2020/oct/30/treasury-rejects-theory-eat-out-to-help-out-caused-rise-in-covid

Kangas, A. and Salmenniemi, S. 2016. 'Decolonizing Knowledge: Neoliberalism beyond the Three Worlds'. *Distinktion: Journal of Social Theory*, 17 (2): 210–27.

Kirkup, J. 2012. 'David Cameron: Build Your Way Out of Recession with Home Improvements'. *The Telegraph*, 5 September 2012. www.telegraph.co.uk/news/9524089/David-Cameron-build-your-way-out-of-recession-with-home-improvements.html

Klein, N. 2007. *The Shock Doctrine: The Rise of Disaster Capitalism.* London: Allen Lane.

Krugman, P. 2015. 'The Case for Cuts Was a Lie. Why Does Britain Still Believe It?' *The Guardian*, 29 April 2015. www.theguardian.com/business/ng-interactive/2015/apr/29/the-austerity-delusion

Kuznets, S. 1955. 'Economic Growth and Income Inequality'. *American Economic Review*, 45 (1): 1–28.

Maatsch, A. 2013. 'Are We All *Austerian* Now? An Analysis of National Parliamentary Parties' Positioning on Anti-Crisis Measures in the Eurozone'. *Journal of European Economic Policy*, 21 (1): 96–115.

Mason, P. 2014. 'Thomas Piketty's Capital: Everything You Need to Know about the Surprise Bestseller'. *The Guardian*, 28 April 2014. www.theguardian.com/books/2014/apr/28/thomas-piketty-capital-surprise-bestseller

McCluskey, L. 2014. 'Len McCluskey on Capital in the Twenty-First Century: 'Manna from Heaven'. *The Guardian*, 28 April 2014. www.theguardian.com/politics/2014/apr/28/len-mccluskey-capital-21st-century-manna-from-heaven

Moody, O. 2019. 'Britons Take a Generous View of Filthy Rich'. *The Times*, 11 February, 2019. www.thetimes.co.uk/article/britons-take-a-generous-view-of-filthy-rich-20chv2vjv

Mueller, B. 2019. 'What Is Austerity and How Has It Effected British Society'. *The New York Times*, 24 February 2019. www.nytimes.com/2019/02/24/world/europe/britain-austerity-may-budget.html

Mullen, A. 2018. 'Media Performance in the 'Age of Austerity': British Newspaper Coverage of the 2008 Financial Crisis and Its Aftermath, 2008–2010'. *Journalism*, 22 (4): 993–1011.

Oxfam. 2013. 'A Cautionary Tale: The True Cost of Austerity and Inequality in Europe'. *Oxfam Briefing Paper 174.* September 2013.

Palast, G. 2001. 'IMF's Four Steps to Damnation'. *The Guardian*, 29 April 2001. www.theguardian.com/business/2001/apr/29/business.mbas

Parenteau, R. 2015. 'Goebbelnomics – Austerian Duplicity and the Dispensing of Greece'. *Naked Capitalism*. 19 March 2015. www.nakedcapitalism.com/2015/03/rob-parenteau-goebbelnomics-austerian-duplicity-dispensing-greece.html

Peet, R. 2009. *Unholy Trinity: The IMF, World Bank, and WTO*. London: Zed Books.

Piketty, T. 2006. 'The Kuznets Curve: Yesterday and Tomorrow'. In: *Understanding Poverty*. Edited by A.V. Banerjee, R. Bénabou, and D. Mookherjee. Oxford: Oxford University Press, pp. 63–72.

Piketty, T. 2014 [2013]. *Capital in the Twenty-First Century*. Translated by A. Goldhammer. Cambridge: Harvard University Press.

Piketty, T. 2020 [2019]. *Capital and Ideology*. Translated by A. Goldhammer. Cambridge: Harvard University Press.

Quijano, A. 2000. 'Coloniality of Power and Eurocentricism in Latin America'. *International Sociology*, 15 (2): 215–32.

Salam, R. 2014. 'Will the Future Be Dominated by Immortal Quadrillionaires?'. *National Review*, 28 March 2014. www.nationalreview.com/the-agenda/will-future-be-dominated-immortal-quadrillionaires-reihan-salam/

Scott, J. 2015. *One Precariat Place*. CreateSpace Independent Publishing Platform.

Sennett, R. 1998. *The Corrosion of Character*. London and New York: W. W. Norton and Company.

Sennett, R. 2006. *The Culture of the New Capitalism*. New Haven: Yale University Press.

Sennett, R. 2008. *The Craftsman*. New Haven: Yale University Press.

Sennett, R. and Cobb, J. 1972. *The Hidden Injuries of Class*. New York: Alfred A. Knopf.

Shuchman, D. 2014. 'Thomas Piketty Revives Marx for the 21st Century'. *The Wall Street Journal*, 21 April 2014. www.wsj.com/articles/SB10001424052702303825604579515452952131592

Silva, P. 1987. *Estado, neoliberalismo y politica agrarian en Chile 1973–1981*. Amsterdam: CEDLER.

Silva, P. 1988. 'The State, Politics and Peasant Unions in Chile'. *Journal of Latin American Studies*, 20 (2): 433–52.

Solow, R. 2017. 'Thomas Piketty is Right'. In: *After Piketty: The Agenda for Economics and Inequality*. Edited by H. Boushey, B. DeLong, and M. Steinbaum. Cambridge: Harvard University Press, pp. 48–59.

Standing, G. 2011. *The Precariat: The New Dangerous Class*. London: Bloomsbury.

Story, L. and Dash, E. 2009. 'Bankers Reaped Lavish Bonuses during Bailouts'. *The New York Times*, 30 July 2009. www.nytimes.com/2009/07/31/business/31pay.html

Tett, G. 2009. *Fool's Gold: How Unrestrained Greed Corrupted a Dream, Shattered Global Markets and Unleashed a Catastrophe*. London: Little, Brown.

Toyama, K. 2012. 'The Rise and Fall and Rise (Literally) of the Most Important Curve in Economics'. *The Atlantic*, 30 April 2012. www.theatlantic.com/business/archive/2012/04/the-rise-and-fall-and-rise-literally-of-the-most-important-curve-in-economics/256530/

Toynbee, P. and Walker, D. 2020. *The Lost Decade 2010–2020 and What Lies Ahead for Britain*. London: Guardian Faber Publishing.

12 The End of Capitalism

Contemporary Critiques of Capitalism

Karl Marx wrote that capitalism was born in the 'blood and fire' of primitive accumulation. In *The Communist Manifesto* [1848], he predicted that its imminent overthrow would be equally cataclysmic: a proletarian revolution of world-historical significance was on the immediate horizon. In this regard, Marx was evidently wrong. Capitalism remains, a century and a half later. Yet, this belief that capitalism is in the late stages of terminal decline is common to many of the subsequent theorists of capitalism (Streeck 2016a: 3). Repurposing Mark Twain's epigram, reports of capitalism's imminent death have long been greatly exaggerated. The question of capitalism's demise, and of what follows in its stead, has stalked theories of capitalism for centuries.[1] A further question has rapidly emerged, borne out of this sense of capitalism's impending self-destruction: what should critics of capitalism do about it? Theories of the end of capitalism have typically elided into the politico-strategic realm: the question changes from 'what is going to happen?' to, in Lenin's (1902) words, *What is to be Done?*

Following the rise of post-modernism and the collapse of the Soviet Union, the confident answers once provided by both Leninist and orthodox Marxists to these questions are treated with almost universal suspicion. There is today a widespread rejection of metanarratives and the foundational notion of progress is increasingly questioned (Allen 2016). Calls for revolutionary change are rejected as unfeasible and doomed to authoritarian-capture, while the claims made by the evolutionary socialist tradition are seen as being discredited by history. In this regard, both the theories of Eduard Bernstein (1961 [1899]) and Auguste Blanqui (2018 [1868]) seem *de passe*: neither revolution nor evolution offers the answer to the question of how to steer post-capitalist transition. Yet, as we argue in this chapter, the loss of faith in grand narratives and the relative demise of politico-strategic theory has not stopped contemporary theorists from predicting capitalism's imminent demise. Rather, there remains a clear echo of Marx 'the glorious harbinger' in the widespread belief in the imminent end of capitalism.[2] We stress that the central theorists discussed in this chapter, Wolfgang Streeck, Slavoj Žižek, Shoshana Zuboff, McKenzie Wark and Paul Mason, all present capitalism as a system in the final stages of terminal decline. However, many of today's leading scholars of capitalism suggest that what will follow neoliberalism will be *worse* than the status quo; the future is not necessarily emancipatory and progressive. While there is increasing agreement that capitalism is entering a 'prolonged period of social entropy' (Streeck 2016a: 13), precisely what will follow, and what should be done, remains contested.

In this chapter, we draw out unifying and contested ideas across the contemporary literature on the end of capitalism. We start by commenting on Slavoj Žižek's *Living in the End Times* [2010] which underscores this sense of capitalism's impending decline. Central

DOI: 10.4324/9781351017671-13

to Žižek's book is the idea that western societies are processing a repressed collective grief for the loss of capitalism. People are unable to come to terms with capitalism's failure; yet they are unable to ignore its hastening self-destruction. Likewise, Wolfgang Streeck's *How Will Capitalism End?* [2016] is predicated on the belief that capitalism is a failing system, living out its final days. Streeck wrote that the requirement for perpetual economic growth led to capitalism destroying the democratic preconditions which have enabled its survival. Next we discuss the work of Shoshana Zuboff, McKenzie Wark and Paul Mason, all of whom suggest that technological progress has brought neoliberal capitalism to its conclusion. Zuboff and Wark offer particularly dystopian visions of the future. For Zuboff, neoliberalism is being replaced by a form of 'surveillance capitalism', a system dominated by the commodification of personal information for profit. The extraction of 'behavioural surplus' is becoming the dominant imperative, displacing the primacy of the extraction of surplus value. Such 'behavioural surplus' relates to capturing the data related to multiple aspects of human interaction, including that which is intuitively irrelevant and disconnected from the primary concerns of market actors. For Zuboff, such developments presage nothing short of an authoritarian capitalist dystopia: there are actors who seek total knowledge and who desire total control. Wark diverges from Zuboff in arguing that our current social order is actually already 'something worse' than hitherto existing capitalisms. With the rise of big data and algorithmic governance, Wark argues that the existing economy privileges an emergent ruling class of *vectorialists* who are not bourgeois in their class position. In keeping with Zuboff's analysis, this new class does not extract surplus value from labour, rather their power comes from their ability to navigate and control the movement of data and information. Before concluding, we engage with an author who offers a more optimistic prospect for the post-capitalist future. For Paul Mason, technological advances will lead to the obsolescence of many capitalist imperatives. Mason argues that in a future world without scarcity and of instantaneous, effortless production, capitalism simply withers away: there is no surplus value to extract and no unmet demand to respond to. We show how Mason's analysis provides an interesting counterpoint to the dystopian predictions of Wark and Zuboff.

To conclude, we comment on two political-strategic responses to the enduring question 'what is to be done about the end of capitalism?' In keeping with Mason's faith in technological emancipation, we engage first with the growing accelerationist current. We discuss the work of Srnicek and Williams, which embraces technological innovation, deterritorialization and increasing social complexity. Such an embrace of the future will enable the contradictions of capitalism to be sublated. However, this view is far from universal as it requires a temporary compromise with growth-based capitalism, a policy which ecological-Marxists, such as Andreas Malm, find unconscionable. In contrast, drawing on the work of Franz Fanon and Karl Marx, Malm argues for a campaign of sabotage against the carbon-capitalist infrastructure. Despite Malm's explicit politico-strategic injunctions, a central theme uniting this chapter is the lack of certainty in responses to the age-old Leninian question, just 'what is to be done?' A widespread sense that capitalism is in the final stages of its decline remains evident (Wallerstein et al. 2013). What will follow, and what we should do about it, remains highly contested.

Slavoj Žižek: The End Times of Capitalism

If the rockstar economist in the aftermath of the financial crash was Thomas Piketty, Slavoj Žižek is undisputedly the rockstar philosopher of the 'end times' of capitalism (see

Self 2017). No contemporary book on capitalism's critics would be complete without some engagement with the work of the enigmatic Slovenian psychoanalyst. Žižek has popularized the critique of capitalism amongst a new generation. His idiosyncratic Hegelian-Lacanian analysis is presented in numerous books (Žižek 1989, 2008, 2009, *inter alia*) and even in feature-length documentary films (Fiennes et al. 2006, 2013). His rockstar academic status is undeniable, despite the fact that his work is often stiflingly inaccessible. However, what is clear throughout Žižek's writing is his certainty that capitalism is in terminal decline and that it is rapidly 'approaching its apocalyptic zero-point' (Žižek 2010: x).

In *Living in the End Times*, Žižek's argument is that capitalism is dying yet people are unable to accept this reality. Capitalist realism collides with capitalism's unmistakable death rattle. The vast majority of people are hit with a confused, disconcerting and unacknowledged grief when they consider their social existence. If it is easier to imagine the end of the world than it is to imagine the end of capitalism (see Fisher 2009), yet capitalism is clearly ending, a psychic trauma ensues as people struggle to process the discordance of their reality. There is a repressed collective mourning for the end of capitalism. To develop this argument, Žižek turns to the five stages of grief outlined by Elisabeth Kübler-Ross (2005). Žižek argues that we are slowly, and at different rates, moving through these stages of grieving as we try and grapple with the contradiction: capitalism is immortal and it is dying. It should be stressed that Žižek's text is somewhat inaccessible and this abstracted argument is never presented in explicit, clear prose. Indeed, critics of Žižek have long accused him of a range of charges, including obfuscation, methodological imprecision, even outright racism (see Moller-Nielsen 2019).

In earlier work, Žižek (2008) identified a possible revolutionary actor, a class representing the 'universal individual'. These are 'the slum people', those who are left outside capitalism insofar as the system has effectively given up all claims to support their uplift. They have been abandoned to their fate and as such, for Žižek, the fate of capitalism becomes inextricably connected with their own. In *In Defence of Lost Causes* [2008], Žižek argued that the possibility for revolutionary change lies in the alliance of the 'slum peoples' and the progressive elements of the proletariat. Yet, in *Living in the End Times*, there is no such focus on a revolutionary subject; the death is capitalism is simply a fact to be stated. That said, while there is no revolutionary actor, there remains a clear humanist focus throughout the text. The primary concern of the book, at least at an explicit level, is how people deal with the reality of capitalism's demise. In this regard, Žižek's analysis of capitalism is depth-psychological as much as it is sociological.

The first of Kubler-Ross' stages of grieving is ideological denial. The subject refuses to accept that capitalism is ending: there is a dogmatic reassertion of the inherent 'naturalness' of market mechanisms and of the stability of the capitalist way of life. There is also a deliberate attempt to foster and fetishize other conflicts to displace the reality of capitalism's demise. We must talk of anything but the death! In this regard, Žižek comments on the much-discussed contradictions of liberal (in)tolerance and the challenges of multiculturalism. Žižek argues that in both responses, outright denial and deliberate displacement, there is an ideological shrouding of the demise of capitalism, which is capably supported by the culture industry. Hollywood films serve to maintain the magic of capitalist realism. Hollywood is thus the 'ideological battlefield' which requires considered examination. For Žižek, the underlying message of popular films such as Batman and Kung Fu Panda is to be aware of, but then subvert, repress and ignore, the contradictions inherent in the failing social order. Both Batman and Kung Fu Panda are shown to be injunctions to lie, an ideological injunction to conceal the truth, to acknowledge the falsity of your world but then to return to the illusion. In an earlier interview, Žižek argued that Kung Fu Panda (a children's movie) was 'a really dangerous film', 'ideology at its purest' (Žižek and Stein 2008); as it prescribes repression of the awareness of social contradictions. Hollywood obscures and normalizes the contradictions of the present, teaching us to repress our awareness of the incoming economic and ecological Armageddon.

The second phase of grief identified by Kübler-Ross is anger. Such anger is typically misplaced, eliding with the denial identified above. Today one may think of both the rage of Capitol Hill rioters in Washington, DC, but equally of the liberal contempt of Trump.[3] Žižek encourages the reader to think of the anger against religious extremism and against cancel culture as being, at least in part, equally displaced and misunderstood. As Howard Beale declares in Sidney Lumet's 1976 classic, *Network*, we are all 'mad as hell' and 'are not going to take it anymore!' But, as per Beale's proclamation, the 'it' which people 'won't take any more' remains unclear. For Žižek, the true genesis of the 'it', if not the displaced content which ultimately becomes fetishized, is capitalism.

The third phrase of grief is bargaining. Such bargaining is insufficient and unconsciously offered. We buy hybrid cars to offset incoming environmental cataclysm, forgetting the vast insufficiency of this futile gesture. We will read of rising sea levels and recycle carrier bags. Theoretically and intellectually this bargaining presents itself: we see a pseudo return of interest in Marx (as discussed in the preceding chapter). Increasingly, even liberals admit that there maybe is something to Marx's ideas after all. Tellingly, Marx appeared on the cover of *Time Magazine* in 2009. However, as with our analysis of Piketty in the preceding chapter, this Marxian renaissance is often more symbolic than substantive. It is an unconscious, inconsequential return to Marx, a desire to return a debased signifier to circulation. Such symbolic-Marxism is the functional equivalent of recycling milk bottles in Richmond to offset the building of a hundred coal power stations in China. It is not merely futile, it serves to retard genuine resolution and *anagnorisis*. In short, with this third phase of grief, bargaining, we see the rise, both politically and theoretically, of symbolic, structurally inconsequential posturing, which impedes true self and world-awareness.

The penultimate stage of grief is depression, which leads on naturally from such futile bargaining. One may well ask 'If China is building hundreds of new coal power stations, why bother with anything?' The emerging pandemic of 'climate anxiety' could be well captured by this phase (see McKibben 2021). There is an awareness that capitalism's death knell has sounded, that little can be done. We thus see a spike in mental health conditions, of anxiety, depression, suicide. For a disaffected youth, there is a lack of purpose, a widespread ennui and an inter-generational exasperation. Why bother explaining anything to 'boomers'?

Finally, we reach the last stage: acceptance. People realize that the basis for a new social formation exists, latent within the present. The end of capitalism is not the end of the world. A new form of subjectivity also exists, emerging from the rubble of the end times, an entirely new form social life may be about to emerge. A wide variety of sources are deployed by Žižek to demonstrate a new fascination with emerging subjects, from the science-fiction TV drama series *Heroes* to a resurgence of interest in Kafkaesque fiction. Yet, while there are some signs of 'acceptance', the earlier stages of the grieving vastly predominate. We are a long way from genuine collective acceptance.

Tellingly, Žižek does not even attempt to justify his assertion that capitalism is in terminal decline. It is the accepted point of departure for his analysis. Capitalism is reaching an 'apocalyptic zero-point'; we simply have to accept this if we are to accompany him beyond the foreword. The four horsemen of this particular apocalypse: climatic crisis, economic inequalities, the biogenetic revolution and increasingly ossified social cleavages are referred to, but there is no attempt to justify their existence and significance. It is as if that time has passed. Rather, the cycle of grief is what structures *Living in the End Times*. These four horsemen are not representing speculative possible futures: we must admit to their current reality as a *sine qua non* for any contemporary theorization of capitalism. We simply must accept that we are 'living in the end times'. For Žižek, there is some possible hope for the future; there remains some vestigial communist horizon. However, the immediate forecast is apocalyptic. We remain rooted in a collective repressed grief, which elides denial, anger, unconscious bargaining and depression. Time to actively shape the future in a progressive and rational direction is running out.

Wolfgang Streeck: Capitalism's Democratic Deficit

While Žižek is summarily dismissed by many liberal and conservative commentators as an eccentric iconoclast, it is hard to subject Streeck to the same caricature. Streeck was at one point a key adviser to the government of Gerhard Schröder and has held various senior positions within German academia. As a result, his work is given serious consideration in outlets such as the *Financial Times* and the *Times Literary Supplement* (Wolf 2016; Collier 2016). While such reviews disagree with Streeck's ultimate conclusion, it is notable that such establishment outlets seriously engage with his position. Throughout his career, Streeck's analysis has been unflinching, even when it leads to his entering into clear conflict with other progressive voices. Memorably, he criticized Angela Merkel's 'open door policy' to refugees as a ploy to let in masses of labourers to prevent workers for organizing and to drive down the rising cost of labour (Streeck 2016b). This adds to the interest his analysis holds for centre-right readers; this is not an academic seeking adulation from the 'woke' gallery. As Chakraborty (2016) comments, when Streeck is 'barking last orders for our way of life' many technocrats, as well as progressives, pay attention.

In *How Will Capitalism End? Essays on a Failing System* [2016], Streeck presented a clear argument: that the tension which has long existed between capitalism and democracy is coming to a head and will lead to the ultimate collapse of capitalism. This is not the only threat which capitalism faces, Streeck argues, however it is increasingly the most serious. In an earlier influential paper in the *New Left Review*, Streeck argued that five fundamental problems were plaguing contemporary capitalism: the rise of oligarchies, lack of growth, the demise of the public sphere, the anarchy of the international system and escalating corruption. However, in *How Will Capitalism End*, it is the conflict between capitalism and democracy which Streeck argues is responsible for capitalism's impending demise. One can read Streeck's analysis as being somewhat Polanyian, insofar as he is concerned with the background conditions which are required for capitalism to remain embedded within the social order. These background conditions have always included liberal democracy, or at the very least, some semblance of it. For Streeck, it is a fundamental prerequisite for liberal capitalism to flourish. Capitalism has survived because it has been resisted, and thereby the worst excesses it encourages have been kept at bay.

Streeck argues that the conditions which capitalism requires to survive are being eaten away by capitalism itself: it has become a victim of its own success. The veneer of democratic legitimacy which liberal democracy invests capitalism with is being lost, and lost quickly. For Streeck, capitalism has survived and flourished *because* it has been opposed, not in spite of it. The demos has been a vital stabilizing counterweight to the market. This is no longer the case in neoliberalism: the vehicles for resistance to capital are unable to wield institutional mechanisms and have been largely co-opted by the right. To underscore this point, Streeck recalls Thatcher's statement that her greatest achievement was not defeating trade unionists but in digging the foundations for New Labour. There is no longer any meaningful opposition to neoliberalism. As a result, Streek predicts that inequality will continue to spiral until the market loses any semblance of legitimacy.

Streeck grounded his argument in historical precedent. He argued that after the crises of liberal capitalism in the nineteenth century a democratic countermovement emerged which produced the modern liberal reforms (in the UK, these occurred in earnest between 1906 and 1914). This was crucial in enabling capitalism's survival and repressing communist revolt. In the aftermath of the First World War, an attempt was made at reinstituting full-blooded liberal capitalism, which proved unviable. What followed was fascism and war, there was no possibility of a return to a Victorian-era capitalism in the aftermath of 1929. The market had to concede to democratic demands or risk total displacement by an altogether divergent way of life: fascism or communism. Therefore, following the Second World War, space was afforded to the democratic critique of capitalism. As discussed in Chapter 6, Keynesianism triumphed, which enabled an awkward, yet peaceful, co-existence between labour and capital.

The neoliberal revolution destroyed this *entente cordiale*. For Streeck, neoliberalism has rapidly consumed all counterforces; all democratic resistance has been tamed and eroded (see also Brown 2015). In the past, there was always some public sphere countermovement, some democratic resistance to capitalism. Today, Streeck argues, neoliberalism has achieved a remarkable, unprecedented hegemony. The power of neoliberal ideology is simply too strong. Free-market economies have destroyed the charade of the democratic nature of capitalism. In the UK, as we write, a bill is proceeding through parliament which will place further curbs on the right to protest: the Police, Crime, Sentencing and Courts Bill 2021. This is entirely in alignment with the path Streeck predicted: even peaceful democratic resistance is increasingly delegitimized and only neoliberal imperatives are afforded standing. Inequalities spiral and the residual democratic opposition is sabotaged by the organs of neoliberalism itself: the right-wing press assaults any attempt at democratic resistance. As a result, for Streeck, capitalism is destroying itself as it eradicates the essential preconditions which enable its reproduction.

For Streeck, as neoliberalism advances, it destroys *all* the mechanisms which can stabilize it: not merely a healthy public sphere, but the state itself. Here, Streeck's analysis falls into conflict with many others on the left. For Streeck, a key non-market force which stabilizes capitalism is the state; however, neoliberalism remorselessly destroys *all* non-market forces, the state being no exception. The state, argues Streeck, is simply being overpowered. While the state has often been utilized to embed neoliberalism, the 'state people' (*staatsvolk*) retain at least some degree of democratic accountability, something which the 'market people' (*marktsvolk*) do not. For Streeck, the history of neoliberalism has been one of the *staatsvolk* being outgunned by the *marktsvolk*. This naturally leads into a support for a state-based counterattack against the undemocratic international bodies which aid the flow of capital, be it the World Bank, the International Monetary Fund or the European Union. Indeed, for Streeck (2019), the European Union is best theorized as being a 'liberal empire'. Streeck's support for the nation-state and democratic national governance has led to heated debates, especially during the Brexit referendum and its aftermath (see Habermas 2015; Šumonja 2018; Tooze 2017).

Streeck's prediction is that neoliberal subjectivity has become so ingrained, that neoliberal logics have become so normalized and that the possible democratic counterforces have so etiolated that capitalism will move into a bloated period of excess and decay. Its collapse will mirror the decline and fall of the Roman Empire rather than the French Revolution. The proletariat will not rise, as the subject-object of history; they will not attain their world-historical destiny in the overthrow of the bourgeoisie. Rather, what will ultimately kill off capitalism will be its gluttony. As all resistance to capital is culled, democratic countermovements fail and inequalities skyrocket. No cure exists, no group remains which is capable of mounting resistance.

While Streeck's work has long been explosively debated, most notably in exchanges with Habermas and liberal-internationalists (Šumonja 2018), contemporary scholars have recently identified subtle theoretical weaknesses in Streeck's argument. For example, Samuel Sadian (2022) draws out a troubling economism and historical imprecision within Streeck's analysis of the depoliticization of the demos. The basic argument presented by Streeck is that neoliberal reform has led to generalized depoliticization: neoliberalism gave us consumerism and as such the people rapidly abandoned fights for a more just and rational future. We bought consumerism and disposed of politics. Sadian has argued this account is historically reductive; the consumerist ethos which emerged in the 1970s cannot simply be attributed to the emerging neoliberal order. The transition to neoliberalism was in reality grounded upon a range of normative and epistemic shifts which were already underway: such as the idea of the sovereignty of the consumer and a new focus on consumer welfare. Yet, while the transition to a depoliticized demos may not have occurred precisely in the manner Streeck outlines, Sadian rightly remains sympathetic to Streeck's broader claims. Uniting Streeck's insights with those of his critics we can conclude that consumerism, neoliberalism, depoliticization and authoritarianism are definitely connected; however, they exist as part of a broader and more complex social web. Regardless of its particular nodes, this web is undeniably following trends which Streeck outlines: the demos is increasingly depoliticized, there is no clear counter-power to the dominant socio-economic logic of the day, neoliberalism.

Authoritarian Neoliberalism

Streeck is not the only theorist of contemporary capitalism to draw attention to its increasingly anti-democratic realities and to predict its movement towards further authoritarianism. Ian Bruff (2014) has written at length about 'authoritarian neoliberalism' and there is a rapidly growing literature which develops and utilizes this concept (see Bruff and Tansel 2019; Jessop 2019; Springer 2017; Harrison 2019, *inter alia*). Bruff is quick to qualify that he does not believe that earlier phases of neoliberalism were somehow not authoritarian. Rather, for Bruff, the authoritarian tendencies which had always been present within neoliberalism are now fully evident. To support market imperatives, states increasingly sideline democratic due process. The repressive arms of the state are brazenly deployed to protect market institutions at a regional, national and international level. Coercion has replaced consent and democratic oversight of the market has been effectively quashed (see Jessop 2019).

While these authoritarian realities of contemporary neoliberalism may seem both abundantly evident and of real importance, the particular framing of 'authoritarian neoliberalism' advanced by Bruff is, by the author's own admission, somewhat 'messy' (see Bruff and Tansel 2019). This is presented as being a virtue rather than a flaw: Bruff is keen to reject strict typologies and neat classifications. As Bruff argues, authoritarianism today relies upon both consent and coercion; it functions at both a global and a local level and occurs across space and time. As such, to capture commonalities while mindful of particularities, a deliberately fluid approach is encouraged. The study of 'authoritarian neoliberalism' thus seeks to elide the boundaries between politics and culture, state and society, and serves to challenge the binary of formal and informal social action (see Bruff 2014). This flexibility purportedly better captures the ever changing nature of hegemony, the dynamism of power and the constant dialectic between power and resistance. To critics, in contrast, this is simply conceptual imprecision which should be worked through, rather than embraced. Predictably, more precise typologies have been developed and applied by other theorists (see Gallo 2021).

Importantly, Bruff does not argue that the state is necessarily getting bigger. Rather, authoritarianism develops despite, and to some extent because, the state is shrinking. There has been an apparent curtailing of state power; for example, cuts have been made to police budgets across the Global North. But, as Laub (2021) argues, the reduction in police numbers has led to increasingly authoritarian tactics being implemented. Policing by consent is harder to achieve on a low budget, as a result, entire estates are increasingly framed as 'suspect', requiring surveillance, and effectively criminalized (Laub 2021). In a further irony, Laub observes that as austerity hits police budgets, the implicit remit of the police has vastly expanded. As social care and mental health provisions are severely reduced in austerity budgets, the police force becomes the de facto state agent of last resort. When there is nobody left to aid the acutely mentally ill or to care for homeless children, the police end up functioning as ill-equipped social workers and first-aid responders. As McNicoll (2015) writes, children are routinely detained in police cells as a 'substitute' for adequate health and social care facilities. This needs to be grasped as a crucial reality of authoritarian neoliberalism: the reliance on carceral and coercive institutions to carry out even the most delicate of state obligations is not some contingent anomaly, it is a direct result of fiscal policy.

Both Streeck and Bruff point to the increasingly authoritarian nature of neoliberal societies. We agree that these trends require considered attention. Other commentators, such as Zuboff and Wark, however, would rightly also suggest that to understand the increasingly authoritarian direction of society one must engage in detail with recent technological developments. The next three authors we turn to, Shoshana Zuboff, McKenzie Wark and Paul Mason, all focus on technology when contemplating possible post-capitalist futures. In this regard, these authors all point to the ways in which the digital revolution may move us beyond conventional capitalist economics (see Morozov 2019). However, as we discuss, these three authors present very different visions of what the future may hold. While Zuboff and Wark envision dystopian authoritarianisms, Mason believes in the emancipatory potential of technological progress.

Shoshana Zuboff: Surveillance Capitalism

For Shoshana Zuboff (2019a), we are at the dawn of a new age of primitive accumulation; these are the early days of 'surveillance capitalism'. Zuboff paints a totalitarian vision of what such a future has in store, which she expands upon at length in *The Age of Surveillance Capitalism* [2019]. Her thesis is that capitalism remains, at least for the foreseeable future; however, it undergoes a mutation. Indeed, she writes that this mutation is already substantially underway and the new breed of capitalism is fast becoming dominant. It is ripping through existing capitalist logics like 'an invasive species with no natural predators' (Zuboff 2019b: 10). Market forces are reorienting society towards the mass commodification of personal information, which is exchanged for profit. This is a new form of capitalism and one which Zuboff argues foreshadows a totalitarian eclipse of democracy and an erasure of agency. Consciously making parallels to Marx's insights on the development of capitalism, Zuboff argues that she is writing on the cusp of this new and dangerous form of life emerging. In this regard, Zuboff's work is somewhat hyperbolic: the 'surveillance capitalism' she envisages is horrific and totalitarian, the worst fears of Orwell and Koestler realized (see Delanty and Harris 2021).

The origins of this new dystopia were held to lie with the team at Google's *AdWords*, where a fateful serendipity changed the course of the internet. Large amounts of data were being collected by Google, with initially no clear purpose; however, Google employees suddenly realized that this data could provide powerful insights into the behaviour of its users. Before long, Google realized that such information could be deployed to enable forms of targeted advertising which could provide a lucrative revenue stream, a real boon in the aftermath of the 2002 dot-com crash. The technologies required for targeted advertising, and which were further refined with 'behavioural nudging', were rapidly developed and soon became a central feature of the internet.

Crucially, our data is collected from us without any compensation. In this regard, the gathering of big data represents a new form of primitive accumulation. We provide a valuable resource to capitalists without any reward. For Zuboff, it is not merely Google which is driving this new form of extraction, rather Facebook is held to be equally significant. While Zuboff is clear these are not the only agents driving the move to surveillance capitalism, she stresses that these are the most significant players that extract 'behavioural surplus' for analysis and resale. As a result, the real customers who sustain Google and Facebook are not its everyday users, but those who use the data they harvest: principally, advertizers. This represents a move towards what Zuboff deems 'economies of action', the aim is no longer to predict what users will do, but to get customers to buy their products. In short, predicting behaviour is a vital prerequisite for shaping behaviour.

Such targeted advertising is not merely the benign case where Mr Smith repeatedly enters 'nice cakes near me' into Google five times in a day and is soon helpfully presented with an advert pointing to a 50% discount from a friendly patisserie. Rather, surveillance capitalism truly taps into the internet of things; it utilizes all data points at its disposal. Surveillance capitalism works most effectively through the seamless interconnectivity of multiple data points. As such, it functions so as to optimally determine the timing of 'the appearance of a BUY button on your phone with the rise of your endorphins at the end of your run' (2019b: 17); your smart watch works in harmony with targeted push notifications. Such underhand 'nudging' is not restrained solely to buying cakes. As the Cambridge Analytica scandal demonstrated, political campaigners are able to use equally sophisticated predictive analytic models to determine when to pitch messages to particular audiences. Capitalism rewrites social norms as ever more data points are incorporated within a matrix of data harvesting, behavioural prediction and 'nudging'. As digital technologies become ever more ingrained in our lives, bodies and cities (see Ceco 2019), the reach of such predictive technology grows ever further. We are on the cusp of normalizing virtual reality headsets, smart cities, holographic phones, smart cars. For Zuboff, this 'internet of things' constitutes the ingredients of a dark dystopia in which our capacities for agentival action are eroded by optimally timed behaviour nudges.

An important case study discussed by Zuboff (2019a: 308–18) is that of Pokémon Go. Pokémon Go is an augmented reality game played on mobile phones in which the real-world (and real time) position of players impacts their on-screen experience. As such, to achieve certain rewards in the game, the user needs to be in a certain place in the real world at a certain time: i.e. I may need to be at Victoria Station at 5 pm to engage in certain on-screen game play. The ease with which such interactive games enable companies to both observe and manipulate user behaviour has been subject to extensive discussion (see Varghese 2019). The game app enables the software's owner, Niantic, to track user's locations and to access content on their device, even when the mobile was on standby mode. Pokémon Go simultaneously enabled the harvesting of spectacular swathes of data and provided nudges to drive users to particular locations. This occurred both explicitly and implicitly: users could enjoy the gimmick of purchasing a 'Pokémon Go Frappuccino' from Starbucks. Equally, various companies got their locations sponsored, paying Niantic to drive footfall in their direction without this being obvious to players (Tynan 2016). For those who share Zuboff's fears for a world of surveillance capitalism, Pokémon Go is something to most definitely avoid (see Owen 2016).

Cory Doctorow's (2020) work offers an important analysis of Zuboff's ideas and is worthy of engagement. Doctorow agrees with much of what Zuboff states; however, he offers some valuable qualifications. For Doctorow, Zuboff risks overemphasizing the 'surveillance' and underplaying the 'capitalism' in her 'surveillance capitalism' framing. There is undeniably a dystopian edge to *The Age of Surveillance Capitalism* and Doctorow is quick to call out her tendency to hyperbole. As Doctorow pithily frames it: we are not yet under the threat of mind control rays from Google HQ which destroy human agency. Indeed, Doctorow is keen to suggest that the mega power of Facebook and Google which Zuboff describes remains vastly exaggerated. Targeted advertising is actually limited in efficacy. While people are commonly presented with adverts tailored to their desires, we are equally often bombarded by redundant and inaccurate suggestions. As a result, Google and Facebook have not got surveillance capitalism sewn up; there remain numerous avenues of resistance.

Doctorow warns that there may even be a certain utility for capitalist companies in the populace believing technology is leading the way. Rather, for Doctorow, the enemy of democracy is presented to be, not unregulated surveillance, but unregulated capitalism. Ever since the Reagan era, anti-trust legislation has been eroded, it is this, far more than technical innovation, which enabled the rise of the technical titans Google and Facebook. The legal and political system needs to be critiqued: we do not simply need to learn more about algorithmic governmentality, rather, we need to pay attention to the nexus between capital and the executive which has led to the systematic dismantling of regulatory constraints. The idea that some clever unstoppable algorithms are blasting their way through outmoded economic models is useful propaganda for Facebook and Google. Rather, Doctorow reminds us that technological advances are part of a broader political and economic landscape which has enabled new forms of accumulation to thrive.

McKenzie Wark: Capital Is Dead

While Doctorow argues that Zuboff is too negative in her assessment, Wark conversely argues that Zuboff does not go far enough. In *Capital Is Dead: Is This Something Worse* [2019], Wark claims that we have already moved beyond capitalism. We are witnessing the birth of a new mode of production altogether, not merely a new variant of capitalism.

Zuboff is clear, 'surveillance capitalism' is a new force, however, the fundamental logics of capitalism remain. In contrast, for Wark, we are witnessing something entirely different, a new mode of production is emerging, with new class relationships forming. This is not to say that capitalism is no longer the primary mode of production. Rather, as per Marx's identification of capitalism emerging within a still broadly feudal society, Wark identifies a post-capitalist mode of production emerging within the ruins of capitalist society.

For Wark, the conceptual utility of 'capitalism' is wearing thin. We are forced to apply countless modifiers for the term to have sufficient capture. There is 'surveillance' capitalism, 'racial' capitalism, 'post-capitalism', 'cognitive' capitalism, 'platform' capitalism, the list is endless. As Wark provocatively comments, if we need to add countless prefixes to 'capitalism' for it to be an accurate reflection of the current economy, we need to accept that it is time to develop a new and more efficacious conceptual arsenal. Perhaps, says Wark, the reason we are unable to simply speak of 'capitalism' anymore, and we search for so many modifiers, is because 'capitalism' no longer captures the emerging dominant force of our social world. There are perhaps new classes in the making, with new dominant actors who do not achieve mastery on the basis of the same norms and dynamics as before. For Wark, it is time to embrace the possibility that technological development has opened the doors to a new mode of production altogether.

With clear initial parallels with Zuboff, Wark argues that the production and control of information is now central to the economy in the way that the production of physical commodities was in the nineteenth century. Information has created a new powerful class, whose dominance is sustained in a different way to before, in a manner which is no longer capitalist. This new ruling class does not own factories or shop floors, estates or fleets, rather they own information and their power stems from their ability to control access to both the data itself and the infrastructure through which such data is operationalizable. Increasingly, these actors are not even spatially temporally located; they exist 'in the web'.

Wark adopts a clear Marxist approach to further their analysis. Notably, this is not Marxism as per the *substantive* content of Marx's texts. Rather, this is Marxism as methodology, utilizing historical materialism as a living and adaptive perspective for studying political economy. What is required, says Wark, is an analysis of the digital economy which is attuned to the power gradients and class relations of the actually existing conjuncture. The substantive answer produced by Wark, when such a perspective is adopted, is a radical new take on the social world. In place of the binary of capitalist and bourgeois which Marx theorized as the central class agonism of capitalism, predicated on the forced extraction of surplus value from labourers, Wark identifies a new class relationship. Today we live in an informational political economy in which the extraction of 'surplus information' is the primary dynamic. Such informational surplus is utilized to construct models which can predict and influence future behaviour, similar to Zuboff's account above. What differentiates Wark's account from Zuboff's is that Wark argues this new relation has transcended capitalism, a new class antagonism has *already* emerged which cannot be captured by the proletariat-bourgeoisie agonism. Rather, Wark identifies a new class conflict existing between a class of *hackers* and *vectorialists*. The 'hackers' are the creative actors, those who design, write and produce all manner of content, all forms of data. The *vectorialists* are the new dominant class, they are those who own and control information. As Wark argues, 'the dominant ruling class of our time no longer maintains its rule through the ownership of the means of production as capitalists do. Nor through the ownership of land as landlords do' (2019: 5) Rather, it is the power to abstract and connect data which provides the *vectorialists* with their privileged social position. The *vectorialist* class is defined by their exercise of power over the mechanisms which link the content produced by the hackers with the broader flow, communication and consumption of information.

Wark is not suggesting that there are no longer any farmers, miners or other traditional labourers. Rather they argue that in the Global north the dominant class antagonism has changed, we see a world increasingly divided between *hackers* and *vectorialist*, with 'earlier' modes of production migrating to the global South. The Global North moves into an entirely new mode of production, one in which data capture and transfer is central to the economy. For Wark, the powerful economic class no longer seeks to produce content and extract surplus value, rather it seeks to steal data and offer to the market the potentiality for total direction. Under the guise of offering friendly personalization features, this new class of *vectorialists* monitors your sleep cycle and your sex drive, it 'nudges' and 'suggests', monitors and influences. In Wark's theory, everyone, including capitalists, is already increasingly subsumed within this new socio-economic reality.

Paul Mason: Post-Capitalism and Post-Work

Paul Mason agrees with Wark that we already see the signs of a post-capitalist future emerging. Likewise, Mason argues that such transitions are deeply connected with the development of new technologies which are reshaping production and consumption. However, that is where the similarities end. While Wark, like Zuboff, predicts a dystopian, totalitarian future growing out of the ashes of neoliberalism, Mason sees a post-capitalist world full of hope and progressive possibilities. As per the title of his latest book, Mason contends that there remains a *Clear Bright Future* [2019] for humanity.

Mason's key work on the end of capitalism is *Post-Capitalism: A Guide to Our Future* [2015]. Here, Mason argues that the signs of a more rational and just economy are already emerging as post-capitalist models such as co-operatives and digital freeware challenge past notions of ownership. Importantly, this positive future does not emerge solely from the developments of the new, but also out of the failures of the old. Like Streeck's argument detailed above, Mason contends that this post-capitalist future in part erupts out of capitalism's extravagant successes. Indeed, like Streeck, Mason argues that neoliberalism has killed the democratic conditions which enabled capitalism to thrive. In Part One, Mason argues that capitalism has travelled through various waves of boom and bust, the so-called Kondratieff cycles (see Chapter 8). While in the past capitalists relied on technological innovation to recover from the slumps, the neoliberal revolution brought about a new response to economic downturn: austerity. Rather than investment and support for new development, which would have enabled technological progress to restart, the neoliberal adoption of austerity was fundamentally opposed to their own long-term interests. Mason argues throughout *Post-Capitalism* that this neoliberal strategy is simply unsustainable: poor economic performance and spiralling inequalities do not augur well for any social system. For Mason, capitalism is further threatened by the fact that such egregious and irrational ownership structures will increasingly exist side by side with new, progressive forms of ownership made possible by technical developments. In a world of digital socialism (see Morozov 2019) and productive surplus how could the masses accept the spiralling material inequalities and poor economic performance of neoliberal policy? A central part of Mason's argument is therefore that the public will demand an alternative to capitalism. Technological progress will spur new economic formations which will be evidently preferable to all forms of capitalism, especially increasingly inequitable neoliberalism. Such an analysis, however, seems frustrated by a central argument put forward by Streeck: there is no meaningful agent capable of enacting such a transformation. For political resentment to transform into political praxis, some critical agency is needed. As neoliberalism tightens its grip further, it erodes the possibilities for critical consciousness.

But Mason offers a further, and more intriguing, argument, in the favour of a progressive post-capitalist future. Crucially, with advances in technology, we will soon move into a surplus-based economy. Capitalism has historically operated on the basis of scarcity; goods and services are in limited supply, which, in relation to the extent of the demand, determines their price. In orthodox capitalist economics, these are the fundamental market categories: supply and demand. But, Mason argues, we can see social realms emerging in which supply is infinite and in which demand is always met (see also Bastani 2020). This will not impact every sector, there will still be 'just in time' supply chains and limited natural resources. However, the changes across sectors more broadly will be substantial and socio-politically significant. For Mason, it will fundamentally challenge the most basic norms and understandings of value within society. In this regard, Mason points to the ease with which computers enable a wide range of resources to be copied, almost infinitely, at little-to-no cost or labour time. As the digital revolution gathers further pace, new technologies will emerge enabling limitless and effortless production. In sum, supply will swamp demand. With the rise of 3D printing and of open source digital models, scarcity and thereby capitalism may soon be a thing of the past (see Schröter 2020).

Mason's argument is that the post-capitalist future will emerge as the basic axioms of capitalism will no longer be relevant when the cost of production is negligible and the supply is limitless. When we have intelligent machines which cost nothing to replace, capitalism fails to operate (Mason 2015a: 166). Not only will supply swamp demand by the organic composition of capital will be negligible, as Marx teaches, this is where capitalists derive profit from. Technological development thus leads to the total obsolesce of central capitalist imperatives. Mason's work could be seen as a radical technologically centric reworking of Marx's analysis of the tendency of profit to fall; however, Mason's twist is that the technical apparatuses of the future will be so advanced that the term 'profit' itself becomes meaningless. In such an environment, the need for toil, the need to labour, becomes greatly reduced. The post-capitalist future is thus likely to be a post-work future too (see Srnicek and Williams 2016, Hines 2019, Mason 2021).

Mason is correct to argue that we can see post-capitalist tendencies manifest within today's economy. However, he fails to engage with the reality that we can also identify early signs of capitalist countermovements in response to the challenge to market logics posed by the new economies. There is intense interest in a variety of projects which ultimately seek to defend property rights by artificially retaining a fictive scarcity value in a world of infinite production. An important example here is the rise of so-called non-fungible tokens (more commonly known as NFTs). A NFT is a chain of code which is stored on a blockchain which can be sold. Such a chain of code is presented as being proof of ownership of the 'original' item of property, be it anything from an innocent GIF, a revolutionary folk song or a pornographic video. The particular link between the NFT and the actual art work remains loose. The presence of the NFT does not stop other actors from copying the video file, GIF etc. Also, little stops 'illegitimate' actors from claiming that *their* NFT is the true proof of ownership associated with the asset. The NFT is perhaps best understood as being an emerging deed of ownership, which is related to the fungible digital object. The problem, however, is that while the token is non-fungible, the item which it refers to remains effortlessly fungible, typically it is limitlessly and freely reproducible via two keyboard commands: Ctrl + C followed by Ctrl + V.

The rise of NFTs demonstrates two things. First, it shows that capitalists are indeed faced with the problem Mason identifies: without scarcity, something new is desperately required to retain the logic of the market. However, where Mason falls short is in anticipating the speed and determination of capitalists to invent false conditions of scarcity. The UK Chancellor of the Exchequer, Rishi Sunak, has already officially endorsed NFTs; he has even instructed the Bank of England to create an NFT (Partington 2022). The curious question for the future is whether NFTs are ultimately held to be an absurd bubble, functionally akin to the first 'non-fungible' craze: the mania to purchase 'non-fungible tulips' in 1630s' Amsterdam (see Reyburn 2021).

The foregoing analysis is perhaps doing Mason a disservice; he could not possibly have been expected to predict precisely how capitalists would respond to changing conditions. Indeed, Mason is actually impressively future-oriented in his work, something which we admire. Mason is unusual amongst contemporary critics of capitalism in offering clear politico-strategic considerations to further post-capitalism. In this regard, Mason develops 'five principles of transition' which are:

(i) the importance of using data and simulations to consider the best directions for future change,
(ii) environmental sustainability in all actions,
(iii) the need for an always 'bigger picture' when considering transition which extends beyond the merely economic,
(iv) the need to avoid singular, myopic visions, and
(v) the need to unlock the power of information.

Mason discusses these at length across his wider work (see Mason 2019a, 2020). Notably, making accessible and actionable suggestions is something which Streeck, Zizek, Wark, Zuboff steer clear of. For Mason, we should encourage and promote the expansive use of data modelling of future alternative societies, we need to end offshore banking, promote creative commons and co-operatives, we need to re-regulate the financial sector and we need to implement a universal basic income (see Mason 2015b). Mason thus offers an important counterweight to Zuboff and Wark in that he presents an optimistic vision for a concrete post-capitalist future.

Conclusion: What Is To Be Done?

In the 1960s, the literature on the future of capitalism had a remarkably different inflection; it was intimately associated with teleological narratives and revolutionary-strategy. The question of 'what happens next?' was inextricably linked to concerns of political action. For many on the left the demise of capitalism was simply a historical inevitability, as Khrushchev memorably framed it, 'history is on our side … we will bury you'. There was a sense that time was all socialists needed, capitalism would simply dig its own grave. As our discussion in this chapter has shown, while the belief in such fixed teleology has declined, there remains an unerring commonality across the literature that neoliberal capitalism's days are numbered. While few mainstream commentators discuss the political-strategic realities of post-capitalist transition, it would be a gross exaggeration to suggest Mason is the only theorist who contemplates such concerns today. As such, we conclude this chapter reflecting on two of the more radical strains of thought which present ways in which the end of capitalism could be accelerated.

One significant, but loose, grouping of theorists who seek to advance the end of capitalism is the 'accelerationists'. As Mackay and Avanessian (2014: 4) define it, accelerationism seeks to expedite the 'uprooting, alienating, decoding, abstractive tendencies' of capitalism, with the aim of furthering the existing instabilities and contradictions of capitalism so as to hasten the system's demise. For Srnicek and Williams (2016), the left needs to get better at 'embracing the future', in identifying the transitional possibilities latent within technology and within more complex social formations. In contrast to a strategy built around resisting change and asserting the primacy of the local and national, accelerationists believe that the left needs to embrace deterritorialization (Srnicek and Williams 2016, Deleuze and Guattari 1972). To expedite the decay of capitalism, the left must support the broader trend towards globalization and complexity, it must jettison its 'folk politics' of direct action and affect. In short, accelerationists reject the idea that more modernity and more progress equates to ever more secure and entrenched capitalism. Rather, to bring capitalism to an end, accelerationists argue that such progress needs to be embraced and expedited. More progress does not mean more capitalism, rather it means more contradictions and more possibilities for rupture (see CCRU 2017). Some accelerationists even speak of the goal of reaching the 'technological singularity' (Land 2011), a point at which technical development becomes unstoppable and in which radical social change becomes inevitable.

The accelerationist position has clear advantages. For example, while many political strategies and critical theories have sought in vain to identify an area outside of capitalism in which to invest, be it 'recognition', 'language', 'affect', 'local struggle' or 'identity', accelerationists do not attempt such a futile exercise (see Thompson 2016). Rather, accelerationists are alert to the complexity of social power and admit that trying to theorize capitalism from 'outside' is methodologically impossible. Accelerationists, conversely, seek to embrace the totalizing tendencies of capitalism, to encourage change, to advance progress. This, however, leads to obvious rejoinders. Perhaps the most obvious rebuttal is that it brings a political imperative to temporarily adopt the dynamics of a system which is irrational and inequitable. Accelerationism seems to suggest that left actors should become neoliberal bankers to hasten the end of neoliberalism. This seems surreal at best and self-servingly pragmatic at worst, enabling anti-capitalists to theoretically justify getting filthy rich *from* capitalism in the name of revolution.

It should be stressed that there is no coherent accelerationist philosophy, rather the term represents a broad variety of ideas and themes. Theorists as diverse as Baudrillard, Deleuze and Guattari, Nick Land,[4] Mark Fisher, and Srnicek and Williams may all be considered 'accelerationist' despite holding very divergent understandings of both capitalism and accelerationism.[5] However, what accelerationist theory is united upon, and which we consider worthy of note, is the need to challenge the left's tendency towards reactionary localism and to embrace, rather than resist, a future of change and complexity. As such, the left must gain technical competence and attempt to steer, rather than halt, the deterritorializing paths of the future.

There are many across the political spectrum who find the accelerationist response to capitalism reprehensible. For Andreas Malm, and other ecological-Marxists, any policy which requires embracing the carbon capitalist system, even temporarily, is deeply flawed. What is required, for Malm at least, is immediate and active resistance to bring about a decarbonized economy, as quickly as possible. In *How to Blow Up a Pipeline: Learning to Fight in a World on Fire*, Malm argues for the need to engage in violent physical acts of sabotage. The fundamental conditions required for life on earth are being destroyed by capitalism, hence we need to radically expedite carbon capitalism's end. In this regard, Malm produces a stinging indictment of non-violent action and the fetishization of pacifistic tactics, as per the style of Extinction Rebellion. Rather, Malm argues, we need to engage actively in sabotaging carbon-capitalist infrastructure, cutting the tyres of 4 x 4 vehicles, blockading oil refineries. Malm stresses, however, that such sabotage is not reckless, gleeful, wanton destruction. Rather it is a particular type of political violence which has proven effective in the past. In sum, Malm argues that the time of the Gandhian protest movement has passed, the time of the Fanonian sabotage movement has come.

Malm calls for 'intelligent sabotage', arguing somewhat counterintuitively, that it can be done 'softly' with care and precision. The absolute non-violence of mainstream anti-capitalist movements is held to be retarding the cause of anti-capitalism. Yet the 'general demise of revolutionary politics' (2021: 70), which Malm laments, is not irreversible. Rather, there exists both theoretical and political justifications for taking up a campaign of sabotage. Increasingly there are groups ready to take such action (see Webb 2022). Malm justifies his call to arms on the basis that the framing of 'violent' protest is always highly politicized. One could thus say that 'pacificism' has never really existed, rather the question is always what exactly counts as 'violence'. Engels (1969 [1845]) famously wrote of capitalism as a system of 'social murder' [*sozialer Mord*] where the ruling class places the poor and vulnerable in a position where they will inevitably meet an early and unnatural death. The decisions made repeatedly by the international capitalist elite, to perpetuate carbon capitalism despite the obvious and foreseeable fatal outcomes, arguably exemplifies Engels' analysis. Yet, where Engels wrote of the deaths of 'hundreds' and 'thousands', the death toll caused by perpetuating carbon capitalism will be unspeakably higher.

In conclusion, the question as to 'what follows capitalism?' remains highly debated. The question 'what is to be done?' is less often addressed today, but perhaps it is even more divisive when responses are offered. There could hardly be a greater strategic divide between the suggestions presented by Malm and by Srnicek and Williams. Yet, with the noteworthy exception of Mason's optimistic post-capitalism, the resounding answer to the question 'what follows neoliberalism?' seems terrifyingly clear and bleak. There is an unusually broad accord that things are likely to get much, much worse: the future is likely to be a time of monsters.

Notes

1 This is in part because, as Wolfgang Streeck (2016a: 1–3) argued, theories of capitalism are often theories of ever worsening crises.

2 This phrase originally comes from Marx's *On the Paris Commune* and has been repeatedly repurposed to suggest a theorist or event presaging the new.

3 Consider, for example, Hilary Clinton's comments about 'the deplorables' (those who vote for Trump).

4 It should be noted that Nick Land's work has taken a distinctly reactionary turn after his earlier work exploring accelerationism with the Cybernetic Culture Research Unit (CCRU).

5 Marx is often cited as having accelerationist tendencies and these appear most evidently within his 1848 speech on Question of Free Trade where he writes: 'In a word, the free trade system hastens the social revolution. It is in this revolutionary sense alone, gentlemen, that I vote in favour of free trade'.

References

Allen, A. 2016. *The End of Progress: Decolonizing the Normative Foundations of Critical Theory*. New York: Columbia University Press.

Bastani, A. 2020. *Fully Automated Luxury Communism*. London: Verso.

Bernstein, E. 1961 [1899]. *Evolutionary Socialism: A Criticism and Affirmation*. New York: Schocken.

Blanqui, A. 2018 [1868]. 'Instructions for an Armed Uprising'. In: *The Blanqui Reader: Political Writings, 1830–1880*. Edited by P. Hallward and P. Le Goff. Translated by M. Abidor, P. Hallward and P. Le Goff. London: Verso, pp. 202–230.

Brown, W. 2015. *Undoing the Demos: Neoliberalism's Stealth Revolution*. New York: Zone Books.

Bruff, I. 2014. 'The Rise of Authoritarian Neoliberalism'. *Rethinking Marxism*. 26 (1): 113–29.

Bruff, I. and Tansel, C. B. 2019. 'Authoritarian Neoliberalism: Trajectories of Knowledge Production and Praxis'. *Globalizations*, 16 (3): 233–44.

CCRU. 2017. *Writings 1997–2003*. Falmouth: Urbanomic.

Ceco, L. 2019. "Surveillance Capitalism': Critic Urges Toronto to Abandon Smart City Project'. *The Guardian*. 6 June 2019. www.theguardian.com/cities/2019/jun/06/toronto-smart-city-google-project-privacy-concerns

Chakraborty, A. 2016. 'Wolfgang Streeck: The German Economist Calling Time on Capitalism'. *The Guardian*, 9 December 2016. www.theguardian.com/books/2016/dec/09/wolfgang-streeck-the-german-economist-calling-time-on-capitalism

Collier, P. 2016. 'How to Save Capitalism from Itself'. *Times Literary Supplement*, 13 May 2016. www.the-tls.co.uk/articles/how-to-save-capitalism/

Delanty, G. and Harris, N. 2021. 'Critical Theory and the Question of Technology: The Frankfurt School Revisited'. *Thesis Eleven*, 166 (1): 88–108.

Deleuze, G. and Guattari, F. 1977 [1972]. *Anti-Oedipus: Capitalism and Schizophrenia*. Translated by T. Hurley, M. Seem and H. Lane. New York: Viking Press.

Doctorow, C. 2020. *How to Destroy Surveillance Capitalism*. Medium: One Zero.

Engels, F. 1969 [1845]. *The Condition of the Working-Class in England*. London: Panther Books.

Fiennes, S., Wilson, J. and Žižek, S. 2013. *The Pervert's Guide to Ideology*. New York: Zeitgeist Films.

Fiennes, S., Žižek, S., Rosenbaum, M., Misch, M., Wieser, R., Schnorr, R., Shepherd, E. and Myers, T. 2006. *The Pervert's Guide to Cinema*. London: Mischief Films.

Fisher, M. 2009. *Capitalist Realism*. London: Zero Books.

Gallo, E. 2021. 'Three Varieties of Authoritarian Neoliberalism: Rule by the Experts, the People, the Leader'. *Competition & Change*, https://doi.org/10.1177/10245294211038425

Habermas, J. 2015. *The Lure of Technocracy*. Cambridge: Polity Press.

Harrison, G. 2019. 'Authoritarian Neoliberalism and Capitalist Transformation in Africa: All Pain, No Gain'. *Globalizations*, 16 (3): 274–88.

Hines, A. 2019. 'Getting Ready for a Post-Work Future'. *Foresight and STI Governance*, 13 (1): 19–30.

Jessop, B. 2019. 'Authoritarian Neoliberalism: Periodization and Critique'. *South Atlantic Quarterly*, 118 (2): 343–61.

Kübler-Ross, E. and Kessler, D. 2005. *On Grief and Grieving: Finding the Meaning of Grief through the Five Stages of Loss*. New York: Scribner.

Land, N. 2011. *Fanged Noumena: Collected Writings 1987–2007*. Falmouth: Urbanomic.

Laub, M. 2021. 'Policing Authoritarian Neoliberalism in South London'. Political Geography, 90. Online first.

Lenin, V. I. 2017 [1902]. *What Is to Be Done? Burning Questions of Our Movement*. Bishop Auckland: Aziloth Books.

Mackay, R. and Avanessian, A. 2014. *#Accelerate: The Accelerationist Reader*. Falmouth: Urbanomic.

Malm, A. 2021. *How to Blow Up a Pipeline: Learning to Fight in a World on Fire*. London: Verso.

Mason, P. 2015a. *PostCapitalism: A Guide to Our Future*. London: Allen Lane.

Mason, P. 2015b. 'Paying Everyone a Basic Income Would Kill Off Low-paid Menial Work'. *The Guardian*, 1 February 2015. www.theguardian.com/commentisfree/2015/feb/01/paying-everyone-a-basic-income-would-kill-off-low-paid-menial-jobs

Mason, P. 2019a. 'Time for PostCapitalism'. *Social Europe*, 1 July 2019. https://socialeurope.eu/time-for-postcapitalism

Mason, P. 2019b. *Clear Bright Future: A Radical Defence of the Human Being*. London: Penguin.

Mason, P. 2020. 'The Postcapitalist Transition: Policy Implications for the Left'. *Political Quarterly*, 91 (2): 287–98.

Mason, P. 2021. 'Labour Must Embrace a Post-work Future or Condemn Itself to Irrelevance'. *The New Statesman*, 28 April 2021. www.newstatesman.com/politics/2021/04/labour-must-embrace-post-work-future-or-condemn-itself-irrelevance

McKibben, B. 2021. 'Climate Anxiety Makes Good Sense'. *The New Yorker*, 5 May 2021. www.newyorker.com/news/annals-of-a-warming-planet/climate-anxiety-makes-good-sense

McNicoll, A. 2015. 'Vulnerable Children Detained in Police Cells as 'Substitute' for Health and Social Care'. *Community Care*, 10 March 2015. www.communitycare.co.uk/2015/03/10/police-cells-used-substitute-health-social-care/

Moller-Nielsen, T. 2019. 'What is Žižek for?'. *Current Affairs*, 18 October 2019. www.currentaffairs.org/2019/10/what-is-Žižek-for

Morozov, E. 2019. 'Digital Socialism? The Calculation Debate in the Age of Big Data'. *New Left Review*, 116/117. 33–67.

Network. 1976. Lumet, S. [Feature Film]. MGM.

Owen, P. 2016. 'Oliver Stone Says 'Pokemon Go' Is 'Surveillance Capitalism'. *The Wrap*, 21 July 2016. www.thewrap.com/oliver-stone-says-pokemon-go-is-surveillance-capitalism/

Partington, R. 2022. 'Rishi Sunak Asks Royal Mint to Create NFT'. *The Guardian*, 4 April 2022. www.theguardian.com/technology/2022/apr/04/rishi-sunak-asks-royal-mint-to-create-nft

Reyburn, S. 2021. 'Art's NFT Question: Next Frontier in Trading, or a New Form of Tulip?' *The New York Times*, 30 March 2021. www.nytimes.com/2021/03/30/arts/design/nft-bubble.html

Sadian, S. 2023 forthcoming. 'Wolfgang Streeck on Consumption, Depoliticisation and Neoliberal Capitalism'. *European Journal of Social Theory*. https://doi.org/10.1177/13684310221097016

Schröter, J. 2020. 'Imaginary Economies: The Case of the 3D Printer'. *Review of Evolutionary Political Economy*, 1. 357–70.

Self, W. 2017. 'The Courage of Hopelessness by Slavoj Žižek Review – How the Big Hairy Marxist Would Change the World'. *The Guardian*, 28 April 2017. www.theguardian.com/books/2017/apr/28/courage-of-hopelessness-slavoj-zizek-review

Springer, S. 2017. 'Klepto-neoliberalism: Authoritarianism and Patronage in Cambodia'. In: *States of discipline: Authoritarian neoliberalism and the contested reproduction of capitalist order.* Edited by C. B. Tansel. London: Rowman & Littlefield, pp. 235–54.

Srnicek, N. and Williams, A. 2016. *Inventing the Future: Postcapitalism and a World without Work.* London: Verso.

Streeck, W. 2016a. *How Will Capitalism End?* London: Verso.

Streeck, W. 2016b. *'Exploding Europe: Germany, the Refugees and the British Vote to Leave'*. Sheffield: SPERI. No. 31.

Streeck, W. 2019. 'The European Union Is a Liberal Empire, and It Is about to Fall'. *LSE Brexit Blog.* Published online 6 March 2019.

Šumonja, M. 2018. 'The Habermas-Streeck Debate Revisited: Syriza and the Illusions of the Left-Europeanism'. *Capital and Class*, 43 (3): 437–58.

Tansel, C. B. and Bruff, I. (eds.) 2020. *Authoritarian Neoliberalism: Philosophies, Practices, Contestations.* Abingdon: Routledge.

Thompson, M. J. 2016. *The Domestication of Critical Theory*. London: Rowman and Littlefield.

Tooze, A. 2017. 'A General Logic of Crisis'. *London Review of Books*, 5 January 2017. www.lrb.co.uk/the-paper/v39/n01/adam-tooze/a-general-logic-of-crisis

Tynan, D. 2016. 'Welcome to the Pokeconomy: How Businesses Are Riding the Pokemon Craze'. *The Guardian*, 15 July 2016. www.theguardian.com/technology/2016/jul/15/pokemon-go-businesses-sponsored-location-lure-modules

Varghese, S. 2019. 'Pokemon Go Was a Warning about the Rise of Surveillance Capitalism'. *Wired*, 3 February 2019. www.wired.co.uk/article/the-age-of-surveillance-capitalism-facebook-shoshana-zuboff

Wallerstein, I., Collins, R. Mann, M. Drerluguian G. and Calhoun, C. 2013. *Does Capitalism Have a Future?* Oxford: Oxford University Press.

Wark, M. 2019. *Capital is dead: Is This Something Worse?* London:Verso.

Webb, S. 2022. 'Environmental Activists Let Down Tyres on "Hundreds" of SUVs across Britain'. *Independent*, 8 March 2022. www.independent.co.uk/climate-change/news/air-pollution-suv-tyres-britain-b2048361.html

Wolf, M. 2016. 'Martin Wolf: The Case against the Collapse of Capitalism'. *Financial Times*, 2 November 2016. www.ft.com/content/7496e08a-9f7a-11e6-891e-abe238dee8e2

Žižek, S. 1989. *The Sublime Object of Ideology*. London:Verso.

Žižek, S. 2008. *In Defence of Lost Causes*. London:Verso.

Žižek, S. 2009. *First as Tragedy, Then as Farce*. London:Verso.

Žižek, S. 2010. *Living in the End Times*. London:Verso.

Žižek, S. and Stein, J. D. 2008. 'What did Slavoj Žižek Think of 'Kung Fu Panda' Anyway?' *Vulture*, 12 September 2008. www.vulture.com/2008/09/what_did_slavoj_Žižek_think_of.html

Zuboff, S. 2019a. *The Age of Surveillance Capitalism: The Fight for a Human Future at the New Frontier of Power*. London: Profile Books.

Zuboff, S. 2019b. 'Surveillance Capitalism and the Challenge of Collective Action'. *New Labor Forum*, 28 (1): 10–29.

Index

For Product Safety Concerns and Information please contact our EU representative GPSR@taylorandfrancis.com Taylor & Francis Verlag GmbH, Kaufingerstraße 24, 80331 München, Germany